for
Katelyn, Jesse,
Kathleen, and Michael

Discovering AutoCAD

Release 14

MARK DIX
and
PAUL RILEY

CAD Support Associates

PRENTICE HALL, Upper Saddle River, NJ 07458

Library of Congress Cataloging-in-Publication Data

Dix, Mark
    Discovering AutoCAD, release 14 / Mark Dix and Paul Riley.
        p.   cm.
    Includes index.
    ISBN 0-13-080183-6 (pbk)
    1. Computer graphics.   2. AutoCAD (Computer file)   I. Riley,
Paul   II. Title
    T385.D.632   1998
    604.2'0285'5369--dc21   98-26045
                                                                 CIP

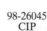

Acquisitions Editor: **Eric Svendsen**
Editor-in-chief: **Marcia Horton**
Managing editor: **Bayani Mendoza De Leon**
Vice-president of production and manufacturing: **David W. Riccardi**
Production editor: **Katharita Lamoza**
Art director: **Michele Giusti**
Cover design: **Jayne Conte**
Manufacturing buyer: **Donna Sullivan**

© 1999, by Prentice-Hall, Inc.
Simon & Schuster / A Viacom Company
Upper Saddle River, New Jersey 07458

The author and publisher of this book have used their best efforts in preparing this book. These efforts include the development, research, and testing of the theories and programs to determine their effectiveness. The author and publisher make no warranty of any kind, expressed of implied, with regard to these programs or the documentation contained in this book. The author and publisher shall not be liable in any event for incidental or consequential damages in connection with or arising out of, the furnishing, performance, or use of these programs.

Printed in the United States of America

10 9 8 7 6 5 4 3 2

ISBN 0-13-080183-6

AutoCAD, AutoLISP, and 3D Studio are registered trademarks of Autodesk, Inc. dBase III is a registered trademark of Ashton-Tate. DMP-61, DMP-29, and Houston Instrument are trademarks of Amtek, Inc. IBM is a registered trademark of International Business Machines Corporation. LaserJet II is a trademark of Hewlett-Packard. LOTUS 1-2-3 is a trademark of Lotus Development Corporation. MultiSync is a registered trademark of NEC Information Systems, Inc. MS-DOS and Windows are trademarks of Microsoft Corporation. Summagraphics is a registered trademark of Summagraphics Corporation. Zenith is a trademark of Zenith Data Systems, Inc.

The AutoCAD Primary Screen Menu Hierarchy and Pull Down Menus are reprinted with the permission of Autodesk, Inc. The AutoCAD Table Menu, Screen Menu, and Pull-Down Menu are reprinted from the AutoCAD Reference Manual with permission from Autodesk, Inc.

Prentice-Hall International (UK) Limited, London
Prentice-Hall of Australia Pty. Limited, Sydney
Prentice-Hall Canada, Inc., Toronto
Prentice-Hall Hispanoamericana, S.A., Mexico
Prentice-Hall of India Private Limited, New Delhi
Prentice-Hall of Japan, Inc., Tokyo
Simon & Schuster Asia Pte. Ltd., Singapore
Editoria Prentice-Hall do Brasil, Ltda., Rio de Janeiro

CONTENTS

PREFACE

AutoCAD and the personal computer world in general have come a long way since we began work on our first book back in 1986. We were working in version 2.6 at that time and were delighted with the enhancements we could add when Release 9 came out in time for us to use it for the first published edition of Discovering AutoCAD. Although the scope of AutoCAD and the changes that have occurred in the twelve years since have been phenomenal, some things do not change. Drawing on a CAD system is still a skill that can be learned only through many hours of practice. Like driving a car or playing a musical instrument, it cannot be learned by reading about it or watching someone else do it.

Accordingly, this book, like all our previous books, takes a very active approach to teaching AutoCAD. It is designed as a teaching tool and a self-study guide and assumes that readers will have access to a CAD workstation. It is organized around drawing exercises or tasks that offer the reader a demonstration of the commands and techniques being taught at every point, with illustrations that show exactly what to expect on the computer screen when steps are correctly completed. While the focus is on the beginning AutoCAD user, we have found over the years that experienced CAD operators also look to our books for tips, suggestions, and clear explanations of AutoCAD commands and principles.

The AutoCAD world is full of books, many of which do little more than duplicate the function of the *AutoCAD Command Reference*. In this text we strive to present an *optimal learning sequence*. Topics are carefully grouped so that readers will progress logically through the AutoCAD command set. Explanations are straightforward and focus on what is relevant to actual drawing procedures. Most important, drawing exercises are included at the end of every chapter so that newly learned techniques are applied to practical drawing situations immediately. The level of difficulty increases steadily as skills are acquired through experience and practice. At the end of this book we have included additional drawing projects for those who want the extra challenge.

All figures and working drawings have been prepared using AutoCAD. Drawing exercises at the end of all chapters are reproduced in a large, clearly dimensioned format on each right-hand page with accompanying tips and suggestions on the left-hand page. Drawing suggestions offer time-saving tips and explanations on how to use new techniques in actual applications. The book is not a drafting manual, yet the drawings include a wide range of applications. While the focus is on mechanical drawings, there are also architectural drawings in most chapters and anyone completing all the drawings will be well equipped to move on to more advanced and specialized applications.

We would like to thank the many people who have helped us in the preparation of this book. To begin with, thanks to Eric Svendsen, our editor at Prentice Hall, for his encouragement and support, and to Katharita Lamoza, for her expert production editing.

We are grateful to a number of people at Autodesk, Inc., for the use of software and support. Thanks to Houston Instruments for the use of plotters and to Summagraphics for the use of digitizers.

We are grateful to Mike Pilarella for technical advice and support, and to John Williams at Mount Ida College for his interest in this project and his commitment to CAD education.

Thanks to Brian Cook, Jeremy O'Hara, and Matt Rose for classroom testing this manuscript.

Mark Dix and Paul Riley

INTRODUCTION TO RELEASE 14

Release 14 is a pleasure to work with. Performance improvements along with enhancements in object snap, object property definitions, startup routines, and online help, to name a few, make it far superior to any previous AutoCAD release. Most tools that you will need are readily available in the pull-down menus and toolbars of the default screen setup, and additional toolbars are easily accessed through the toolbar dialog box. With Release 14, AutoCAD has also moved completely into the world of Windows 95. There is no longer a DOS version and the Windows elements will be familiar and comfortable for anyone who has used other Windows 95 applications. With these enhancements, new learners should be able to master techniques more smoothly and quickly than with any other release of AutoCAD.

Varieties of CAD

This book takes the reader through a broad range of essential AutoCAD drawing techniques. Part I (Chapters 1–6) focuses on 2D drawing and editing procedures using lines, arcs, and circles with multiple layers, linetypes, and colors. Part II (Chapters 7–11) adds text and dimensions to drawings along with blocks, polylines, and other complex 2D entities. Part III (Chapters 12–14) moves into the exciting world of 3D, including wireframe, surface, and solid modeling.

AutoCAD has become the industry standard software for computer-aided drafting and design. It is widely used for the preparation of all types of drawings that previously would have been created on a drafting board. Its "open architecture" allows companies and third-party developers to customize it for specific applications, so that productivity is further enhanced.

AutoCAD is a full 3D package capable of a tremendous range of both 2D and 3D applications. It is useful to think in terms of a hierarchy of complexity in the use of CAD. On the first level is 2D drafting. This is the world for which AutoCAD was originally developed. Two-dimensional drawings in AutoCAD can be stored, edited, and plotted to any scale or paper size. The windowing, layering, and multiple viewport capabilities of AutoCAD allow a single drawing to produce a variety of different plots, depending on the type of information required. Through the process of attribute extraction, 2D drawings also can be used in conjunction with database programs to produce numerical data for cost estimates and bills of materials (see Chapter 10). 2D drawing techniques are the subject of Chapters 1–11. However, everything learned in the 2D chapters will be useful in 3D, and nothing will need to be relearned.

The second level in this hierarchy is 3D wireframe modeling. This is the focus of Chapter 12. Wireframe models share with 2D drawings an emphasis on precise dimensioning, which can be used in communicating design specifications for manufacturing as well as for cost estimates and bills of materials. There is no attempt in either 2D drafting or wireframe modeling to represent the physical qualities of the object being drawn. Rather, the emphasis is on a precise mathematical description of outlines, boundaries, and edges. A wireframe model may be viewed from any angle and can be used to produce 2D orthographic projections, which may be plotted simultaneously.

Surface modeling is the third level. A surface model not only shows the outline of objects, it also attempts to fill in between the lines. Surface models are explored in Chapter 13. One of the primary uses of surface modeling is to produce realistic shaded renderings that simulate the effect of light and shadow on real surfaces. AutoCAD Release 14 includes full rendering capabilities, which are introduced in Chapter 14.

Finally, solid modeling is the fourth level of CAD. Solid models can be constructed by combining and subtracting basic solid shapes. In some applications, the goal of solid modeling is to represent not only the shapes but also interior characteristics of solid objects. Solid modeling is used by engineering firms to perform finite element analysis (FEA). FEA allows designers and engineers to simulate and predict the behavior of 3D objects based on mathematical representations of their interior physical properties. In Chapter 14 we offer a substantial introduction to Release 14 solid modeling and rendering.

PART I
BASIC TWO-DIMENSIONAL ENTITIES

1 Lines

COMMANDS

DRAW	**EDIT**	**FILE**	**VIEW**
LINE	REDO	NEW	UCSICON
	U	SAVE	
		SAVEAS	
		OPEN	

OVERVIEW

This chapter will introduce you to some of the tools you will use whenever you draw in AutoCAD. You will begin to find your way around Release 14 for menus and toolbars, and you will learn to control basic elements of the Drawing Window. You will produce drawings involving straight lines and learn to undo your last command with the U command. Your drawings will be saved, if you wish, using the SAVE or SAVEAS commands.

TASKS

1.1   Beginning a New Drawing

When you load Release 14 you will find yourself in the Drawing Window with the Start Up dialog box open. The Drawing Window is where you do most of your work with AutoCAD. You can begin a new drawing or open a previously saved file. In this task you will begin a new drawing and ensure that your Drawing Window shows the "Start from Scratch" default settings we have used in preparing this chapter.

⊕   From the Windows 95 Start Up screen, choose Programs, then the AutoCAD Release 14 folder, and then the AutoCAD Release 14 program.

Or, if your system has an AutoCAD Release 14 shortcut icon on the Windows 95 desktop, double click on the icon to start AutoCAD.

⊕   Wait ...

When you see the Release 14 screen with the Start Up dialog box in the foreground, as shown in Figure 1-1, you are ready to begin.

The Start Up dialog box gives you several options, including the use of a Wizard, which guides you through setup; a template, which uses a previously saved template drawing as the basis for your new drawing; and starting from scratch. For our purposes it will be best to start from scratch to ensure that your Drawing Window shows the same settings as are used in this chapter. We will explore other possibilities later.

You should see your cursor arrow somewhere on the screen. If you do not see it, move your pointing device to the middle of your drawing area or digitizer. When you see the arrow, you are ready to proceed.

⊕   Click on "Start from Scratch".

Figure 1-1

Figure 1-2

⊕ Click on "English" in the Select Default Setting box.

⊕ Click on Okay to exit the dialog and start your new drawing.

Pressing Enter will also work.

The dialog box will disappear and your screen should resemble Figure 1-2. You are now ready to proceed to Task 1.2.

1.2 Exploring the Drawing Window

You are looking at the AutoCAD Drawing Window. There are many ways that you can alter it to suit a particular drawing application. To begin with, there are a number of features that can be turned on and off using your mouse or the F-keys on your keyboard. Note that the six function keys and their functions are listed at the bottom of every drawing in this chapter, so it is not necessary to memorize them now. You will learn them best through repeated use.

The Screen

The Release 14 Drawing Window has many features that are common to all Windows 95 programs. At the top of the screen you will see the title bar, with the AutoCAD Release 14 icon on the left and the standard Windows 95 minimize, maximize, and close buttons on the right. Next to the word "AutoCAD" you will also see "[Drawing]". This is AutoCAD's default drawing name. When you have named and saved your drawing, the drawing name will appear in the brackets. This drawing name is also displayed at the bottom of the screen on the Windows 95 taskbar.

Below the title bar you will see Release 14's pull-down menu bar, including the titles for the File, Edit, View, Insert, Format, Tools, Draw, Dimension, Modify, and Help pull-down menus. Pull-down menus are discussed later in this task.

The next line down is the standard toolbar. This toolbar is one of many toolbars that can be displayed on the Release 14 screen. The use of toolbars will also be discussed later in this chapter and in Chapter 3.

The next line is the Object Properties toolbar, which displays the current layer and linetype. It also includes tools for changing other object properties. Layers and linetypes are discussed in Chapter 4.

Below these toolbars you will see the drawing area on the right with the Draw and Modify toolbars positioned vertically on the left.

Below the drawing area and along the right side of the screen you will see scroll bars. These work like the scroll bars in any Windows application. Clicking on the arrows or clicking and dragging the square sliders will move your drawing to the left or right, up or down within the drawing area. You should have no immediate need for this function.

Beneath the scroll bar you will see the command prompt area. Typed commands are one of the basic ways of working in AutoCAD.

At the bottom of the Drawing Window is the status bar, with the coordinate display on the left and six mode indicators (Snap, Grid, Ortho, Osnap, Model, and Tile) in the middle. The coordinate display and mode indicators are discussed shortly.

Finally, the bottom of your screen will show the Windows 95 taskbar, with the Start button on the left and any open applications following. You should see the Release 14 icon and the name of your drawing here, as at the top of your screen.

> **Tip:** You can expand your drawing window slightly if you wish by hiding the Windows 95 taskbar. This can be done by pointing to the top of the taskbar and dragging it down off the bottom of the screen. It will move down, leaving only the top edge showing. To get it back, point to this top edge again and drag it upward.

Switching Screens

⊕ Press F2.

This brings up the AutoCAD text window. AutoCAD uses this window to display text that will not fit in the command area. As soon as the text window opens, Windows 95 adds a button for it on the taskbar at the bottom of the screen. Now you can open and close the text window using the taskbar buttons or F2.

⊕ Press F2 again, or click on the AutoCAD—[Drawing] button on the taskbar.

This brings you back to the Drawing Window. Once used, the AutoCAD Text Window operates like an open application. It remains "open" but may be visible or invisible until you close it using the close button in the upper right corner.

⊕ Press F2 or the AutoCAD text window button to view the text window again.

⊕ Click on the close button (X) in the upper right corner of the text window to close the text window.

Note: Sometimes AutoCAD switches to the text window automatically when there is not enough room in the command area for prompts or messages. If this happens, use F2 when you are ready to return to the drawing area.

The Mouse

Your pointing device has many functions and will handle most of your interaction with the AutoCAD drawing window. Given the toolbar and menu structure of AutoCAD and Windows 95, a two-button mouse is sufficient for most applications. In this book we will assume two buttons. If you have a digitizer and a more complex pointing device, the two button functions will be present along with other functions that we will not address.

On a common two-button mouse the left button will be used for point selection, object selection, and menu or tool selection. All mouse instructions refer to this left button, unless specifically stated otherwise. The right button functions as an alternative to the enter key on the keyboard and, when used in the right context, calls pop-up menus or help windows. Learning how and when to use these right-button functions can immediately increase your efficiency. We will point them out as we go along.

Cross Hairs and Pickbox

You should see a small cross with a box at its intersection somewhere in the display area of your screen. If you do not see it, move your pointing device until it appears. The two perpendicular lines are the cross hairs, or screen cursor, which tell you where your pointing device is located on your digitizer or mouse pad.

The small box at the intersection of the cross hairs is called the pickbox and is used to select objects for editing. You will learn more about the pickbox later.

Move the pointer and see how the cross hairs move in coordination with your hand movements.

⊕ Move the pointer so that the cross hairs move to the top of the screen.

When you leave the drawing area, your cross hairs will be left behind and you will see an arrow pointing up and to the left. The arrow will be used as in other Windows 95 applications to select tools and to pull down menus from the menu bar.

Note: Here and throughout this book we show the Release 14 Windows 95 versions of AutoCAD screens in our illustrations. If you are working with another version, your screen may show significant variations.

⊕ Move the cursor back into the drawing area and the selection arrow will disappear.

Toolbars and Pull-Down Menus

There are 17 toolbars available in the standard AutoCAD Release 14 toolbar dialog box. Toolbars can be created and modified. They can be moved, resized, and reshaped. They are a convenience, but they can also make your work and your drawing area overly cluttered. For our purposes you will not need more than a few of the available toolbars.

The Coordinate Display

The coordinate display at the bottom left of the status line keeps track of coordinates as you move the pointer. The coordinate display is controlled using the F6 key.

Move the cross hairs around slowly and keep your eye on the three numbers at the bottom of the screen. They should be moving very rapidly through four-place decimal numbers. When you stop moving, the numbers will be showing coordinates for the location of the pointer. These coordinates are standard coordinate values in a three-dimensional coordinate system originating from (0,0,0) at the lower left corner. The first value is the x value, showing the horizontal position of the cross hairs, measuring left to right. The second value is y, or the vertical position of the cross hairs, measured from bottom to top. Points also have a z value, but it will always be 0 in two-dimensional drawing and can be ignored until you begin to draw in 3D (Chapter 12). *In this book we will usually not include the z value if it is 0, as it will be until we get into 3D drawings.*

⊕ Press F6.

The numbers will freeze and the coordinate display will turn gray.

⊕ Move the cross hairs slowly.

Now when you move the cross hairs you will see that the coordinate display does not change. You will also see that it is grayed out. The display is now in static mode, in which the numbers will only change when you select a new point by pressing the pickbutton on your cursor. Try it.

⊕ Move the cross hairs to any point on the screen and press the left button on your mouse. The left button is the pickbutton.

Notice that the first two numbers in the coordinate display change, but the display is still grayed out.

⊕ Move the cross hairs to another point on the screen.

You will see that AutoCAD opens a box on the screen, as shown in Figure 1-3. This is the **object selection window**. It will have no effect now since there are no objects on your screen. Object selection is discussed in Chapter 2.

AutoCAD prompts for the other corner of the box. You will see this in the command area:

                    Other corner:

⊕ Pick a second point.

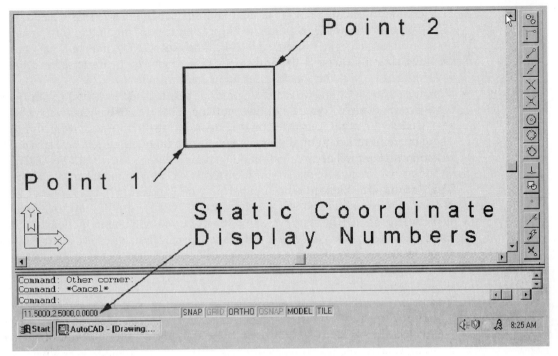

Figure 1-3

This will complete the object selection window. Notice the change in the static coordinate display numbers.

⊞ Press F6 to return the coordinate display to dynamic mode.

The coordinate display actually has two different dynamic modes, but this will not be apparent until you enter a drawing command such as LINE (Task 1.3), which asks for point selection.

Note: The units AutoCAD uses for coordinates, dimensions, and for measuring distances and angles can be changed at any time using the UNITS command (Chapter 2). For now we will accept the AutoCAD default values, including the four-place decimals. In the next chapter we will be changing to two-place decimals. *The F-keys are switches only; they cannot be used to change settings.*

The Grid

⊞ Press F7 or double click on the word GRID on the status bar.

This will turn on the grid. When the grid is on, the word "GRID" will become black on the status bar.

The grid is simply a matrix of dots that helps you find your way around on the screen. It will not appear on your drawing when it is plotted, and it may be turned on and off at will. You may also change the spacing between dots using the GRID command, as we will be doing in Chapter 2.

The grid is presently set up to emulate the shape of an A-size (9×12 inch) piece of paper. There are 10 grid points from bottom to top, numbered 0 to 9, and 13 points from left to right, numbered 0 to 12. The AutoCAD command that controls the outer size and shape of the grid is LIMITS, which will be discussed in Chapter 4. Until then we will continue to use the present format.

You should be aware from the beginning that there is no need to scale Auto-CAD drawings while you are working on them. That can be handled when you get ready to plot or print your drawing on paper. You will always draw at full-scale, where one unit of length on the screen equals one unit of length in real space. This full-scale drawing space is called "model space." Notice the word "MODEL" on the status bar, indicating that you are currently working in model space. The actual size of drawings printed out on paper may be handled in "paper space." When you are in paper space you will see the word "PAPER" on the status bar in place of the word "MODEL". For now, all your work will be done in model space, and you do not need to be concerned with paper space. The word "TILE" at the right of the status bar also affects model space and paper space, but is of no concern to you at this point.

Snap

⊹   Press F9 or double click on the word "SNAP" on the status bar.
SNAP should become black, indicating that the snap mode is now on.

⊹   Move the cross hairs slowly around the drawing area.
Look closely and you will see how the cross hairs jump from point to point. If your grid is on, notice that it is impossible to make the cross hairs touch a point that is not on the grid. Try it.

You will also see that the coordinate display shows only values ending in 0.0000 or 0.5000.

⊹   Press F9 or double click on SNAP again.
Snap should now be off and SNAP will be grayed out on the status bar again.

If you move the cursor in a circle now, you will see that the cross hairs move more smoothly, without jumping. You will also observe that the coordinate display moves rapidly through a full range of four-place decimal values again.

F9 turns snap on and off. With snap off you can, theoretically, touch every point on the screen. With snap on you can move only in predetermined increments. With the Start from Scratch default settings snap is set to a value of 0.5000 so that you can move only in half unit increments. In the next chapter you will learn how to change this setting using the SNAP command. For now we will leave the snap setting alone. A snap setting of 0.5000 will be adequate for the drawings at the end of this chapter.

Using an appropriate snap increment is a tremendous timesaver. It allows for a degree of accuracy that is not possible otherwise. If all the dimensions in a drawing fall into 1-inch increments, for example, there is no reason to deal with points that are not on a 1-inch grid. You can find the points you want much more quickly and accurately if all those in between are temporarily eliminated. The snap setting will allow you to do that.

Ortho

F8 turns ortho mode on and off. You will not observe the ortho mode in action until you have entered the LINE command, however. We will try it out at the end of Task 1.3.

The User Coordinate System Icon

At the lower left of the screen you will see the User Coordinate System (UCS) icon (see Figure 1-2). These two perpendicular arrows clearly indicate the directions of the x and y axes, which are currently aligned with the sides of your screen. In Chapter 12, when you begin to do 3D drawings, you will be defining your own coordinate systems, which can be turned at any angle and originate at any point in space. At that time you will find that the icon is a very useful visual aid. However, it is hardly necessary in two-dimensional drawing and may be distracting. For this reason you may want to turn it off now and keep it turned off until you actually need it.

⊕ Type "ucsicon".

Notice that the typed letters are displayed on the command line to the right of the colon.

⊕ Press the enter key on your keyboard.

AutoCAD will show the following prompt on the command line:

ON/OFF/All/Noorigin/ORigin <ON>:

As you explore AutoCAD commands you will become familiar with many prompts like this one. It is simply a series of options separated by slashes (/). For now we only need to know about "On" and "Off".

⊕ Type "off" and press enter.

The UCS icon will disappear from your screen. Anytime you want to see it again, type "ucsicon" and then type "on". Alternatively, you can click on "View" on the menu bar, then highlight "Display" and "Ucsicon" and click "On". This will turn the icon on if it is off and off if it is on.

1.3 Exploring Command Entry Methods

You can communicate drawing instructions to AutoCAD by typing or by selecting items from a toolbar, a pull-down menu, or a tablet menu. Each method has its advantages and disadvantages depending on the situation. Often a combination of two or more methods is the most efficient way to carry out a complete command sequence. The instructions in this book are not always specific about which to use. All operators develop their own preferences.

Each method is described briefly. You do not have to try them all out at this time. Read them over to get a feel for the possibilities and then proceed to the LINE command. As a rule, we suggest learning the keyboard procedure first. It is the most basic, the most comprehensive, and changes the least from one release of AutoCAD to the next. But do not limit yourself by typing everything. As soon as you know the keyboard sequence, try out the other methods to see how they vary and how you can use them to save time. Ultimately, you will want to type as little as possible and use the differences between the menu systems to your advantage.

The Keyboard and the Command Line

The keyboard is the most primitive and fundamental method of interacting with AutoCAD. Toolbars, pull-down menus, and tablet menus all function by automating basic command sequences as they would be typed on the keyboard. It is therefore useful to be familiar with the keyboard procedures even if the other methods are sometimes faster.

As you type commands and responses to prompts, the characters you are typing will appear on the command line after the colon. Remember that you must press enter to complete your commands and responses. The command line can be moved and reshaped, or you can switch to the text screen using F2 when you want to see more lines, including previously typed entries.

It is useful to know that some of the most often used commands, such as LINE, ERASE, and CIRCLE, have "aliases." These one- or two-letter abbreviations are very handy. A few of the most commonly used aliases are shown in Figure 1-4. In Release 14 there are a large number of two-letter aliases, which we will introduce as we go along.

Pull-Down Menus

Pull-down menus and toolbars have the advantage that instead of typing a complete command, you can simply "point and shoot" to select an item. In Release 14, the pull-down menus contain most commands that you will use regularly. Menu selections and toolbar selections often duplicate each other.

Pull-down menus work here as they do in any Windows 95 application. To use a menu, move the cross hairs up into the menu bar so that the selection arrow appears. Then move the arrow to the menu heading you want. Select it with the pick-

COMMAND ALIAS CHART		
LETTER + ENTER		= COMMAND
A	⏎	ARC
C	⏎	CIRCLE
E	⏎	ERASE
L	⏎	LINE
M	⏎	MOVE
P	⏎	PAN
R	⏎	REDRAW
Z	⏎	ZOOM

Figure 1-4

Figure 1-5

button (the left button on your mouse). A menu will appear. Run down the list of items to the one you want. Press the pickbutton again to select the item (see Figure 1-5). Items followed by a triangle have "cascading" submenus. Submenus open automatically when an item is highlighted. Picking an item that is followed by an ellipsis (…) will call up a dialog box.

Dialog boxes are familiar features in many Windows and Macintosh programs. They require a combination of pointing and typing that is fairly intuitive. We will discuss many dialog boxes in detail as we go along.

Toolbars

Toolbars are also a standard Windows feature. They are comprised of buttons with icons that give one-click access to commands. Seventeen toolbars can be opened from the Toolbars dialog box at the bottom of the View pull-down menu.

Once opened, toolbars can "float" anywhere on the screen, or can be "docked" along the edges of the drawing area. Toolbars can be a nuisance, since they cover portions of your drawing space, but they can be opened and closed quickly. Beyond the Standard, Object Properties, Draw, and Modify toobars, which are open by default, you will probably only wish to open a toolbar if you are doing a whole set of procedures involving one toolbar. In dimensioning an object, for example, you may wish to have the Dimensioning toolbar open. Do not use too many toolbars at once, and remember that you can move toolbars or use the scroll bars to move your drawing right, left, up, and down behind the toolbars.

Figure 1-6

The icons used on toolbars are also a mixed blessing. One picture may be worth a thousand words, but with so many pictures, you may find that a few words can be very helpful as well. As in other Windows applications, you can get a label for an icon simply by allowing the selection arrow to rest on the button for a moment without selecting it. These labels are called "Tooltips". Try this:

⊕ Position the selection arrow on the top button of the Draw toolbar, as shown in Figure 1-6, but do not press the pickbutton.

You will see a yellow label that says "Line", as shown in Figure 1-6. This label identifies this button as the LINE command button.

When a tooltip is displayed, you will also see a phrase in the status bar in place of the coordinate display. This phrase will describe what the tool or menu item does and is called a "Helpstring." The LINE helpstring says "Creates straight line segments: line". The word following the colon identifies the command as you would type it in the command area.

Tablet Menus

If you are using a digitizer with a tablet (as opposed to a mouse) you may have a tablet menu available. With any good menu system there should be a large number of commands and subcommands available on the tablet, and you will not have to search through submenus or toolbars to find them. The major disadvantage of the tablet menu is that in order to use it you must take your eyes off the screen.

On a digitizing tablet simply move the pointing device over the item you want and press the pickbutton (see Figure 1-7).

Now let's get started drawing.

Figure 1-7

1.4   Drawing and Undoing Lines

> **GENERAL PROCEDURE**
>
> 1. Type "L", select Line from the Draw menu, or select the Line tool from the Draw toolbar.
> 2. Pick a start point.
> 3. Pick an end point.
> 4. Pick another end point to continue in the LINE command, or press enter or the enter button on your mouse to exit the command.

Now it is time to enter the LINE command and start drawing.

⊕   Type "L" or select the Line icon from the Draw toolbar, or Line under Draw on the pull-down menu (remember to press enter if you are typing).

Look at the command area. You should see this, regardless of how you enter the command:

From point:

This is AutoCAD's way of asking for a start point.

Also, notice that the pickbox disappears from the cross hairs when you have entered a drawing command.

Most of the time when you are drawing you will want to point rather than type. To do this you need to pay attention to the grid and the coordinate display.

⊕   If snap is off switch it on (F9 or double click on SNAP).

⊕   Move the cursor until the display reads "1.0000, 1.0000, 0.000". Then press the pickbutton.

Now AutoCAD will ask for a second point. You should see this in the command area:

To point:

Rubber Band

There are two new things to be aware of. One is the "rubber band," which extends from the start point to the cross hairs on the screen. If you move the cursor, you will see that this visual aid stretches, shrinks, or rotates like a tether, keeping you connected to the start point. You will also notice that when the rubber band and the cross hairs overlap (i.e., when the rubber band is at 0, 90, 180, or 270 degrees), they both disappear in the area between the cross hairs and the start point, as illustrated in Figure 1-8. This may seem odd at first, but it is actually a great convenience. You will find many instances where you will need to know that the cross hairs and the rubber band are exactly lined up.

Figure 1-8

Absolute (*xyz*) and Polar Coordinates

The other thing to watch is the coordinate display. If it is off (no change in coordinates when the cursor moves), press F6 to turn it on. Once it is on it will show either absolute coordinates or polar coordinates. Absolute coordinates are the familiar coordinate numbers discussed previously. They are distances measured from the origin (0,0,0) of the coordinate system at the lower left corner of the grid. If your display shows three four-digit numbers, then these are the absolute coordinates.

If your display shows something like "4.2426<45,0.0000", it is set on polar coordinates.

⊞   Press F6 and move your cursor.

Which type of coordinates is displayed?

⊞   Press F6 and move your cursor again.

Observe the coordinate display. You will see that there are three coordinate display modes: static (no change until you select a point), *xyz* (*x*, *y*, and *z* values separated by a comma), and polar (length<angle, *z*).

⊞   Press F6 once or twice until it shows polar coordinates.

Polar coordinates are in a length, angle, *z* format and are given relative to the last point you picked. They look something like this: 5.6569<45,0.0000. There are three values here: 5.6569, 45, and 0.0000. The first number (5.6569) is the distance from the starting point of the line to the cross hairs. The second (45) is an angle of rotation, measuring counterclockwise, with 0 degrees being straight out to the right. The third value (0.0000) is the *z* coordinate, which will remain zero in 2D drawing. In LINE, as well as most other draw commands, polar coordinates are very useful because the first number will give you the length of the segment you are currently drawing.

⊞   Press F6 to read *xyz* coordinates.

Figure 1-9

⊕ Pick the point (8.0000,8.0000,0.0000).

Your screen should now resemble Figure 1-9. AutoCAD has drawn a line between (1,1) and (8,8) and is asking for another point.

To point:

This will allow you to stay in the LINE command to draw a whole series of connected lines if you wish. You can draw a single line from point to point, or a series of lines from point to point to point to point. In either case, you must tell AutoCAD when you are finished by pressing enter or the enter-equivalent button on the cursor, or the space bar.

Note: When you are drawing a continuous series of lines, the polar coordinates on the display are given relative to the most recent point, not the original starting point.

⊕ Press enter or the space bar to end the LINE command.

You should be back to the "Command:" prompt again, and the pickbox will have reappeared at the intersection of the cross hairs.

Space Bar, Enter Key, and Enter Button

In most cases AutoCAD allows you to use the space bar as a substitute for the enter key or the enter button on your mouse. This is often a convenience, since the space bar is easy to locate with one hand while the other hand is on the pointing device. For example, the LINE command can be entered without removing your right hand from your pointing device by typing the "L" on the keyboard and then hitting the space bar, both with the left hand. The major exception to the use of the space bar as an enter key is when you are entering text in the TEXT, DTEXT, or MTEXT commands (Chapter 7). Since a space may be part of a text string, the space bar must have its usual significance there.

Tip: Hitting the space bar, the enter key, or the enter button on your pointing device at the command prompt will repeat the last command entered. This is a major convenience, and we recommend that you use it often.

Relative Coordinates and "@"

Besides typing or showing absolute *xyz* coordinates, AutoCAD allows you to enter points using coordinates relative to the last point selected. To do this, use the "@" symbol. For example, after picking the point (1,1) in the last exercise you could have specified the point (8,8) by typing "@7,7", since the second point is over 7 and up 7 from the first point. Or, using polar coordinates relative to (1,1), you could, in theory, type "@9.8995<45". All of these methods would give the same results.

Direct Distance Entry

Another convenient drawing method, new in Release 14, is called Direct Distance Entry. In this method, you pick the first point and then show the direction of the line segment you wish to draw, but instead of picking the other end point you type in a value for the length of the line. Try it:

⊕ Repeat the LINE command by pressing enter, the space bar, or the enter (right) button on your mouse.

AutoCAD prompts for a first point.

Tip: If you press enter, the space bar, or the enter button at the "From point:" prompt, AutoCAD will select the last point entered, so that you can begin drawing from where you left off.

⊕ Press enter, the space bar, or the enter button on your mouse to select the point (8,8,0), the end point of the previously drawn line.

AutoCAD prompts for a second point.

⊕ Pull the rubber band diagonally down to the right, as shown in Figure 1-10.

Figure 1-10

Figure 1-11

Figure 1-12

Moving along the diagonal set of grid points will put you at a −45 degree angle, as shown. The length of the rubber band does not matter, only the direction.

⊕   With the rubber band stretched out as shown, type "3".

⊕   Press enter, or hit the space bar.

AutoCAD will draw a 3.0000 line segment at the angle you have shown.

⊕   Press enter, the enter button on your pointing device, or the space bar to exit the LINE command.

Your screen should resemble Figure 1-11.

Undoing Commands with U

⊕   To undo the line you just drew, type "U" <enter> or select the Undo tool from the Standard toolbar, as shown in Figure 1-12.

U undoes the last command, so if you have done anything else since drawing the line, you will need to type "U" <enter> more than once. In this way you can walk backward through your drawing session, undoing your commands one by one.

⊕   To bring the line back, type "REDO" <enter> or select the Redo tool, which is to the right of the Undo tool on the Standard toolbar.

REDO only works immediately after U, and it only works once. That is, you can only REDO the last U and only if it was the last command executed.

Note: The Undo tool actually executes a command called U. AutoCAD also has an UNDO command that can be entered at the command line. UNDO is more elaborate than U, which is *not* an alias for UNDO. REDO can be used to reverse either U or UNDO. Also note that R is *not* an alias for REDO.

✦ Before going on, enter U twice, or as many times as necessary to undo any lines you have drawn and leave your drawing area blank.

Ortho

Before completing this section, we suggest that you try the ortho mode.

✦ Type "L" <enter> or select Line or the Line tool.
✦ Pick a starting point. Any point near the center of the screen will do.
✦ Press F8 or double click on the word ORTHO and move the cursor in slow circles.

Notice how the rubber band jumps between horizontal and vertical without sweeping through any of the angles between. Ortho forces the pointing device to pick up points only along the horizontal and vertical quadrant lines from a given starting point. With ortho on you can select points at 0, 90, 180, and 270 degrees of rotation from your starting point only (see Figure 1-13).

The advantages of ortho are similar to the advantages of snap mode, except that it limits angular rather than linear increments. It ensures that you will get precise and true right angles and perpendiculars easily when that is your intent. Ortho will become more important as drawings grow more complex. In this chapter it is hardly necessary, though it will be convenient in drawings 1 and 3.

The Esc key

✦ While still in the LINE command, press the "Esc" (escape) key.

This will abort the LINE command and bring back the "Command": prompt. Esc is used to cancel a command that has been entered. Sometimes

Figure 1-13

it will be necessary to press Esc twice to exit a command and return to the command prompt.

1.5 Saving and Opening Your Drawings

Saving drawings in Release 14 is just like saving a file in most other Windows 95 applications. Use SAVE to save an already named drawing. Use SAVEAS to name a drawing as you save it or save a named drawing under a new name. In all cases, a .dwg extension is added to file names to identify them as AutoCAD files. This is automatic when you name a file.

The SAVE Command

To save your drawing without leaving the drawing window, select "Save" from the File pull-down menu, or select the Save tool from the Standard toolbar, as shown in Figure 1-14.

If the current drawing is already named, Release 14 will save it without intervening dialog. If it is not named, it will open the SAVEAS dialog box and allow you to give it a name before it is saved. SAVEAS is described following.

The SAVEAS Command

To rename a drawing or to give a name to a previously unnamed drawing type "Saveas", select "Saveas…" from the File pull-down menu, or, in an unnamed drawing, select the Save tool from the Standard Toolbar.

Any of these methods will call the Save Drawing As dialog box (see Figure 1-15). The cursor will be blinking in the area labeled "Files:", waiting for you to enter a file name. Include a drive designation, (i.e., "A:1-1") if you are saving your work on a floppy disk. AutoCAD will add the .dwg extension automatically. SAVEAS will also allow you to save different versions of the same drawing under different names while continuing to edit.

OPENing Saved Drawings

To open a previously saved drawing, type "open", select "Open" from the File pull-down menu, or select the Open tool from the Standard toolbar, as shown in Figure 1-16.

Once you have saved a drawing you will need to use the OPEN command to return to it later. Entering the OPEN command by any method will bring up the Select File dialog box shown in Figure 1-17. You can select a file directory in the

Figure 1-14

Figure 1-15

Figure 1-16

Figure 1-17

box at the left and then a file from the box at the right. When you select a file, Release 14 will show a preview image of the selected drawing in the Preview image box at the right. This way you can make sure that you are opening the drawing you want.

Exiting the Drawing Window

To leave AutoCAD, open the File pull-down menu and select "Exit" or click the Windows 95 close button (X) at the upper right of the screen. If you have not saved your current drawing, AutoCAD will ask you if you wish to save your changes before exiting.

1.6   Review Material

Questions

Before going to the drawings, quickly review the following questions and problems. Then you should be ready for Drawing 1.

1. What function key opens and closes the text window?
2. What are the three different modes of the coordinate display and how does each mode appear? How do you switch between modes?
3. Explain and describe the differences among absolute, relative, and polar coordinates.
4. You have just entered the point (1,1,0) and you now wish to enter the point two units straight up from this point. How would you identify this point using absolute, relative, and polar coordinates?
5. What is the value and limitation of having SNAP on?
6. Name three different ways to enter the LINE command.
7. Name and describe three different methods of point selection in AutoCAD.
8. What does the U command do?
9. What is the main limitation of the REDO command?
10. What key do you use to cancel a command?
11. What command would you use to save a new version of a drawing under a new file name? How would you enter it?

Drawing Problems

1. Draw a line from (3,2) to (4,8) using the keyboard only.
2. Draw a line from (6,6) to (7,5) using the mouse only.
3. Draw a line from (6,6) to (6,8) using the direct distance method.
4. Undo (U) all lines on your screen.
5. Draw a square with corners at (2,2), (7,2), (7,7), and (2,7). Then erase it using the U command as many times as necessary.

Tip: Closing a Set of Lines

For drawing an enclosed figure like the one in Problem 5, the LINE command provides a convenient Close option. "Close" will connect the last in a continuous series of lines back to the starting point of the series. In drawing a square, for instance, you would simply type "C" <enter> in lieu of drawing the last of the four lines. For this to work, the whole square must be drawn without leaving the LINE command.

1.7 Drawing 1-1: Grate

Before beginning, look over the drawing page. Notice the F-key reminders and other drawing information at the bottom. The commands on the right are the new commands you will need to do this drawing. They are listed with their toolbar or menu locations in parentheses.

The first two drawings in this chapter are given without dimensions. Instead, we have drawn them as you will see them on the screen, against the background of a half-unit grid. All of these drawings were done using a half-unit snap, and all points will be found on one-unit increments.

DRAWING SUGGESTIONS

- If you are beginning a new drawing, type or select "New…" and then select Start from Scratch in the Startup dialog box. Notice that Release 14 remembers your last selection and it becomes the default. Because of this you may be able simply to press enter or select okay to Startup.
- Remember to watch the coordinate display when searching for a point.
- Be sure that grid, snap, and the coordinate display are all turned on.
- Draw the outer rectangle first. It is six units wide and seven units high, and its lower left-hand corner is at the point (3.0000,1.0000). The three smaller rectangles inside are 4×1.
- The Close option can be used in all four of the rectangles.

IF YOU MAKE A MISTAKE—U

The U command works nicely within the LINE command to undo the last line you drew, or the last two or three if you have drawn a series.

- Type "U" <enter>. The last line you drew will be gone or replaced by the rubber band, awaiting a new end point. If you want to go back more than one line, type "U" <enter> again, as many times as you need.
- If you have already left the LINE command, U will still work, but instead of undoing the last line, it will undo the last continuous series of lines. In Grate this could be the whole outside rectangle, for instance.
- Remember, if you have mistakenly undone something, you can get it back by typing "REDO" <enter>. You cannot perform other commands between U and REDO.

U is quick, easy to use, and efficient as long as you always spot your mistakes immediately after making them. Most of us, however, are more spontaneous in our blundering. We may make mistakes at any time and not notice them until the middle of next week. For us, AutoCAD provides more flexible editing tools, like ERASE, which is introduced in the next chapter.

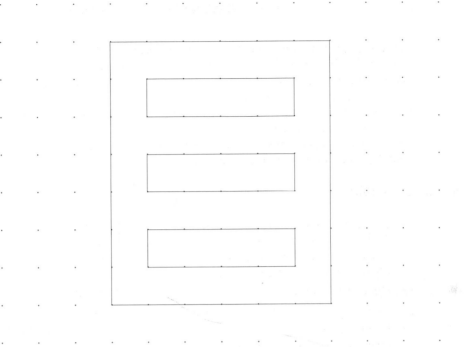

GRATE

Drawing 1—1

F1	F2	F6	F7	F8	F9
HELP	TEXT/GRAPHICS SCREEN	ABSOLUTE/OFF/POLAR COORDS	ON/OFF GRID	ON/OFF ORTHO	ON/OFF SNAP

1.8 Drawing 1-2: Design

This design will give you further practice with the LINE command.

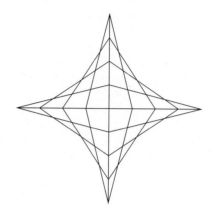

DRAWING SUGGESTIONS

- If you are beginning a new drawing, type or select "New…" and then check the Start Up dialog box to ensure that you Start from Scratch.
- Draw the horizontal and vertical lines first. Each is eight units long.
- Notice how the rest of the lines work—outside point on horizontal to inside point on vertical, then working in, or vice versa.

REPEATING A COMMAND

Remember, you can repeat a command by pressing enter, the enter button on your cursor, or the space bar at the Command: prompt. This will be useful in this drawing, since you have several sets of lines to draw.

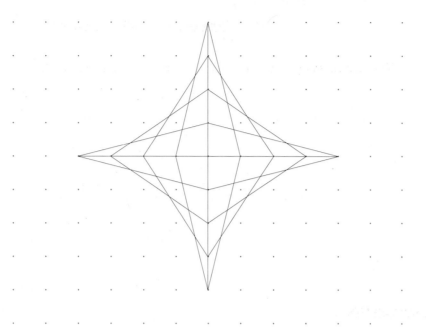

DESIGN # 1

Drawing 1—2

F1	F2	F6	F7	F8	F9
HELP	TEXT/GRAPHICS SCREEN	ABSOLUTE/OFF/POLAR COORDS	ON/OFF GRID	ON/OFF ORTHO	ON/OFF SNAP

1.9   Drawing 1-3: Shim

This drawing will give you further practice in using the LINE command. In addition, it will give you practice in translating dimensions into distances on the screen. Note that the dimensions are only included for your information; they are not part of the drawing at this point. Your drawing will appear like the reference drawing that follows. Dimensioning is discussed in Chapter 8.

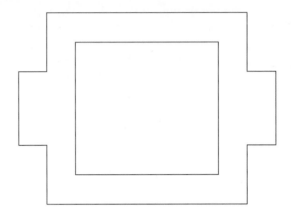

DRAWING SUGGESTIONS

- If you are beginning a new drawing, type or select "New..." and Start from Scratch.
- It is most important that you choose a starting point that will position the drawing so that it fits on your screen. If you begin with the bottom left-hand corner of the outside figure at the point (3,1), you should have no trouble.
- Read the dimensions carefully to see how the geometry of the drawing works. It is good practice to look over the dimensions before you begin drawing. Often the dimension for a particular line may be located on another side of the figure or may have to be extrapolated from other dimensions. It is not uncommon to misread, misinterpret, or miscalculate a dimension, so take your time.

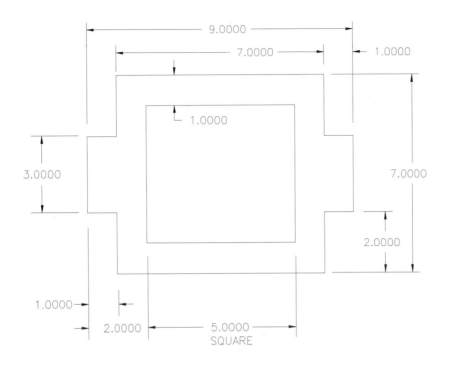

SHIM
Drawing 1–3

F1	F2	F6	F7	F8	F9
HELP	TEXT/GRAPHICS SCREEN	ABSOLUTE/OFF/POLAR COORDS	ON/OFF GRID	ON/OFF ORTHO	ON/OFF SNAP

1.10   Drawing 1-4: Stamp

This drawing will give you practice in point selection. You can begin anywhere and use any of the point selection methods introduced in this chapter. We recommend that you try them all.

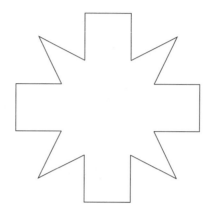

DRAWING SUGGESTIONS

- If you are beginning a new drawing, type or select "New..." and Start from Scratch.
- Choose your first point carefully so that the drawing will fit on the grid.
- The entire drawing can be done without leaving the LINE command if you wish.
- If you do leave LINE, remember that you can repeat LINE by pressing enter or the space bar, and then select the last point as a new start point by pressing enter or the space bar again.
- Plan to use point selection by typing, by pointing, and by direct distance entry. Make use of absolute, relative, and polar coordinates.

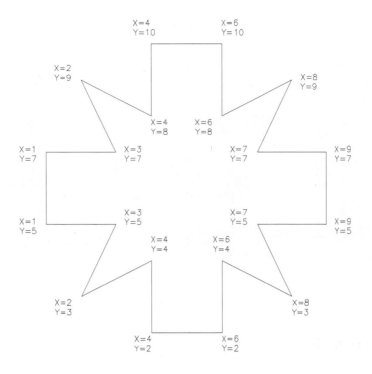

X=4
Y=10

X=6
Y=10

X=2
Y=9

X=8
Y=9

X=4
Y=8

X=6
Y=8

X=1
Y=7

X=3
Y=7

X=7
Y=7

X=9
Y=7

X=1
Y=5

X=3
Y=5

X=7
Y=5

X=9
Y=5

X=4
Y=4

X=6
Y=4

X=2
Y=3

X=8
Y=3

X=4
Y=2

X=6
Y=2

STAMP

Drawing 1—4

F1	F2	F6	F7	F8	F9
HELP	TEXT/GRAPHICS SCREEN	ABSOLUTE/OFF/POLAR COORDS	ON/OFF GRID	ON/OFF ORTHO	ON/OFF SNAP

2

Circles and Drawing Aids

COMMANDS

TOOLS	**DRAW**	**MODIFY**	**VIEW**	**FORMAT**	**HELP**
DDRMODES	CIRCLE	ERASE	REDRAW	UNITS	HELP
DIST		OOPS			
GRID					
SNAP					

OVERVIEW

In this chapter you will learn to change the spacing of the grid and the snap. You will also change the units in which coordinates are displayed. You will explore the CIRCLE command and AutoCAD's HELP features, and learn to delete objects selectively using ERASE. You will also learn to measure and mark distances on the screen using the DIST command. Finally, you will begin to learn AutoCAD plotting and printing procedures.

TASKS

2.1 Changing the GRID setting
2.2 Changing the SNAP setting
2.3 Changing UNITS
2.4 Drawing CIRCLES giving center point and radius
2.5 Drawing CIRCLES giving center point and diameter
2.6 Accessing AutoCAD HELP features

2.7 Using the ERASE command
2.8 Using the DIST command
2.9 Plotting or printing a drawing
2.10 Review material
2.11 Drawing 2-1: Aperture Wheel
2.12 Drawing 2-2: Roller
2.13 Drawing 2-3: Fan Bezel
2.14 Drawing 2-4: Switch Plate
2.15 Drawing 2-5: Gasket

2.1 Changing the GRID Setting

GENERAL PROCEDURE

1. Type "Grid" or select "Drawing Aids" from the Tools menu.
2. Enter a new value.

When you begin a new drawing from scratch in Release 14, the grid and snap are set with a spacing of 0.5000. In Chapter 1 all drawings were done without altering the grid and snap spacings from the default value. Frequently you will want to change this, depending on your application. You may want a 10-foot snap for a building layout, or a 0.010-inch snap for a printed circuit diagram. The grid may match the snap setting or may be set independently.

⊕ To begin, open a new drawing by typing "new" or selecting New from the File menu or the Standard toolbar, and then selecting Start from Scratch and English units in the StartUp dialog box.

Once again, this ensures that you begin with the settings we have used in preparing this chapter.

⊕ Using F7 and F9, or double clicking on the status bar, be sure that GRID and SNAP are both on.

⊕ Type "grid".

We will no longer remind you to press enter after typing a command or response to a prompt. Do not use the pull-down menu or toolbar yet. We will get to those procedures momentarily.

The command area prompt will appear like this, with options separated by slashes (/):

> Grid spacing(X) or ON/OFF/Snap/Aspect <0.5000>:

You can ignore the options for now. The number <0.5000> shows the present setting. AutoCAD uses this format (<default>) in many command sequences to show you a current value or default setting. It usually comes at the end of a series of options. Pressing the enter key or space bar at this point will confirm the default setting.

⊕ In answer to the prompt, type "1" and watch what happens (of course you remembered to press enter).

The screen will change to show a one-unit grid.

⊕ Move the cursor around to observe the effects of the new grid setting.

The snap setting has not changed, so you still have access to all half-unit points, but the grid shows only single-unit increments.

⊕ Try other grid settings. Try 2, 0.25, and 0.125.

Remember that you can repeat the last command, GRID, by pressing enter, the space bar, or the enter key on your pointing device.

⊕ What happens when you try 0.05?

Figure 2-1

When you get too small (smaller than 0.106 on our screen), the grid becomes too dense to display, but the snap can still be set smaller.

Using the Drawing Aids Dialog Box

You can also change grid and snap settings using a dialog box. The procedure is somewhat different, but the result is the same. Select "Tools" from the pull-down bar and then "Drawing Aids…" from the menu. This method will call the Drawing Aids dialog box shown in Figure 2-1. DDRMODES is the command that calls up this dialog box, so you can actually open it from the keyboard as well. Most dialog boxes are called by a command name beginning with DD, which stands for "Dynamic Dialog."

Look at the Drawing Aids dialog box. It contains some typical features, including check boxes, edit boxes, and radio buttons.

Check Boxes

You can turn ortho, snap, and grid on and off by moving the arrow inside the appropriate check box and pressing the pickbutton. A checked box is on, while an empty box is off. Notice that there are seven other check boxes in the area on the left under "Modes". We will only have use for the snap and grid settings at this point.

On the lower right you will see a box for isometric snap and grid control. We will have no use for these until Chapter 11. But notice the boxes in the lower line of the isometric snap/grid area labeled "Left", "Top", and "Right". These are examples of radio buttons, which are discussed in Task 3.

Also notice the "Help…" box at the bottom right. Again, any box with an ellipsis (…) calls another dialog box that will overlay the current one. Picking this box would activate the HELP command, discussed later in this chapter.

Edit Boxes

The snap and grid settings are shown in edit boxes. Edit boxes contain text or numerical information that can be edited as you would in a text editor. You can highlight the entire box to replace the text, or point anywhere inside to do partial editing.

To change the grid or snap setting, use the following procedure:

1. Move the arrow into the box in the table where the change is to be made ("X Spacing" under "Snap" or "Grid").
2. Double click to highlight the entire number.
3. Type a new value and press enter. Notice that the *y* spacing changes automatically when you enter the *x* spacing (see note following).
4. Click on the OK box at the bottom to confirm changes, or "Cancel" to cancel changes.

> **Note:** The dialog box has places to set both *x* and *y* spacing. It is unlikely that you will want to have a grid or snap matrix with different horizontal and vertical increments, but the capacity is there if you do. Also notice that you can change the snap angle. Setting the snap angle to 45, for example, would turn your snap and grid at a 45 degree angle. When you turn the grid or snap angle, you may also want to designate *x* and *y* base points around which to rotate. This is the function of the *x* and *y* base point settings.

⊞ Before going on to Task 2, use the dialog box to set the grid back to 0.5000.

2.2 Changing the SNAP Setting

GENERAL PROCEDURE

1. Type "Snap" or select "Drawing Aids" from the Tools pull-down menu.
2. Enter a new snap value.

Whether you are typing or using one of your menus, the process for changing the snap setting is the same as changing the grid. In fact, the two are similar enough to cause confusion. The grid is only a visual reference. It has no effect on selection of points. Snap is invisible, but it dramatically affects point selection. Grid and snap may or may not have the same setting.

⊞ The grid should be set to 0.5000 from the previous task before you begin.

⊞ Type "snap" or open the Drawing Aids from the Tools menu.

If you are typing, the prompt will appear like this, with options separated by slashes (/):

    Snap spacing(X) or ON/OFF/Aspect/Rotate/Style <0.5000>:

⊞ Type "1".

This makes the snap setting larger than the grid setting. Move the cursor around the screen and you will see that you can only access half of the grid points. Clearly this type of arrangement is not too useful.

⊕ Try other snap settings. Try 2, 0.25, and 0.125.

⊕ Set the snap to 0.05.

Remember what happened when you tried to set the grid to 0.05?

⊕ Move the cursor and watch the coordinate display.

Observe how the snap setting is reflected in the available coordinates. How small a snap will AutoCAD accept?

⊕ Try 0.005.

Move the cursor and observe the coordinate display.

⊕ Try 0.0005.

You could even try 0.0001, but this would be like turning snap off, since you are only going to four decimal places anyway. The point is that unlike the grid, which is limited by the size of your screen, you can set snap to any value you like.

⊕ Finally, before you leave this task, set the snap to 0.25 and the grid to 0.5.

This is the most efficient type of arrangement. With the grid set "coarser" than the snap, you can still pick exact points easily, but the grid is not so dense as to be distracting.

Note: If you wish to keep snap and grid the same, set the grid to "0" in the Drawing Aids dialog box, or enter the GRID command and then type "s", for the Snap option. The grid will then change to match the snap and will continue to change any time you reset the snap. To free the grid, just give it its own value again using the GRID command or the dialog box.

2.3 Changing UNITS

GENERAL PROCEDURE

1. Type "Units", or select "Units ..." from the Format menu.
2. Answer the prompts.
3. Press F2, if necessary, to return to the drawing window.

⊕ Type "Units".

Do not use the pull-down menu yet.

Presto! The text window appears and covers the drawing window. We told you this would happen. The command area is too small to display the complete UNITS sequence, so the drawing window has been temporarily overlaid by the text window. What function key will bring it back?

What you now see looks like this:

REPORT FORMATS:	**(EXAMPLES)**
1. Scientific	1.55E + 01
2. Decimal	15.50
3. Engineering	1'—3.50"
4. Architectural	1'—3 1/2"
5. Fractional	15 1/2

With the exception of Engineering and Architectural formats, these formats can be used with any basic unit of measurement. For example, decimal mode works for metric units as well as English units.

```
Enter choice, 1 to 5 <2>:
```

✚ Type "2" or simply press enter, since the default system, and the one we will use, is number 2, decimal units.

Through most of this book we will stick to decimal units. Obviously, if you are designing a house you will want architectural units. If you are building a bridge you may want engineering-style units. You might want scientific units if you are doing research.

Whatever your application, once you know how to change units, you can do so easily and at any time. However, as a drawing practice you will want to choose appropriate units when you first begin work on a new drawing.

AutoCAD should now be showing the following prompt:

```
Number of digits to right of decimal point, (0 to 8) <4>:
```

We will use two-place decimals because they are practical and more common than any other choice.

✚ Type "2" in answer to the prompt for the number of decimal places you wish to use.

AutoCAD now gives you the opportunity to change the units in which angles are measured. In this book we will use all of the default settings for angle measure, since they are by far the most common. If your application requires something different, the UNITS command or the DDUNITS dialog box is the place to change it.

The default system is standard degrees without decimals, measured counterclockwise, with 0 being straight out to the right (3 o'clock), 90, straight up (12 o'clock), 180 to the left (9 o'clock), and 270 straight down (6 o'clock).

✚ Press enter four times, or until the "Command:" prompt reappears.

Be careful not to press enter again, or the UNITS command sequence will be repeated.

Looking at the coordinate display, you should now see values with only two digits to the right of the decimal. This setting will be standard in this book.

We suggest that you experiment with other choices to get a feel for the options that are available to you. You should also try the Units Control dialog box described next.

Figure 2-2

The Units Control Dialog Box

Activate the Units Control dialog box by picking "Units..." from the Format pull-down menu. You will see the command DDUNITS entered on the command line, and the dialog box shown in Figure 2-2 will appear. This box shows all of the settings that are also available through the UNITS command sequence. There are two dialog box features here that we have not discussed previously.

Radio Buttons

First are the radio buttons in the columns labeled "Units" and "Angles". Radio buttons are used with lists of settings that are mutually exclusive. You should see that the Decimal button is shaded in the format column. All other buttons in this column are not shaded. You can switch settings by simply picking another button, but you can have only one button on at a time. Radio buttons are used here because you can use only one format at a time.

Pop-Down Lists

The second new feature is the pop-down lists at the bottom of the units and angles columns. You should try these out to see how they function. You can change the precision (number of place values shown) by picking the arrow at the right of the box and then picking a setting, such as "0.000" for three place decimals, from the list that appears.

Experiment as much as you like with the dialog box. None of your changes will be reflected in the drawing until you click on the OK button or press enter on the keyboard.

⊞   When you are through experimenting, be sure to leave your units set for two-place decimals, your angle measure set for zero-place decimal degrees, and your angle zero direction set to East.

Note: All dialog boxes can be moved on the screen. This is done by clicking in the gray title area at the top of the dialog box, holding down the pickbutton, and dragging the box across the screen.

2.4 Drawing Circles Giving Center Point and Radius

GENERAL PROCEDURE

1. Type "c", select Circle from the Draw menu, or select the Circle tool from the Draw toolbar.
2. Pick a center point.
3. Enter or show a radius value.

Circles can be drawn by giving AutoCAD three points on the circle's circumference, two points that determine a diameter, two tangents and a radius, a center point and a radius, or a center point and a diameter. In this chapter we will use the latter two options.

We will begin by drawing a circle with radius 3 and center at the point (6,5). Then we will draw two smaller circles centered at the same point. Later we will erase them using the ERASE command.

⊕   Grid should be set to 0.5, snap to 0.25, and units to two-place decimal.

⊕   Type "c", select Circle from the Draw menu, or select the Circle tool from the Draw toolbar, illustrated in Figure 2-3.

The prompt that follows will look like this:

            3P/2P/TTR/<Center point>:

⊕   Type coordinates or point to the center point of the circle you want to draw. In our case it will be the point (6,5).

Figure 2-3

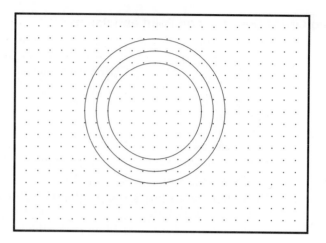

Figure 2-4

AutoCAD assumes that a radius or diameter will follow and shows the following prompt:

Diameter/<Radius>:

If we type or point to a value now, AutoCAD will take it as a radius, since that is the default.

⊕   Type "3" or show by pointing that the circle has a radius of 3.

Notice how the rubber band works to drag out your circle as you move the cursor.

⊕   If your coordinate display is not showing polar coordinates, press F6 once or twice until you see something like "3.00<0, 0.00". When you are ready, press the pickbutton to show the radius end point.

You should now have your first circle complete.

⊕   Draw two more circles using the same center point, radius method. They will be centered at (6,5) and have radii of 2.50 and 2.00.

The results are illustrated in Figure 2-4.

2.5   Drawing Circles Giving Center Point and Diameter

GENERAL PROCEDURE

1. Type "c", select Circle from the Draw menu, or select the Circle tool from the Draw toolbar.
2. Pick a center point.
3. Type "d".
4. Enter or show a diameter value.

We will draw three more circles centered on (6,5) having diameters of 2, 1.5, and 1. Drawing circles this way is almost the same as the radius method, except you will not use the default, and you will see that the rubber band works differently.

⊕ Press enter or the space bar to repeat the CIRCLE command.

⊕ Indicate the center point (6,5) by typing coordinates or pointing.

⊕ Answer the prompt with a "d", for diameter.

Notice that the cross hairs are now outside the circle you are dragging on the screen (see Figure 2-5). This is because AutoCAD is looking for a diameter, but the last point you gave was a center point. So the diameter is being measured from the center point out, twice the radius. Move the cursor around, in and out from the center point, to get a feel for this.

⊕ Point to a diameter of 2.00, or type "2".

You should now have four circles.

⊕ Draw two more circles with diameters of 1.0 and 1.5

When you are done, your screen should look like Figure 2-6.

Figure 2-5

Figure 2-6

2 POINT

Pick two points.
Line between is used as
diameter to construct circle.

3 POINT

Pick three points.
Arc through all three is
completed to form circle.
Circle is visible on screen
after second point selection.

TANGENT, TANGENT, RADIUS

Select two objects on the
screen ("Tangent Specs").
Type or show radius length.
AutoCAD constructs the
circle that has the given
radius and is tangent to
both objects.

TANGENT, TANGENT, TANGENT

Select three objects on the
screen ("Tangent Specs").
Autocad constructs the circle
that is tangent to the three
objects.

Figure 2-7

Sit back and admire your work, because we are about to erase it. In the meantime, studying Figure 2-7 and using the HELP command, as discussed in the next task, will give you a good introduction to the remaining options in the CIRCLE command.

2.6 Accessing AutoCAD HELP Features

> **GENERAL PROCEDURE**
>
> 1. Press F1, open the Help menu and select AutoCAD Help Topics, or select the Help tool from the Standard toolbar.
> 2. Click on the Index tab.
> 3. Type the name of a command or topic.
> 4. Highlight the item you want.
> 5. Press enter or click on Display.

The Release 14 HELP command gives access to a complete library of Auto-CAD references and information. The procedures are standard Windows 95 help procedures and give you access to the *AutoCAD Command Reference*, the *AutoCAD User's Guide*, the *AutoCAD Customization Guide*, the *AutoCAD Installation Guide*, and the *Release 14 Tutorial*. In this task we will focus on the use of the Index feature, which pulls information from all of the references, depending on the topic you select. For demonstration, we will look at the CIRCLE command.

⊕ **To begin you should be at the command prompt.**

HELP is context sensitive, meaning that it will go directly to the *AutoCAD Command Reference* if you ask for help while in the middle of a command sequence. You should try this later.

⊕ **Press F1, open the Help menu and select AutoCAD Help topics ..., or select the question mark at the right end of the Standard toolbar.**

This will open the AutoCAD Help dialog box shown in Figure 2-8. If the Contents tab is showing, you will see the list of available references. These

Figure 2-8

contain the same information as the actual AutoCAD manuals, and you can look through their contents as you would with the books. It is usually quicker to use the Index, however.

⊕ If necessary, click on the Index tab.

You should see the Index as shown in Figure 2-8. The list of topics is very large, so it is rare that you will use the scroll bar on the right. Most often you will type in a command or topic. The list will update as you type, so often you will not need to type the complete word or command.

⊕ Type "Cir".

If you do this slowly, one letter at a time, you will see how the index follows along. When you have typed "cir" you will be at the Circle (Draw menu) options entry. Adding the rest of the letters "cle" will have no further effect.

The entry we want is the CIRCLE command entry, which is just below the Draw menu options.

⊕ Double click on "CIRCLE command" or highlight it and then press enter or click on display.

This will call up a second smaller dialog box with three options. We want the first option.

⊕ Double click on "CIRCLE command" again, or press enter or click on display.

AutoCAD will display the CIRCLE command page from the *AutoCAD Command Reference*, as shown in Figure 2-9. Additional information on items on this page is available for words shown in green.

⊕ Click on "TTR".

This will call up the page for the Tangent, Tangent, Radius option of the CIRCLE command, shown in Figure 2-10.

⊕ To exit HELP, click on the close button, the *x* in the upper right corner of the Help window.

This terminates the HELP command and brings you back to the command prompt. The HELP feature contains a vast amount of information. You are encouraged to access it at any time to expand your knowledge of AutoCAD.

2.7 Using the ERASE Command

GENERAL PROCEDURE

1. Type "e", select Erase from the Modify menu, or select the Erase tool from the Modify toolbar.
2. Select objects.
3. Press enter to carry out the command.

or

1. Select objects.
2. Type "e", select Erase from the Modify menu, or select the Erase tool from the Modify toolbar.

Figure 2-9

AutoCAD allows for many different methods of editing and even allows you to alter some of the basics of how edit commands work. Fundamentally, there are two different sequences for using most edit commands. These are called the Noun/Verb and the Verb/Noun methods.

In earlier versions of AutoCAD, most editing was carried out in a verb/noun sequence. That is, you would enter a command, such as ERASE (the verb), then select objects (the nouns), and press enter to carry out the command. This method is still perfectly reasonable and effective, but AutoCAD now allows you to reverse the verb/noun sequence. You can use either method as long as "Noun/Verb" selection is enabled in your drawing.

In this task we will explore the traditional verb/noun sequence and then introduce the noun/verb or "pick first" method along with some of the many methods for selecting objects.

Verb/Noun Editing

⊞ To begin this task you should have the six circles on your screen, as shown previously in Figure 2-6.

  We will use verb/noun editing to erase the two outer circles.

Figure 2-10

Figure 2-11

⊕ Type "e", select Erase from the Modify menu, or select the Erase tool
from the Modify toolbar, as shown in Figure 2-11.

The cross hairs will disappear, but the pickbox will still be on the screen
and will move when you move your cursor.

Also notice the command area. It should be showing this prompt:

Select objects:

This is a very common prompt. You will find it in all edit commands and
many other commands as well.

⊕ Move your cursor so that the outer circle crosses the pickbox.

Tip: In many situations you may find it convenient or necessary to turn snap
off (F9) while selecting objects, since this gives you more freedom of motion.

⊕ Press the pick button.

The circle will be highlighted (dotted). This is how AutoCAD indicates that an object has been selected for editing. It is not yet erased, however. You can go on and add more objects to the selection set and they, too, will become dotted.

⊕ Use the box to pick the second circle. It too should now be dotted.

⊕ Press enter, the space bar, or the enter-equivalent button on your pointing device to carry out the command.

This is typical of the verb/noun sequence in most edit commands. Once a command has been entered and a selection set defined, a press of the enter key is required to complete the command. At this point the two outer circles should be erased.

Noun/Verb Editing

Now let's try the noun/verb sequence.

⊕ Type "u" to undo the ERASE and bring back the circles.

⊕ Use the pickbox to select the outer circle.

The circle will be highlighted, and your screen should now resemble Figure 2-12. Those little blue boxes are called "grips." They are part of AutoCAD's autoediting system, which we will begin exploring in Chapter 3. For now you can ignore them.

⊕ Pick the second circle in the same fashion.

The second circle will also become dotted, and more grips will appear.

⊕ Type "e", select Erase from the Modify menu, or select the Erase tool from the Modify toolbar.

Your two outer circles will disappear as soon as you press enter or pick the tool.

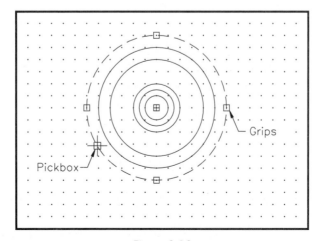

Figure 2-12

The two outer circles should now be gone. As you can see, there is not a lot of difference between the two sequences. One difference that is not immediately apparent is that there are numerous selection methods available in the older verb/noun system that cannot be activated when you pick objects first. We will get to other object select methods momentarily, but first try out the OOPS command.

OOPS!

⊕   Type "oops" and watch the screen.

If you have made a mistake in your erasure, you can get your selection set back by typing "oops". OOPS is to ERASE as REDO is to UNDO. You can use OOPS to undo an ERASE command, as long as you have not done another ERASE in the meantime. In other words, AutoCAD only saves your most recent ERASE selection set.

You can also use U to undo an ERASE, but notice the difference: U simply undoes the last command, whatever it might be; OOPS works specifically with ERASE to recall the last set of erased objects. If you have drawn other objects in the meantime, you can still use OOPS to recall a previously erased set. But if you tried to use U, you would have to backtrack, undoing any newly drawn objects along the way.

Other Object Selection Methods

You can select individual entities on the screen by pointing to them one by one, as we have done previously, but in complex drawings this will often be inefficient. AutoCAD offers a variety of other methods, all of which have application in specific drawing circumstances. In this exercise we will select circles by the "windowing" and "crossing" methods, by indicating "last" or "L", meaning the last entity drawn, and by indicating "previous" or "P" for the previously defined set. There are also options to add or remove objects from the selection set and other variations on windowing and crossing. We suggest that you study Figure 2-13 to learn about other methods. The number of selection options available may seem a bit overwhelming at first, but time learning them will be well spent. These same options appear in many AutoCAD editing commands (MOVE, COPY, ARRAY, ROTATE, MIRROR) and should become part of your CAD vocabulary.

Selection by Window

Window and crossing selections, like individual object selection, can be initiated without entering a command. In other words, they are available for noun/verb selection. Whether you select objects first or enter a command first, you can force a window or crossing selection simply by picking points on the screen that are not on objects. AutoCAD will assume you want to select by windowing or crossing and will ask for a second point.

OBJECT SELECTION METHOD	DESCRIPTION	ITEMS SELECTED
(W) WINDOW		THE ENTITIES WITHIN THE BOX
(C) CROSSING		THE ENTITIES CROSSED BY OR WITHIN THE BOX
(P) PREVIOUS		THE ENTITIES THAT WERE PREVIOUSLY PICKED
(L) LAST		THE ENTITY THAT WAS DRAWN LAST
(R) REMOVE		REMOVES ENTITIES FROM THE ITEMS SELECTED SO THEY WILL NOT BE PART OF THE SELECTED GROUP
(A) ADD		ADDS ENTITIES THAT WERE REMOVED AND ALLOWS FOR MORE SELECTION AFTER THE USE OF REMOVE
ALL		ALL ENTITIES CURRENTLY VISIBLE ON THE DRAWING
(F) FENCE		THE ENTITIES CROSSED BY THE FENCE
(WP) WPOLYGON		THE ENTITIES WITHIN THE THE POLYGON
(CP) CPOLYGON		THE ENTITIES CROSSED BY OR WITHIN THE PLOYGON

Figure 2-13

Let's try it. We will show AutoCAD that we want to erase all of the inner circles by throwing a temporary selection window around them. The window will be defined by two points moving left to right that serve as opposite corners of a rectangle. Only entities that lie completely within the window will be selected. See Figure 2-14.

⊕ Pick point 1 at the lower left of the screen, as shown. Any point in the neighborhood of (3.5,1) will do.

AutoCAD will prompt for another corner:

Other corner:

⊕ Pick point 2 at the upper right of the screen, as shown.

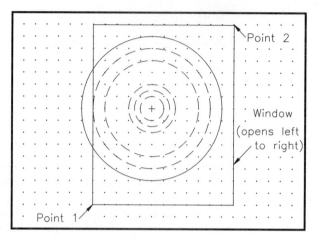

Figure 2-14

Any point in the neighborhood of (9.5,8.5) will do. To see the effect of the window, be sure that it crosses the outside circle, as in Figure 2-14.

⊕ Type "e" or select the Erase tool.

   The inner circles should now be erased.

⊕ Type or select "oops" to retrieve the circles once more. Since ERASE was the last command, typing "U" will work equally well.

Selection by Crossing Window

Crossing is an alternative to windowing that is useful in many cases where a standard window selection could not be performed. The selection procedure is the same, but a crossing box opens to the left instead of to the right and all objects that cross the box will be chosen, not just those that lie completely inside the box.

   We will use a crossing box to select the inside circles.

⊕ Pick point 1 close to (8.0,3.0), as in Figure 2-15.

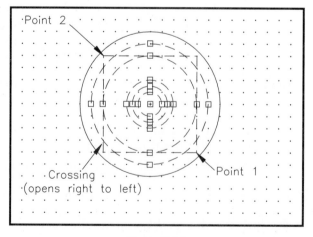

Figure 2-15

AutoCAD prompts:

Other corner:

⊕ Pick a point near (4.0,7.0).

This point selection must be done carefully to demonstrate a crossing selection. Notice that the crossing box is shown with dotted lines, whereas the window box was shown with solid lines.

Also, notice how the circles are selected: those that cross and those that are completely contained within the box, but not those that lie outside.

At this point we could enter the ERASE command to erase the circles, but instead we will demonstrate how to use the Esc key to cancel a selection set.

⊕ Press the Esc key on your keyboard.

This will cancel the selection set. The circles will no longer be highlighted, but you will see that the grips are still visible. To get rid of the grips you will need to cancel again.

⊕ Press Esc again.

The grips should now be gone as well.

Selecting the "Last" Entity

AutoCAD remembers the order in which new objects have been drawn during the course of a single drawing session. As long as you do not leave the drawing, you can select the last drawn entity using the "last" option. If you leave the drawing and return later, this information will no longer be available.

⊕ Type "e" or select the Erase tool.

Notice that there is no way to specify "last" before you enter a command. This option is only available as part of a command procedure. In other words, it only works in a verb/noun sequence.

⊕ Type "L".

The inner circle should be highlighted.

⊕ Press enter to carry out the command.

The inner circle should be erased.

Selecting the "Previous" Selection Set

The P or previous option works with the same procedure, but it selects the previous selection set rather than the last drawn entity. If the difference is not obvious to you now, don't worry: It will become clear as you work more with edit commands and selection sets.

Remove and Add

Together, the remove and add options form a switch in the object selection process. Under ordinary circumstances, whatever you select using any of the aforementioned options will be added to your selection set. By typing "r" at the "Select objects:" prompt you can switch over to a mode in which everything you pick is deselected or removed from the selection set. Then by typing "a" you can return to the usual mode of adding objects to the set.

Undoing a Selection

The ERASE command and other edit commands have an internal undo feature, similar to that found in the LINE command. By typing "u" at the "Select objects:" prompt you can undo your last selection without leaving the edit command you are in and without undoing previous selections. You can also type "u" several times to undo your most recent selections one by one. This allows you to back up one step at a time without having to cancel the command and start all over again.

ALL

"All" is a powerful option that should be used with care. By typing "all" at the "Select objects:" prompt you can select all objects currently visible in your drawing.

Fence

Type "f" at the "Select objects:" prompt and AutoCAD will prompt for a series of "fence points." These points will define a series of line segments called a fence. Any entity that the fence crosses or touches will be selected. This is a very useful option in tight, complex areas.

WPolygon and CPolygon

Type "wp" for "window polygon" or "cp" for "crossing polygon" at the "Select objects:" prompt. AutoCAD will ask for a series of polygon points. These will become the vertices of an irregular polygon of as many sides as you like. Objects will be - selected as in window and crossing selections. That is, a window polygon will select only objects that lie completely within the window. A crossing polygon will select objects inside and objects that cross the polygon.

Group

Using the GROUP command, you can define a set of objects as a named group. Once defined, a group may be selected as a unit using the group option and the group name. Groups are discussed in Chapter 10.

Other Options

If you hit any key other than the ones AutoCAD recognizes, at the "Select objects:" prompt you will see the following:

```
                    Expects a point
```

or

```
Window/Last/Crossing/Box/All/Fence/WPolygon/Cpolygon/Group/Add/
   Remove/Multiple/Previous/Undo/AUto/SIngle
Select objects:
```

Along with the options already discussed, you will see Box, Multiple, AUto, and SIngle. These options mostly are used in programming customized applications. Look up the SELECT command in the *AutoCAD Command Reference* for additional information.

2.8   Using the DIST Command

GENERAL PROCEDURE

1. Type "Dist" or open the Tools menu, highlight Inquiry, and select Distance.
2. Pick first point.
3. Pick second point.
4. Read information in command area or use blips as guide points.

   The DIST command is one of AutoCAD's most useful inquiry commands. Inquiry commands give you information about your drawing. DIST works like a simple LINE command procedure, but it gives you distances instead of actually drawing a line.
   There are two principal uses of the DIST command. The most obvious is that it may be used to measure distances or the lengths of linear objects on the screen. The second use is less obvious and will require a change in the setting of the BLIPMODE system variable. In Release 14, BLIPMODE is set to off by default. If you turn it on, AutoCAD will place a small cross on the screen any time you select a point. You will not need these indicators most of the time, but they can be helpful. With the DIST command they can be used as guide points for drawing lines, circles, or other entities. This "guide point" method is introduced later in the drawing suggestions for Drawing 2-4, "Switch Plate."
   The following exercise will introduce you to blips, the REDRAW command, and the DIST command.

BLIPS

⊕   Open the Tools menu and select Drawing Aids ...

⊕   In the Drawing Aids dialog box click the Blips check box on the left under Modes.

⊕   Click on OK.

   This changes the setting of the BLIPMODE system variable. With the Blips box checked AutoCAD will display a blip any time you select a point. You will see this as we use the DIST command.

⊕   Type "Dist" or open the Tools menu, highlight Inquiry, and select Distance.

AutoCAD will prompt you to pick a point:

First point:

⊕   Pick a point anywhere near the middle of the screen.

Notice that AutoCAD gives you a blip at the first point and a rubber band, just as if you were drawing a line. You are also prompted for a second point:

Second point:

⊕   Pick any other point on the screen.

A blip is placed at the second point as well, but no line is drawn between the two points.

You should see something like this in the command prompt area:

```
Distance = 5.00 Angle in XY Plane = 53, Angle from XY Plane = 0
Delta X = 3.00, Delta Y = 4.00, Delta Z = 0.00
```

All of this information can be useful, depending on the situation. "Distance" gives the straight-line distance between the two selected points. "Angle in XY Plane" gives the angle that a line between the two points would make within the coordinate system in which 0 degrees represents a horizontal line out to the right. "Angle from XY Plane" is a 3D feature and will always be 0 in 2D drawings. "Delta X" is the horizontal displacement, which may be either positive or negative. Similarly, "Delta Y" is the vertical displacement. "Delta Z" is the displacement in the z direction. It will always be 0 until we begin to explore AutoCAD's 3D drawing capabilities in Chapter 12.

Compare what is on your screen with Figure 2-16.

Figure 2-16

REDRAW

Whenever Blips are on, you may also want to use the Redraw command. Redraw quickly removes blips when you no longer want them.

⊕   Type "r".

    The blips from the DIST command will be removed.

    Blipmode is still on so that new objects points would be marked with blips. To turn blips off, remove the check from the blips box.

⊕   Open the Drawing Aids dialog box from the Tools menu.

⊕   Click in the Blips box to remove the check.

2.9   Plotting or Printing a Drawing

GENERAL PROCEDURE

1. Type Ctrl-p, select the Print tool from the Standard toolbar, or select Print from the File pull-down menu.
2. Click on "Window…".
3. Pick two points to define a window.
4. See that "Scaled to Fit" is checked.
5. Prepare printer or plotter.
6. Click on "OK".

AutoCAD's printing and plotting capabilities are extensive and complex. In this book we will introduce you to them a little bit at a time. These presentations are intended to get your work out on paper efficiently. You will find discussions of plotting and printing in Chapters 2, 3, 4, 5, 6, and 8, before the review material and drawings.

In this chapter, we will show you how to do a very simple plot procedure. This procedure assumes that you do not have to change devices or configuration details. It should work adequately for the drawings in this chapter. One of the difficulties is that different types of plotters and printers work somewhat differently. We will try to present procedures that will work on whatever equipment you are using, assuming that it is appropriately configured to begin with.

We suggest that you now open the Plot Configuration dialog box and work through this section without actually plotting anything. Then come back to the general procedure after you have completed one of the drawings in this chapter that you want to print out.

⊕   Type Ctrl-p, select the Print tool from the Standard toolbar, or select "Print…" from the File menu.

    Any of these methods will call up the "Plot Configuration" dialog box illustrated in Figure 2-17. You will become very familiar with it as you work

Figure 2-17

through this book. It is one of the most important working spaces in Auto-CAD. It contains many options and will call many subdialogs, but for now we are going to look at only two settings.

Look at the box on the lower left labeled "Additional Parameters". The line of radio buttons on the left allows you to tell AutoCAD what part of your drawing you want to plot. For our purposes we will use "Window". For this exercise you will define a window around an object you have drawn. Windowing allows you to plot any portion of a drawing simply by defining the window. AutoCAD will base the size and placement of the printed drawing on the window you have defined on the screen. For now, any object will do.

⊕ Click on "Window..." at the bottom middle of the Additional Parameters box.

This will call up the Window Selection dialog box illustrated in Figure 2-18. It contains the x and y coordinates of the two corners of your window selec-

Figure 2-18

tion. To ensure that you get the window you want, you need to pick the two points, or type in the coordinates if you know them. We will pick points, using Drawing 2-1 to illustrate.

⊕ Click on "Pick <" at the top left of the dialog box.

AutoCAD will temporarily close the Plot Configuration dialog box so that you can pick points. You will be prompted:

First corner:

⊕ Pick a point similar to point 1 in Figure 2-19. For this drawing, a point in the neighborhood of (1.5,.25) will do.

⊕ Pick a point similar to point 2 in Figure 2-19. For this drawing, a point in the neighborhood of (10.5,8.75) will do.

As soon as you have picked the second point, AutoCAD will display the Window Selection box again, showing the coordinates you have chosen.

⊕ Click on "OK".

This will bring you back to the Plot Configuration dialog box. You are essentially done at this point. But before plotting, there is one thing to check. Look at the box at the middle right labeled "Scale, Rotation, and Origin". It should not be necessary to worry about any of these parameters at this point. If the "Scaled to Fit" box is checked, as it should be by default, then AutoCAD will plot your drawing at maximum size based on paper size and the window you have defined.

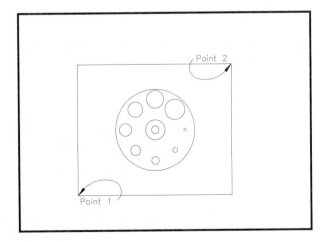

Figure 2-19

⊕ If "Scaled to Fit" is not checked, click in the box to check it.

⊕ If you are not actually going to print a drawing at this point, click on Cancel to close the Plot Configuration dialog box.

At this point the exercise is complete. You should come back to it when you have a drawing ready to plot.

⊕ If you are ready to proceed with a plot, look at your printer or plotter. Make sure that it is on and ready and that the paper is ready to go.

⊕ Click on "OK".

This sends the drawing information out to be printed. You can sit back and watch the plotting device at work. If you need to cancel for any reason, click on the Cancel button.

For now, that's all there is to it. If your plot does not look perfect—if it is not centered, for example—don't worry, you will learn all you need to know about plotting in later chapters.

2.10 Review Material

Questions

1. Which is likely to have the smaller setting GRID or SNAP? Why? What happens if the settings are reversed?
2. Why do some dialog box areas use check boxes while others use radio buttons?
3. How do you switch from decimal units to architectural units?
4. Where is 0 degrees located in AutoCAD's default units setup? Where is 270 degrees? Where is −45 degrees?
5. How do you enter the CIRCLE command?
6. Why does the rubber band touch the perimeter of the circle when you are using the radius option, but not when you are using the diameter option?
7. How does AutoCAD know when you want a crossing selection instead of a window selection?
8. What is the difference between a "Last" selection and a "Previous" selection?
9. What is the difference between noun/verb and verb/noun editing?
10. How do you access the AutoCAD HELP index?

Drawing Problems

1. Use HELP to look up the CMDDIA system variable. If this variable were changed to 0 instead of 1, what would happen when you select the Print tool?
2. Use the 3P option to draw a circle that passes through the points (3,3), (6,6), and (9,3).
3. Using the 2P option, draw a second circle with a diameter from (9,3) to (12,3).
4. Using the TTR option, draw a third circle tangent to the first two with a radius of 1.50.

2.11   Drawing 2-1: Aperture Wheel

This drawing will give you practice drawing circles using the center point, radius method. Refer to the table below the drawing for radius sizes. With snap set at 0.25, some of the circles can be drawn by dragging and pointing. Other circles have radii that are not on a snap point. These circles can be drawn easily by typing in the radius.

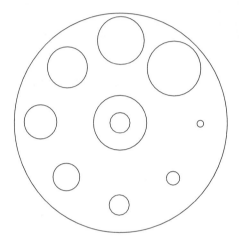

DRAWING SUGGESTIONS

GRID = 0.50
SNAP = 0.25

- A good sequence for doing this drawing would be to draw the outer circle first, followed by the two inner circles (h and c). These are all centered on the point (6.00,4.50). Then begin at circle a and work around clockwise, being sure to center each circle correctly.

- Notice that there are two circles c and two h. This simply indicates that the two circles having the same letter are the same size.

- Remember, you may type any value you like and AutoCAD will give you a precise graphic image, but you cannot always show the exact point you want with a pointing device. Often it is more efficient to type a few values than to turn snap off or change its setting for a small number of objects.

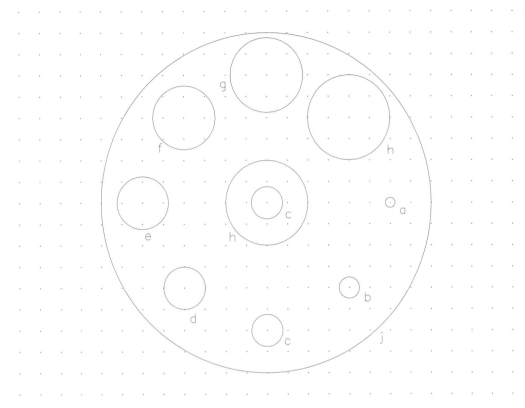

LETTER	a	b	c	d	e	f	g	h	j
RADIUS	.12	.25	.38	.50	.62	.75	.88	1.00	4.00

APERTURE WHEEL

Drawing 2-1

2.12   Drawing 2-2: Roller

This drawing will give you a chance to combine lines and circles and to use the center point, diameter method. It will also give you some experience with smaller objects, a denser grid, and a tighter snap spacing.

> **Note:** Even though units are set to show only two decimal places, it is important to set the snap using three places (0.125) so that the grid is on a multiple of the snap (0.25 = 2 × 0.125). AutoCAD will show you rounded coordinate values, like 0.13, but will keep the graphics on target. Try setting snap to either 0.13 or 0.12 instead of 0.125, and you will see the problem for yourself.

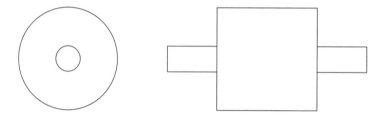

DRAWING SUGGESTIONS

GRID = 0.25
SNAP = 0.125

- The two views of the roller will appear fairly small on your screen, making the snap setting essential. Watch the coordinate display as you work and get used to the smaller range of motion.
- Choosing an efficient sequence will make this drawing much easier to do. Since the two views must line up properly, we suggest that you draw the front view first, with circles of diameter 0.25 and 1.00, and then use these circles to position the lines in the right side view.
- The circles in the front view should be centered in the neighborhood of (2.00,6.00). This will put the upper left-hand corner of the 1 × 1 square at around (5.50,6.50).

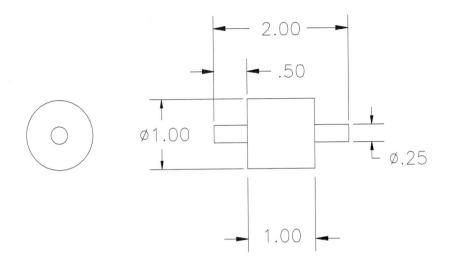

ROLLER

Drawing 2–2

2.13   Drawing 2-3: Fan Bezel

This drawing should be easy for you at this point. Set grid to 0.50 and snap to 0.25 as suggested, and everything will fall into place nicely.

DRAWING SUGGESTIONS

$$GRID = 0.50$$
$$SNAP = 0.25$$

- Notice that the outer figure is a 6 × 6 square and that you are given diameters for the circles.
- You should start with the lower left-hand corner of the square somewhere near the point (3.00,2.00) if you want to keep the drawing centered on your screen.
- Be careful to center the large inner circle at the center of the square.

FAN BEZEL

Drawing 2-3

2.14   Drawing 2-4: Switch Plate

This drawing is similar to the last one, but the dimensions are more difficult, and a number of important points do not fall on the grid. The drawing will give you practice using grid and snap points and the coordinate display. Refer to the table below the drawing for dimensions of the circles, squares, and rectangles inside the 7 × 10 outer rectangle. The placement of these smaller figures is shown by the dimensions on the drawing itself.

DRAWING SUGGESTIONS

GRID = 0.50
SNAP = 0.25

- Turn ortho on to do this drawing.
- A starting point in the neighborhood of (1,1) will keep you well positioned on the screen.

GUIDE POINTS WITH DIST

The squares, rectangles, and circles in this drawing can be located easily using DIST to set up guide points. For example, set a first point at the lower left corner of the outer rectangle, as in Reference 2-4b. Then set the second point at 1.25 to the right along the bottom of the rectangle. Now repeat the DIST command and use this second point as the new first point. Set the new second point 2.00 up, and you will have a blip right where you want to begin the c rectangle. Look for other places to use this technique in this drawing.

THE RECTANG COMMAND

The RECTANG command is a quick and easy way to draw rectangles. Type or select the command and then pick two points at opposite corners of the rectangle you want to draw. This is just like creating a selection window, but the window remains as a single entity called a polyline. Polylines are discussed in Chapter 10. Type "Rectang" or select the Rectangle tool from the Draw toolbar.

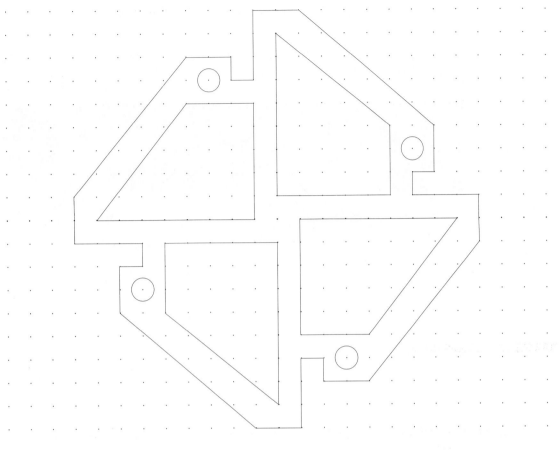

GASKET
Drawing 2-5

3 Layers, Colors, and Linetypes

COMMANDS

DATA	**VIEW**	**MODIFY**
DDLMODES	PAN	CHAMFER
LAYER	REGEN	FILLET
LTSCALE	VPORTS	
	ZOOM	

OVERVIEW

So far all the drawings you have done have been on a single white layer called "0". In this chapter you will create and use three new layers, each with its own associated color and linetype. You will also learn to FILLET and CHAMFER the corners of previously drawn objects, to magnify portions of a drawing using the ZOOM command, and to move between adjacent portions of a drawing with the PAN command.

TASKS

3.1   Creating New Layers

GENERAL PROCEDURE

1. Select the Layer tool from the Object Properties toolbar or "Layers..." from the Format pull-down menu.
2. Click on "New".
3. Type in a layer name.
4. Repeat for other new layers.
5. Click on "OK" to leave the dialog box.

Layers allow you to treat specialized groups of entities in your drawing separately from other groups. For example, all of the dimensions in this book were drawn on a special dimension layer so that we could turn them on and off at will. We turned off the dimension layer to prepare the reference drawings for Chapters 1 through 7, which are shown without dimensions. When a layer is turned off, all the objects on that layer become invisible, though they are still part of the drawing database and can be recalled at any time.

It is common to put dimensions on a separate layer, and there are many other uses of layers as well. Fundamentally, layers are used to separate colors and linetypes, and these, in turn, take on special significance depending on the drawing application. It is standard drafting practice, for example, to use small, evenly spaced dashes to represent objects or edges that would, in reality, be hidden from view. On a CAD system with a color monitor, these hidden lines can also be given their own color to make it easy for the designer to remember what layer he or she is working on.

In this book we will use a simple and practical layering system, most of which will be presented in this chapter. You should remember that there are many systems in use and countless possibilities. AutoCAD allows as many as 256 different colors and as many layers as you like.

You should also be aware that linetypes and colors are not restricted to being associated with layers. It is possible to mix linetypes and colors on a single layer. But while this may be useful for certain applications, we do not recommend it at this point.

⊕   Open a new drawing using the Start from Scratch option to ensure that you are using the same defaults as those used in this chapter.

The Layer Control Dialog Box (DDLMODES)

In this instance we will introduce the dialog box procedures first because they are more efficient than the command line methods. The main advantage of using the dialog box is that a table of layers will be displayed in front of you as you make changes, and you will be able to make several changes at once.

⊕   Select the Layer tool from the Object Properties toolbar, as shown in Figure 3-1, or select "Layers..." from the Format pull-down menu.

Figure 3-1

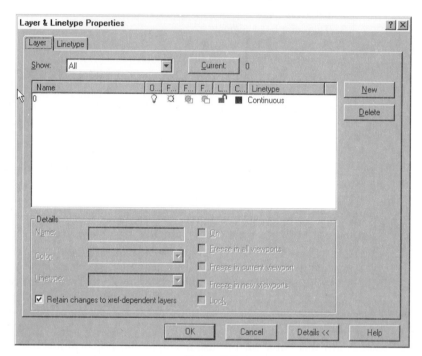

Figure 3-2

Either method will call the Layer and Linetype Properties dialog box illustrated in Figure 3-2. This is a tabbed "index card" style box, like the Help topics dialog presented in the preceding chapter. There are only two tabs, Layers and Linetypes. Yours should be showing the Layers card. The large open rectangle in the middle shows the names and properties of all layers defined in the current drawing. Layering systems can become very large and complex, and for this reason there is a system to limit the layer names shown in the name window. This is controlled by the box at the top left, which currently says "All", meaning that all layers are shown. To the right of this box, the current layer is identified. Once we have defined new layers, we will be able to use the Current button to change the current layer.

In the layer name list window, you will see that "0" is the only defined layer. The icons on the line after the layer name show the current state of various properties of that layer. We will get to this shortly.

Now we will create three new layers. In Release 14 this is extremely easy.

⊕ Click on "New", to the right of the list window.

The newly defined layer, Layer1, will be entered immediately in the layer name window. You will see that it is currently defined with characteristics identical to layer 0. We will alter these momentarily. But first give this layer a new name and then define two more layers.

Layer names may be up to 31 characters long. We have chosen single-digit numbers as layer names because they are easy to type and we can match them to AutoCAD's color numbering sequence.

⊕ Type "1" for the layer name.

"Layer1" will change to simply "1".

⊕ Click on "New" again.

A second new layer will be added to the list. It will again have the default name "Layer1". Change it to "2".

⊕ Type "2" for the second layer name.

⊕ Click on "New" once more.

⊕ Type "3" for the third layer name.

At this point your layer name list should show layers 0, 1, 2, and 3, all with identical properties.

3.2   Assigning Colors to Layers

GENERAL PROCEDURE

1. Select the Layers tool from the Object Properties toolbar, or select "Layers…" from the Format menu.
2. Select a layer name.
3. Click on the color icon.
4. In the Color dialog box, type a color name or number, or select a color from the color chart.
5. Click on "OK".

We now have four layers, but they are all pretty much the same. Obviously, we have more changes to make before our new layers will have useful identities.

Layer 0 has some special features, which will be discussed in Chapter 10. Because of these it is common practice to leave it defined the way it is. We will begin our changes on layer 1.

⊕ (If for any reason you have left the Layer and Linetype Properties dialog box, reenter it by selecting the Layers tool from the Object properties toolbar or "Layers …" from the Format menu.)

Before you can change the qualities of a layer, you must select it in the layer name box.

⊕ Move the cursor arrow anywhere on the layer 1 line and click to select layer 1.

Figure 3-3

The layer name will be highlighted.

✛ Click on the white square under "C".

The C is for color. The columns may be made wider, if you wish, so that the complete heading is visible. Clicking on the white square in the color column will call the Select Color dialog box illustrated in Figure 3-3. There are nine standard colors at the top, followed by gray shades and a palette of colors.

AutoCAD can display up to 256 different color shades. The nine standard colors shown at the top of the box are numbered 1 through 9 and are the same for all color monitors. Color numbers 10–249 are shown in the full color palette, and numbers 250–255 are the gray shades shown in between.

✛ Select the red box, the first of the nine standard colors at the top of the box.

✛ Click on "OK".

You will now see that layer 1 is defined with the color red in the layer name list box.

Next we will assign the color yellow to layer 2.

✛ Click on the layer 2 line.

2 should now be highlighted.

✛ Click on the white square under Color and assign the color yellow (color #2) to layer 2 in the Select Color dialog box.

✛ Click on OK.

✛ Select layer 3 and set this layer to green, color #3.

Look at the layer list. You should now have the layers 1, 2, and 3 defined with the colors red, yellow, and green.

3.3   Assigning Linetypes

GENERAL PROCEDURE

1. Select the Layer tool from the Object Properties toolbar or "Layers..." from the Format menu.
2. Click in the Linetype column of the layer you want to set.
3. In the Select Linetype dialog box, select a linetype. If necessary, load linetypes first.
4. Click on "OK".
5. Click on "OK" again to exit the Layer and Linetype dialog box.

AutoCAD has a standard library of linetypes that can be assigned easily to layers. There are 45 standard types in addition to continuous lines. If you do not assign a linetype, AutoCAD will assume you want continuous lines. In addition to continuous lines, we will be using hidden and center lines. We will put hidden lines in yellow on layer 2 and center lines in green on layer 3.

⊕   (If for any reason you have left the Layer and Linetype dialog box, reenter it by selecting the Layer tool from the Object Properties toolbar.)

⊕   Click on "Continuous" in the Linetype column of the layer 2 line.

This will select layer 2 and call up the Select Linetype dialog box illustrated in Figure 3-4. The box containing a list of loaded linetypes currently only shows the continuous linetype. We can fix this by selecting the "Load..." button at the bottom of the dialog box.

Note: Make sure that you actually click on the word "continuous". If you click on one of the icons, you may turn a layer off or freeze it so that you cannot draw on it. These other properties are discussed at the end of the next task.

⊕   Click on "Load...".

Figure 3-4

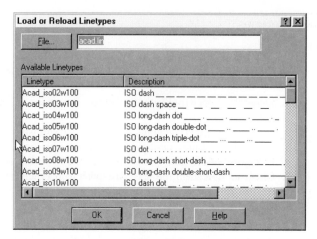

Figure 3-5

This will call a second dialog box, the Load or Reload Linetypes box illustrated in Figure 3-5. Here you can pick from the list of linetypes available from the standard "acad" file or from other files containing linetypes, if there are any on your system. You also have the option of loading all linetypes from any given file at once. The linetypes are then defined in your drawing, and you can assign a new linetype to a layer at any time. This makes things easier. It does, however, use up more memory.

For our purposes we will load only the hidden and center linetypes we are going to be using.

⊕ Scroll down until you see the Center linetype.

⊕ Click on "Center" in the Linetype column at the left.

⊕ Scroll down again until you see the "Hidden" linetype on the list.

⊕ Hold down the Ctrl key and click on "Hidden" in the Linetype column.

The Ctrl key lets you highlight two separated items in a list.

⊕ Click on "OK" to complete the loading process.

You should now see the center and hidden linetypes added to the list of loaded linetypes. Now that these are loaded, we can assign them to layers.

⊕ Click on "Hidden" in the linetype column.

⊕ Click on "OK" to close the box.

You should see that layer 2 now has the hidden linetype.

Next assign the center linetype to layer 3.

⊕ Click on "Continuous" in the linetype column of the layer 3 line.

⊕ In the Select Linetype dialog box, select the Center linetype.

⊕ Click on OK.

Examine your layer list again. It should show layer 2 with the hidden linetype and layer 3 with the center linetype.

⊕ Click on OK to exit the Layer and Linetype dialog box.

3.4   Changing the Current Layer

GENERAL PROCEDURE

1. Open the Layer list from the Object Properties toolbar.
2. Select one layer name.

or

1. Select the Make Object's Layer Current tool from the Object Properties toolbar.
2. Select an object on the layer you wish to make current.

To draw new entities on a layer, you must make it the currently active layer. Previously drawn objects on other layers that are turned on will be visible also and will be plotted, but new objects will go on the current layer.

You can make a layer current through the Layer and Linetype dialog box, but a quicker method is to use the layer list on the Object Properties toolbar.

⊕   Click anywhere in the current layer list box on the Object Properties toolbar.

This will open the list, as shown in Figure 3-6.

⊕   Select Layer 1.

Layer 1 will replace layer 0 as the current layer on the Object Properties toolbar. At this point we suggest that you try drawing some lines to see that you are, in fact, on layer 1 and drawing in red, continuous lines.

When you are satisfied with the red lines you have drawn, leave them on the screen and switch to layer 2.

⊕   Click anywhere in the Layer Control box on the Object Properties toolbar.

⊕   Click on the layer 2 line.

Layer 2 will become the current layer. Now draw more lines and see that they are "hidden" yellow lines.

⊕   Make layer 3 the current layer and draw some green center lines.

Finally, we will use another method to make layer 1 current before moving on.

Figure 3-6

Figure 3-7

⊕ Select the Make Object's Layer Current tool from the Object Properties toolbar, as shown in Figure 3-7.

This tool allows us to make a layer current by selecting any object on that
layer. AutoCAD will show this prompt:

```
Select object whose layer will become current:
```

⊕ Select any red, continuous line drawn on layer 1.

Layer 1 will replace layer 3 in the current layer box.

Other Properties in the Layer and Linetype Box

There are several other properties that may be set in the Layer and Linetype box.
These settings probably will not be useful to you until later on, but we introduce
them briefly here for your information.

Layers can be turned on or off with the light bulb icon. On and off status affects only the visibility of objects on a layer. Objects on layers that are off are not
visible or plotted, but are still in the drawing and are considered when the drawing is "regenerated." Regeneration is the process by which AutoCAD translates
the precise numerical data that make up a drawing file database into the less precise values of screen graphics. Regeneration can be a slow process in large, complex drawings. As a result it may be useful not to regenerate all layers all the time.
This is where the Freeze and Thaw options come in. Frozen layers are not only invisible but are ignored in regeneration. Thaw reverses this setting. Thawed layers
will always be regenerated. Freeze and Thaw properties are set using the sun icon,
for freezing and thawing layers in a complete drawing, or the sun and window icon,
for freezing and thawing only in the current viewport. Layers are thawed by default
as indicated by the yellow sun.

Lock and Unlock, the remaining setting, does not affect visibility but does affect
availability of objects for editing. Objects on locked layers are visible but cannot
be edited. Unlocking reverses this setting. This property is set with the lock icon.

Deleting Layers

You can delete layers using the Delete button in the Layer and Linetype dialog
box. However, you cannot delete layers that have objects drawn on them. Also,
you cannot delete the current layer or layer 0.

3.5   Editing Corners Using FILLET

GENERAL PROCEDURE

1. Type "f" or select the Fillet tool from the Modify toolbar or Fillet from the Modify menu.
2. Type "r" for radius.
3. Enter a radius value.
4. Press Enter to repeat the FILLET command.
5. Select two lines that meet at a corner.

Now that you have a variety of linetypes to use, you can begin to do some more realistic mechanical drawings. All you will need is the ability to create filleted (rounded) and chamfered (cut) corners. The two work similarly, and AutoCAD makes them easy. Fillets may also be created between circles and arcs, but the most common usage is the type of situation demonstrated here.

⊕   Erase any lines left on the screen from previous exercises.

⊕   If you have not already done so, set Layer 1 as the current layer.

⊕   Draw a 5 × 5 square on your screen, as in Figure 3-8.

We will use this figure to practice fillets and chamfers. Exact coordinates and lengths are not significant.

⊕   Type "f", select the Fillet tool from the Modify toolbar, or select Fillet from the Modify menu.

Depending on your monitor, you may have to move the toolbar from its docked position to see the Fillet tool, which is at the bottom of the Modify toolbar. Undock the toolbar by clicking in the gray area and dragging the toolbar to the middle of the screen. Once the toolbar is floating, you will be able to select the fillet tool, as shown in Figure 3-9. Moving the toolbar is

Figure 3-8

Figure 3-9

cumbersome, however, so if you do have to do this, typing "f" or selecting from the Modify menu is preferable.

A prompt with options will appear as follows:

```
(TRIM mode) Current fillet radius = 0.50
Polyline/Radius/Trim<Select first object>:
```

Polylines are discussed in Chapter 9. Trim mode is discussed at the end of this exercise.

The first thing you must do is determine the degree of rounding you want. Since fillets are really arcs, they can be defined by a radius.

⊕ Type "r".

AutoCAD prompts:

```
Enter fillet radius <0.50>:
```

The default is 0.50.

⊕ Type "0.75" or show two points 0.75 units apart.

You have set 0.75 as the current fillet radius for this drawing. You can change it at any time. Changing will not affect previously drawn fillets.

⊕ Press Enter or the space bar to repeat FILLET.

The prompt is the same as before, but the radius value has changed:

```
(TRIM mode) Current fillet radius = 0.75
Polyline/Radius/Trim<Select first object>:
```

You will notice that you have the pickbox on the screen now without the cross hairs.

⊕ Use the pickbox to select two lines that meet at any corner of your square.

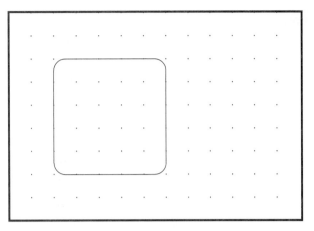

Figure 3-10

Behold! A fillet! You did not even have to press Enter. AutoCAD knows that you are done after selecting two lines.

⊞ Press Enter or the space bar to repeat FILLET. Then fillet another corner.

We suggest that you proceed to fillet all four corners of the square. When you are done, your screen should resemble Figure 3-10.

Trim Mode

Trim mode allows you to determine whether or not you want AutoCAD to remove square corners as it creates fillets and chamfers. Examples of fillets created with Trim mode on and off are shown in Figure 3-11. In most cases, you will want to leave trim mode on. To turn it off, enter FILLET and select "No Trim" from the screen menu, or type "t" for "Trim" and then "n" for "No Trim".

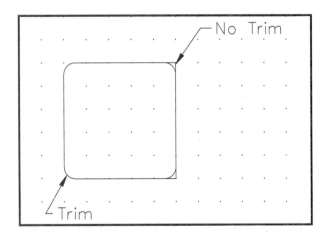

Figure 3-11

3.6 Editing Corners Using CHAMFER

GENERAL PROCEDURE

1. Type "Cha", select the Chamfer tool from the Modify toolbar, or select Chamfer from the Modify menu.
2. Type "d" for the "Distance" option.
3. Enter a chamfer distance.
4. Press Enter to repeat the CHAMFER command.
5. Select two lines that meet at a corner.

The CHAMFER command sequence is almost identical to the FILLET command, with the exception that chamfers may be uneven. That is, you may cut back farther on one side of a corner than on the other. To do this you must give Auto-CAD two distances instead of one.

⊕ Prepare for this exercise by undoing all your fillets using the U command as many times as necessary.

⊕ Type "cha" or select Chamfer from the Modify menu.

Here again, you may have to have the Modify toolbar in a floating position in order to select the Chamfer tool, shown previously in Figure 3-9.

AutoCAD prompts:

```
(TRIM mode) Current chamfer Dist1 = 0.50, Dist2 = 0.50
Polyline/Distance/Angle/Trim/Method/<Select first line>:
```

⊕ Type "d".

The next prompt will be

```
                Enter first chamfer distance <0.50>:
```

⊕ Type "1".

AutoCAD asks for another distance:

```
                Enter second chamfer distance <1.00>:
```

The first distance has become the default and most of the time it will be used. If you want an asymmetric chamfer, enter a different value for the second distance.

⊕ Press enter to accept the default, making the chamfer distances symmetrical.

⊕ Press Enter to repeat the CHAMFER command.

⊕ Answer the prompt by pointing to a line this time.

⊕ Point to a second line, perpendicular to the first.

You should now have a neat chamfer on your square. We suggest that you continue this exercise by chamfering the other three corners of your square. When you are done, your screen should resemble Figure 3-12.

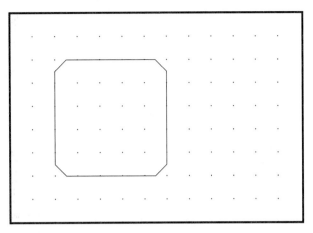

Figure 3-12

3.7 ZOOMing Window, Previous, and All

GENERAL PROCEDURE

1. Type "z" or select a Zoom tool from the Standard toolbar.
2. Enter a ZOOM method or magnification value.
3. Enter values or points, if necessary, depending on choice of method.

The capacity to zoom in and out of a drawing is one of the more impressive benefits of working on a CAD system. When drawings get complex, it often becomes necessary to work in detail on small portions of the drawing space. Especially with a small monitor, the only way to do this is by making the detailed area larger on the screen. This is done easily with the ZOOM command.

⊕ You should have a square with chamfered corners on your screen from the previous exercise.

We will demonstrate zooming using the window, all, previous, and realtime options.

⊕ Type "z" or select the Zoom Window tool from the Standard toolbar, as illustrated in Figure 3-13.

The prompt that follows includes the following options:

```
All/Center/Dynamic/Extents/Previous/Scale(X/XP)/
Window/<Realtime>:
```

Figure 3-13

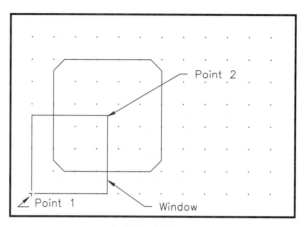

Figure 3-14

If you have used the Zoom Window tool, the Window option will be entered automatically. As in ERASE and other edit commands, you can force a window selection by typing "w" or selecting "Window". However, this is unnecessary. The windowing action is automatically initiated if you pick a point on the screen after entering ZOOM.

⊕ Pick a point just below and to the left of the lower left-hand corner of your square (point 1 in Figure 3-14).

AutoCAD asks for another point:

Other corner:

You are being asked to define a window, just as in the ERASE command. This window will be the basis for what AutoCAD displays next. Since you are not going to make a window that exactly conforms to the screen size and shape, AutoCAD will interpret the window this way: Everything in the window will be shown, plus whatever additional area is needed to fill the screen. The center of the window will become the center of the new display.

⊕ Pick a second point near the center of your square (point 2 in the figure).

The lower left corner of the square should now appear enlarged on your screen, as shown in Figure 3-15.

Figure 3-15

Figure 3-16

⊕ Using the same method, try zooming up further on the chamfered corner of the square. If snap is on, you may need to turn it off (F9).

Remember that you can repeat the ZOOM command by pressing Enter or the space bar.

At this point, most people cannot resist seeing how much magnification they can get by zooming repeatedly on the same corner or angle of a chamfer. Go ahead. After a couple of zooms the angle will not appear to change. An angle is the same angle no matter how close you get to it. But what happens to the spacing of the grid and snap as you move in?

When you are through experimenting with window zooming, try zooming to the previous display.

Zoom Previous

⊕ Press Enter to repeat the ZOOM command, or select the Zoom Previous tool, as shown in Figure 3-16.

⊕ If you repeated the command by pressing enter, type "p".

You should now see your previous display.

AutoCAD keeps track of up to 10 previous displays.

⊕ ZOOM "Previous" as many times as you can until you get a message that says

No previous display saved.

Zoom All

ZOOM All zooms out to display the whole drawing. It is useful when you have been working in a number of small areas of a drawing and are ready to view the whole scene. You do not want to have to wade through previous displays to find your way back. ZOOM All will take you there in one jump.

To see it work, you should be zoomed in on a portion of your display before executing ZOOM All.

⊕ Press Enter or type "z" to repeat the ZOOM command and zoom in on a window within your drawing.

⊕ Press Enter or type "z" to repeat ZOOM again.

⊕ Type "a" for the All option.

Note: The Zoom Window tool also has a flyout that includes tools for all of the ZOOM command options, including ZOOM All, as shown in Figure 3-17. Flyouts are toolbar features that make additional tools available. Any tool button that has a small black triangle in one corner will open a flyout. To

Figure 3-17

open a flyout, hold down the pickbutton while the arrow is on the tool. Then run down or across the flyout to the tool you want. When the tool button is "down," release the pickbutton.

3.8 Using Realtime ZOOM and PAN

GENERAL PROCEDURE

1. Pick the PAN Realtime or ZOOM Realtime tool from the Standard toolbar.
2. Use the cursor to move objects (PAN) or increase or decrease magnification (ZOOM).
3. Use enter or the space bar to exit the command.

Release 14 has new Realtime ZOOM and PAN features. Realtime means that you will see changes in display and magnification dynamically as you make adjustments. As soon as you start to use ZOOM, you are likely to need PAN as well. While ZOOM allows you to magnify portions of your drawing, PAN allows you to shift the area you are viewing in any direction.

In Windows you have the option of panning with the scroll bars at the edges of the drawing area, but the PAN command allows more precision and flexibility. In particular, it allows diagonal motion. We will use the PAN Realtime tool first and then the ZOOM Realtime tool.

⊕　Type "p" or select the Pan tool from the Standard toolbar (as illustrated in Figure 3-18).

With either method, you will see the PAN command cursor representing a hand with which you can move objects on the screen. When the mouse but-

Figure 3-18

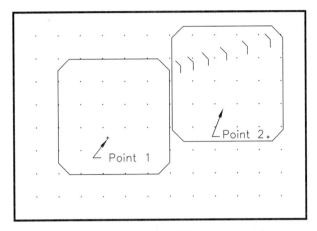

Figure 3-19

ton is not depressed, the hand will move freely across the screen. When you move the mouse with the pickbutton held down, the complete drawing display will move along with the hand.

⊕ Move the hand near the middle of the screen without holding down the pickbutton.

⊕ Hold down the pickbutton and move the cursor diagonally up and to the right, as illustrated in Figure 3-19.

⊕ Release the pickbutton to complete the PAN procedure.

Experiment with Realtime PAN, moving objects up, down, left, right, and diagonally. You should also compare the effect of using the scroll bars with the PAN command.

Realtime ZOOM

Any time that you are in either the ZOOM or PAN command, you can access a pop-up menu by pressing the right button on your cursor. Try it.

⊕ Without leaving PAN, press the right button on your mouse.

This will call up the pop-up menu illustrated in Figure 3-20. Pop-up lists are context specific. They are called only from within certain commands and contain options that are useful in specific conditions. This menu is useful while you are panning and zooming. In particular, it will allow you to switch quickly between realtime PAN and realtime ZOOM.

Figure 3-20

Figure 3-21

⊕ Select Zoom from the pop-up menu.

The menu will vanish and the realtime ZOOM cursor will appear. As illustrated in Figure 3-21, this represents a magnifying glass with a + sign above and a − sign below.

⊕ Without pressing the pickbutton, move the zoom cursor near the bottom of the screen.

As with the PAN cursor, you will be able to move freely when the pickbutton is not held down.

⊕ Press the pickbutton down and move the cursor upward.

With the pickbutton down, upward motion will increase magnification, enlarging objects on the screen.

⊕ Move up and down to see the effects of zoom cursor movement.

Release the pickbutton to complete the process. When you release the button you will not exit the command. This is important because it may take several trips up or down the screen to indicate the amount of magnification you want. Moving the cursor halfway up the screen will produce a 100% magification.

Continue to experiment with Realtime ZOOM and PAN until you feel comfortable. Then exit the command.

⊕ To exit, press ESC, the space bar, or the enter key.

You can also press the right button to open the pop-up menu and then select Exit.

Transparent Commands

If you have used the toolbar or the menu to enter the ZOOM and PAN commands, you may have noticed that they place an apostrophe and an underline before the name of the command. If you select the Pan tool, for example, you will see the following in the command area:

Command: '_pan

The apostrophe is a command modifier that makes the command transparent. This means that you can enter it in the middle of another command sequence, and when you are done you will still be in that sequence. For example, you can pan while drawing a line. This is a convenience if you already have selected the first point and then realize that the second point will be off the screen. A sample procedure using transparent PAN would be as follows:

1. Type "l" or select "Line".
2. Pick a first point.

3. Type "'p" (notice the apostrophe) or select the Pan tool.
4. Move the display as you wish.
5. Exit PAN.
6. Pick a second point to complete the line.

The underline character (_) you see after the apostrophe and before many commands that AutoCAD sends to the command line is added to commands in menu systems to ensure that AutoCAD interprets the commands in English. Foreign language versions of AutoCAD have their own command names but can still use menus developed in English, as long as the underline is there as a flag.

3.9   Creating Multiple Viewports in 2D (Optional)

GENERAL PROCEDURE

1. Highlight "Tiled Viewports" from the View pull-down menu.
2. Select one, two, three, or four viewports.

Although it may not be critical at this point, you have the ability to create multiple viewports, or windows, on your screen. You can position viewports anywhere on the screen, vary their size, and plot any configuration of viewports. These features are most useful in 3D drawings and will be discussed later in this book.

Multiple viewports also may be used in 2D to allow you to view different parts of a drawing or a complete drawing and a zoomed portion simultaneously. With multiple viewports you have the advantage of switching views less frequently, but this must be weighed against the disadvantage of working in smaller viewing windows.

There are two types of viewports: tiled and nontiled. Tiled viewports cover the whole screen and do not overlap. They must be plotted one at a time. Nontiled viewports can be placed in any configuration on the screen and can be plotted as they appear on the screen. They can only be created in paper space.

In this exercise we will create a simple tiled two-viewport configuration with a full view in one window and a zoomed view in the other.

⊕   To begin this exercise, you should have a full view of the chamfered square, as shown previously in Figure 3-12.

⊕   Open the View pull-down menu and highlight "Tiled Viewports".
    This will open a cascading submenu, as shown in Figure 3-22.

⊕   Pick "2 Viewports".
    AutoCAD will prompt:

    Horizontal/<Vertical>:

⊕   Press enter to accept the default, vertical.
    Your screen will be redrawn, as shown in Figure 3-23.

⊕   Now move your cursor back and forth between the two windows.

Figure 3-22

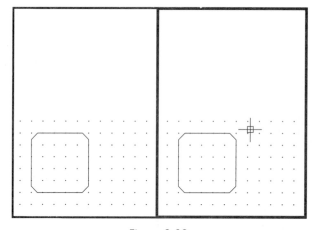

Figure 3-23

You will see the cross hairs whenever you are in the right viewport and an arrow when you are in the left viewport. You will also notice that the right viewport is surrounded by a black border. This indicates that the right viewport is currently active. You can perform drawing or editing in the current viewport only. However, any changes you make will be immediately reflected in all viewports.

⊕ Move the cursor to the left viewport and press the pickbutton.

The cross hairs will appear on the left. The left viewport is now active and its border will be black. If you move back to the right you will see the arrow. Often you can switch viewports while you are in the middle of a command sequence. With some commands, such as ZOOM and PAN, this will not work.

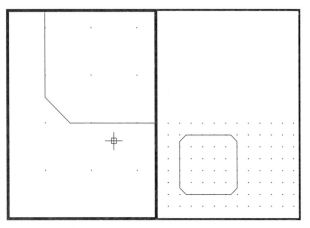

Figure 3-24

⊕   With the left viewport active, enter the ZOOM command and zoom in on a window around the lower left corner of the square.

Your screen should now resemble Figure 3-24.

To complete this exercise, you may want to do some simple drawing and editing in each viewport and observe how your changes appear in both viewports.

None of the two-dimensional drawings in this book will require multiple viewports, but you may try them at any time if you wish. If you want more information, look up Viewports in the *AutoCAD User's Guide*.

3.10   Using Plot Preview

GENERAL PROCEDURE

1. Type CTRL-P or select the Print tool from the Standard toolbar, or select Print from the File pull-down menu.
2. Change parameters as needed.
3. Select Partial or Full preview.
4. Select "Preview…".

The plot preview feature of the Plot Configuration dialog box is an essential tool in carrying out efficient plotting and printing. Plot configuration is complex, and the odds are good that you will waste time and paper by printing drawings directly without first previewing them on the screen. In this task we are still significantly limited in our use of plot configuration parameters, but learning to use the plot preview will make all of your future work with plotting and printing more effective.

As in Chapter 2, we suggest that you work through this task now with whatever objects are on your screen, and return to it after you have done one of the drawings at the end of this chapter.

⊕   To begin this task you should have objects or a drawing on your screen ready to preview.

Any drawing will do, but we will illustrate using Drawing 3-4.

⊕   Type CTRL-P, or select the Print tool from the Standard toolbar or Print from the File menu.

This will open the Plot Configuration dialog box. Plot Preview is at the lower right of the dialog box. There are two types of preview, "Partial" and "Full". A partial preview will show you an outline of the effective plotting area in relation to the paper size but will not show an image of the plotted drawing.

Note: We will address paper sizes in the next chapter. For now, we will assume that your plot configuration is correctly matched to the paper in your printer or plotter. If you do not get good results with this task, the problem may very well lie here.

Partial Preview

Partial previews are quick and should be accessed frequently as you set plot parameters, which affect how paper will be used and oriented to print your drawing. Full previews take longer and may be saved for when you think you have got everything right.

We will look at a partial preview first.

⊕   If the "Partial" radio button is not selected in your dialog box, select it now.

⊕   Click on "Preview …".

You will see a preview image similar to the one shown in Figure 3-25. The exact image will depend on your plotting device, so it may be different from the one shown here. The elements of the preview will be the same, however.

Figure 3-25

The red rectangle represents your drawing paper. It may be oriented in landscape (horizontally) or portrait (vertically). Typically, printers are in portrait, and plotters in landscape.

The blue rectangle inside the red one illustrates the effective plotting area. It is quite possible that the blue and red rectangles will overlap. The blue represents the size and shape of the area that AutoCAD can actually use given the shape of the drawing in relation to the size and orientation of the paper. The effective area is dependent on many things, as you will see. We will leave it as is for now and return to it later when you begin to alter the plot configuration.

In one corner of the red rectangle you will see a small triangle. This is the rotation icon. It shows the corner of the plotting area where the plotter will begin plotting (the origin).

⊕　Click on "OK" to exit the preview box.

Full Preview

⊕　Click on the "Full" radio button to switch to a full preview.

⊕　Click on "Preview ...".

The dialog box will disappear temporarily and you will see a preview similar to the one in Figure 3-26. We have used Drawing 3-4 to illustrate. You will see whatever drawing you are previewing, with orientation and placement depending on your plotting device.

Figure 3-26

This image represents your drawing on paper as it is now configured for printing. The ZOOM Realtime cursor appears to allow you to zoom in or out on aspects of the preview. By clicking on the right button, you can access the zoom and pan pop-up list demonstrated earlier in this chapter. Panning and zooming in the preview has no effect on the plot parameters. You may want to experiment with this feature now.

⊕ When you are done experimenting, press ESC or the enter key or space bar to return to the Plot Configuration dialog box.

This ends our initial preview of your drawing. In ordinary practice, if everything looked right in the preview you would move on to plot or print your drawing now by clicking on "OK". In the chapters that follow, we will explore the rest of the plot configuration dialog box and will use plot preview extensively as we change plot parameters. For now, get used to using plot preview. If things are not coming out quite the way you want, you will be able to fix them soon.

3.11 Review Material

Questions

1. What function(s) can be performed directly from the Layer list on the Object Properties toolbar? What functions can be performed from the Layer and Linetype dialog box?
2. What linetype is always available when you start a drawing from scratch in AutoCAD? What must you do to access other linetypes?
3. How many colors are available in AutoCAD?
4. How many different layers does AutoCAD allow you to create?
5. Name three ways to change the current layer.
6. You have been working in the Layer and Linetype dialog box, and when you return to your drawing you find that some objects are no longer visible. What happened?
7. Why is it often necessary to enter the FILLET and CHAMFER commands twice to create a single fillet or chamfer?
8. What is a transparent command? How do you make a command transparent when entering it at the command line?
9. What happens to the grid when you zoom way out on a drawing?
10. Name one limitation of scroll bars that the PAN command does not have.
11. What is the difference between a partial and a full plot preview?

Drawing Problems

1. Make layer 3 current and draw a green center line cross with two perpendicular lines, each two units long and intersecting at their midpoints.

2. Make layer 2 current and draw a hidden line circle centered at the intersection of the cross drawn in Problem 1, with radius of two units.

3. Make layer 1 current and draw a red square two units on a side centered on the center of the circle. Its sides will run tangent to the circle.

4. Use a window to zoom in on the objects drawn in Problems 1, 2, and 3.

5. Fillet each corner of the square with a 0.125 radius fillet.

3.12   Drawing 3-1: Mounting Plate

This drawing will give you experience using center lines and chamfers. Since there are no hidden lines, you will have no need for layer 2, but we will continue to use the same numbering system for consistency. Draw the continuous lines in red on layer 1 and the center lines in green on layer 3.

DRAWING SUGGESTIONS

GRID = 0.5
SNAP = 0.25
LTSCALE = 0.5

LTSCALE

The size of the individual dashes and spaces that make up center lines, hidden lines, and other linetypes is determined by a global setting called "LTSCALE". By default it is set to a factor of 1.00. In smaller drawings this setting will be too large and will cause some of the shorter lines to appear continuous regardless of what layer they are on.

To remedy this, change LTSCALE as follows:

1. Type "ltscale" or select "Linetypes" and then "Global Linetype Scale" from the Options pull-down menu.
2. Enter a value.

For the drawings in this chapter use a setting of 0.50. See Figure 3-27 for some examples of the effect of changing LTSCALE.

Note: In manual drafting it would be more common to draw the center lines first and use them to position the circles. Either order is fine, but be aware that what is standard practice in pencil and paper drafting may not be efficient or necessary on a CAD system.

———— — ———— LTSCALE = 1.00

—— – ———— – — LTSCALE =   .50

— – — – — – — – LTSCALE =   .25

Figure 3-27

.25 x .25 CHAMFER
4 PLACES

Ø.75
4 HOLES

4.00

2.50

3.00

3.00

Ø2.00

5.50   6.50

3.25

1.75

.50

.50   →

7.00

8.00

Ø.50
4 HOLES

MOUNTING PLATE

DRAWING 3-1

3.13   Drawing 3-2: Stepped Shaft

This two-view drawing uses continuous lines, center lines, chamfers, and fillets. You may want to zoom in to enlarge the drawing space you are actually working in, and pan right and left to work on the two views.

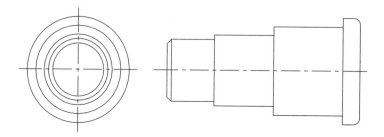

DRAWING SUGGESTIONS

GRID = 0.25
SNAP = 0.125
LTSCALE = 0.5

- Center the front view in the neighborhood of (2,5). Then the right side view will have a starting point at about (5,4.12), before the chamfer cuts this corner off.
- Draw the circles in the front view first, using the vertical dimensions from the side view for diameters. Save the inner circle until after you have drawn and chamfered the right side view.
- Draw a series of rectangles for the side view, lining them up with the circles of the front view. Then chamfer two corners of the leftmost rectangle and fillet two corners of the rightmost rectangle.
- Use the chamfer on the side view to line up the radius of the inner circle.
- Remember to set the current layer to 3 before drawing the center line through the side view.

.12 5 FILLET

.12 5 X .125
CHAMFER

ø1.750   ø2.000   ø2.750   ø3.25

1.375   1.75   2.00   .50

5.625 REF

STEPPED SHAFT
Drawing 3-2

3.14   Drawing 3-3: Base Plate

This drawing uses continuous lines, hidden lines, center lines, and fillets. The side view should be quite easy once the front view is drawn. Remember to change layers when you want to change linetypes.

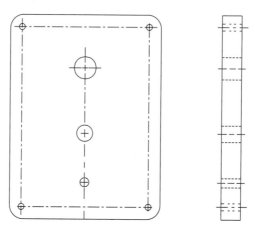

DRAWING SUGGESTIONS

GRID = 0.25
SNAP = 0.125
LTSCALE = 0.5

- Study the dimensions carefully and remember that every grid increment is 0.25, while snap points not on the grid are exactly halfway between grid points. The four circles at the corners are 0.38 (actually 0.375 rounded off) over and in from the corner points. This is three snap spaces (0.375 = 3 × 0.125).
- Position the three circles along the center line of the rectangle carefully. Notice that dimensions are given from the center of the screw holes at top and bottom.
- Use the circle perimeters to line up the hidden lines on the side view, and the centers to line up the center lines.

.375 FILLET
4 PL

Ø.25
4 PL

4.75

1.25
REF

2.00

3.50

Ø.75

Ø.50

Ø.25

6.25

5.50

.75

.375

2.00

4.00

.38

.50

BASE PLATE
Drawing 3-3

3.15 Drawing 3-4: Bushing

This drawing will give you practice with chamfers, layers, and zooming. Notice that because of the smaller dimensions here, we have recommended a smaller LTSCALE setting.

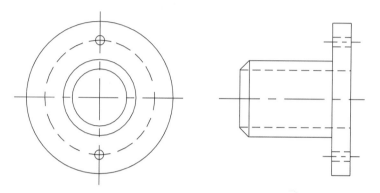

DRAWING SUGGESTIONS

GRID = 0.25
SNAP = 0.125
LTSCALE = 0.25

- Since this drawing will appear quite small on your screen, it would be a good idea to ZOOM in on the actual drawing space you are using and use PAN if necessary.
- Notice that the two 0.25-diameter screw holes are 1.50 apart. This puts them squarely on grid points that you will have no trouble finding.

REGEN

When you zoom you may find that your circles turn into many-sided polygons. AutoCAD does this to save time. These time savings are not noticeable now, but when you get into larger drawings they become significant. If you want to see a proper circle, type "Regen". This command will cause your drawing to be regenerated more precisely from the data you have given.

You may also notice that REGENs happen automatically when certain operations are performed, such as changing the LTSCALE setting after objects are already on the screen.

Ø.25 THRU
2 HOLES EQ SP
ON Ø1.50 B.C

.75 DIA
THRU

.25

Ø1.00

Ø2.00

1.50

.12 x .12 CHAMFER

BUSHING
DRAWING 3-4

3.16   Drawing 3-5: Half Block

This cinder block is the first project using architectural units in this book. Set units, grid, and snap as indicated, and everything will fall into place nicely.

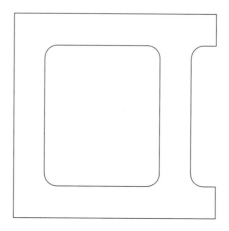

DRAWING SUGGESTIONS

UNITS = Architectural

smallest fraction = 4 (1/4″)

GRID = 1/4″

SNAP = 1/4″

- Start with the lower left corner of the block at the point (0′—1″, 0′—1″) to keep the drawing well placed on the display.
- After drawing the outside of the block with the $5\frac{1}{2}$″ indentation on the right, use the DIST command to locate the inner rectangle $1\frac{1}{4}$″ in from each side.
- Set the FILLET radius to 1/2″ or 0.5. Notice that you can use decimal versions of fractions. The advantage is that they are easier to type.
- You can use MULTIPLE FILLET to fillet the six corners.

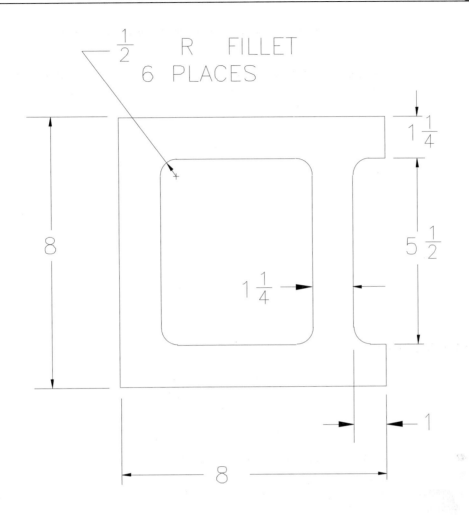

HALF BLOCK

Drawing 3–5

3.17   Drawing 3-6: Packing Flange

This drawing uses continuous lines, hidden lines, center lines, and fillets. The side view should be quite easy once the front view is drawn. Remember to change layers when you want to change linetypes.

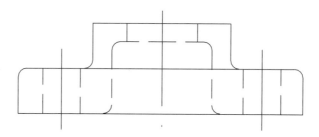

DRAWING SUGGESTIONS

GRID = 1/4
SNAP = 1/8
LTSCALE = 0.5

- Study the dimensions carefully and remember that every grid increment is 1/4, while snap points not on the grid are exactly halfway between grid points. Notice that the units should be set to fractions.
- Begin this drawing by drawing the outline and then the three center lines in the top view. Then proceed by drawing all circles.
- The circles can be drawn using center and diameter. Position the center of the circle where the center lines cross and type in the diameter.
- Use the top view to line up all the lines on the front view.

$1\frac{1}{8}$ DRILL
2 HOLES

$5\frac{3}{4}$

$1\frac{1}{2}$ FILLET

6

$1\frac{3}{16}$

$8\frac{3}{8}$

$4\frac{1}{8}$ DIA

$2\frac{1}{8}$ DIA

$\frac{1}{4}$ FILLET

$2\frac{5}{8}$

$2\frac{1}{8}$

$1\frac{5}{16}$

3 DIA

PACKING FLANGE
DRAWING 3-6

4

Template Drawings

COMMANDS

MODIFY	DATA
ARRAY (rectangular)	LIMITS
COPY	
MOVE	

OVERVIEW

In this chapter you will learn some real timesavers. If you have grown tired of defining the same three layers, along with units, grid, snap, and ltscale, for each new drawing, read on. You are about to learn how to use template drawings. With templates, you can begin each new drawing with whatever setup you want.

In addition, you will learn to reshape the grid using the LIMITS command and to COPY, MOVE, and ARRAY objects on the screen so that you do not have to draw the same thing twice. We will begin with LIMITS, since we will want to change the limits as part of defining your first template.

TASKS

4.1 Setting LIMITS

GENERAL PROCEDURE

1. Open a new drawing using the Quick Setup Wizard.
2. Enter a width.
3. Enter a length.
4. Click Done to exit the Quick Setup dialog box.

You have changed the density of the screen grid many times, but always within the same 12×9 space, which basically represents an A-size sheet of paper. Now you will learn how to change the shape by setting new limits to emulate other sheet sizes or any other space you want to represent. But first, a word about model space and paper space.

Model Space and Paper Space

Model space is an AutoCAD concept that refers to the imaginary space in which we create and edit objects. In model space, objects are always drawn full scale (1 screen unit = 1 unit of length in the real world). The alternative to model space is paper space, in which screen units represent units of length on a piece of drawing paper. Paper space is most useful in plotting multiple views of 3D drawings. In Part I of this book all of your work will be done in model space.

In this exercise we will reshape our model space to emulate different drawing sheet sizes. This will not be necessary in actual practice. With AutoCAD you can scale your drawing to fit any drawing sheet size when it comes time to plot. Model space limits should be determined by the size and shapes of objects in your drawing, not by the paper you are going to use when you plot.

The Quick Setup Wizard

Limits can be set from within a drawing using the LIMITS command. When you are beginning a new drawing, however, a quicker way is to use a drawing setup wizard. Wizards are standard Windows 95 features that guide you through setup functions in all kinds of applications. We will use the Quick Setup Wizard to begin this drawing and set 18×12 limits.

⊕ Start AutoCAD or begin a new drawing.

If the Create New Drawing dialog box is not showing, open the File menu and select New, or select the New tool from the Standard toolbar.

⊕ In the Create New Drawing dialog box click the Use a Wizard button on the left.

⊕ Highlight Quick Setup in the Select a Wizard box.

⊕ Click on OK.

This will bring up the Quick Setup tabbed dialog box illustrated in Figure 4-1. Our illustration shows the Step 2 Area card on top because this is where

Figure 4-1

you will set new limits. The Step 1 Units card will allow you to select decimal units, the default, but will not allow you to set the number of decimal places to use. For this you will need to continue using the UNITS command for now.

⊕ Click on the Step 2 Area card to bring it to the top.

⊕ Double click in the Width box to highlight the number 12.0000.

⊕ Type "18".

The number in the width box should now read 18.0000. Also, the number at the bottom of the preview image on the right will change to 18.0000.

⊕ Double click in the Length box and type "12".

The length box and the preview image will show 12.0000.

⊕ Click on Done to exit the Quick Setup Wizard.

Your screen should resemble Figure 4-2, showing an 18 × 12 grid.

After we are finished exploring the LIMITS command, we will create the new settings we want and save this drawing as your B-size template.

We suggest that you continue to experiment with setting limits and that you try some of the possibilities listed in Figure 4-3, which is a table of sheet sizes. Notice that there are two sets of standards commonly in use. Sometimes the standard you use will be determined by your plotter. This is particularly true for the larger sheet sizes. Some plotters that plot on C-size paper, for example, will take a 24 × 18 inch sheet but not a 22 × 17.

Now that you are already in a drawing, you may wish to use the LIMITS command to try other settings.

The LIMITS command

The LIMITS command changes the grid area in the same way as the Quick Setup Wizard, except that it is used after a drawing has already been opened and uses

Figure 4-2

SHEET SIZE		"X" DIM	"Y" DIM
A	*	11"	8.5"
		12"	9 "
B	*	17"	11"
		18"	12"
C	*	22"	17"
		24"	18"
D	*	34"	22"
		36"	24"
E	*	44"	34"
		48"	36"

SELECT FROM CHART
UPPER RIGHT CORNER

*ANSI Y14.1 STANDARD

"Y" DIM

SIZE
SHEET

LOWER LEFT CORNER
SETTING STAYS AT 0,0

"X" DIM

Figure 4-3

coodinate values for the lower left and upper right corners of the grid in place of widths and lengths of the grid boundaries. To use LIMITS, follow this procedure:

1. Type "Limits" or select "Drawing Limits" from the Format menu.
2. Type coordinates for the lower left corner—for example, (0,0).
3. Type coordinates for the upper right corner—for example, (18,12).

The Off and On options in the LIMITS command control what happens when you try to draw outside of the defined limits. With LIMITS off, nothing will happen. With LIMITS on, AutoCAD will not accept any attempt to begin an entity outside of limits, notifying you with the message "Attempt to draw outside of limits". You can extend objects beyond the limits as long as they were started within them. By default, LIMITS is off.

⊕ When you are done experimenting, return LIMITS to (0,0) and (18,12), using the LIMITS command, and then ZOOM All.

You are now in the drawing that we will use for your template, so it is not necessary to begin a new drawing for the next section.

4.2   Creating a Template

GENERAL PROCEDURE

1. Define layers and change settings (grid, snap, units, limits, ltscale, etc.) as desired.
2. Save the drawing, giving it an appropriate name for a template.

To make your own template, so that new drawings will begin with the settings you want, all you have to do is create a drawing that has those settings and then tell AutoCAD that this is the drawing you want to use to define your initial drawing setup. The first part should be easy for you now, since you have been doing your own drawing setup for each new drawing in this book.

⊕ Make changes to the present drawing as follows:

GRID:	1.00 ON (F7)	COORD:	ON (F6)
SNAP:	0.25 ON (F9)	LTSCALE:	0.5
UNITS:	2-place decimal	LIMITS:	(0,0) (18,12)

Note: If you use the Quick Setup Wizard to set limits, you will still have to set the grid and snap as shown, since the wizard uses a 0.70 grid and snap spacing when you set to 18×12.

⊕ Load all linetypes from the ACAD file using the following procedure.
1. Open the Linetype dialog box from the Format menu.
2. Click on Load to open the Load dialog box.

3. Highlight the first Linetype on the list.
4. Scroll down to the end of the list.
5. Hold down the shift key as you highlight the last linetype on the list.
6. With all linetypes highlighted, click on OK.
7. Click on OK in the Layer and Linetype dialog box, or click on the Layer tab to define layers.

⊕ **Create the following layers and associated colors and linetypes.**

Remember that you can make changes to your template at any time. The layers called "text," "hatch," and "dim" will not be used until Chapters 7 and 8, in which we introduce text, hatch patterns, and dimensions to your drawings. Creating them now will save time and avoid confusion later.

Layer 0 is already defined.

Layer Name	On/Off	Color	Linetype
0	On	7 (white)	Continuous
1	On	1 (red)	Continuous
2	On	2 (yellow)	Hidden
3	On	3 (green)	Center
Text	On	4 (cyan)	Continuous
Hatch	On	5 (blue)	Continuous
Dim	On	6 (magenta)	Continuous

⊕ **When all changes are made, save your drawing as "B".**

Note: Do not leave anything drawn on your screen or it will come up as part of the template each time you open a new drawing. For some applications this may be useful. For now we want a blank template.

If you have followed instructions up to this point, B.dwg should be on file. Now we will use it as the template for a new drawing.

4.3 Selecting a Template Drawing

GENERAL PROCEDURE

1. Select Save As... from the File menu.
2. Enter your template drawing name in the File Name edit box.
3. Select "Drawing Template File (*.dwt)" in the Save as type list box.
4. Click on Save.
5. Type a template description in the Template Description box.
6. Click on OK.

The procedure for designating a template drawing involves saving the drawing as a template file. The template file will be given a .dwt extension and placed in the

Figure 4-4

template file folder. It will automatically become the default template until you select another template.

+ To begin this task you should be in the B drawing created in the last task. All the drawing changes should be made as described.
+ Open the File menu and select Save As...

This will call up the familiar Save Drawing As dialog box shown in Figure 4-4. The edit box in the middle holds the name of the current drawing. If you have not named the drawing, it will be called "Drawing".

+ Double click in the File name box to highlight the drawing name.
+ Type "B" for the new name.

Below the file name box is the Save as type box. This box will list four different options for saving the drawing. Drawing Template File is the last.

+ Highlight "Drawing Template File (*.dwt)", and click on it so that it shows up in the list box.

This will also open the Template file folder automatically. You will see that there are many templates already there. These are supplied by Auto-CAD and may be useful to you later. At this point it is more important to learn how to make your own.

Once your drawing name ("B") is in the name box and the Save as type box shows Drawing Template File, you are ready to save.

+ Click on Save.

This will call up a Template Description box, as illustrated in Figure 4-5. Here you can specify a description that will appear in the Create New Drawing dialog box whenever this template is used.

+ Type "B size template, blank page".

This will indicate that this is your B template and that there is no title block or other objects drawn in the template.

+ Click on OK.

Figure 4-5

The task of creating the drawing template is now complete. All that remains is to create a new drawing using the template to see how it works.

⊕ Open the File menu and select New, or pick the New tool from the standard toolbar.

This will bring up the Create New Drawing dialog box. Whatever method you used last will be retained as the default. In this case you want to start with the Use a Template option.

⊕ Click on "Use a Template."

The heading of the box will change to "Use a Template" and a list of available templates will appear at the right.

⊕ If B is not highlighted, highlight it as the template you wish to use.

Notice the template description.

⊕ Click on OK to begin the drawing.

4.4 Using the MOVE Command

GENERAL PROCEDURE

1. Type "m", select the Move tool from the Modify toolbar, or select Move from the Modify menu.
2. Define a selection set. (If noun/verb selection is enabled, you can reverse steps 1 and 2.)
3. Choose the base point of a displacement vector.
4. Choose a second point.

The ability to copy and move objects on the screen is one of the great advantages of working on a CAD system. It can be said that CAD is to drafting as word processing is to typing. Nowhere is this analogy more appropriate than in the cut-and-paste capacities that the COPY and MOVE commands give you.

⊕ Draw a circle with a radius of 1 somewhere near the center of the screen (9,6), as shown in Figure 4-6.

Figure 4-6

Figure 4-7

As discussed in Chapter 2, AutoCAD allows you to pick objects before or after entering an edit command. In this exercise we will use MOVE both ways, beginning with the verb/noun method. We will use the circle you have just drawn, but be aware that the selection set could include as many entities as you like and that a group of entities can be selected with a window or crossing box.

⊕ Type "m", select Move from the Modify menu, or select the Move tool from the Modify toolbar, as shown in Figure 4-7.

You will be prompted to select objects to move.

⊕ Point to the circle.

As in the ERASE command, your circle will become dotted.

In the command area, AutoCAD will tell you how many objects have been selected and prompt you to select more. When you are through selecting objects you will need to press Enter to move on.

⊕ Press Enter.

AutoCAD prompts

               `Base point or displacement:`

Most often you will show the movement by defining a vector that gives the distance and direction you want the object to be moved. To define movement with a vector, all AutoCAD needs is a distance and a direction. Therefore, the base point does not have to be on or near the object you are moving. Any point will do, as long as you can use it to show how you want your objects moved. This may seem strange at first, but it will soon become natural. Of

Figure 4-8

course, you may choose a point on the object if you wish. With a circle, the center point may be convenient.

⊕ Point to any location not too near the right edge of the screen.

AutoCAD will give you a rubber band from the point you have indicated and will ask for a second point:

Second point of displacement:

As soon as you begin to move the cursor, you will see that AutoCAD also gives you a circle to drag so you can immediately see the effect of the movement you are indicating. An example of how this may look is shown in Figure 4-8. Let's say you want to move the circle 3.00 to the right. Watch the coordinate display and stretch the rubber band out until the display reads "3.00 < 0" (press F6 or double click on the coordinate display to get polar coordinates).

⊕ Pick a point 3.00 to the right of your base point.

The rubber band and your original circle disappear, leaving you a circle in the new location.

Now, if ortho is on, turn it off (F8) and try a diagonal move. This time we will use the previous option to select the circle.

⊕ Type "m" or select the Move tool, or press Enter to repeat the command.

AutoCAD follows with the "Select objects:" prompt.

⊕ Reselect the circle by typing "p" for previous.

⊕ Press Enter to end the object selection process.

⊕ Select a base point.

⊕ Move the circle diagonally in any direction you like.

Figure 4-9 is an example of how this might look.

⊕ Try moving the circle back to the center of the screen.

It may help to choose the center point of the circle as a base point this time, and choose a point at or near the center of the grid for your second point.

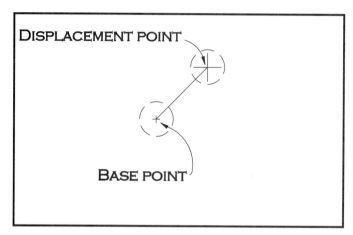

Figure 4-9

Moving with Grips

You can use grips to perform numerous editing procedures without ever entering a command. This is probably the simplest of all editing methods, called autoediting. It does have some limitations, however. In particular, you can only select by pointing, windowing, or crossing.

⊕ Point to the circle.

The circle will become highlighted and grips will appear.

Notice that grips for a circle are placed at quadrants and at the center. In more involved editing procedures the choice of which grip or grips to use for editing is significant. In this exercise you will do fine with any of the grips.

⊕ Move the pickbox slowly over one of the grips.

If you do this carefully you will notice that the pickbox "locks onto" the grip as it moves over it. You will see this more clearly if snap is off (F9).

⊕ When the pickbox is locked on a grip, press the pick button.

The selected grip will become filled and change colors (from blue to red).

In the command area you will see this:

```
** STRETCH **
<Stretch to point>/Base point/Copy/Undo/eXit:
```

Stretching is the first of a series of five autoediting modes that you can activate by selecting grips on objects. The word "stretch" has many meanings in AutoCAD, and they are not always what you would expect. We will explore the stretch autoediting mode and the STRETCH command in Chapter 6. For now, we will bypass stretch and use the MOVE mode.

Release 14 has a convenient pop-up menu for use in grip editing.

⊕ Click the enter button on your mouse.

This will call up the pop-up menu shown in Figure 4-10. It contains all of the grip edit modes plus several other options.

Figure 4-10

⊕ Select Move in the pop-up menu box.

The pop-up list will disappear and you will be in Move mode. Move the cursor and you will see a rubber band from the selected grip to the same position on a dragged circle.

⊕ Pick a point anywhere on the screen.

The circle will move where you have pointed.

Moving by Typing a Displacement

There is one more way to use the MOVE command. Instead of showing AutoCAD a distance and direction, you can type a horizontal and vertical displacement. For example, to move the circle three units to the right and two units up, you would use the following procedure (there is no autoediting equivalent for this procedure):

1. Press Esc twice to remove grips.
2. Pick the circle.
3. Type "m" or select the Move tool.
4. Type "3, 2" in response to the prompt for base point or displacement.
5. Press Enter in response to the prompt for a second point.

4.5   Using the COPY Command

```
                        GENERAL PROCEDURE

1. Type "Copy" or select the Copy tool from the Modify toolbar (not Copy to Clipboard,
   which is on the Standard toolbar).
2. Define a selection set (steps 1 and 2 can be reversed if noun/verb selection is enabled).
3. Choose a base point.
4. Choose a second point.
```

Figure 4-11

The COPY command works so much like the MOVE command that you should find it easy to learn at this point, and we will give you fewer instructions. The main difference is that the original object will not disappear when the second point of the displacement vector is given. There is the additional option of making multiple copies of the same object, which we will explore in a moment.

First, we suggest that you try making several copies of the circle in various positions on the screen. Try using both noun/verb and verb/noun sequences.

⊞   To initiate COPY, type "co" or select Copy from the Modify menu, or the Copy tool from the Modify toolbar, as shown in Figure 4-11.

Notice that "c" is not an alias for COPY. Also notice that there is a Copy to Clipboard tool on the Standard toolbar that initiates the COPYCLIP command. This tool has a very different function. It is used to copy objects to the Windows 95 Clipboard and then into other applications. It has no effect on objects within your drawing, other than to save them on the clipboard.

When you are satisfied that you know how to use the basic COPY command, move on to the Multiple copy option.

The Multiple Copy Option

This option allows you to show a series of vectors starting at the same base point, with AutoCAD placing copies of your selection set accordingly.

⊞   Type "co" or select the Copy tool from the Modify toolbar.
⊞   Point to one of the circles on your screen.
⊞   Press Enter to end the selection process.
⊞   Type "m" for the Multiple option.
⊞   Show AutoCAD a base point.
⊞   Show AutoCAD a second point.

You will see a new copy of the circle. Notice also that the prompt for a "Second point of displacement" has returned in the command area. Auto-CAD is waiting for another vector, using the same base point as before.

⊞   Show AutoCAD another second point.
⊞   Show AutoCAD another second point.

Repeat as many times as you wish. If you get into this you may begin to feel like a magician pulling rings out of thin air and scattering them across the screen. The results will appear something like Figure 4-12.

Figure 4-12

Copying with Grips

The grip editing system includes a variety of special techniques for creating multiple copies in all five modes. The function of the Copy option will differ depending on the grip edit mode. For now we will use the Copy option with the Move mode, which provides a shortcut for the same kind of process you just went through with the COPY command.

Since you should have several circles on your screen now, we will take the opportunity to demonstrate how you can use grips on more than one object at a time. This can be very useful if your drawing contains two or more objects that maintain the same relationship with each other at different locations in your drawing.

⊕ Pick any two circles.

The circles you pick should become highlighted, and grips should appear on both, as illustrated in Figure 4-13.

Figure 4-13

⊕ Pick any grip on either of the two highlighted circles.

The grip should change colors. This time we will not use the pop-up menu. In the command area you will see the grip edit prompt for the Stretch mode:

```
** STRETCH **
<Stretch to point>/Base point/Copy/Undo/eXit:
```

⊕ Press enter or the space bar.

(Do not press the enter key on your mouse.) This will bring you to the MOVE mode prompt:

```
** MOVE**
<Move to point>/Base point/Copy/Undo/eXit:
```

⊕ Type "c" to initiate copying.

The prompt will change to

```
** MOVE (multiple) **
<Move to point>/Base point/Copy/Undo/eXit:
```

You will find that all copying in the grip editing system is multiple copying. Once in this mode AutoCAD will continue to create copies wherever you press the pickbutton until you exit by typing "x" or pressing Enter.

⊕ Move the cursor and observe the two dragged circles.

⊕ Pick a point to create copies of the two highlighted circles, as illustrated in Figure 4-14.

⊕ Pick another point to create two more copies.

⊕ When you are through, press Enter to exit the grip editing system.

⊕ Press Esc twice to remove grips.

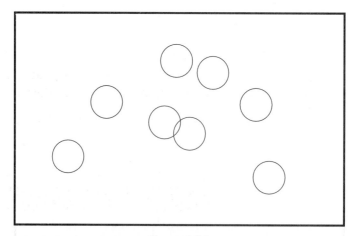

Figure 4-14

4.6   Using the ARRAY Command—Rectangular Arrays

GENERAL PROCEDURE

1. Type "Ar" or select the Array tool from the Modify toolbar or Array from the Modify menu.
2. Define a selection set. (Steps 1 and 2 can be reversed if noun/verb editing is enabled.)
3. Press Enter to end selection.
4. Type "r" for rectangular.
5. Enter the number of rows in the array.
6. Enter the number of columns.
7. Enter the distance between rows.
8. Enter the distance between columns.

The ARRAY command gives you a powerful alternative to simple copying. An array is a repetition in matrix form of the same figure. This command takes an object or group of objects and copies it a specific number of times in mathematically defined, evenly spaced locations.

There are two types of arrays. Rectangular arrays are linear and defined by rows and columns. Polar arrays are angular and based on the repetition of objects around the circumference of an arc or circle. The dots on the grid are an example of a rectangular array; the lines on any circular dial are an example of a polar array. Both types are common. We will explore rectangular arrays in this chapter and polar arrays in the next.

In preparation for this exercise, erase all the circles from your screen. This is a good opportunity to try the ERASE All option.

⊕   Type "e" or select the Erase tool from the Modify toolbar.

⊕   Type "all".

⊕   Press Enter.

⊕   Now draw a single circle, radius 0.5, centered at the point (2,2).

⊕   Type "Ar" or select Array from the Modify menu, or the Array tool from the Modify toolbar, as shown in Figure 4-15.

You will see the "Select objects" prompt.

Figure 4-15

⊕ Point to the circle.

⊕ Press Enter to end the selection process.

AutoCAD will ask which type of array you want:

Rectangular or Polar array (R/P) <R>:

⊕ Type "r", or you can press Enter if R is the default.

AutoCAD will prompt you for the number of rows in the array.

Number of rows (---) <1>:

The (---) is to remind you of what a row looks like (i.e., it is horizontal). The default is 1. So if you press Enter you will get a single row of circles. The number of circles in the row will depend, then, on the number of columns you specify. We will ask for three rows instead of just one.

⊕ Type "3".

AutoCAD now asks for the number of columns in the array:

Number of columns (|||) <1>:

Using the same format (|||), AutoCAD reminds you that columns are vertical. The default is 1 again. What would an array with three rows and only one column look like?

We will construct a five-column array.

⊕ Type "5".

Now AutoCAD needs to know how far apart to place all these circles. There will be 15 of them in this example—three rows with five circles in each row. AutoCAD prompts

Unit cell or distance between rows (---):

"Unit cell" means that you can respond by showing two corners of a window. The horizontal side of this window would give the space between columns; the vertical side would give the space between rows. You could do this exercise by showing a 1 × 1 window. We will use the more basic method of typing values for these distances. The distance between rows will be a vertical measure.

⊕ Type "1".

AutoCAD now asks for the horizontal distance between columns:

Distance between columns (|||):

⊕ Type "1" again.

You should have a 3 × 5 array of circles, as shown in Figure 4-16.

Notice that AutoCAD builds arrays up and to the right. This is consistent with the coordinate system, which puts positive values to the right on the horizontal *x* axis, and upward on the vertical *y* axis. Negative values can be used to create arrays in other directions.

We will use the array now on your screen as the selection set to create another array. We will specify an array that has three rows and three columns,

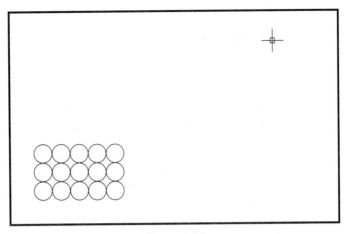

Figure 4-16

with 3.00 between rows and 5.00 between columns. This will keep our circles touching without overlapping.

⊕ Press Enter to repeat the ARRAY command.

⊕ Using a window, select the whole array of 15 circles.

⊕ Press Enter to end the selection process.

⊕ Type "r".

⊕ Type "3" for the number of rows.

⊕ Type "3" for the number of columns.

⊕ Type "3" for the distance between rows.

⊕ Type "5" for the distance between columns.

You should have a screen full of circles, as in Figure 4-17.

When you are ready to move on, use the U command to undo the last two arrays.

⊕ Type "u" to undo the second array.

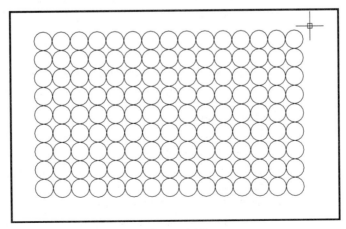

Figure 4-17

⊕ Type "u" again to undo the first array.

Now you should be back to your original circle centered at (2,2). Notice that the U command works nicely to undo an incorrectly drawn array quickly. This is important to know, because it is easy to make mistakes creating arrays. Be aware, however, that for other purposes the objects in an array are treated as separate entities, just as if you had drawn them one by one.

Try using some negative distances to create an array down and to the left.

⊕ First, use the MOVE command or grips to move your circle to the middle of the screen.

⊕ Type "Ar" or select the Array tool.

⊕ Select the circle by pointing or typing "L" for last.

⊕ Press Enter to end the selection process.

⊕ Type "r" or press Enter.

⊕ Type "3" for the number of rows.

⊕ Type "3" for the number of columns.

⊕ Type "−2" for the distance between rows.

⊕ Type "−2" for the distance between columns.

Your array should be built down and to the left. The −2 distance between rows causes the array to be built going down. The −2 distance between columns causes the array to be built across to the left.

4.7 Changing Plot Configuration Parameters

In the previous chapter you began using the plot preview feature of the Plot Configuration Dialog box. In this chapter we encourage you to continue to learn about plot configuration by exploring several more areas of the dialog box. We have used no specific drawing for illustration. Now that you know how to use plot preview, you can observe the effects of changing plot parameters with any drawing you like and decide at any point whether you actually want to print out the results. We will continue to remind you to look at a plot preview after making any change in configuration. This is the best way to learn about plotting.

We will start with device selection and move on to pen parameters and additional parameters. In the next chapter we will complete the introduction to the dialog box with paper size, orientation, scaling, rotation, and origin.

⊕ To begin this exploration, you should have a drawing or drawn objects on your screen so that you can observe the effects of various configuration changes you will be making.

⊕ Type "Ctrl-p", select "Print..." from the File pull-down menu, or select the Print tool from the Standard toolbar.

This will open up the Plot Configuration dialog box.

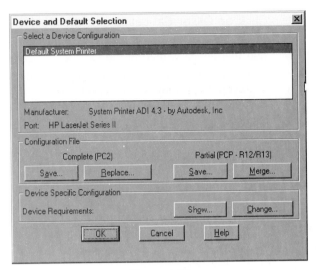

Figure 4-18

Device and Default Information

The device box should contain the name of the printer or plotter you are planning to use. If not, you can get a list of available options through the subdialog illustrated in Figure 4-18.

⊞   Click on "Device and Default Selection..." or type "d".

You should see a dialog box similar to the one shown in Figure 4-18. The list of devices will be your own, of course. If there is a need to change plotters or printers, you can do so by selecting from the list. If the device you want is not on the list, you will need to make sure the device driver is properly installed and then use the CONFIG command to add it to the list. See the *AutoCAD Installation Guide* for additional information.

Along with the list of available plotting devices, this dialog box allows you to save plotting specifications to ASCII files and get them back later. AutoCAD automatically saves your most recent plot parameters in a file called ACAD.cfg. However, for more permanent storage, you can create a separate file. Such files are saved with a "pc2" extension for complete configuration files or "pcp" (plot configuration parameter) for partial configuration files. There are many parameters to deal with in plotting, including as many as 256 pen colors. So saving a set of parameters to a file may be far more efficient than specifying them manually each time you plot. You may have one set of parameters for one device and another set for a different device. Pcp files save only device-independent information, while pc2 files save all configuration information.

In addition, some plotting devices have special configuration requirements not needed or not available on other devices. If this is the case with your device, the boxes under "Device Specific Configuration" will be accessible. The specific parameters and options will be determined by the device driver for your plotter. See the *AutoCAD Installation Guide* if you need additional information.

⊕   Click on OK or Cancel to exit the Device and Default Selection dialog.

This will bring you back to the Plot Configuration dialog box. Assuming that the device named in the Device and Default Information box is the correct one, you are ready to move on. However, if you have made any changes, we recommend that you do a plot preview. Changing devices may bring about changes in paper size and orientation, for example, and you will see these changes reflected graphically in the partial and full previews.

Pen Parameters

If you are using a plotter with multiple pens, you can assign colors, linetypes, widths, and speeds to each pen individually. If you are using a printer, you will find that the Pen Assignments box is grayed out. If you do have access, we suggest you look at the Pen Assignment dialog now, even though you may not want to make changes.

⊕   Click on "Pen Assignments..." or type "p".

This will call the dialog box shown in Figure 4-19. If you select any pen, you will see its color, number, linetype, speed, and width displayed in the Modify Values box at the right. Changes can be made in these edit boxes in the usual manner.

The specifications made here are designed to relate pen numbers on your plotter to pen colors. If pen numbers are correctly related to pen colors, then layers will automatically be plotted in their assigned colors. The linetypes assigned to layers in AutoCAD are also plotted automatically and do not need to be assigned to pens at this point.

Note: If your plotter supports multiple linetypes, you will reach another dialog box showing numbered linetypes by clicking on "Feature Legend...". These are not to be confused with the linetypes created within your Auto-CAD drawing associated with layers. They should be used in special applica-

Figure 4-19

tions to vary the look of "continuous" AutoCAD lines only. Otherwise you will get a confused mixture of linetypes when your plotter tries to break up lines that AutoCAD has already drawn broken.

⊕   Click on OK or Cancel to exit the "Pen Assignments" dialog box.

Additional Parameters

This is a crucial area of the dialog box that allows you to specify the portion of your drawing to be plotted. You have some familiarity with this from Chapter 2, where you plotted using a window selection. Changes here will have a significant impact on the effective plotting area. Be sure to use plot preview any time you make changes in these parameters.

Also available in this area are hidden line removal (for 3D drawings); fill area adjustment, which affects the way pen width is interpreted when drawing wide lines; and plotting to a file instead of to an actual plotter. These are discussed briefly at the end of this section.

The radio buttons on the left show the options for plotting area. "Display" will create a plot using whatever is actually on the screen. If you used the ZOOM command to enlarge a portion of the drawing before entering PLOT and then selected this option, AutoCAD would plot whatever you have zoomed in on. "Extents" refers to the actual drawing area in which you have drawn objects. It may be larger or smaller than the limits of the drawing. Drawing limits, as you know, are specified using the LIMITS command or a setup Wizard. If you are using our standard B-size template, they will go from (0,0) to (18,12). "View" will be accessible only after you have defined views in the drawing using the VIEW command (Chapter 11). "Window" will not be accessible until you define a window (if you have defined a window in a previous drawing, it may be saved in ACAD.cfg, the plot configuration file).

⊕   As an exercise, we suggest that you try switching among Display, Extents, Limits, and Window selections and use plot preview to see the results. Use both partial and full previews to ensure that you can clearly see what is happening.

Whenever you make a change, also observe the changes in the boxes showing Plotted Inches = Drawing Units. Assuming that "Scaled to Fit" is checked, you will see significant changes in these scale ratios as AutoCAD adjusts scales according to how much area it is being asked to plot.

A few words about the other "Additional Parameters" options before moving on. "Hide Lines" is relevant only to 3D drawings. Lines that would be obstructed from the current point of view on a 3D surface or solid model can be removed from the display using the HIDE command. When it comes to plotting, however, they will not be removed unless the "Hide Lines" box is checked. Hidden line removal is discussed in Chapter 13.

"Adjust Area Fill" is only relevant in drawings that must be precise to specifications less than a pen's width. In these cases, you can tell your plotter to compensate for pen width when it draws thick lines, such as wide polylines, solids, and traces (Chapter 9).

"Plot to File" saves the plot information so that it can be used later or sent to another site for plotting. Plots saved to a file are given the same name as the drawing but with a .plt extension. This may be a more efficient way to plot if, for example, a number of files can be plotted at one time using a plot spooler. Plot spoolers are software programs that plot a series of plot files one after another. Release 14 has its own plot spool utility called Autospool.

We will explore the last two areas of Plot Configuration, "Paper Size and Orientation" and "Scale, Rotation, and Origin," in the next chapter. In the meantime, you should continue to experiment with plotting and plot previewing as you complete the drawings at the end of this chapter.

4.8 Review Material

Questions

1. What command is automated through the step 2 (area) tab of the Quick Setup Wizard?
2. Name at least five settings that would typically be included in a Template drawing.
3. Where are template drawings stored in a standard AutoCAD file configuration? What extension is given to template file names?
4. What is the value of using a template drawing?
5. What is the main difference between the command procedure for MOVE and that for COPY?
6. What is the main limitation of grip editing?
7. What do you have to do to remove grips from an object once they are displayed?
8. How do you access the grip edit pop-up menu?
9. Explain how arrays are a special form of copying.
10. What is a rectangular array? What is a polar array?
11. Why is it important to do a partial plot preview after changing printing devices or after switching radio buttons in the additional parameters area of the plot configuration dialog box?

Drawing Problems

1. Create a C-size drawing template using an ANSI standard sheet size, layers, and other settings as shown in this chapter. Use your B template to make this process easier.

2. Open a drawing with your new C-size template and draw a circle with a two-unit radius centered at (11,8).
3. Using grips, make four copies of the circle, centered at (15,8), (11,12), (7,8), and (11,4).
4. Switch to layer 2 and draw a 1 × 1 square with lower left corner at (1,1).
5. Create a rectangular array of the square with 14 rows and 20 columns, one unit between rows, and one unit between columns.

4.9   Drawing 4-1: Pattern

All the drawings in this chapter will use your B template. Do not expect, however, that you will never need to change settings. Layers will stay the same throughout this book, but limits will change from time to time, and grid and snap will change frequently.

This drawing will give you practice using the COPY command. There are numerous ways in which the drawing can be done. The key is to try to take advantage of the repetition in the pattern by copying in an efficient manner. The following figures suggest one way it can be done.

DRAWING SUGGESTIONS

GRID = 0.5
SNAP = 0.25

- Begin with a 6 × 6 square. Then draw the first set of lines as in Reference 4-1a.
- Copy the first set down 0.5 to produce Reference 4-1b.
- Draw the first set of V-shaped lines. Then use a multiple copy to produce Reference 4-1c.
- Finally, make a single copy of all the lines you have so far, using a window or crossing box for selection. (Be careful not to select the outside lines.) Watch the displacement carefully and you will produce Reference 4-1d, the completed drawing.

(a)

(b)

(c)

(d)

.50 TYP

.50 TYP

.25

.50 TYP

.25

.50 TYP

.50 TYP

6.00 SQ

PATTERN

Drawing 4-1

4.10   Drawing 4-2: Grill

This drawing should go very quickly if you use the ARRAY command.

DRAWING SUGGESTIONS

GRID = 0.5
SNAP = 0.25

- Begin with a 4.75 × 4.75 square.
- Move in 0.25 all around to create the inside square.
- Draw the rectangle in the lower left-hand corner first; then use the ARRAY command to create the rest.
- Also remember that you can undo a misplaced array using the U command.

GRILL
Drawing 4-2

4.11 Drawing 4-3: Weave

As you do this drawing, watch AutoCAD work for you and think about how long it would take to do by hand! The finished drawing will look like Reference 4-3. For clarity, the drawing shows only one cell of the array and its dimensions.

DRAWING SUGGESTIONS

GRID = 0.5
SNAP = 0.25

- Draw the 6 × 6 square; then zoom in on the lower left using a window. This will be the area shown in the lower left of the dimensioned drawing.
- Observe the dimensions and draw the line patterns for the lower left corner of the weave. You could use the COPY command in several places if you like, but the time gained will be minimal. Don't worry if you have to fuss with this a little to get it correct; once you've got it right the rest will be easy.
- Use ARRAY to repeat the lower left-hand cell in an 8 × 8 matrix.
- If you get it wrong, use U and try again.

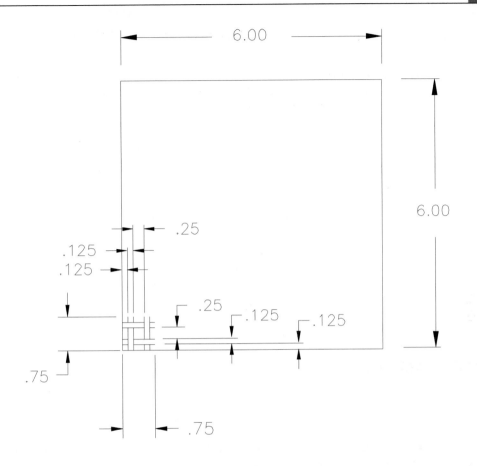

WEAVE

Drawing 4-3

4.12   Drawing 4-4: Test Bracket

This is a great drawing for practicing much of what you have learned up to this point. Notice the suggested snap, grid, ltscale, and limit settings, and use the ARRAY command to draw the 25 circles on the front view.

DRAWING SUGGESTIONS

GRID = 0.5
SNAP = 0.25
LTSCALE = 0.50
LIMITS = (0,0) (24,18)

- Be careful to draw all lines on the correct layers, according to their linetypes.
- Draw center lines through circles before copying or arraying them; otherwise you will have to go back and draw them on each individual circle or repeat the array process.
- A multiple copy will work nicely for the four 0.50-diameter holes. A rectangular array is definitely desirable for the twenty-five 0.75-diameter holes.

CREATING CENTER MARKS
WITH THE DIMCEN SYSTEM VARIABLE

There is a simple way to create the center marks and center lines shown on all the circles in this drawing. It involves changing the value of a dimension variable called "dimcen" (dimension center). Dimensioning and dimension variables are discussed in Chapter 8, but if you would like to jump ahead, the following procedure will work nicely in this drawing.

1. Type "dimcen". The default setting for dimcen is 0.09, which will cause AutoCAD to draw a simple cross as a center mark. Changing it to 2.09 will tell AutoCAD to draw a cross that reaches across the circle.
2. Type "2.09".
3. After drawing your first circle, and before arraying it, type "dim". This will put you in the dimension command.
4. Type "cen", indicating that you want to draw a center mark. This is a very simple dimension feature.
5. Point to the circle.

TEST BRACKET

Drawing 4—4

4.13   Drawing 4-5: Floor Framing

This architectural drawing will require changes in many features of your drawing setup. Pay close attention to the suggested settings.

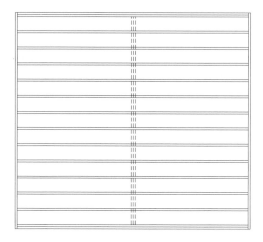

DRAWING SUGGESTIONS

> UNITS = Architectural, smallest fraction = 1″
> LIMITS = 36″, 24″
> GRID = 1′
> SNAP = 2″
> LTSCALE = 12

- Be sure to use foot (′) and inch (″) symbols when setting limits, grid, and snap (but not ltscale).
- Begin by drawing the 20′ × 17′-10″ rectangle, with the lower left corner somewhere in the neighborhood of (4′,4′).
- Complete the left and right 2 × 10 joists by copying the vertical 17′-10″ lines 2″ in from each side. You may find it helpful to use the arrow keys when working with such small increments.
- Draw a 19′-8″ horizontal line 2″ up from the bottom and copy it 2″ higher to complete the double joists.
- Array the inner 2 × 10 in a 14-row by 1-column array, with 16″ between rows.
- Set to layer 2 and draw the three 17′-4″ hidden lines down the center.

2 x 10 (2)

2 x 10 (2)

2X10−16"O.C.

2 x 10

2 x 10

2 x 10 (2)

17'−6"

17'−10"

20'−0"

FLOOR FRAMING

Drawing 4−5

4.6 Drawing 4-6: Threaded Shaft

The finished drawing should be the top and front view. Draw the circular view first. This will be the top view. Use the top view to line up the front view. Do not dimension unless instructed to do so.

   This drawing includes a typical application of rectangular array and copy commands.

DRAWING SUGGESTIONS

GRID = 1/4
SNAP = 1/8
LIMITS = (0,0) (18,12)
LTSCALE = 0.5

- Draw the circles in the top view and use these to line up the horizontal lines in the front view.
- Pay particular attention to the detail drawing when designing the acme screw thead. Draw the outline of the zig-zag shape on each side for one thread and then connect the lines, creating the full thread. Be sure the zig-zag on opposite sides is offset by one thread before drawing the angular lines.
- Now that one thread is created, a simple array will complete the whole thread $6\frac{3}{4}$ long.
- Complete the drawing by drawing shaft lines and the square shape at the top end.

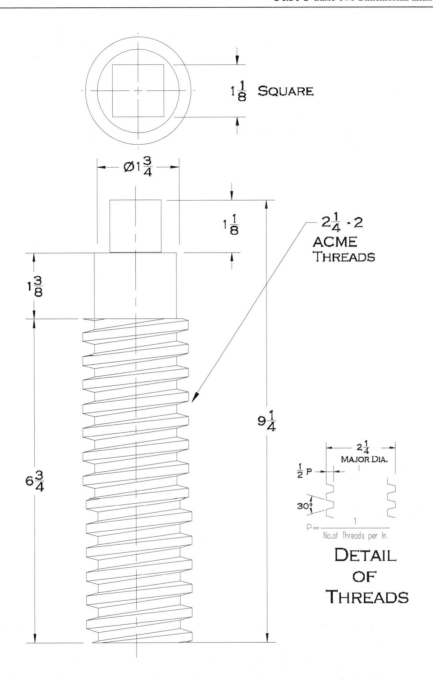

$1\frac{1}{8}$ SQUARE

$\varnothing 1\frac{3}{4}$

$1\frac{1}{8}$

$2\frac{1}{4}$ - 2
ACME
THREADS

$1\frac{3}{8}$

$9\frac{1}{4}$

$6\frac{3}{4}$

$2\frac{1}{4}$
MAJOR DIA.

$\frac{1}{2}$ P

30°

$P = \dfrac{1}{\text{No.of Threads per In.}}$

DETAIL
OF
THREADS

THREADED SHAFT
DRAWING 4-6

5

Arcs and Polar Arrays

COMMANDS

DRAW	**MODIFY**
ARC	ARRAY (polar)
	MIRROR
	ROTATE

OVERVIEW

So far, every drawing you have done has been composed of lines and circles. In this chapter you will learn a third major entity, the ARC. In addition, you will expand your ability to manipulate objects on the screen. You will learn to ROTATE objects and create their MIRROR images. But first, we will pick up where we left off in Chapter 4 by showing you how to create polar arrays.

TASKS

5.1   Creating Polar Arrays

GENERAL PROCEDURE

1. Type "Ar", select the Array tool from the Modify toolbar, or select Array from the Modify menu.
2. Define a selection set. (Steps 1 and 2 can be reversed if noun/verb selection is enabled.)
3. Type "p" for "polar".
4. Pick a center point.
5. Enter the number of items to be in the array (or press Enter).
6. Enter the angle to fill (or 0).
7. Enter the angle between items.
8. Tell whether or not to rotate items.

The procedure for creating polar arrays is lengthy and requires some explanation. The first two steps are the same as in rectangular arrays. Step 3 is also the same, except that you respond with "p" instead of "r". From here on the steps will be new. First you will pick a center point, and then you will have several options for defining the array.

There are three qualities that define a polar array, but two are sufficient. A polar array is defined by two of the following: (1) a certain number of items, (2) an angle that these items span, and (3) an angle between each item and the next. However you define your polar array, you will have to tell AutoCAD whether or not to rotate the newly created objects as they are copied.

⊕   Begin a new drawing using the B template.

⊕   In preparation for this exercise, draw a vertical 1.00 line at the bottom center of the screen, near (9.00,2.00), as shown in Figure 5-1.

   We will use a 360 degree polar array to create Figure 5-2.

⊕   Type "Ar", select Array from the Modify menu, or select the Array tool from the Modify toolbar, as illustrated in Figure 5-3.

Figure 5-1

Figure 5-2

Figure 5-3

⊕ Select the line.

⊕ Type "p".

So far, so good. Nothing new up to this point. Now you have a prompt that looks like this:

Base/Specify center point of array:

Rectangular arrays are not determined by a center, so we did not encounter this prompt before. Polar arrays, however, are built by copying objects around the circumferences of circles or arcs, so we need a center to define one of these. We will also need to specify whether objects should be rotated as they are copied. The Base option would allow us to determine how objects are rotated. For this array, show a center point.

⊕ Pick a point directly above the line and somewhat below the center of the screen.

Something in the neighborhood of (9.00,4.50) will do. The next prompt is

Number of items:

Remember that we have a choice of two out of three among number of items, angle to fill, and angle between items. This time we will give AutoCAD the first two.

⊕ Type "12".

Now that AutoCAD knows that we want 12 items, all it needs is either the angle to fill with these or the angle between the items. It will ask first for the angle to fill:

Angle to fill (+=ccw,-=cw) <360>:

The symbols in parentheses tell us that if we give a positive angle, the array will be constructed counterclockwise; if we give a negative angle, it will be constructed clockwise. Get used to this; it will come up frequently.

The default is 360 degrees, meaning an array that fills a complete circle.

If we did not give AutoCAD an angle (that is, if we responded with a "0"), we would be prompted for the angle between. This time around we will give 360 as the angle to fill.

⊕ Press Enter to accept the default, a complete circle.

AutoCAD now has everything it needs, except that it doesn't know whether we want our lines to retain their vertical orientation or to be rotated along with the angular displacement as they are copied. AutoCAD asks

Rotate objects as they are copied? <Y>:

Notice the default, which we will accept.

⊕ Press Enter or type "y".

Your screen should resemble Figure 5-2. Now let's try some of the other options. We will define an array that has 20 items placed 15 degrees apart and not rotated.

⊕ Type "U" to undo the first array.

⊕ Type "Ar" or select the Array tool.

⊕ Select the line again.

⊕ Press Enter to end object selection.

⊕ Type "p".

⊕ Pick the same center point as before.

⊕ Type "20" for the number of items.

⊕ Type "0" for the angle to fill.

As mentioned, this response tells AutoCAD to issue a prompt for the angle between items:

Angle between items (+=ccw,-=cw):

The symbols in parentheses are familiar from the "angle to fill" prompt. Notice that there is no default angle here.

⊕ Type "15" for the angle between items.

All that remains is to tell AutoCAD not to rotate the lines as they are copied.

⊕ Type "n".

Your screen should now resemble Figure 5-4.

Try one more and then you will be on your own with polar arrays. For this one, define an array that fills 270 degrees moving clockwise and has 30 degrees between each angle, as in Figure 5-5.

⊕ Undo the last array.

⊕ Repeat the first four steps, up to the "number of items" prompt.

⊕ Press Enter to skip the "Number of items" prompt.

This tells AutoCAD to issue the other two prompts instead.

Figure 5-4

Figure 5-5

⊕ Type "−270" for the angle to fill.

What will the negative angle do?

⊕ Type "30" for the angle between.

⊕ Press Enter to rotate items as they are copied.

Your screen should resemble Figure 5-5.

This ends our discussion of polar arrays. With the options AutoCAD gives you, there are many possibilities that you may want to try out. As always, we encourage experimentation. When you are satisfied, erase everything on the screen in preparation for learning the ARC command.

5.2   Drawing Arcs

GENERAL PROCEDURE

1. Type "a", select the Arc tool from the Draw toolbar, or select Arc from the Draw menu.
2. Type or show where to start the arc, where to end it, and what circle it is a portion of, using any of the 11 available methods.

Learning AutoCAD's ARC command is an exercise in geometry. In this section we will give you a firm foundation for understanding and drawing arcs so that you will not be confused by all the options that are available. The information we give you will be more than enough to do the drawings in this chapter and most drawings you will encounter elsewhere. Refer to the *AutoCAD Command Reference* and the chart at the end of this section (Figure 5-8) if you need additional information.

AutoCAD gives you eight distinct ways to draw arcs, eleven if you count variations in order. With so many choices, some generalizations will be helpful.

First, notice that every option requires you to specify three pieces of information: where to begin the arc, where to end it, and what circle it is theoretically a part of. To get a handle on the range of options, look at the list of options from the Arc submenu.

⊕   Open the Draw menu and select Arc to open the cascading submenu illustrated in Figure 5-6.

Figure 5-6

For clarity, we have numbered the options one through eleven in the figure. Notice that options 8, 9, and 10 are simply reordered versions of 2, 3, and 4. This is how we end up with eleven options instead of eight.

More important, "start" is always included. In every option, a starting point must be specified, though it does not have to be the first point given.

The options arise from the different ways you can specify the end and the circle from which the arc is cut. The end may be shown as an actual point (all End options) or inferred from a specified angle or length of chord (all Angle and Length options).

The circle that the arc is part of may be specified directly by its center point (all Center options) or inferred from other information, such as a radius length (Radius options), an angle between two given points (Angle options), or a tangent direction (the Start, End, Direction, and Continue options).

With this framework in mind, we will begin by drawing an arc using the simplest method, which is also the default, the three-points option. The geometric key to this method is that any three points not on the same line determine a circle or an arc of a circle. AutoCAD uses this in the CIRCLE command (the 3P option) as well as in the ARC command.

⊕ Type "a" or select the Arc tool from the Draw toolbar, as shown in Figure 5-7.

AutoCAD's response will be this prompt:

> Center/<Start point>:

Accepting the default by specifying a point will leave open all those options in which the start point is specified first.

If you instead type a "c", AutoCAD will prompt for a center point and follow with those options that begin with a center.

⊕ Select a starting point near the center of the screen.

AutoCAD prompts

> Center/End/<Second point>:

We will continue to follow the default three-point sequence by specifying a second point. You may want to refer to the chart (Figure 5-8) as you draw this arc.

⊕ Select any point one or two units away from the previous point. Exact coordinates are not important.

Once AutoCAD has two points, it gives you an arc to drag. By moving the cursor slowly in a circle and in and out, you can see the range of what the third point will produce.

Figure 5-7

AutoCAD also knows now that you have to provide an end point to complete the arc, so the prompt has only one option:

> End point:

Any point you select will do, as long as it produces an arc that fits on the screen.

⊕ Pick an end point.

As you can see, three-point arcs are easy to draw. It is much like drawing a line, except that you have to specify three points instead of two. In practice, however, you do not always have three points to use this way. This necessitates the broad range of options in the ARC command. The dimensions you are given and the objects already drawn will determine what options are useful to you.

Next, we will create an arc using the start, center, end method, the second option illustrated in Figure 5-8.

⊕ Type "U" to undo the three-point arc.

⊕ Type "a" or select the Arc tool.

⊕ Select a point near the center of the screen as a start point.

The prompt that follows is the same as for the three-point option, but we will not use the default this time:

> Center/End/<Second point>:

We will choose the Center option.

Tip: If you choose options from the Draw menu, you will find some steps automated. If you select "Start,Center,End" for example, the "c" will be entered automatically.

⊕ Type "c", if necessary.

This tells AutoCAD that we want to specify a center point next, so we see this prompt:

> Center:

⊕ Select any point roughly one to three units away from the start point.

The circle from which the arc is to be cut is now clearly determined. All that is left is to specify how much of the circle to take, which can be done in one of three ways, as the prompt indicates:

> Angle/Length of chord/<End point>:

We will simply specify an end point by typing coordinates or pointing. But first, move the cursor slowly in a circle and in and out to see how the method works. As before, there is an arc to drag, and now there is a radial direction rubber band as well. If you pick a point anywhere along this rubber band, AutoCAD will assume that you want the point where it crosses the circumference of the circle.

Note: Here, as in the polar arrays in this chapter, AutoCAD is building arcs counterclockwise, consistent with its coordinate system.

Figure 5-8

⊕ Select an end point to complete the arc.

We will draw one more arc, using the start, center, angle method, before going on. This method has some peculiarities in the use of the rubber band that are typical of the ARC command and can be confusing. An example of how the start, center, angle method may look is shown in Figure 5-8.

⊕ Type "u" to undo the last arc.

⊕ Type "a" or select the Arc tool.
AutoCAD will ask for a center or start point:

                    Center/<Start point>:

⊕ Pick a start point near the center of the screen.
AutoCAD prompts:

                    Center/End/<Second point>:

⊕ Type "c".
AutoCAD prompts for a center point:

                            Center:

⊕ Pick a center point one to three units below the start point.
AutoCAD will prompt, as before,

                    Angle/Length of chord/<End point>:

⊕ Type "a" to indicate that you will specify an angle.

You can type an angle specification or show an angle on the screen. Notice that the rubber band now shows an angle only; its length is insignificant.
The indicated angle is being measured from the horizontal, but the actual arc
begins at the start point and continues counterclockwise, as illustrated in Figure 5-8. The prompt reads

                        Included angle:

⊕ Type "45" or show an angle of 45 degrees.
(Remember, you can use F6 to change to polar coordinates that will show
the angle.)

Now that you have tried three of the basic methods for constructing an arc, we
strongly suggest that you study the chart in Figure 5-8 and then try out the other options. The notes in the right-hand column will serve as a guide to what to look for.

The differences in the use of the rubber band from one option to the next can
be confusing. You should understand, for instance, that in some cases the linear
rubber band is only significant as a distance indicator; its angle is of no importance
and is ignored by AutoCAD. In other cases it is just the reverse; the length of the
rubber band is irrelevant, while its angle of rotation is important.

> **Tip:** One additional trick you should try out as you experiment with arcs is
> as follows: If you press Enter or the space bar at the "Center/<Start point>"
> prompt, AutoCAD will use the end point of the last line or arc you drew as
> the new starting point and construct an arc tangent to it. This is the same as
> the Continue option on the pull-down menu.

This completes the present discussion of the ARC command. Constructing arcs,
as you may have realized, can be tricky. Another option that is available and often
useful is to draw a complete circle and then use the TRIM or BREAK commands
to cut out the arc you want. BREAK and TRIM are introduced in the next chapter.

5.3 Using the ROTATE Command

GENERAL PROCEDURE

1. Type "Ro", select Rotate from the Modify menu, or select the Rotate tool from the Modify toolbar.
2. Define the selection set. (Steps 1 and 2 can be reversed if noun/verb selection is enabled.)
3. Pick a base point.
4. Indicate an angle of rotation.

ROTATE is a fairly straightforward command, and it has some uses that might not be apparent immediately. For example, it frequently is easier to draw an object in a horizontal or vertical position and then ROTATE it rather than drawing it in a diagonal position.

In addition to the ROTATE command, there is a rotate mode in the grip edit system, which we will introduce later in this section.

⊕ In preparation for this exercise, clear your screen and draw a horizontally oriented arc near the center of your screen, as in Figure 5-9. Exact coordinates and locations are not important.

We will begin by rotating the arc to the position shown in Figure 5-10.

⊕ Select the arc.

⊕ Type "Ro", select Rotate from the Modify menu, or select the Rotate tool from the Modify toolbar, as shown in Figure 5-11.

You will be prompted for a base point:

Base point:

This will be the point around which the object is rotated. The results of the rotation, therefore, are dramatically affected by your choice of base point. We will choose a point at the left tip of the arc.

Figure 5-9

Figure 5-10

Figure 5-11

⊕ Point to the left tip of the arc.

The prompt that follows looks like this:

<Rotation angle>/Reference:

The default method is used to indicate a rotation angle directly. The object will be rotated through the angle specified and the original object will be deleted.

Move the cursor in a circle and you will see that you have a copy of the object to drag into place visually. If ortho or snap are on, turn them off to see the complete range of rotation.

⊕ Type "90" or point to a rotation of 90 degrees (use F6 if your coordinate display is not showing polar coordinates).

The results should resemble Figure 5-10.

Notice that when specifying the rotation angle directly like this, the original orientation of the selected object is taken to be 0 degrees. The rotation is figured counterclockwise from there. However, there may be times when you want to refer to the coordinate system in specifying rotation. This is the purpose of the "Reference" option. To use it, all you need to do is specify the present orientation of the object relative to the coordinate system, and then tell AutoCAD the orientation you want it to have after rotation. Look at Figure 5-12. To rotate the arc as shown, you either can indicate a rotation of −45 degrees or tell AutoCAD that it is presently oriented to 90 degrees and you want it rotated to 45 degrees. Try this method for practice.

Figure 5-12

⊕   Press Enter to repeat the ROTATE command.
⊕   Select the arc.
⊕   Press Enter to end selection.
⊕   Choose a base point at the lower tip of the arc.
⊕   Type "r".
    AutoCAD will prompt for a reference angle:

                    Reference angle <0>:

⊕   Type "90".
    AutoCAD prompts for an angle of rotation:

                    Rotation angle:

⊕   Type "45".
    Your arc should now resemble the solid arc in Figure 5-12.

Rotating with Grips

Rotating with grips is simple, and there is a useful option for copying, but your choice of object selection methods is limited, as always, to pointing and windowing. Try this:

⊕   Pick the arc.
    The arc will become highlighted and grips will appear.
⊕   Pick the center grip.
⊕   Press the enter (right) button on your pointing device.
⊕   Select "Rotate" from the pop-up menu.
    Move your cursor in a circle and you will see the arc rotating around the grip at the center of the arc.
⊕   Now type "b" or press the right button again and select "Base pt" from the pop-up menu.

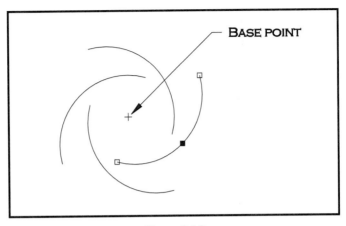

Figure 5-13

Base point will allow you to pick a base point other than the selected grip.

⊕ Pick a base point above and to the left of the grip, as shown in Figure 5-13.

Move your cursor in circles again. You will see the arc rotating around the new base point.

⊕ Type "c" or open the pop-up menu and select "Copy".

Notice the Command area prompt, which indicates that you are now in a rotate and multiple copy mode.

⊕ Pick a point showing a rotation angle of 90 degrees, as illustrated by the top arc in Figure 5-13.

⊕ Pick a second point showing a rotation angle of 180 degrees, as illustrated by the arc at the left in the figure.

⊕ Pick point 3 at 270 degrees to complete the design shown in Figure 5-13.

⊕ Press enter or the space bar to exit the grip edit mode.

This capacity to create rotated copies is very useful, as you will find when you do the drawings at the end of this chapter.

5.4 Creating Mirror Images of Objects on the Screen

GENERAL PROCEDURE

1. Type "Mi", select Mirror from the Draw menu, or the Mirror tool from the Modify toolbar.
2. Define a selection set. (Steps 1 and 2 can be reversed if noun/verb selection is enabled.)
3. Point to two ends of a mirror line.
4. Indicate whether or not to delete the original object.

Figure 5-14

Figure 5-15

There are two main differences between the command procedures for Mirror and Rotate. First, to mirror an object you will have to define a mirror line; second, you will have an opportunity to indicate whether you want to retain the original object or delete it. In the Rotate sequence the original is always deleted.

There is also a mirror mode in the grip edit system, which we will explore later in this section.

⊕ To begin this exercise, undo the rotate copy process of the former exercise so that you are left with a single arc. Rotate it and move it to the left so that you have a bowl-shaped arc placed left of the center of your screen, as in Figure 5-14.

Except where noted, you should have snap and ortho on to do this exercise.

⊕ Select the arc.

⊕ Type "Mi", select Mirror from the Draw menu, or select the Mirror tool from the Modify toolbar, as shown in Figure 5-15.

Now AutoCAD will ask you for the first point of a mirror line:

First point of mirror line:

A mirror line is just what you would expect; the line serves as the "mirror," and all points on your original object will be reflected across the line at an equal distance and opposite orientation.

We will show a mirror line even with the top of the arc, so that the end points of the mirror images will be touching.

⊕ Select a point even with the left end point of the arc, as in Figure 5-16.

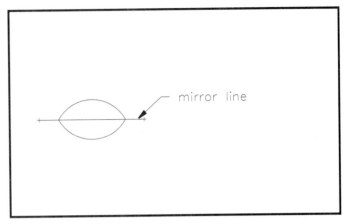

Figure 5-16

You are prompted to show the other end point of the mirror line:

Second point:

The length of the mirror line is not important. All that matters is its orientation. Move the cursor slowly in a circle, and you will see an inverted copy of the arc moving with you to show the different mirror images that are possible, given the first point you have specified. Turn ortho off to see the whole range of possibilities; then turn it on again to complete the exercise.

We will select a point at 0 degrees from the first point, so that the mirror image will be directly above the original arc and touching at the end points, as in Figure 5-16.

⊕ Select a point directly to the right (0 degrees) of the first point.

The dragged object will disappear until you answer the next prompt, which asks if you want to delete the original object or not.

Delete old objects? <N>:

This time around we will not delete the original.

⊕ Press Enter to retain the old object.

Your screen will look like Figure 5-16, without the mirror line in the middle.

Now let's repeat the process, deleting the original this time and using a different mirror line.

⊕ Press Enter to repeat the MIRROR command.

⊕ Select the original (lower) arc.

⊕ Press Enter to end selection.

We will create a mirror image above the last one by choosing a mirror line slightly above the two arcs, as in Figure 5-17.

⊕ Select a first point of the mirror line slightly above and to the left of the figure.

⊕ Select a second point directly to the right of the first point.

⊕ Type "y", indicating that you want the old object, the lower arc, deleted.

Your screen should now resemble Figure 5-18.

Figure 5-17

Figure 5-18

Mirroring with Grips

The Mirror grip edit mode works exactly like the rotate mode, except that the rubber band will show you a mirror line instead of a rotation angle. The option to retain or delete the original is obtained through the copy option, just as in the Rotate mode. Try it.

⊕ Select the two arcs on your screen by pointing or windowing.

The arcs will be highlighted and grips will be showing.

⊕ Pick any of the grips.

⊕ Press the enter button on your mouse and pick Mirror from the pop-up menu.

Move the cursor and observe the dragged mirror images of the arcs. Notice that the rubber band operates as a mirror line, just as in the Mirror command.

⊕ Type "b" or press the enter button again and select "Base point".

This frees you from the selected grip and allows you to create a mirror line from any point on the screen. Notice the "Base point:" prompt in the command area.

⊕   Type "c" or open the cursor menu and select "Copy".

As in the Rotate mode, this is how you retain the original in a grip edit mirroring sequence.

⊕   Pick a base point slightly below the arcs.

⊕   Pick a second point to the right of the first.

Your screen should resemble Figure 5-19.

⊕   Press enter or the space bar to exit grip edit mode.

We suggest that you complete this exercise by using the Mirror grip edit mode with the copy option to create Figure 5-20.

Figure 5-19

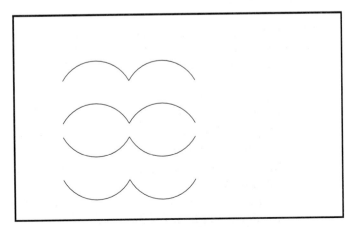

Figure 5-20

5.5 Changing Paper Size, Orientation, Plot Scale, Rotation, and Origin

This discussion will complete our exploration of the basic features of the Plot Configuration dialog box. The parameters involved will dramatically impact the results of your hard copy output. In particular, putting all of these variables together with each other and with previously discussed parameters takes a lot of skill and knowhow. You can gain this expertise through experience with actual plotting and plot previewing. As you become more comfortable with what is going on, it is especially valuable experience to plot using more than one device and different paper sizes.

⊕   Type Ctrl-P or select the Print tool from the standard tool bar to open the Plot Configuration dialog box.

Paper Size and Orientation

This box gives critical information and choices about the size and orientation of your drawing sheet. To begin with, you can choose to see information presented in inches or millimeters by selecting one of the two radio buttons. Inches is the default.

⊕   Click on "MM".

You will see that both the plot area and the scale values are changed to reflect metric units.

⊕   Click on "Inches".

On the right you will see a rectangle showing the orientation of the paper in the plotting device. It will be either landscape (horizontal) or portrait (vertical). This orientation is part of the device driver and cannot be changed directly. If you want to plot horizontally when your device is configured vertically, or viceversa, you must rotate the plot using the Rotation and Origin dialog described in the next subsection.

The plot area is shown below the radio buttons and is also determined by the plotting device. The default size will be the maximum size available on your printer or plotter. If you are using a printer, for example, you may have the equivalent of an A-size sheet. In this case the plot area will be close to 8.00×11.00.

⊕   Click on "Size...".

This will open the Paper Size dialog box shown in Figure 5-21. (If you are using a printer with only one paper size, this dialog box may be inaccessible.) The standard sizes listed in the box on the left are device specific and will depend on your plotter. The "USER" boxes on the right allow you to define plotting areas of your own. This means, for example, that you can plot in a 5.00×5.00 area on an 8.00×11.00 or larger sheet of paper.

Paper size can be changed by picking any of the sizes on the list at the left.

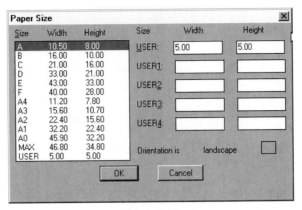

Figure 5-21

⊕ Change the paper size, if you wish, and then click on "OK" to exit the dialog.

If you have changed sizes, the new size will be named next to the Size box, and the new plot area will be listed below. The change also may be reflected in the scale box ("Plotted Inches = Drawing Units").

If you have changed paper sizes, we suggest that you do a plot preview.

Paper size is one of the important factors in determining effective plotting area.

Scale, Rotation, and Origin

Plots can be scaled to fit the available plot area or given an explicit scale of paper units to drawing units. "Scaled to Fit" is the default, as shown by the check in the check box. With this setting, the area chosen for plotting in the Additional Parameters box (Display, Extents, Limits, etc.) will be plotted as large as possible within the plot area specified in the Paper Size and Orientation box. Fitting the chosen area to the available plot area will dictate the scale shown in the edit boxes. Plotted inches or millimeters are shown in relation to drawing units. If either the area to be plotted or the paper size is changed, the change will be reflected in the scale boxes.

If "Scaled to Fit" is not checked, the scale will default to 1 = 1. In this case drawing units will be considered equivalent to paper size units. A 1-to-1 scale is definitely preferred when plotting from Paper Space (Chapter 6). Other scales can be specified explicitly by typing in the edit boxes. When you change the drawing scale, the area to be plotted may be affected. If the area is too large for the paper size given the scale, then only a portion of the chosen area will be plotted. If the area becomes smaller than the available paper, some blank space will be left. Changing scales should be followed by a partial preview.

The area of the paper that is actually used for plotting may also be affected by the rotation and origin of the plot. If your device is configured with paper oriented vertically (portrait style), and you want to plot horizontally (landscape), then you will need to rotate 90 degrees. This is done with the radio buttons in the Plot Rotation and Origin dialog box.

Figure 5-22

⊕ Click in the Rotation and Origin box.

This will call the dialog box shown in Figure 5-22. You can rotate to 0, 90, 180, or 270 degrees as shown. Rotating a plot by 90 degrees will have a significant impact on the relationship between paper size and effective drawing area.

This box will also allow you to change the origin of the plot. Plots usually originate in the lower left-hand corner of the page, but you can alter this. For example, let's say you wanted to plot a 5 × 5 area in the upper right of an 8 × 11 sheet landscape orientation. You could do this by creating a 5 × 5 "User" paper size and then moving its origin from (0,0) to (6,3).

⊕ Change the plot rotation if you wish, and then Click on OK to exit the dialog box.

At this point, you have been through all the major parameters of plot configuration. It is important that you gain experience in using the configuration parameters available. When you have a drawing ready, open the plot configuration dialog box and make whatever adjustments you think are necessary. You should access at least one partial and one full preview along the way. When everything looks right, check your plotting device and paper and then click on "OK" to start it rolling.

5.6 Review Material

Questions:

1. What factors define a polar array? How many are needed to define an array?
2. What factors define an arc? How many are needed for any single method?
3. What is the difference between the three-point option in the CIRCLE command and the three-point option in the ARC command?
4. Explain the significance of the rubber band in the Start, Center, Angle and the Start, End direction methods.
5. How would you use the reference option to rotate a line from 60 degrees to 90 degrees? How would you accomplish the same rotation without using reference?
6. What is the purpose of the base point option in the grip edit Rotate mode?
7. Why does Mirror require a mirror line where Rotate only requires a single point?
8. How do you create a landscape plot if your printer prints in portrait orientation?

9. What would happen if a drawing created with our B template were printing with a 1-to-1 scale on an A-size printer? What feature of the Plot Configuration dialog box would you use to find out if you weren't sure?
10. How would you print within a 3×3 area in the lower left corner of an 8.5×11 piece of paper?

Drawing Problems:

1. Draw an arc starting at (10,6) and passing through (12,6.5) and (14,6).
2. Create a mirrored copy of the arc across the horizontal line passing through (10,6).
3. Rotate the pair of arcs from problem 2 45 degrees around the point (9,6).
4. Create a mirrored copy of the pair of arcs mirrored across a vertical line passing through (9,6).
5. Create mirrored copies of both pairs of arcs mirrored across a horizontal line passing through (9,6).
6. Erase any three of the four pairs of arcs on your screen and re-create them using a polar array.

5.7   Drawing 5-1: Flanged Bushing

This drawing makes use of a polar array to draw eight screw holes in a circle. It also reviews the use of layers and linetypes.

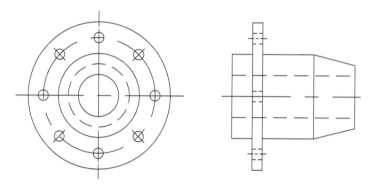

DRAWING SUGGESTIONS

GRID = 0.25
SNAP = 0.25
LTSCALE = 0.50
LIMITS = (0,0) (12,9)

- Draw the concentric circles first, using dimensions from both views. Remember to change layers as needed.
- Once you have drawn the 2.75-diameter bolt circle, use it to locate one of the bolt holes. Any of the circles at a quadrant point (0, 90, 180, or 270 degrees) will do.
- Draw a center line across the bolt hole, and then array the hole and the center line 360 degrees. Be sure to rotate the objects as they are copied; otherwise, you will get strange results from your center lines.

FLANGED BUSHING

Drawing 5-1

5.8   Drawing 5-2: Guide

There are six arcs in this drawing, and while some of them could be drawn as fillets, we suggest that you use the ARC command for practice. By drawing arcs you will also avoid a common problem with fillets. Since fillets are designed to round intersections at corners, creating a fillet in the middle of a line will erase part of that line unless you turn Trim mode off. This would affect the center line on the left side of the front view of this drawing, for example.

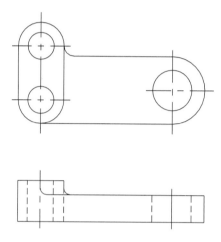

DRAWING SUGGESTIONS

GRID = 0.25
SNAP = 0.125
LTSCALE = 0.50
LIMITS = (0,0) (12,9)

- The three large arcs in the top view all can be drawn easily using Start, Center, End.
- The smaller 0.375 arc in the top view could be drawn by filleting the top arc with the horizontal line to its right. However, we suggest you try an arc giving start, center, end or start, center, angle. Note that you can easily locate the center by moving 0.375 to the right of the end point of the upper arc.
- The same method will work to draw the 0.25 arc in the front view. Begin by dropping a line down 0.25 from the horizontal line. Start your arc at the end of this line, and move 0.25 to the right to locate its center. Then the end will simply be 0.25 down from the center (or you could specify an angle of 90 degrees).
- Similarly, the arc at the center line can be drawn from a start point 0.25 up from the horizontal. It will have a radius of 0.25 and make an angle of 90 degrees.

.375 R

1.25 R

2.00

.375

.875 R
2 PLACES

1.00 DIA THRU,
2 PLACES

1.50 DIA
THRU

.25 R

1.50

1.00

5.00

GUIDE
Drawing 5-2

5.9 Drawing 5-3: Dials

This is a relatively simple drawing that will give you some good practice with polar arrays and the ROTATE and COPY commands.

Notice that the needle drawn at the top of the next page is only for reference; the actual drawing includes only the plate and the three dials with their needles.

DRAWING SUGGESTIONS

GRID = 0.25
SNAP = 0.125
LTSCALE = 0.50
LIMITS = (0,0) (18,12)

- After drawing the outer rectangle and screw holes, draw the leftmost dial, including the needle. Draw a 0.50 vertical line at the top and array it to the left (counterclockwise—a positive angle) and to the right (negative) to create the 11 larger lines on the dial. Use the same operation to create the 40 small (0.25) markings.
- Complete the first dial and then use a multiple copy to produce two more dials at the center and right of your screen. Be sure to use a window to select the entire dial.
- Finally, use the ROTATE command to rotate the needles as indicated on the new dials. Use a window to select the needle, and rotate it around the center of the dial.

Detail of pointer

DIALS
Drawing 5–3

5.10   Drawing 5-4: Alignment Wheel

This drawing shows a typical use of the MIRROR command. Carefully mirroring sides of the symmetrical front view will save you from duplicating some of your drawing efforts. Notice that you will need a small snap setting to draw the vertical lines at the chamfer.

DRAWING SUGGESTIONS

$$GRID = 0.25$$
$$SNAP = 0.125$$
$$LTSCALE = 0.50$$
$$LIMITS = (0,0) \ (12,9)$$

- There are numerous ways to use Mirror in drawing the front view. As the reference shows, there is top–bottom symmetry as well as left–right symmetry. The exercise for you is to choose an efficient mirroring sequence.
- Whatever sequence you use, consider the importance of creating the chamfer and the vertical line at the chamfer before this part of the object is mirrored.
- Once the front view is drawn, the right side view will be easy. Remember to change layers for center and hidden lines and to line up the small inner circle with the chamfer.

ALIGNMENT WHEEL
Drawing 5—4

5.11   Drawing 5-5: Hearth

Once you have completed this architectural drawing as it is shown, you might want to experiment with filling in a pattern of firebrick in the center of the hearth. The drawing itself is not complicated, but little errors will become very noticeable when you try to make the row of 4×8 bricks across the bottom fit with the arc of bricks across the top, so work carefully.

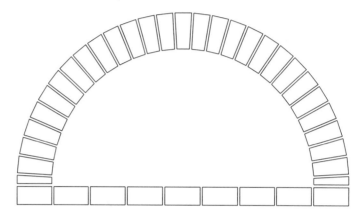

DRAWING SUGGESTIONS

UNITS = Architectural
            Smallest fraction = 8 (1/8")
LIMITS = (0,0) (12',9')
GRID = 1'
SNAP = 1/8"

- Zoom in to draw the wedge-shaped brick indicated by the arrow on the right of the dimensioned drawing. Draw half of the brick only and mirror it across the center line as shown. (Notice that the center line is for reference only.) It is very important that you use Mirror so that you can erase half of the brick later.
- Array the brick in a 29-item, 180-degree polar array.
- Erase the bottom halves of the end bricks at each end.
- Draw a new horizontal bottom line on each of the two end bricks.
- Draw a 4×8 brick directly below the half brick at the left end.
- Array the 4×8 brick in a one-row, nine-column array, with 8.5" between columns.

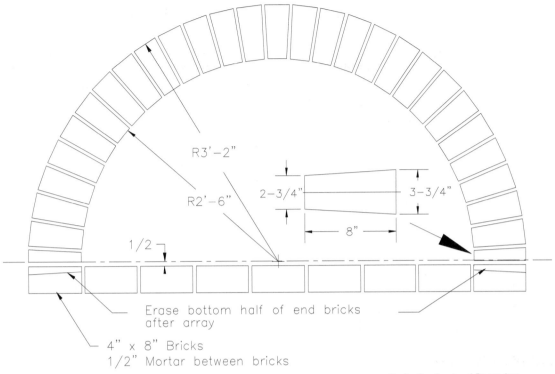

R3'-2"

R2'-6"

2-3/4"

3-3/4"

8"

1/2

Erase bottom half of end bricks
after array

4" x 8" Bricks
1/2" Mortar between bricks

Drawing Compliments of Thomas Casey

HEARTH

Drawing 5-5

5.12   Drawing 5-6: Slotted Flange

This drawing includes a typical application of polar arrays and arcs. The finished drawing should consist of the top view and front view. The center lines and outline of the large circle in the top view are shown in the reference drawing. Do not dimension unless instructed to do so.

Location of Top View

Location of Front View

DRAWING SUGGESTIONS

- Begin by drawing the circles in the top view. Use the circles to line up the vertical lines in the front view.
- The small arcs in the slots can be drawn on a center line and rotated and copied into place using grips.
- A quick method for drawing the vertical lines in the front view is to use a quadrant object snap beginning from all the circles in the top view to make guide lines.

Ø1.50 THRU
2.000 C'BORE X .50 DEEP

RO.25
8 PLACES

Ø3.00

Ø7.50

3.58

RO.50

Ø0.50 THRU
4 HOLES

0.20

R2.375

50°

R2.8750

20°

SLOTTED FLANGE
DRAWING 5-6

6 Object Snap

COMMANDS

MODIFY	**TOOLS**
BREAK	OSNAP
TRIM	
EXTEND	
STRETCH	
LENGTHEN	

OVERVIEW

This chapter will continue to expand your repertoire of editing commands. You will learn to BREAK entities on the screen into pieces so that they may be manipulated or erased separately. You will also learn to shorten entities using the TRIM command, or to lengthen them with the EXTEND command. But most important, you will begin to use a very powerful tool called Object Snap that will take you to a new level of accuracy and efficiency as a CAD operator.

TASKS

6.1   Selecting Points with Object Snap (Single-Point Override)

GENERAL PROCEDURE

1. Enter a drawing command, such as LINE, CIRCLE, or ARC.
2. Hold down the CTRL key and press the enter button on the mouse.
3. Select an object snap mode from the cursor menu.
4. Point to a previously drawn object.

Some of the drawings in the last two chapters have pushed the limits of what you can accomplish accurately on a CAD system with incremental snap alone. Object snap is a related tool that works in a very different manner. Instead of snapping to points defined by the coordinate system, it snaps to geometrically specifiable points on objects that you already have drawn.

Let's say you want to begin a new line at the end point of one that is already on the screen. If you are lucky, the end point may be on a snap point, but it is just as likely not to be. Turning snap off and moving the cursor to the apparent end point may appear to work, but when you zoom in you probably will find that you have missed the point. Using object snap is the only precise way, and it is as precise as you could want. Let's try it.

⊹ To prepare for this exercise, draw a 6 × 6 box with a circle inside, as in Figure 6-1.

Exact sizes and locations are not important; however, the circle should be centered within the square.

⊹ Now enter the LINE command (type "L" or select the Line tool).

We are going to draw a line from the lower left corner of the square to a point on a line tangent to the circle, as shown in Figure 6-2. This task would be extremely difficult without object snap. The corner is easy to locate, since you probably have drawn it on snap, but the tangent may not be.

Figure 6-1

Figure 6-2

Figure 6-3

We will use an end point object snap to locate the corner and a tangent object snap to locate the tangent point. When AutoCAD asks for a point, you can type the abreviated name of an object snap mode, or select an object snap mode from the handy cursor menu.

⊕ At the "From point:" prompt, instead of specifying a point, type "end" or hold down the CTRL key and press the enter button on your cursor.

This will open the pop-up cursor menu illustrated in Figure 6-3.

⊕ If you are using the cursor menu, select "Endpoint".

Entering "Endpoint" by either of these methods tells AutoCAD that you are going to select the start point of the line by using an end point object snap rather than by direct pointing or entering coordinates.

Now that AutoCAD knows that we want to begin at the end point of a previously drawn entity, it needs to know which one.

⊕ Move the cursor near the lower left corner of the square.

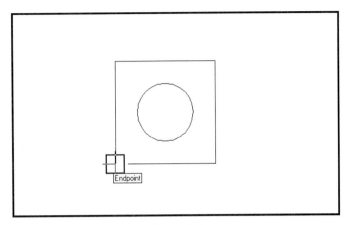

Figure 6-4

When you are close to the corner, AutoCAD will recognize the end point of the lines there and indicate this with a yellow box surrounding the end point. This object snap symbol is called a marker. There are different-shaped markers for each type of object snap. If you let the cursor rest here for a moment, a tooltip-like label will appear, naming the type of object that has been recognized, as shown in Figure 6-4. This label is called a snaptip. Also notice that if the cross hairs are inside the marker, they will lock onto the end point. This action can be turned on or off and is called the magnet setting. You do not have to be locked on to the end point, however. As long as the end point marker is showing, the end point will be selected.

⊕ With the end point object snap marker showing, press the pickbutton.

The yellow end point box and the snaptip will disappear, and there will be a rubber band stretching from the lower left corner of the square to the cursor position. In the command area you will see the To point prompt.

We will use a tangent object snap to select the second point.

⊕ At the "To point:" prompt, type "tan" or select "Tangent" from the cursor menu (shift + enter button to open the cursor menu).

⊕ Move the cursor to the right and position the cross hairs so that they are near the lower right side of the circle.

When you approach the tangent area, you will see the yellow tangent marker, as shown in Figure 6-5. Here again, if you let the cursor rest you will see a snaptip.

⊕ With the tangent marker showing, press the pickbutton.

AutoCAD will locate the tangent point and draw the line.

⊕ Press Enter to exit the LINE command.

Your screen should now resemble Figure 6-2.

We will repeat the process now, but start from the midpoint of the bottom side of the square instead of its end point.

⊕ Repeat the LINE command.

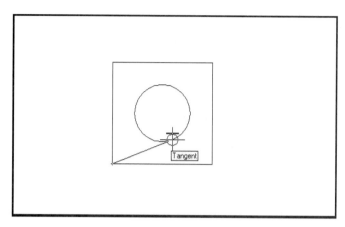

Figure 6-5

⊕ At the prompt for a point, select "Midpoint" from the cursor menu.

⊕ Position the aperture anywhere along the bottom side of the square so that a yellow triangle, the midpoint marker, appears at the midpoint of the line.

⊕ Press the pickbutton.

⊕ At the prompt for a second point, select "Tangent" from the cursor menu.

⊕ Position the aperture along the right side of the circle so that the tangent symbol appears and press the pickbutton.

⊕ Press Enter or the space bar to exit the LINE command.

At this point your screen should resemble Figure 6-6.

That's all there is to it. Remember the steps: (1) Enter a command; (2) when AutoCAD asks for a point, type or select an object snap mode; and (3) position the cross hairs near an object to which the mode can be applied and let AutoCAD find the point.

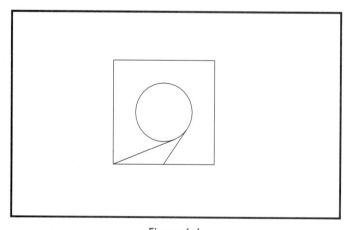

Figure 6-6

6.2 Selecting Points with OSNAP (Running Mode)

GENERAL PROCEDURE

1. Type "os" or pick "Object Snap Settings..." from the Tools menu.
2. Type or select one or more OSNAP modes.
3. Enter drawing commands.
4. If more than one marker appears, cycle through using the tab key.

So far we have been using object snap one point at a time. Since object snap is not constantly in use for most applications, this single-point method is probably most common. But if you find that you are going to be using one or a number of object snap types repeatedly and will not need to select many points without them, there is a way to keep object snap modes on so that they affect all point selection. These are called running object snap modes. We will use this method to complete the drawing shown in Figure 6-7. Notice how the lines are drawn from midpoints and corners to tangents to the circle. This is easily done with object snap.

⊕ Type "os" or select "Object Snap Settings..." from the Tools menu.
You will see the dialog box illustrated in Figure 6-8. At the top is a list of object snap modes with check boxes. At the bottom is a box with a scroll bar where you can change the object snap aperture size.

You will find a description of all of the object snap modes on the chart in Figure 6-9, but for now we will be using three: midpoint, tangent, and intersect. Midpoint and tangent you already know. Intersect snaps to the point where two entities meet or cross. We will use intersect instead of end point to select the remaining three corners of the square.

⊕ Click on the check boxes next to "Midpoint", "Tangent", and "Intersection".

⊕ Click on OK.

Figure 6-7

Figure 6-8

⊕ Enter the LINE command.

⊕ Position the aperture so that the lower right corner is within the box.

A yellow X, the intersection marker, will appear.

⊕ With the intersection marker showing, press the pickbutton.

AutoCAD will select the intersection of the bottom and the right sides and give you the rubber band and the prompt for a second point.

⊕ Move the cross hairs up and along the right side of the circle until the tangent marker appears.

⊕ With the tangent marker showing, press the pickbutton.

AutoCAD will construct a new tangent from the lower right corner to the circle.

⊕ Press Enter to complete the command sequence.

⊕ Press Enter again to repeat LINE so you can begin with a new start point.

We will continue to move counterclockwise around the circle. This should begin to be easy now.

⊕ Position the aperture along the right side of the square so that the midpoint triangle appears.

⊕ With the midpoint marker showing, press the pickbutton.

AutoCAD snaps to the midpoint of the side.

⊕ Move up along the upper right side of the circle so that the tangent marker appears.

⊕ With the tangent marker showing, press the pickbutton.

⊕ Press Enter to exit LINE.

TYPE	APPEARANCE	DESCRIPTION
CENter		Pick circumference of circle or arc Snaps to center point
ENDpoint		Pick line or arc Snaps to nearest end point
INSert	(See Chapter 10)	Pick any point of a block Snaps to insertion point
INTersection		Intersection must be within the aperture Snaps to crossing or meeting point of arcs, lines, circles, and snaps to corners of traces and solids
APParent Inter		Snaps to apparent intersection of 2 objects. Objects may or may not intersect in 3D space Apparent intersection and intersection cannot be in effect at the same time
MIDpoint		Pick line or arc Snaps to midpoint
NEArest		Pick line, circle, or arc Snaps to nearest point on selected object
NODe		Point must be within aperture Snaps to nearest point
PERpendicular		Pick line, circle, or arc Snaps to point perpendicular to the object from the last point selected
QUAdrant		Pick arc or circle Snaps to nearest quadrant point: 0, 90, 180, or 270 degrees
QUIck	(Modifies other modes)	Speeds up point search With QUIck on, AutoCAD accepts the first appropriate point it finds rather than exploring all options
TANgent		Pick circle or arc Snaps to point on line tangent to the object from the last point selected

Figure 6-9

⊕ Press Enter again to repeat LINE and continue around the circle drawing tangents like this: upper right corner to top of circle, top side midpoint to top left of circle, upper left corner to left side, left side midpoint to lower left side.

Remember that running osnap modes should give you both speed and accuracy, so push yourself a little to see how quickly you can complete the figure.

Your screen should now resemble Figure 6-7.

Before going on, we need to turn off the running osnap modes.

⊕ Type "os" or select "Object Snap Settings..." from the Tools menu.
⊕ Click on the Clear All box.
⊕ Click on OK to exit the dialog box.

Tip: One of the object snap modes is called None, meaning no object snap. F3 is the function key equivalent of None. F3 or None can be used while running object snaps are in effect and you wish to select a point that the object snap modes would interfere with. None (or F3) works like a single-point override in reverse. It overrides the running object snaps for a single point or selection.

Now we will move on to five useful and important new editing commands: BREAK, TRIM, EXTEND, STRETCH, and LENGTHEN. Before leaving Object Snap, be sure to study the chart in Figure 6-9.

6.3 BREAKing Previously Drawn Objects

GENERAL PROCEDURE

1. Type "Break" or select Break from the Modify menu.
2. Select an object to be broken.
3. Show the first point of the break.
4. Show the second point of the break.

The BREAK command allows you to break an object on the screen into two entities, or to cut a segment out of the middle or off the end. The command sequence is similar for all options. The action taken will depend on the points you select for breaking. BREAK works on lines, circles, arcs, traces, and polylines (traces and polylines are discussed in Chapter 9).

⊕ In preparation for this section, clear your screen of any objects left over from Task 2 and draw a 5.0 horizontal line across the middle of your screen, as in Figure 6-10.

Exact lengths and coordinates are not important. Also, be sure to turn off any running object snap modes that may be on from the last exercise.

Figure 6-10

Figure 6-11

AutoCAD allows for four different ways to break an object, depending on whether the point you use to select the object is also to be considered a break point. You can break an object at one point or at two points, and you have the choice of using your object selection point as a break point.

We begin by breaking the line you have just drawn into two independent lines using a single break point, which is also the point used to select the line.

⊕   Type "Break" or select the Break tool from the Modify menu.

There is also a Break tool on the Modify toolbar, as shown in Figure 6-11, but it is at the bottom of the toolbar in the docked position and may be hidden behind the command prompt. If this is the case, you can access it by moving the toolbar to a floating position.

Be aware that the noun/verb or pick first sequence does not work with BREAK.

AutoCAD will prompt you to select an object to break:

```
Select object:
```

You may select an object in any of the usual ways, but notice that you can only break one object at a time. If you try to select more—with a window, for example—AutoCAD will give you only one. Because of this you will best indicate the object you want to break by pointing to it.

Tip: Object snap modes work well in edit commands such as BREAK. If you wish to break a line at its midpoint, for example, you can use the midpoint object snap mode to select the line and the break point.

⊕   Select the line by picking any point near its middle. (The exact point is not critical; if it were, we could use a midpoint object snap.)

The line has now been selected for breaking, and since there can be only one object, you do not have to press Enter to end the selection process, as you often do in other editing commands. AutoCAD will prompt as follows:

Enter second point (or F for first point):

When you are selecting an object by pointing, AutoCAD will assume that the point you use for selection is also the first point of the break. It will be most efficient, therefore, if you do select the object with a break point. Then you can proceed by selecting the second point immediately. If not, type "f" and you will be prompted for the first break point, as the parentheses tell you.

Having selected the object and the first break point, we now want to select a point that will break the object in two without erasing anything. To do this, simply pick the same point again.

⊕ Point to the same point that you just used to select the line, or type "@".

The "@" symbol is shorthand for the last point entered.

The break is complete. To demonstrate that the line is really two lines now, we will select the right half of it for our next break.

⊕ Press Enter or the space bar to repeat the BREAK command.
⊕ Point to the line on the right side of the last break.

The right side of the line should become dotted, as in Figure 6-12. Clearly, the original line is now being treated as two separate entities.

We will shorten the end of this dotted section of the line. Assume that the point you just used to select the object is the point where you want it to end; now all you need to do is to select a second point anywhere beyond the right end of the line.

⊕ Select a second point beyond the right end of the line.

Your line should now be shortened, as in Figure 6-13.

Next we will cut a piece out of the middle of the left side.

⊕ Press Enter or the space bar to repeat BREAK.
⊕ Select the left side of the original line with a point toward the left end.

Figure 6-12

Figure 6-13

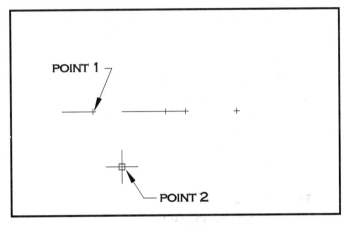

Figure 6-14

We want to cut a piece out of the middle of the left side, so the next point needs to be to the right of the first point, but still toward the middle of the left-hand line.

Note: It is not necessary that the second point be on the line at all. It could be above or below it, as in Figure 6-14. AutoCAD will break the line along a perpendicular between the point we choose and the line we are breaking. The same system would apply if we were breaking a polyline or a trace. An arc or a circle would be broken along a line between the selected point and the center of the arc or circle.

⊕ Select a second point on or off the line, somewhat to the right of the first point.

Your line should now have a piece cut out, as in Figure 6-14. Notice that there are now three lines on the screen, one to the left and two to the right of the last break.

BREAK is a very useful command, but there are times when it is cumbersome to shorten objects one at a time. The TRIM command has some limitations that

BREAK does not have, but it is much more efficient in situations where you want to shorten objects at intersections.

6.4 Shortening Objects with the TRIM Command

GENERAL PROCEDURE

1. Type "Tr" or select Trim from the Modify menu or the Trim tool from the Modify toolbar.
2. Select a cutting edge or edges.
3. Press Enter to end the cutting edge selection process.
4. Select object to trim.
5. Select other objects to trim.
6. Press Enter to return to "Command" prompt.

The TRIM command works wonders in many situations where you want to shorten objects at their intersections with other objects. It will work with lines, circles, arcs, and polylines (see Chapter 9). The only limitation is that you must have at least two objects and they must cross or meet. If you are not trimming to an intersection, use BREAK.

⊕ In preparation for exploring TRIM, clear your screen and then draw two horizontal lines crossing a circle, as in Figure 6-15. Exact locations and sizes are not important.

First we will use the TRIM command to go from Figure 6-15 to Figure 6-16.

⊕ Type "Tr" or select Trim from the Modify menu or the Trim tool from the Modify toolbar, as shown in Figure 6-17.

The first thing AutoCAD will want you to specify is at least one cutting edge. A cutting edge is an entity you want to use to trim another entity. That is, you want the trimmed entity to end at its intersection with the cutting edge.

Select cutting edge(s): (Projmode = UCS, Edgemode = No extend)
Select objects:

Figure 6-15

Figure 6-16

Figure 6-17

The first line reminds you that you are selecting edges first—the objects you want to trim will be selected later. The option of selecting more than one edge is a useful one, which we will get to shortly. The notations in parentheses are relevant to 3D drawing and need not concern you at this point. For your information, Projmode and Edgemode are system variables that determine the way AutoCAD will interpret boundaries and intersections in 3D space.

For now we will select the circle as an edge and use it to trim the upper line.

⊕ **Point to the circle.**

The circle becomes dotted and will remain so until you leave the TRIM command. AutoCAD will prompt for more objects until you indicate that you are through selecting edges.

⊕ **Press Enter or the space bar to end the selection of cutting edges.**

You will be prompted for an object to trim:

    <Select object to trim>/Project/Edge/Undo:

We will trim off the segment of the upper line that lies outside the circle on the left. The important thing is to point to the part of the object you want to remove, as shown in Figure 6-16.

⊕ **Point to the upper line to the left of where it crosses the circle.**

The line is trimmed immediately, but the circle is still dotted, and AutoCAD continues to prompt for more objects to trim. Note how this differs from the BREAK command, in which you could only break one object at a time.

Also notice that you have an undo option, so that if the trim does not turn out the way you wanted, you can back up without having to leave the command and start over.

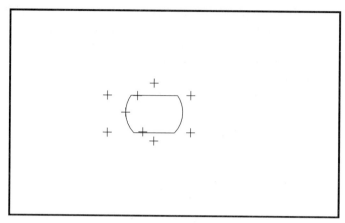

Figure 6-18

⊕ Point to the lower line to the left of where it crosses the circle.
Now you have trimmed both lines.

⊕ Press Enter or the space bar to end the TRIM operation.
Your screen should resemble Figure 6-16.

This has been a very simple trimming process, but more complex trimming is just as easy. The key is that you can select as many edges as you like and that an entity may be selected as both an edge and an object to trim, as we will demonstrate.

⊕ Repeat the TRIM command.

⊕ Select both lines and the circle as cutting edges.
This can be done with a window or with a crossing box.

⊕ Press Enter to end the selection of edges.

⊕ Point to each of the remaining two line segments that lie outside the circle on the right, and to the top and bottom arcs of the circle to produce the band-aid-shaped object in Figure 6-18.

⊕ Press Enter to exit the TRIM command.

6.5 Extending Objects with the EXTEND Command

GENERAL PROCEDURE

1. Type "Ex" or select Extend from the Modify menu or the Extend tool from the Modify toolbar.
2. Select a boundary or boundaries.
3. Press Enter to end the boundary selection process.
4. Select object to extend.
5. Select other objects to extend.
6. Press Enter to return to the command prompt.

If you compare the procedures of the EXTEND command and the TRIM command, you will notice a remarkable similarity. Just substitute the word "boundary" for "cutting edge" and the word "extend" for "trim" and you've got it. These two commands are so quick to use that it is sometimes efficient to draw a temporary cutting edge or boundary on your screen and erase it after trimming or extending.

⊕   Leave Figure 6-18, the band aid, on your screen and draw a vertical line to the right of it, as in Figure 6-19.

We will use this line as a boundary to which to extend the two horizontal lines, as in Figure 6-20.

⊕   Type "Ex" or select Extend from the Modify menu or the Extend tool from the Modify toolbar, as shown in Figure 6-21.

Figure 6-19

Figure 6-20

Figure 6-21

You will be prompted for objects to serve as boundaries:

```
Select boundary edge(s): (Projmode = UCS, Edgemode = No extend)
Select objects:
```

Look familiar? As with the TRIM command, any of the usual selection methods will work. For our purposes, simply point to the vertical line.

⊕ **Point to the vertical line on the right.**

You will be prompted for more boundary objects until you press Enter.

⊕ **Press Enter, the enter button, or the space bar to end the selection of boundaries.**

AutoCAD now asks for objects to extend:

```
<Select objects to extend>/Project/Edge/Undo:
```

⊕ **Point to the right half of one of the two horizontal lines.**

Notice that you have to point to the line on the side closer to the selected boundary. Otherwise AutoCAD will look to the left instead of the right and give you the following message:

```
Object does not intersect an Edge
```

Note also that you only can select objects to extend by pointing. Windowing, crossing, or last selections will not work. Also be aware that arcs and polylines can be extended in the same manner as lines.

⊕ **Point to the right half of the other horizontal line. Both lines should be extended to the vertical line.**

Your screen should resemble Figure 6-20.

⊕ **Press Enter to exit the EXTEND command.**

6.6 Using STRETCH to Alter Objects Connected to Other Objects

---

GENERAL PROCEDURE

1. Type "S" or select the Stretch tool from the Modify toolbar or select Stretch from the Modify menu.
2. Select objects to stretch, using at least one window or crossing selection.
3. Press Enter to end selection.
4. Show the first point of stretch displacement.
5. Show the second point of stretch displacement.

The STRETCH command is a phenomenal timesaver in special circumstances in which you want to move objects without disrupting their connections to other objects. Often STRETCH can take the place of a whole series of moves, trims, breaks, and extends. It is commonly used in such applications as moving doors or windows within walls without having to redraw the walls.

The term "stretch" must be understood to have a special meaning in AutoCAD. When a typical stretch is performed, some objects are lengthened, while others are shortened, and others are simply moved.

There is also a stretch mode in the grip edit system, as we have seen previously. We will take a look at it later in this section.

First, we will do a simple stretch on the objects you have already drawn on your screen. This will give you a good basic understanding of the STRETCH command. Further experimentation on your own is recommended.

⊕ Type "S" or select Stretch from the Modify menu or select the Stretch tool from the Modify toolbar, illustrated in Figure 6-22.

AutoCAD will prompt for objects to stretch in the following manner:

```
Select objects to stretch by crossing-window or crossing-polygon...
Select objects:
```

The first line of this prompt reminds you of a unique quality of the STRETCH command procedure. You must include at least one crossing-window or crossing-polygon selection in your selection set. Beyond that you can include other selection types as well. This ensures that you will include all the objects in an intersection in the stretch procedure. If this is not your intent, you probably should be using a different modifying command.

⊕ Point to the first corner of a crossing box, as shown by point 1 (P1) in Figure 6-23.

Figure 6-22

Figure 6-23

AutoCAD will prompt for a second corner:

```
Other corner:
```

⊕ Point to a second corner, as shown by point 2 (P2) in the figure.

AutoCAD will continue to prompt for objects, so we need to show that we are through selecting.

⊕ Press Enter or the space bar to end the selection process.

Now you will need to show the degree and direction of stretch you want. In effect, you will be showing AutoCAD how far to move the objects that are completely within the box. Objects that cross the box will be extended or shrunk so that they remain connected to the objects that move.

The prompt sequence for this action is the same as the sequence for a move:

```
Base point or displacement:
```

⊕ Pick any point near the middle of the screen, leaving room to indicate a horizontal displacement to the right, as illustrated in Figure 6-24. AutoCAD prompts

```
Second point of displacement:
```

⊕ Pick a second point to the right of the first, as shown in Figure 6-24.

Having ortho on will ensure a horizontal move (F8).

The arcs will be moved to the right and the horizontal lines will be shrunk as shown. Notice that nothing here is literally being stretched. The arcs are being moved and the lines are being compressed. This is one of the ways STRETCH can be used.

Try performing another stretch like the one illustrated in Figures 6-25 and 6-26. Here the lines are being lengthened, while one arc moves and the other stays put, so that the original band aid is indeed stretched.

Figure 6-24

Figure 6-25

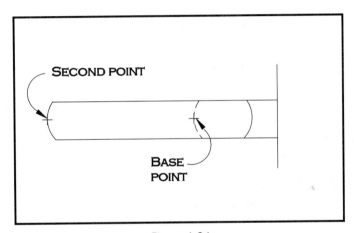

Figure 6-26

Stretching with Grips

Stretching with grips is a simple operation and is best reserved for simple stretches. Stretches like the ones you have just performed with the STRETCH command are possible in grip editing, but they require careful selection of multiple grips. The results are not always what you expect, and it takes more time to complete the process. The type of stretch that works best with grips is illustrated in the following exercise.

⊕ Pick the lower horizontal line.

The line will be highlighted and grips will appear.

⊕ Pick the vertical line.

Now both lines should appear with grips, as in Figure 6-27. We will use one grip on the horizontal line and one on the vertical line to create Figure 6-28.

⊕ Pick the grip at the right end of the horizontal line.

Figure 6-27

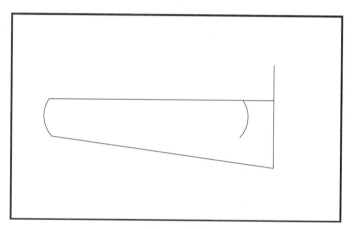

Figure 6-28

As soon as you press the pickbutton, the autoedit system puts you into STRETCH mode and the grip will change color.

In the command area you will see the following:

```
** STRETCH **
<Stretch to point>/Base point/Copy/Undo/eXit:
```

We will stretch the line to end at the lower end point of the vertical line.

⊕ Move the cross hairs slowly downward and observe the screen.

If ortho is off, you will see two rubber bands. One represents the line you are stretching, and the other connects the cross hairs to the grip you are manipulating.

⊕ Pick the grip at the bottom of the vertical line.

Your screen should resemble Figure 6-28. Notice how the grip on the vertical line works like an object snap point.

Try one more grip stretch to create Figure 6-29. You will move the end point of the upper line just as you did the lower.

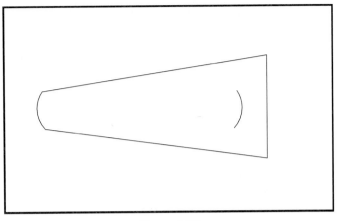

Figure 6-29

In the next task you will learn Release 14's new LENGTHEN command—one more edit command for changing the lengths of lines and arcs.

6.7 Changing Lengths with the LENGTHEN Command

GENERAL PROCEDURE

1. Type "Len" or select the Lengthen tool from the Modify toolbar or select Lengthen from the Modify menu.
2. Type initials to specify a length option.
3. If necessary, type a value.
4. Select an object to lengthen.
5. Select another object or press enter to exit the command.

The LENGTHEN command is new with Release 14. It can be used to lengthen or shorten lines, polylines, and arcs using four different methods. In this exercise we will use two methods to manipulate further the objects in Figure 6-29. We will begin by lengthening and then shortening the vertical line at the right of the figure.

⊕ Type "Len" or select Lengthen from the Modify menu or select the Lengthen tool from the Modify toolbar, illustrated in Figure 6-30.

The prompt that follows shows the different lengthening methods:

DElta/Percent/Total/DYnamic/<Select Object>:

Figure 6-30

Delta lengthens an object by a specified amount, Percent by a percent of the current length. Total changes the current length to a specified value, and Dynamic allows you to change length by cursor movement. If you select an object at this prompt, its current length will be reported in the command area. We will work with Delta and Dynamic.

⊕ Type "de" for the delta option.

AutoCAD prompts

Angle/<Enter delta length (0.00)>:

Angle will allow you to lengthen an arc by a specified angle. To change a linear length, type in a value. A positive value will cause objects to be lengthened, while a negative value will cause shortening.

⊕ Type "1".

AutoCAD prompts you to select an object:

<Select object to change>/Undo:

⊕ Pick a selection point on the upper half of the vertical line.

The object will be lengthened by one unit upward, as shown in Figure 6-31. AutoCAD will continue to prompt for objects. You can select any line, arc, or polyline. Also, you can pick the same line again to add another one unit length. Try it.

⊕ Pick another point on the upper half of the vertical line.

The object will be lengthened again.

Now try lengthening the arc in the middle of the figure.

⊕ Pick a point on the upper half of the arc.

The arc will be lengthened by one unit along a circular path, as shown in Figure 6-31.

Now try the Dynamic option.

⊕ Press enter or the space bar to exit LENGTHEN.

⊕ Press enter or the space bar again to repeat the command.

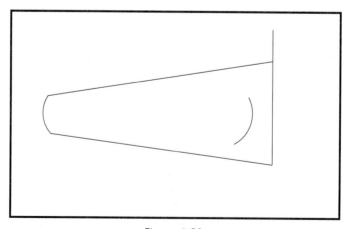

Figure 6-31

⊕ Type "dy" for the Dynamic option.

You are prompted to select objects.

⊕ Select the angled line at the top of the drawing, choosing a point on the right half of the line.

AutoCAD will show a rubber band and will lengthen or shorten the selected line dynamically as you move the cursor.

⊕ Move the cursor back and forth on the screen to get a feel for how the rubber band and cross hairs work in this command option.

⊕ Select any point and observe the resulting change.

⊕ Type "u" to undo the change.

You may wish to continue experimenting with LENGTHEN. We encourage you to try out the percent and total options, to use positive and negative values, and to select arcs and lines to observe the results.

In the next task you will take a giant leap in plotting technique as you begin to use paper space and multiple viewports.

6.8   Plotting from Multiple Viewports in Paper Space

GENERAL PROCEDURE

1. Set "Tilemode" to 0 by typing or by selecting Paper Space from the View menu or double clicking the Model button on the status bar.
2. Use MVIEW to create paper space layout.
3. Switch to model space to position or edit objects in the drawing.
4. Switch to paper space to plot.
5. Type or select "Plot".
6. Preview plot, change parameters, and execute plotting as usual.

In this plotting exercise you will begin to use paper space and multiple floating viewports for the first time. We have used Drawing 6–4 to illustrate. We recommend that you read through this section now and then return to it after you complete Drawing 6-4. The illustrations will make more sense when you have the actual drawing on your screen.

You have a completed drawing on your screen and you are now considering how to present it on paper. In the days of the drafting board, all drawings were committed to paper from the start. This meant that people doing drafting were inevitably conscious of scale, paper size, and rotation from start to finish. When draftspeople first began using CAD systems, they still tended to think in terms of the final hard copy their plotter would produce even as they were creating lines on the screen. But to take full advantage of the powers of a CAD system, it is usually more efficient to conceive of screen images as representing objects at full scale, rather than as potential drawings on a piece of paper. After all, the units on a screen grid can just as easily represent miles as inches. This little world of the screen in which we can think and draw in full scale is called "model space" in AutoCAD lingo.

Using model space to its fullest potential, we can allow ourselves to ignore scale and other drawing paper issues entirely, if we wish, until it is time to plot. At that time, we may want to make use of AutoCAD's "paper space." Paper space overlays model space and allows us to create a paper-scale world on top of the full-scale world in which our drawing has been created.

This is the concept of paper space. In actual practice you may find paper space unnecessary or unwieldy for common two-dimensional plotting. As we have seen in previous plotting exercises, the PLOT command has a very efficient previewing system and scaling features of its own that will allow you to move easily between 2D model space and the sheet of drawing paper waiting in your plotter.

Where paper space really begins to pay off is when you want to create multiple views of a single object and plot them all simultaneously. Model space tiled viewports can only be plotted one at a time. With paper space viewports you can create multiple views of the same object, position them wherever you like, and print the whole configuration as one drawing.

In this task we will create a plot of Drawing 6-4, the "Grooved Hub." The plotted drawing will include the original two views plus two close-up views. This will be done in paper space using three viewports. You should be able to generalize from the techniques demonstrated here to create a variety of multiple-view drawings with whatever drawing you may be working on. Later, when you get into 3D, you will be able to draw an object and view it from different angles, placing different views in different viewports and placing these where you want them in your completed drawing.

⊕   To begin this exercise you should have on your screen a drawing you want to plot showing some close-up views.

We have used Drawing 6-4, shown in Figure 6-32, for illustration.

⊕   Before leaving model space, turn off the grid (F7).

You will see why shortly.

Figure 6-32

To enter paper space, you must change the value of the "Tilemode" variable from 1 ("On") to 0 ("Off"). When Tilemode is on you can only create the type of non-overlapping viewports we showed in Chapter 3. These viewports cannot be moved or plotted simultaneously.

You can change Tilemode at the command line or the Status bar or from the View menu.

⊕ Type "Ti" or select "Paper Space" from the View pull-down menu, or double click the Model button on the status bar.

⊕ If you are working from the command prompt, type "0".

Your screen will go blank and AutoCAD will regenerate your drawing. If "Ucsicon" is "On", you will see the paper space icon in the left-hand corner of your screen. This icon appears in place of the UCS icon whenever you switch to paper space. For this reason it is a good idea to have the icon turned on when you are going back and forth between model and paper spaces.

⊕ If necessary, turn the UCS icon on by opening the View menu, highlighting Display and then UCS icon, and then selecting "on".

You are now looking at a blank sheet of paper in paper space. You can imagine that your drawing is behind the paper space screen. We will need to create viewports before we can see the drawing again. Viewports are like windows from paper space into model space. Until a window is created, you cannot see what is beyond the paper.

But first, we need to think about the paper our drawing will be on. This, after all, is the whole point of paper space. Before opening viewports, we will set up limits and a grid in paper space to emulate the drawing sheet we are going to plot on. For purposes of illustration, let's say that we are going to plot on a D-size sheet of paper. If your plotter will take a D-size sheet, you will be able to find the actual plotting area available by looking in the PLOT dialog paper size list box, as follows.

⊕ Type Ctrl-P or select the Print tool from the Standard toolbar or "Print..." from the File pull-down menu.

⊕ Type "z" or select the "Size..." button.

You will see the Paper Size dialog box illustrated previously in Chapter 5 (Figure 5-21). Ours shows us that the Houston Instruments plotter we are using plots in an area 33.00 by 21.00 on a D-size sheet. If yours is different, or if you have no D-size option, use another sheet size and plotting area from your list. We will also include some instructions for A-size paper as we go along since most people have access to an A-size printer. You should expect to make adjustments, however, if your drawing size does not match ours.

⊕ Cancel the Paper Size dialog or click on OK if you have made changes.

⊕ Cancel the Plot Configuration dialog.

This should bring you back to your blank paper space screen.

⊕ Type "Limits" or select "Drawing Limits..." from the Format menu.

⊕ Set paper space limits to (0,0) and (33,21) or whatever is appropriate for your plotter. If you are working with A-size paper, it will be approximately (12,9) for most printers.

⊕ Turn the grid on (F7).

The grid is now on in paper space and off in model space.

⊕ Zoom All.

⊕ Reset your grid and snap to a 1.00 increment.

Your screen is now truly representative of a D-size drawing sheet. The plot will be made 1-to-1, with one paper space screen unit equaling 1 inch on the drawing sheet. There is little reason to do it any other way, since the whole point of paper space is to emulate the paper on the screen.

Now it is time to create viewports.

⊕ Type "Mv" or select "Model Space (Floating)" from the View pull-down menu.

Either of these methods will enter the MVIEW command. "Floating Viewports" on the View menu will also enter MVIEW but will give you less flexibility in viewport placement.

AutoCAD prompts

ON/OFF/Hideplot/Fit/2/3/4/Restore/<First Point>:

We will deal only with the default option in this exercise. With this option you create a viewport just as you would a selection window.

⊕ Pick a point at the lower left of your screen, as shown in Figure 6-33. Our actual point is (1.00,1.00).

All of the coordinate values in this exercise will need to be adjusted if you are using other than a D-size sheet of paper. Exact correspondence is not critical. As long as your viewports resemble our illustrations, you will be fine.

⊕ Pick a second point up 13 and over 9 from point 1. The coordinate display will show (10.00,14.00).

Your screen will be redrawn with the drawing shown at small scale in the viewport you have just created. We will create a second viewport next.

If you had not turned off the model space grid at this point, you would see model space and paper space grids overlapping. Having both grids on is useless and confusing.

Figure 6-33

Now we will create a second viewport to the right of the first.

⊕ Repeat MVIEW.

⊕ Pick point (13.00,1.00), as shown in Figure 6-33.

⊕ Pick point (31.00,14.00), as shown.

You have now created a second viewport. Notice that the images in the two viewports are the same. Before we go on to create a third viewport, we will create different zoom magnifications inside the two viewports. To do this we need to switch back to model space.

⊕ Type "ms" or double click the "Paper" button on the status bar.

You will see that the paper space icon disappears. You will also see that the viewport on the right is outlined with a thicker border, indicating that it is currently active. If you have not used multiple viewports before, take a moment to explore the way the cursor works. You can have only one viewport active at a time. When the cursor is within that viewport, you will see the cross hairs. Otherwise you will see an arrow. To switch viewports, move the arrow into the desired viewport and press the pickbutton.

⊕ Make the left viewport active.

⊕ Make the right viewport active.

We are going to zoom in so that the two-view drawing fills the right viewport. We could do this by windowing, but we can maintain more precise scale relationships if we use the ZOOM "Center" and "XP" options. We will see the importance of paper space and model space scale relationships in later chapters.

⊕ Type "z" to enter the ZOOM comand.

⊕ Type "c" for the "Center" option.

AutoCAD prompts for a center point.

⊕ Pick a point roughly halfway between the two views in the right viewport.

AutoCAD will prompt for a magnification value.

`Magnification or height <9.4779>:`

Accepting the default would simply center the image in the viewport. We will take an extra step by specifying an "XP" value here. "XP" means "times paper." It allows you to zoom relative to paper space units. If you zoom 1xp, then a model space unit will take on the size of a current paper space unit, which in turn equals 1 inch of drawing paper. We will zoom 2xp (.5xp if you are using A-size paper). This will mean that one unit in the viewport will equal two paper space units, or 2 inches on paper (in A size, one unit will equal 0.5 inch on paper).

⊕ Type "2xp" (or .5xp for A-size paper).

Your right viewport will be redrawn to resemble the one in Figure 6-34. You may need to pan slightly to the left or right to position the image in the viewport. Notice that you cannot use the scroll bars to pan inside a viewport.

Next, we will enlarge the image on the left so that we get a close-up of the left side view.

Figure 6-34

⊕ Make the left viewport active.

⊕ Type "z".

⊕ Type "c".

⊕ Pick a center point in the middle of the left side view.

⊕ Type "4xp" (1xp for A-size paper).

This will create an enlarged image in which one model space unit equals 4 inches in the drawing sheet (1 = 1 A size).

⊕ Pan left or right to position the enlargement in the viewport, as shown in Figure 6-34.

Now that you have the technique, we will create one more enlargement, focusing on the center of the hub.

⊕ Type "Mv" or select "Floating Viewports" from the View pull-down menu and then "1 Viewport".

⊕ Pick point (23.00,15.00).

⊕ Pick point (31.00, 21.00).

Notice that the new viewport is created from the most recent viewport image.

⊕ Use PAN in model space to bring the hub center into the new viewport.

⊕ Zoom on the center of the hub at 6 times paper (1.5xp for an A sheet) in the new viewport.

⊕ Open the View menu and select "Regen All" to regenerate the display and create truer circles.

Your screen should resemble Figure 6-35.

Now we are ready to plot. Plotting a multiple-viewport drawing is no different from plotting from a single view, but you have to make sure you plot from paper space. Otherwise AutoCAD will plot only the currently active viewport.

⊕ Type "ps" or double click on the Model button on the status bar.

⊕ Type CTRL-P or select the Print tool from the Standard toolbar or "Print…" from the File menu.

Figure 6-35

⊕ Click on "Limits" in the Additional Parameters box.

⊕ Click on "Size" in the Paper Size and Orientation box.

We looked into this box for information before, but we canceled the command. Now it is time to choose the paper size we have been preparing for.

⊕ Select the D-size option, or whatever you have chosen for this exercise.

⊕ Click on OK in the Paper Size dialog box.

⊕ If the Scaled to Fit box is selected, click on it so that the check is removed.

When Scaled to Fit is deselected, the scale boxes should show 1 = 1. If not, you should edit them to show 1 = 1.

⊕ Do a partial preview of the plot.

The effective area should match the paper size, because we are set to plot limits, and our limits match the effective drawing area of this paper size for this plotter.

⊕ Do a full preview of the plot.

Your screen should resemble Figure 6-36.

You are now ready to plot.

⊕ Press enter or esc to exit the preview.

⊕ Prepare your plotter. (Make sure you use the right size paper.)

⊕ Click on OK.

⊕ Press Enter and watch it go.

Important: Be sure to SAVE Drawing 6-4 in its multiple-viewport form before leaving this chapter, because we will return to it in Chapter 8 to explore scaling dimensions between model space and paper space.

Figure 6-36

6.9   Review Material

Questions

1. What is the difference between the pickbox and the object snap aperture?
2. At what point in a command procedure would you use an object snap single-point override? How would you signal the AutoCAD program that you want to use an object snap?
3. How do you access the Object Snap cursor menu?
4. Why is there an object snap mode called "None"? What is its function key equivalent?
5. How do you use BREAK to shorten a line at one end? When would you use this procedure instead of the TRIM command? How would you accomplish the same thing with LENGTHEN?
6. You have selected a line to extend and a boundary to extend it to, but Auto-CAD gives you a message that says "Object does not intersect an Edge". What happened?
7. What selection method is always required when you use the STRETCH command?
8. Why is it usual practice to plot 1 to 1 in paper space? Why is it usual practice to designate paper space limits as the area to plot?
9. Why do we use the Zoom XP option when zooming in floating model space viewports?
10. How is CAD different from drafting with regard to issues of scaling and paper size?

Drawing Problems

1. Draw a line from (6,2) to (11,6). Draw a second line perpendicular to the first starting at (6,6).

2. Break the first line at its intersection with the second.

3. There are now three lines on the screen. Draw a circle centered at their intersection and passing through the midpoint of the line going up and to the right of the intersection.

4. Trim all the lines to the circumference of the circle.

5. Erase what is left of the line to the right of the intersction and trim the portion of the circle to the left, between the two remaining lines.

6.10 Drawing 6-1: Bike Tire

This drawing can be done very quickly with the tools you now have. It makes use of one object snap, three trims, and a polar array. Be sure to set the limits large, as suggested.

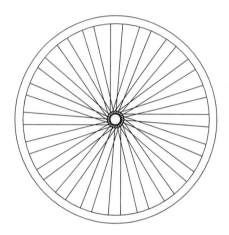

DRAWING SUGGESTIONS

GRID = 1.00
SNAP= 0.25
LIMITS = (0,0) (48,36)

- Begin by drawing the 1.25, 2.50, 24.00, and 26.00 diameter circles centered on the same point near the middle of your display.
- Draw line (a) using a QUADrant object snap to find the first point on the inside circle. The second point can be anywhere outside the 24 circle at 0 degrees from the first point. The exact length of the line is insignificant since we will be trimming it back to the circle.
- Draw line (b) from the center of the circles to a second point anywhere outside the 24 circle at an angle of 14 degrees. Remember to use the coordinate display to construct this angle. This line also will be trimmed.
- Trim lines (a) and (b) using the 24 circle as a cutting edge.
- Trim the other end of line (b) using the 1.25 circle as a cutting edge.
- Construct a polar array, selecting lines (a) and (b). There are 20 items in the array, and they are rotated as they are copied.

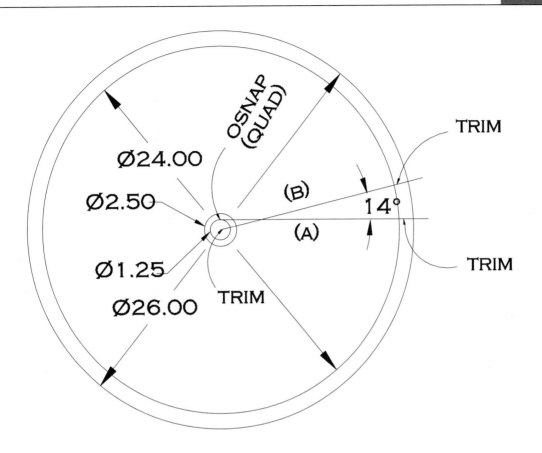

BIKE TIRE

DRAWING 6-1

6.11   Drawing 6-2: Archimedes Spiral

This drawing and the next go together as an exercise you should find interesting and enjoyable. These are not technical drawings, but they will give you valuable experience with important CAD commands. You will be creating a spiral using a radial grid of circles and lines as a guide. Once the spiral is done, you will use it to create the designs in the next drawing, 6-3, "Spiral Designs."

DRAWING SUGGESTIONS

GRID = 0.5
SNAP = 0.25
LIMITS = (0,0) (18,12)
LTSCALE = 0.5

- The alternating continuous and hidden lines work as a drawing aid. If you use different colors and layers, they will be even more helpful.
- Begin by drawing all the continuous circles on layer 0, centered near the middle of your display. Use the continuous circle radii as listed.
- Draw the continuous horizontal line across the middle of your six circles and then array it in a three-item polar array.
- Set to layer 2 for the hidden lines. The procedure for the hidden lines and circles will be the same as for the continuous lines, except that the radii are different and you will array a vertical line instead of a horizontal one.
- Set to layer 1 for the spiral itself.
- Turn on a running object snap to intersection mode and construct a series of three-point arcs. Start points and end points will be on continuous line intersections; second points always will fall on hidden line intersections.
- When the spiral is complete, turn off layers 0 and 2. There should be nothing left on your screen but the spiral itself. Save it or go on to Drawing 6-3.

GROUPING OBJECTS

Here is a good opportunity to use Release 14's GROUP command. GROUP is discussed more fully in Chapter 10, but you will find it useful here. GROUP defines a collection of objects as a single entity so that they may be selected and modified as a unit. The spiral you have just drawn will be used in the next drawing, and it will be easier to manipulate if you GROUP it. For more information, see Chapter 10.

1. Type "Group" or select the Object Group tool from the Standard toolbar.
2. Type "Spiral" for a group name.
3. Click on "New <".
4. Select the six arcs with a window.
5. Press Enter to end selection.
5. Click on OK.

The spiral can now be selected, moved, rotated, and copied as a single entity.

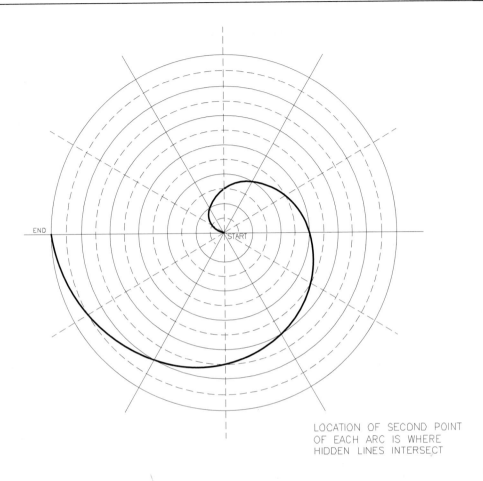

LOCATION OF SECOND POINT
OF EACH ARC IS WHERE
HIDDEN LINES INTERSECT

SOLID CIRCLE RADII	HIDDEN CIRCLE RADII
0.50	0.25
1.00	0.75
1.50	1.25
2.00	1.75
2.50	2.25
3.00	2.75

NOTE: THIS DRAWING IS USED
ON DRAWING 6-3

SAVE THIS DRAWING!

ARCHIMEDES SPIRAL

Drawing 6-2

6.12   Drawing 6-3: Spiral Designs

These designs are different from other drawings in this book. There are no dimensions, and you will use only edit commands now that the spiral is drawn. Below the designs is a list of the edit commands you will need. Don't be too concerned with precision. Some of your designs may come out slightly different from ours. When this happens, try to analyze the differences.

DRAWING SUGGESTIONS

$$\text{LIMITS} = (0,0) \ (34,24)$$

These large limits will be necessary if you wish to draw all of these designs on the screen at once.

In some of the designs and in Drawing 6-4 you will need to rotate a copy of the spiral and keep the original in place. You can accomplish this by using the grip edit rotate procedure with the copy option, or by making a copy of the objects before you enter the ROTATE command. Both procedures are provided next.

HOW TO ROTATE AN OBJECT AND RETAIN THE ORIGINAL

USING GRIP EDIT

1. Select the spiral.
2. Pick the grip around which you want to rotate, or any of the grips if you are not going to use the grip as a base point for rotation.
3. Type "b" or select "Base point", if necessary. In this exercise the base point you choose for rotation will depend on the design you are trying to create.
4. Type "c" or select "Copy".
5. Show the rotation angle.
6. Press Enter to exit the grip edit system.

USING THE ROTATE COMMAND

1. Use COPY to make a copy of the objects you want to rotate directly on top of their originals. In other words, give the same point for the base point and the second point of displacement. When the copy is done, your screen will not look any different, but there will actually be two spirals there, one on top of the other.
2. Enter ROTATE and give "p" in response to the "Select objects:" prompt. This will select all the original objects from the last COPY sequence, without selecting the newly drawn copies.
3. Rotate as usual, choosing a base point dependent on the design you are creating.
4. After the ROTATE sequence is complete, you will need to do a REDRAW before the objects copied in the original position will be visible.

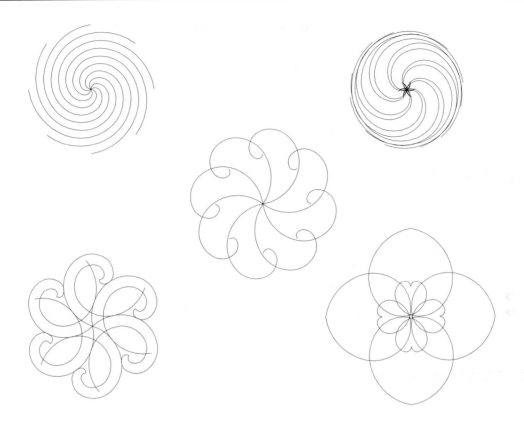

SPIRAL DESIGNS
(Make from Drawing 6-2)

Drawing 6-3

6.13   Drawing 6-4: Grooved Hub

This drawing includes a typical application of the rotation technique just discussed. The hidden lines in the front view must be rotated 120 degrees and a copy retained in the original position. There are also good opportunities to use MIRROR, object snap, and TRIM.

DRAWING SUGGESTIONS

GRID = 0.5
SNAP = 0.0625
LIMITS = (0,0) (12,9)
LTSCALE = 1

- Draw the circles in the front view and use these to line up the horizontal lines in the left side view.
- There are several different planes of symmetry in the left side view, which suggests the use of mirroring. We leave it up to you to choose an efficient sequence.
- A quick method for drawing the horizontal hidden lines in the left side view is to use a quadrant osnap to begin a line at the top and bottom of the 0.62 diameter circle in the front view. Draw this line across to the back of the left side view, and use TRIM to erase the excess on both sides.
- The same method can be used to draw the two horizontal hidden lines in the front view. Snap to the top and bottom quadrants of the 0.25 diameter circle in the left side view as a guide and draw lines through the front view. Then trim to the 2.25 diameter circle and the 0.62 diameter circle.
- Once these hidden lines are drawn, rotate them, retaining a copy in the original position.

PLOTTING IN PAPER SPACE WITH MULTIPLE VIEWPORTS

As you near the completion of Part I, it is time to explore paper space and the use of multiple viewports to plot different views in a drawing. This drawing is used in Task 6.8 to illustrate multiple viewport plotting techniques. Once you have completed the drawing as shown, return to the chapter and create the drawing layout in paper space with two close-up views. *Save the multiple view layout as well because it will be used again in Chapter 8.*

.125 RAD

.25 DIA THRU TO ℄
2 PLACES

.06 X 45° CHAMFER

.625 DIA THRU

⌀3.75

⌀4.00

⌀2.25

.125
.375
.50
1.00
1.50

120°

GROOVED HUB
Drawing 6—4

6.14   Drawing 6-5: Cap Iron

This drawing is of a type of blade used in a wood plane. When wood is planed, the cap iron causes it to curl up out of the plane so that it does not jam. There are several good applications for the TRIM command here.

DRAWING SUGGESTIONS

GRID = 1.00
SNAP = 0.25
LIMITS = (0,0) (18,12)
LTSCALE = 0.25

- The circle with a hidden line outside a continuous line indicates a tapped hole. The dimension is given to the hidden line; the continuous inner line is drawn with a slightly smaller radius that is not specified.
- The figure near the center of the top view that has two arcs with 0.38 radii can be drawn exactly the same way as the band aid discussed earlier in this chapter. Draw a circle and two horizontal lines and then trim it all down.
- The 0.54 and 0.58 arcs in the front view can be drawn using Start, End, Radius.
- The small vertical hidden lines in the front view can be done using a system introduced in the previous drawing. Draw lines down from the figures in the top view and then trim them. For the tapped hole and the arced opening in the middle, you will have to use object snaps to right and left quadrant points to locate the start of these lines.

.312–18 UNC TAPPED HOLE

.75

1.75
.88

.38 R
2 PL

5.00
2.75
2.00
1.25
.18

.50
.50
1.00
.38

.75
1.00

.06

.54
.58

Note:
Save This Drawing
(use on CSA–5C)

CAP IRON
Drawing 6–5

6.15   Drawing 6-6: Deck Framing

This architectural drawing may take some time, although there is nothing in it you have not done before. Notice that the settings are quite different from our standard prototype, so be sure to change them before beginning.

DRAWING SUGGESTIONS

UNITS = Architectural
           Smallest fraction = 1
LIMITS = (0,0) (48,36)
GRID = 1′
SNAP = 2″

- Whatever order you choose for doing this drawing, we suggest that you make ample use of COPY, ARRAY, and TRIM.
- Keep ortho on, except to draw the lines across the middle of the squares.
- With snap set at 2″ it is easy copy lines 2″ apart, as you will be doing frequently to draw the 2 × 80 studs.
- You may need to turn snap off when you are selecting lines to copy, but be sure to turn it on again to specify displacements.
- Notice that you can use ARRAY effectively, but that there are three separate arrays. They are all 16″ on center, but the double boards in several places make it inadvisable to do a single array of studs all the way across the deck. What you can do, however, is to draw, copy, and array all the vertical studs first and then go back and trim them to their various lengths using the horizontal boards as cutting edges.

DECK FRAMING

Drawing 6-6

6.16   Drawing 6-7: Tool Block

In this drawing you will need to take infromation from a three-dimensional drawing and develop it into a three-view drawing. The finished drawing should be composed of of the Top View, Front View, and Side View. The reference drawing shows a portion of each veiw to be developed. You are to complete these views. Do not dimension unless instructed to do so.

DRAWING SUGGESTIONS

- Begin by drawing the top view. Use the top view to line up the front view and side view.
- The slot with the angular lines must be drawn in the front view before the other views. These lines can then be lined up with the top and side view and used as guides to draw the hidden lines.
- Be sure to include all the necessary hidden lines and center lines in each view.

FULL SCREEN CROSS HAIRS

In older versions of AutoCAD the cross hairs extended across the full drawing area. This is usually unnecessary and cumbersome, but it may be useful in aligning points in multiple view drawings. To change the cross hair size follow this procedure:

1. Open the Tools menu and select Preferences ... .
2. From the Preferences dialog box, select the Pointer tab.
3. At the bottom of the Pointer dialog box, change cursor size from 5 percent of screen to 100 percent, or anything in between.
4. Click on OK to exit.

Ø.50 Thru .75
C'Bore .75
x .25 Deep
2 Holes

Ø.500 Thru
C'Bore
Ø1.000 x .25 Deep
2 Holes

1.000
1.00
6.000
3.000
R2.000
1.250
3.750
4.000
R0.500
0.500
2.500
30°
3.000
.625
1.500
7.000
8.000
4.000
6.000

TOOL BLOCK
Drawing 6-7

PART II
TEXT, DIMENSIONS, AND OTHER COMPLEX ENTITIES

7   # Text

COMMANDS

DRAW	**MODIFY**	**DATA**	**OBJECT PROPERTIES**	**TOOLS**
DTEXT	CHANGE	STYLE	DDEMODES	SPELL
MTEXT	CHPROP		MATCHPROP	
TEXT	DDCHPROP			
	DDEDIT			
	DDMODIFY			
	SCALE			

OVERVIEW

This chapter begins Part II of the book. Part I focused on basic 2D entities such as lines, circles, and arcs. In the next five chapters you will be learning to draw a number of AutoCAD entities that are constructed as groups of lines, circles, and arcs. Text, dimensions, polylines, and blocks are all entities made up of basic 2D entities, but you will not have to treat them line by line, arc by arc. Also in Part II, you will continue to learn AutoCAD editing features.

Now it's time to add text to your drawings. In this chapter you will learn to find your way around Release 14's three text commands, TEXT, DTEXT, and MTEXT. In addition, you will learn many new editing commands that are often used with text but that are equally important for editing other objects.

TASKS

7.1 Entering left-justified text using DTEXT

7.2 Using other text justification options

7.3 Entering text on an angle and text using character codes

7.4 Entering paragraph text using MTEXT

7.5 Editing text with DDEDIT

7.6 Modifying text with DDMODIFY

7.7 Using the SPELL command

7.8 Changing fonts and styles

7.9 Changing properties with MATCHPROP

7.10 SCALEing previously drawn entities

7.11 Review Material

7.12 Drawing 7-1: Title Block

7.13 Drawing 7-2: Gauges

7.14 Drawing 7-3: Stamping

7.15 Drawing 7-4: Control Panel

7.16 Drawing 7-5: Tower

7.1   Entering Left-Justified Text Using DTEXT

GENERAL PROCEDURE

1. Type "dt", select the Text tool from the Draw toolbar or Open the Draw menu, highlight Text, and select single-line text.
2. Pick a start point.
3. Answer prompts regarding height and rotation.
4. Enter text on one line and press enter.
5. Enter text on other lines or press enter to exit the command.

Release 14 provides three different commands for entering text in a drawing. TEXT, the oldest of the three, allows you to enter single lines of text at the command prompt. DTEXT uses all of the same options as TEXT but shows you the text on the screen as you enter it and allows you to enter multiple lines of text and to backspace through them to make corrections. MTEXT allows you to type paragraphs of text in a dialog box and then positions them in a windowed area in your drawing. All of these commands have numerous options for placing text and a variety of fonts to use and styles that can be created from them. In the first three tasks we will focus on the basic placement features of the three commands, sticking with the standard style and font.

We will begin with standard text and the DTEXT command. Most of what you learn will apply to the TEXT command as well, but DTEXT has more features and is easier to use.

⊞   To prepare for this exercise, open a new drawing using the B template and draw a 4.00 horizontal line beginning at (1,1). Then create a six-row by one-column array with 2.00 between rows, as shown in Figure 7-1.

These lines are for orientation in this exercise only; they are not essential for drawing text.

Figure 7-1

Figure 7-2

⊕ Type "dt" or open the Draw menu, highlight Text, and then select single-line text, as shown in Figure 7-2.

There is a text tool on the Draw toolbar, but it enters the MTEXT command.

Either of these methods will enter the DTEXT command, and you will see a prompt with three options in the command area:

Justify/Style/<Start point>:

"Style" will be explored in Task 7.8. In this task we will be looking at different options for placing text in a drawing. These are all considered text justification methods and will be listed if you choose the "Justify" option at the command prompt.

First we will use the default method by picking a start point. This will give us left-justified text, inserted left to right from the point we pick.

⊕ Pick a start point at the left end of the upper line.

Look at the prompt that follows and be sure that you do not attempt to enter text yet:

Height <0.20>:

This gives you the opportunity to set the text height. The number you type specifies the height of uppercase letters in the units you have specified for the current drawing. For now we will accept the default height.

⊕ Press Enter to accept the default height (0.20).

The prompt that follows allows you to place text in a rotated position.

Rotation angle <0>:

The default of 0 degrees orients text in the usual horizontal manner. Other angles can be specified by typing a degree number relative to the polar coordinate system or by showing a point. If you show a point, it will be taken as the second point of a baseline along which the text string will be placed. For now we will stick to horizontal text.

⊕ Press Enter to accept the default angle (0).

Now, at last, it is time to enter the text itself. AutoCAD prompts

Text:

Notice also that a small text cursor has appeared at the start point on your screen. Move your cross hairs away from this point and you will see the cursor clearly. This shows where the first letter you type will be placed. This is a feature of DTEXT that you would not find in the TEXT command. For our text we will type the word "Left" since this is an example of left-justified text. Watch the screen as you type and you will see dynamic text at work.

⊕ Type "Left" and press Enter.

(Remember, you cannot use the space bar in place of the enter key when entering text.) Notice that the text cursor jumps down below the line when you hit Enter. Also notice that you are given a second "Text:" prompt in the command area.

⊕ Type "Justified" and press Enter.

The text cursor jumps down again and another "Text:" prompt appears. This is how DTEXT allows for easy entry of multiple lines of text directly on the screen in a drawing. To exit the command, you need to press Enter at the prompt.

⊕ Press Enter to exit DTEXT.

This completes the process and returns you to the command prompt.

Figure 7-3 shows the left-justified text you have just drawn, along with the other options as we will demonstrate them in the rest of this exercise.

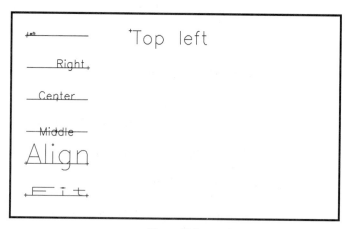

Figure 7-3

Before proceeding with other text justification options, we will demonstrate two additional features of DTEXT.

⊕ Press Enter to repeat the DTEXT command.

If you press Enter again at this point instead of showing a new start point or selecting a justification option, you will go right back to the "Text:" prompt as if you had never left the command. Try it.

⊕ Press Enter.

You will see the "Text:" prompt in the command area and the text box will reappear on the screen just below the word "Justification".

⊕ Type "Text" and press Enter.

At this point you will still be in the DTEXT command with the "Text:" prompt showing. You could press Enter to exit the command or continue typing lines. Instead try this:

⊕ Move the cross hairs to any part of the screen and press the pickbutton.

The text box will move to whatever point you have selected. This means that you can type text in several areas of the screen without ever leaving DTEXT, as long as the text is the same height, angle, and style. You do not even have to press Enter before you move the text box. Try it again.

⊕ Move the cross hairs once again and press the pickbutton.

The text cursor will move wherever you want.

⊕ Type "here" in the new spot.

⊕ Move the text box again and type "and there".

Now, before leaving DTEXT, use the backspace feature to erase the last two lines.

⊕ Backspace through "and there" and "here".

This demonstrates how you can backspace dynamically through text created in DTEXT even if the text is in different areas. However, this only works before you exit the command.

⊕ Press Enter again to exit the command.

Once you have left DTEXT, there are other ways to edit text, which we will explore in Tasks 7.5 and 7.6.

7.2 Using Other Text Justification Options

GENERAL PROCEDURE

1. Type "dt", select the Text tool from the Draw toolbar or Open the Draw menu, highlight Text, and select single-line text.
2. Choose a justification option.
3. Pick a start point.
4. Answer prompts regarding height and rotation.
5. Enter text.

We will now proceed to try out some of the other text placement options, beginning with right-justified text, as shown on the second line of Figure 7-3. We will also specify a change in height.

Right-Justified Text

Right-justified text is constructed from an end point backing up, right to left.

⊕ Repeat the DTEXT command.

You will see the same prompt as before.

⊕ Type "r" for right-justified text.

Now AutoCAD prompts you for an end point instead of a start point:

> End point:

We will choose the right end of the second line.

⊕ Point to the right end of the second line.

This time we will change the height to 0.50. Notice that AutoCAD gives you a rubber band from the end point. It can be used to specify height and rotation angle by pointing, if you like.

⊕ Type ".5" or show a height of 0.50 by pointing.

⊕ Press Enter to retain 0 degrees of rotation.

You are now prompted to enter text.

⊕ Type "Right" and press Enter.

Here you should notice an important fact about the DTEXT command. Initially, DTEXT ignores your justification choice, entering the letters you type from left to right as usual. The justification will be carried out only when you exit the command.

At this point you should have the word "Right" showing to the right of the second line. Watch what happens when you press Enter a second time to exit the command.

⊕ Press Enter.

The text will jump to the left, onto the line. Your screen should now include the second line of text in right-justified position, as shown in Figure 7-3.

Centered Text

Centered text is justified from the bottom center of the text.

⊕ Repeat the DTEXT command.

⊕ Type "c".

AutoCAD prompts

> Center point:

⊕ Point to the midpoint of the third line.

⊕ Press Enter to retain the current height, which is now set to 0.50.

⊕ Press Enter to retain 0 degrees of rotation.

⊕ Type "Center" and press Enter.

Notice again how the letters are displayed on the screen in the usual left-to-right manner.

⊕ Press Enter again to complete the command.

The word "Center" should now be centered, as shown in Figure 7-3.

Middle Text

Middle text is justified from the middle of the text both horizontally and vertically, rather than from the bottom center.

⊕ Repeat DTEXT.

⊕ Type "m".

AutoCAD prompts

> Middle point:

⊕ Point to the midpoint of the fourth line.

⊕ Press Enter to retain the current height of 0.50.

⊕ Press Enter to retain 0 degrees of rotation.

⊕ Type "Middle" and press Enter.

⊕ Press Enter again to complete the command.

Notice the difference between center and middle. Center refers to the midpoint of the baseline below the text. Middle refers to the middle of the text itself, so that the line now runs through the text.

Aligned Text

Aligned text is placed between two specified points. The height of the text is calculated proportional to the distance between the two points, and the text is drawn along the line between the two points.

⊕ Repeat DTEXT.

⊕ Type "a".

AutoCAD prompts

> First text line point:

⊕ Point to the left end of the fifth line.

AutoCAD prompts for another point:

> Second text line point:

⊕ Point to the right end of the fifth line.

Notice that there is no prompt for height. AutoCAD will calculate a height based on the space between the points you chose. There is also no prompt for an angle, because the angle between your two points (in this case 0) will be used. You could position text at an angle using this option.

⊕ Type "Align" and press enter.

⊕ Press Enter again to complete the command.

Notice that the text jumps in size and placement to fill the line.

Text Drawn to Fit between Two Points

The Fit option is similar to the Aligned option, except that the specified text height is retained.

⊕ Repeat DTEXT.

⊕ Type "f".

You will be prompted for two points, as in the "align" option.

⊕ Point to the left end of the sixth line.

⊕ Point to the right end of the sixth line.

⊕ Press Enter to retain the current height.

As in the align option, there will be no prompt for an angle of rotation.

⊕ Type "Fit" and press Enter.

⊕ Press Enter again to complete the command.

This time the text will be stretched horizontally to fill the line without a change in height. This is the difference between fit and align. In the align option, text height is determined by the width you show. With fit, the specified height is retained and the text is stretched or compressed to fill the given space.

Other Justification Options

Before proceeding to the next task, take a moment to look at the list of justification options. The options will be listed on the command line if you enter TEXT or DTEXT and type "J". The command line prompt looks like this:

```
Align/Fit/Center/Middle/Right/TL/TC/TR/ML/MC/MR/BL/BC/BR:
```

The letter options are spelled out in the chart shown in Figure 7-4. We already have explored the first five plus the default Left option. For the others, study the figure. As shown on the chart, T is for top, M is for middle, and B is for bottom. L, C, and R stand for left, center, and right. Notice that it is not necessary to type "J" and see the list before entering the option. Just enter TEXT or DTEXT and then the one or two letters of the option. Let's try one.

⊕ Repeat DTEXT and then type "tl" for the "Top Left" option.

AutoCAD will ask for a "Top/left point". As shown in Figure 7-4, top left refers to the highest potential text point at the left of the word.

⊕ Pick a top left point, as shown in Figure 7-3 above the words "top left".

⊕ Press Enter twice to accept the height and rotation angle settings and arrive at the "Text:" prompt.

⊕ Type "top left" and press Enter.

⊕ Press Enter again to complete the command.

As before, the text will jump into top-left-justified position when you exit the command. Your screen should now resemble Figure 7-3.

TEXT JUSTIFICATION	
<START POINT> TYPE ABBREVIATION	TEXT POSITION + INDICATES START POINT or PICK POINT
A	ALIGN+
F	+FIT+
C	CENTER+
M	MIDDLE
R	RIGHT+
TL	+TOP LEFT
TC	TOP CENTER+
TR	TOP RIGHT+
ML	+MIDDLE LEFT
MC	MIDDLE +CENTER
MR	MIDDLE RIGHT+
BL	BOTTOM LEFT+
BC	BOTTOM +CENTER
BR	BOTTOM RIGHT+

Figure 7-4

7.3   Entering Text on an Angle and Text Using Character Codes

GENERAL PROCEDURE

1. Enter the DTEXT command.
2. Specify justification option, start point, and text height.
3. Speicfy a rotation angle.
4. Enter text, including character codes as needed.

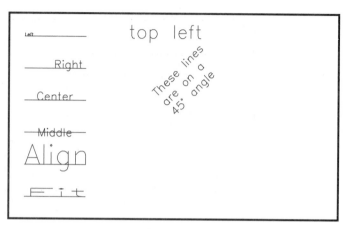

Figure 7-5

We have already seen how you can use DTEXT to enter multiple lines of text. In this task we will explore this further by entering several lines on an angle, adding special character symbols along the way. We will create three lines of left-justified text, one below the other and all rotated 45 degrees, as shown in Figure 7-5.

⊕ Repeat the DTEXT command.

You will see the familiar prompt:

```
Justify/Style/<Start point>:
```

⊕ Pick a starting point near (12.00,8.00), as shown by the blip next to the word "These" in Figure 7-5.

⊕ Type ".3" to specify a smaller text size.

⊕ Type "45" or show an angle of 45 degrees.

Notice that the text box is shown at the specified angle.

⊕ Type "These lines" and press Enter.

The text will be drawn on the screen at a 45-degree angle, and you will be returned to the "Text:" prompt. Notice that the text box on the screen is still at the specified angle.

⊕ Type "are on a" and press Enter.

You should be at the "Text:" prompt.

The Degree Symbol and Other Special Characters

The next line contains a degree symbol. Since you do not have this character on your keyboard, AutoCAD provides a special method for drawing it. Type the text with the %% signs just as shown following and then study Figure 7-6, which lists other special characters that can be drawn in the same way.

Control Codes and Special Characters	
Type at Text Prompt	Text on Drawing
%%O OVERSCORE	O̅V̅E̅R̅S̅C̅O̅R̅E̅
%%U UNDERSCORE	U̲N̲D̲E̲R̲S̲C̲O̲R̲E̲
180%%D	180°
2.00 %%P.01	2.00 ±.01
%%C4.00	⌀4.00

Figure 7-6

⊕ Type "45%%d angle" and press Enter.

DTEXT will initially type the character code directly to the screen, just as you have typed it. When you exit the command, the character code will be translated and redrawn. Watch.

⊕ Press Enter again to complete the command sequence.

Your screen should now resemble Figure 7-5.

7.4 Entering Paragraph Text Using MTEXT

GENERAL PROCEDURE

1. Type "mt", select the Text tool from the Draw toolbar or Open the Draw menu, highlight Text, and select multiline text.
2. Specify options.
3. Pick an insertion point.
4. Pick a second corner.
5. Type text in the dialog box.
6. Click on OK.

The MTEXT command allows you to create multiline text in a dialog box and position it within a defined window in your drawing. Like TEXT and DTEXT, MTEXT has nine options for text justification and its own set of character codes.

We begin by creating a simple left-justified paragraph.

⊕ Type "mt" or select Text and then Multiline text from the Draw menu.

(There is also an Mtext tool on the Draw toolbar, as shown in Figure 7-7, but you may have to move the toolbar to a floating position to access it.) You will see the following prompt in the command area:

```
Attach/Rotation/Style/Height/Direction/<Insertion point>:
```

Figure 7-7

We will discuss options momentarily, after you see how the command works.

Fundamentally, MTEXT lets you define the width of a group of text lines that you will create in a dialog box. When the text is entered using MTEXT, AutoCAD formats it to conform to the specified width and justification method and draws the text on your screen. The width can be defined in several ways. The default method for specifying a width is to draw a window on the screen. This can be misleading. MTEXT does not attempt to place the complete text inside the window, but only within its width. The first point of the window becomes the insertion point of the text. How AutoCAD uses this insertion point depends on the Mtext Justify option. The second window point defines the width and the text flow direction (that is, whether the text lines should be drawn above or below, to the left or right of the insertion point). Exacly how this is interpreted is also dependent on the justification option.

⊕ Pick an insertion point near the middle of your drawing area, in the neighborhood of (9.00,6.00).

AutoCAD will begin a window at the selected point and give you a new prompt:

```
Specify opposite corner or
[Height/Justify/Rotation/Style/Width]:
```

We will continue with the default options by picking a second corner. For purposes of demonstration we suggest a window 3.00 wide, drawn down and to the right.

⊕ Pick a second point 3.00 wide and about 1.00 below the first point.

As soon as you pick the opposite corner, AutoCAD will open the Multiline Text Editor dialog box with the character tab showing, as illustrated in Figure 7-8. The most important feature of this dialog box is the editing area. When you enter text in this area, the text will wrap around as it will be drawn in your drawing, according to the width you have specified.

Figure 7-8

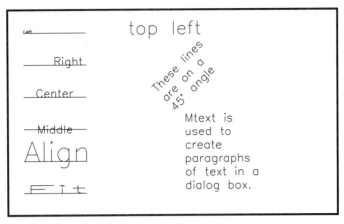

Figure 7-9

Notice that the dialog box also has Property and Find and Replace tabs. Mtext properties include text style, justification, width, and rotation. These can also be set at the command line, as indicated by the previous prompt. Find and Replace works in your as it would in a text editor, only for the text in the edit box.

⊕ Type "Mtext is used to create paragraphs of text in a dialog box."

⊕ Click on "OK" to leave the dialog box.

You will be returned to the drawing window and the new text will be added, as shown in Figure 7-9. Notice that the text you typed has been wrapped around to fit within the 3.00 width window; the 0.30 height of the text has been retained and the 1.00 height of the text window you defined has been ignored.

We will explore other Mtext justification options as an editing procedure using DDMODIFY. But first, we will do some simple text editing with DDEDIT.

7.5 Editing Text with DDEDIT

GENERAL PROCEDURE

1. Type "ddedit", or open the Modify menu, highlight object, and select Text.
2. Select text to edit.
3. Edit text in the Edit text dialog box.
4. Click on OK.

There are several ways to modify text that already exists in your drawing. You can change wording and spelling as well as properties such as layer, style, and justification. Commands that you will use to alter text include CHANGE, CHPROP, DDCHPROP, DDEDIT, and DDMODIFY. CHANGE, DDMODIFY, and DDEDIT can be used to change words as well as text properties; CHPROP AND DDCHPROP can change only properties.

For text editing you will most often use DDEDIT and DDMODIFY. In both cases there will be minor variations in how the commands work depending on whether the text you are editing was created using DTEXT or MTEXT. We will begin with some simple DDEDIT text editing. In Task 7.6 we will use the property modification powers of DDMODIFY to show different justification options of MTEXT paragraphs.

⊕   Type "ddedit" or open the Modify menu, highlight Object, and select Text.

There is also an Edit Text tool that you can access by opening the Modify II toolbar. Regardless of how you enter the command, AutoCAD will prompt you to select an object for editing:

<Select an annotation object>/Undo:

Annotation objects will include all objects that have text, including text, dimensions, and attributes. Dimensions are the subject of Chapter 8. Attributes are discussed in Chapter 10.

We will select one line of the angled text.

⊕   Select the words "These lines" by clicking on any of the letters.

As soon as you select the text, it will appear in a small edit box, as illustrated in Figure 7-10. This is the DDEDIT dialog box for text created with DTEXT and TEXT. If you had selected text created with MTEXT, you would be in the Multline Text Editor. We will demonstrate momentarily. Now add the word "three" to the middle of this line.

⊕   Move the dialog box arrow to the center of the text in the edit box, between "These" and "lines", and press the pickbutton.

The text should no longer be highlighted, and a flashing cursor should be present, indicating where text will be added if you begin typing.

⊕   Type the word "three" and add a space so that the line reads "These three lines".

⊕   Click on "OK".

The dialog box will disappear and your text will be redrawn with the word "three" added, as shown in Figure 7-11.

Now let's try it with the text you created in MTEXT. The first difference you will notice is that since MTEXT creates multiple lines of text as a group, you cannot select a single line of text. When you click, the whole set of lines will be selected.

DDEDIT repeats automatically, so you should have the following prompt in the command area before proceeding:

<Select an annotation object>/Undo:

Figure 7-10

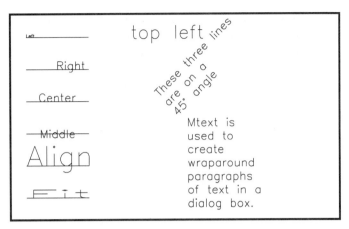

Figure 7-11

If not, repeat DDEDIT.

✣ Select the text beginning with "Mtext is".

This will call up the Multiline Text Editor, with the chosen paragraph showing in the edit area.

✣ Move the screen cursor to the second line, after "create", and press the pickbutton.

You should now have a flashing cursor on the line after "create".

✣ Add "wraparound" so that the paragraph will read "Mtext is used to create wraparound paragraphs of text in a dialog box."

✣ Click on "OK".

You will return to the drawing window, with the new text added and reformatted as shown in Figure 7-11. That's it for DDEDIT. Next we will explore DDMODIFY along with more MTEXT placement options.

7.6 Modifying Text with DDMODIFY

GENERAL PROCEDURE

1. Select Properties... from the Modify menu.
2. Select text to modify (steps 1 and 2 can be reversed if noun/verb editing is enabled in your drawing).
3. Use the dialog box to specify property changes.
4. Click on OK.

DDMODIFY is one of several commands that can be used to change properties of objects in a drawing. It is used with many other kinds of objects besides text. In this exercise you will learn how to use DDMODIFY and at the same time explore the MTEXT justification options. Justification is one of the properties you will be able to modify, and this will be an efficient way to explore the options with-

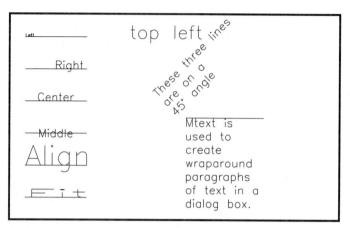

Figure 7-12

out having to input new text. We will end this exercise with a summary of MTEXT placement options.

⊕ Draw a 3.00 line just above the MTEXT paragraph, as shown in Figure 7-12.

This line is only for reference. It should begin at the same snap point that was used as the insertion point for the text. The left end of the line will show the insertion point, and the length will show the width of the paragraph. We have used the point (9.00,6.00) and the 3.00 width.

⊕ Select Properties... from the Modify menu.

The menu selection will actually execute a program called propchk. Both the DDMODIFY command and the program will first check what type of object you have selected and then open the appropriate dialog box. The only difference is that propchk will allow you to select more than one object and then decide what you can do depending on what you have chosen. DDMODIFY will only allow one selection.

⊕ Select the paragraph beginning with "Mtext is".

⊕ Press Enter to end object selection.

You should now see the Modify Mtext dialog box illustrated in Figure 7-13. Take a look at it. The options in the top box, including color, layer, linetype, handle, thickness, and linetype scale, are standard changeable properties for all objects. All DDMODIFY dialog boxes will include these. These are also the common properties that can be changed using CHANGE, CHPROP, or the DDCHPROP dialog box.

The area below the Properties box is unique to text drawn with MTEXT. The content of the text is shown in the middle for reference only. If you wish to edit the contents, click on "Full Editor...". This will call up the Multiline Text Editor and will work much like DDEDIT.

In the area below the text you can modify style, height, direction (horizontal or vertical), justification, paragraph width, and rotation. We will demonstrate two different justification options; other options are illustrated in Figure 7-15, at the end of this exercise.

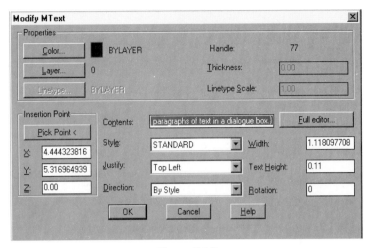

Figure 7-13

⊕ Click on the arrow at the right end of the "Justify" box.

This will open a list box with a list of nine justification options. The list should look familiar to you since it includes some of the same choices as the text justification options introduced previously for DTEXT. The difference is that here you will place and justify multiple lines of text as a group.

Notice that the default justification is Top Left. We will change it to Top Center, the second option on the list.

⊕ Click on "TopCenter".

The list box will close, and "TopCenter" should now be shown in the Justify edit box.

⊕ Click on "OK" to exit MText Properties.

⊕ Click on "OK" again to exit Modify MText.

Your text will be redrawn as shown in Figure 7-14. The paragraph will now be in centered format, with the original insertion point used as a top center point. You may wish to continue with other justification options. Also, study Figure 7-15, which illustrates the options.

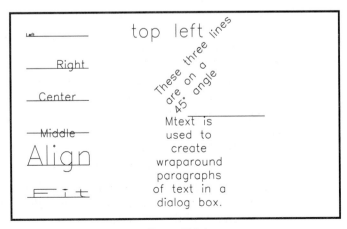

Figure 7-14

MTEXT: ATTACH OPTIONS

OPTIONS	MEANING	EXAMPLE
TL	TOP LEFT	Mtext controls which part of the text boundary aligns at the insertion point. This is an example of Top Left text. Text spill will controls how excess text flows out of the text boundary.
TC	TOP CENTER	Mtext controls which part of the text boundary aligns at the insertion point. This is an example of Top Center text. Text spill controls how excess text flows out of the text boundary.
TR	TOP RIGHT	Mtext controls which part of the text boundary aligns at the insertion point. This is an example of Top Right text. Text spill controls how excess text flows out of the text boundary.
ML	MIDDLE LEFT	Mtext controls which part of the text boundary aligns at the insertion point. This is an example ofthe Middle Left text. Text spill controls how excess text flows out of the text boundary.
MC	MIDDLE CENTER	Mtext controls which part of the text boundary aligns at the insertion point. This is an example of Middle Center text. Text spill controls how excess text flows out of the text boundary.
MR	MIDDLE RIGHT	Mtext controls which part of the text boundary aligns at the insertion point. This is an example of Middle Right text. Text spill controls how excess text flows out of the text boundary.
BL	BOTTOM LEFT	Mtext controls which part of the text boundary aligns at the insertion point. This is an example of Bottom Left text. Text spill controls how excess text flows out of the text boundary.
BC	BOTTOM CENTER	Mtext controls which part of the text boundary aligns at the insertion point. This is an example of Bottom Center text. Text spill controls how excess text flows out of the text boundary.
BR	BOTTOM RIGHT	Mtext controls which part of the text boundary aligns at the insertion point. This is an example of Bottom Right text. Text spill controls how excess text flows out of the text boundary.

Figure 7-15

7.7 Using the SPELL Command

GENERAL PROCEDURE

1. Type "sp", select Spelling from the Tools menu, or select the Spelling tool from the Standard toolbar.
2. Select objects.
3. Press enter to end selection.
4. Use the dialog box to ignore, change, or add words the spell checker does not recognize.

AutoCAD's SPELL command is simple to use and will be very familiar to anyone who has used spell checkers in word processing programs. We will use SPELL to check the spelling of all the text we have drawn so far.

⊕ Type "sp", select Spelling from the Tools menu, or select the Spelling tool from the Standard toolbar, as shown in Figure 7-16.

You will see a "Select objects:" prompt on the command line. At this point you could point to individual objects. Any object may be selected, although no checking will be done if you select a line, for example.

For our purposes we will use an "All" option to check all the spelling in the drawing.

⊕ Type "all".

AutoCAD will continue to prompt for object selection until you press Enter.

⊕ Press Enter to end object selection.

This will bring you to the Check Spelling dialog box shown in Figure 7-17. If you have followed the exercise so far and not misspelled any words along the way, you will see "Mtext" in the Current word box and "Text" as a suggested correction. We will ignore this change, but before you leave SPELL, look at what is available: You can ignore a word the checker does not recognize,

Figure 7-16

Figure 7-17

or change it. You can change a single instance of a word, or change all in-stances in the currently selected text. You can add a word to a customized dictionary or you can change to another dictionary.

⊕ Click on "Ignore".

If your drawing does not contain other spelling irregularities, you should now see an AutoCAD message that says

> Spelling check complete.

⊕ Click on "OK" to end the spell check.

If you have made any corrections in spelling, they will be incorporated into your drawing at this point.

7.8 Changing Fonts and Styles

GENERAL PROCEDURE

1. Type "st" or select Text Style from the Format menu.
2. Change settings in the Text Style dialog box. Specify height, width, and font.
3. Click on New.
4. Type in a name for the new style.
5. Click on OK.
6. Click on Close.

By default, the current text style in any AutoCAD drawing is one called "STANDARD". It is a specific form of a font called "txt" that comes with the soft-ware. All the text you have entered so far has been drawn with the standard style of the "txt" font.

Changing fonts is a simple matter. However, there is room for confusion in the use of the words "style" and "font." You can avoid this confusion if you remem-

Figure 7-18

ber that fonts are the basic patterns of character and symbol shapes that can be used with the TEXT, DTEXT, and MTEXT commands, whereas styles are variations in the size, orientation, and spacing of the characters in those fonts. It is possible to create your own fonts, but for most of us this is an esoteric activity. In contrast, creating your own styles is easy and practical.

We will begin by creating a variation of the STANDARD style you have been using.

⊕ Type "st" or select "Text Style" from the Format menu.

Either method will open the Text Style dialog box shown in Figure 7-18. You will probably see STANDARD listed in the Style name box. However, if anyone has used text commands in your prototype drawing, it is possible that there will be other styles listed. In this case you should open the list with the arrow on the right and select STANDARD, the AutoCAD default style. We will create our own variation of the STANDARD style and call it "VERTI-CAL". It will use the same "txt" character font, but will be drawn down the display instead of across.

⊕ Click in the "Vertical" check box.

We will also give this style a fixed height and a width factor. Notice that the current height is 0.00. This does not mean that your characters will be drawn 0.00 units high. It means that there will be no fixed height, so you will be able to specify a height whenever you use this style. STANDARD currently has no fixed height, so VERTICAL has inherited this setting. Try giving our new "VERTICAL" style a fixed height.

⊕ Double click in the Height edit box and then type ".5".

⊕ Double click in the Width Factor box and type "2".

⊕ Click on "New".

AutoCAD opens a smaller dialog box that asks for a name for the new text style.

⊕ Type "vertical".

⊕ Click on OK.

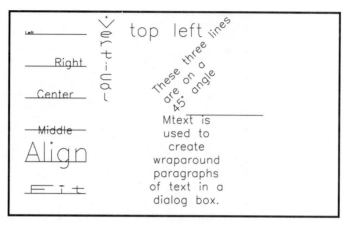

Figure 7-19

This brings you back to the Text Style dialog box, with the new style listed in the style name area.

⊕ Click on Close to exit the Text Style dialog.

The new VERTICAL style is now current. To see it in action you will need to enter some text

⊕ Type "dt" or open the Draw menu, highlight Text, and then highlight Single Line text.

⊕ Pick a start point, as shown by the blip near the letter "V" in Figure 7-19.

Notice that you are not prompted for a height because the current style has height fixed at 0.50.

⊕ Press Enter to retain 270 degrees of rotation.

⊕ Type "Vertical".

⊕ Press Enter to end the line.

Before going on, notice that the DTEXT text placement box has moved up to begin a new column of text next to the word "vertical."

⊕ Press Enter to exit DTEXT.

Your screen should resemble Figure 7-19.

There are now two text styles in the current drawing. Both use the txt font. Next we will create a third style using a different font and some of the other style options.

⊕ Type "st" or select Text Style... from the Format menu.

⊕ Open the font name list by clicking on the arrow.

⊕ Scroll to "Romand.shx" and stop.

Romand stands for "Roman Duplex", an AutoCAD font.

⊕ Click on "romand.shx" to place it in the font name box.

⊕ Click in the Vertical box to remove the check.

⊕ Set the text height to 0.00.

⊕ Set the width factor to 1.

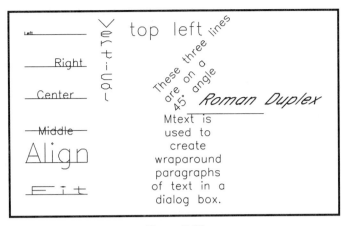

Figure 7-20

- ⊕ Set Obliquing angle to 45.

  This will cause your text to be slanted 45 degrees to the right. For a left slant, you would type a negative number.

- ⊕ Click on New to give the style a name.
- ⊕ In the New text style dialog box, give the style the name "Third".
- ⊕ Click on OK.
- ⊕ Click on Close.

  Now enter some text to see how this slanted Roman Duplex style looks.

- ⊕ Enter the DTEXT command and answer the prompts to draw the words "Roman Duplex" with a 0.50 height, as shown in Figure 7-20.

Switching the Current Style

All new text is created in the current style. The style of previously drawn text can be changed, as we will show later. Once you have a number of styles defined in a drawing, you can switch from one to another by using the Style option of the TEXT and DTEXT commands or by Selecting a text style from the Text Style dialog box.

> **Note:** If you change the definition of a text style, all text previously drawn in that style will be regenerated with the new style specifications.

7.9 Changing Properties with MATCHPROP

GENERAL PROCEDURE

1. Select the Match Properties tool from the Standard toolbar.
2. Select a source object with properties you wish to transfer to another object.
3. If necessary, specify properties you wish to match.
4. Select destination objects.
5. Press enter to end object selection.

MATCHPROP is a very efficient command, new with Release 14, that lets you match all or some of the properties of an object to those of another object. Properties that can be transferred from one object to another, or to many others, include layer, linetype, color, and linetype scale. These settings are common to all AutoCAD entities. Other properties that only relate to specific types of entities are thickness, text style, dimension style, and hatch style. In all cases the procedure is the same.

Here we will use MATCHPROP to change some previously drawn text to the new "Third" style.

⊕   Select the Match Properties tool from the Standard toolbar, as shown in Figure 7-21.

AutoCAD will prompt

Select Source Object:

You can have many destination objects but only one source object.

⊕   Select the text "Roman Duplex", drawn in the last task.

AutoCAD prompts

Settings/<Select Destination Objec(s)>:

At this point you can limit the settings you want to match by typing "s" for settings, or you can select destination objects, in which case all properties will be matched.

⊕   Type "s".

This opens the Property Settings dialog box, shown in Figure 7-22. The Basic properties area on the top shows basic properties that can be changed and the settings that will be used based on the source object you have selected.

At the bottom you will see Dimension, Text, and Hatch in the Special Properties area. These refer to styles that have been defined in your drawing for these types of objects. If any of these is deselected, then Match Properties will ignore styles and will only match the basic properties checked.

Figure 7-21

Figure 7-22

Figure 7-23

⊕ Click on OK to exit the dialog.

AutoCAD returns to the screen with the same prompt as before.

⊕ Select the words "Align" and "Vertical".

These two words will be redrawn in the Third style, as shown in Figure 7-23.

The CHANGE command

The CHANGE command is an older AutoCAD command that has been largely replaced by other editing commands. CHANGE works at the command line and allows you to modify all of the basic text properties, including insertion point, style, height, rotation angle, and the text itself. You can select as many objects as you like and CHANGE will cycle through them. In addition, CHANGE can be used to alter the end points of lines and the size of circles. With lines, CHANGE will perform a function similar to the EXTEND command, but without the necessity of defining an extension boundary. With circles, CHANGE will cause them to be redrawn so that they pass through a designated "change point." The effects of change points on lines and circles are shown in Figure 7-24. Notice in particular the way lines will react to a change point with ortho on.

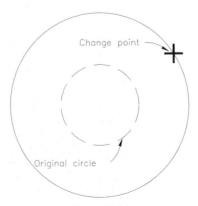

Figure 7-24

7.10 SCALEing Previously Drawn Entities

GENERAL PROCEDURE

1. Type "Sc", select Scale from the Modify menu or select the Scale tool from Modify toolbar.
2. Select objects (steps 1 and 2 can be reversed if noun/verb editing is enabled).
3. Pick a base point.
4. Enter a scale factor.

Any object or group of objects can be scaled up or down using the SCALE command or the grip edit scale mode. In this exercise we will practice scaling some of the text and lines that you have drawn on your screen. Remember, however, that there is no special relationship between SCALE and text and that other types of entities can be scaled just as easily.

⊕ Type "Sc", select Scale from the Modify menu, or select the Scale tool from Modify toolbar, as shown in Figure 7-25.

AutoCAD will prompt you to select objects.

⊕ Use a crossing box (right to left) to select the set of six lines and text drawn in Task 7.1.

⊕ Press Enter to end selection.

Figure 7-25

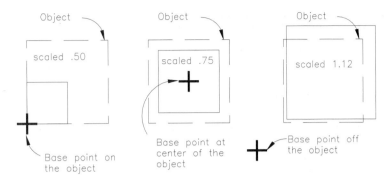

Figure 7-26

You will be prompted to pick a base point:

Base point:

The concept of a base point in scaling is critical. Imagine for a moment that you are looking at a square and you want to shrink it using a scale-down procedure. All the sides will, of course, be shrunk the same amount, but how do you want this to happen? Should the lower left corner stay in place and the whole square shrink toward it? Or should everything shrink toward the center? Or toward some other point on or off the square (see Figure 7-26)? This is what you will tell AutoCAD when you pick a base point.

⊹ Pick a base point at the left end of the bottom line of the selected set (the blip in Figure 7-27).

AutoCAD now needs to know how much to shrink or enlarge the objects you have selected:

<Scale factor>/Reference:

We will get to the reference method in a moment. When you enter a scale factor, all lengths, heights, and diameters in your set will be multiplied by that factor and redrawn accordingly. Scale factors are based on a unit of 1. If you

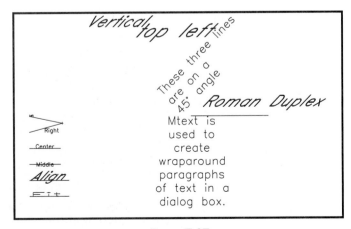

Figure 7-27

enter .5, objects will be reduced to half their original size. If you enter 2, objects will become twice as large.

⊕ Type ".5" and press Enter.

Your screen should now resemble Figure 7-27.

SCALEing by Reference

This option can save you from doing the arithmetic to figure out scale factors. It is useful when you have a given length and you know how large you want that length to become after the scaling is done. For example, we know that two of the lines we just scaled are now 2.00 long (the middle two that we did not alter with CHANGE). Let's say that we want to scale them again to become 2.33 long (a scale factor of 1.165, but who wants to stop and figure that out?). This could be done using the following procedure:

1. Enter the SCALE command.
2. Select the "previous" set.
3. Pick a base point.
4. Type "r" or select "reference".
5. Type "2" for the reference length.
6. Type "2.33" for the new length.

> **Note:** You can also perform reference scaling by pointing. In the preceding procedure, you could point to the ends of the 2.00 line for the reference length and then show a 2.33 line for the new length.

Scaling with Grips

Scaling with grips is very similar to scaling with the SCALE command. To illustrate this, try using grips to return the text you just scaled back to its original size.

⊕ Use a window or crossing box to select the six lines and the text drawn in Task 7.1 again.

There will be a large number of grips on the screen, three on each line and two on most of the text entities. Some of these will overlap or duplicate each other.

⊕ Pick the grip at the lower left corner of the word "Fit," the same point used as a base point in the last scaling procedure.

⊕ Press the enter button on your cursor to open the cursor menu and then select "Scale", or press Enter three times to bypass stretch, move, and rotate at the command prompt.

⊕ Move the cursor slowly and observe the dragged image.

AutoCAD will use the selected grip point as the base point for scaling unless you specify that you want to pick a different base point.

Notice that you also have a reference option as in the SCALE command. Unlike the SCALE command, you also have an option to make copies of your objects at different scales.

As in SCALE, the default method is used to specify a scale factor by pointing or typing.

⊕ Type "2" or show a length of 2.00.

Your text will return to its original size, and your screen will resemble Figure 7-24 again.

⊕ Press Esc twice to clear grips.

Note: Grips can be used to edit text in the usual grip edit modes of moving, copying, rotating, mirroring, and scaling. The stretch mode works the same as moving. Grips cannot be used to reword, respell, or change text properties.

7.11 Review Material

Questions

1. What is the main difference between DTEXT and MTEXT?
2. You have drawn two lines of text using DTEXT and have left the command to do some editing. You discover that a third line of text should have been entered with the first two lines. What procedure will allow you to add the third line of text efficiently so that it is spaced and aligned with the first two, as if you had never left DTEXT?
3. What is the difference between center-justified text and middle-justified text?
4. What is the purpose of "%%" in text entry?
5. In the MTEXT command, what information does AutoCAD take from the two corners of the rectangle you specify before entering text? What else is needed to predict how AutoCAD will interpret these point selections?
6. What aspect of text can be changed with DDEDIT? What aspects of text can be changed with DDMODIFY? What is the purpose of MATCHPROP?
7. How do you check all the spelling in your drawing at once?
8. What is the difference between a font and a style?
9. What can happen if you choose the wrong base point when using the SCALE command?
10. How would you use SCALE to change a 3.00 line to 2.75? How could you use LENGTHEN (Chapter 6) to do the same thing?

Drawing Problems

1. Draw a 6 × 6 square. Draw the word "Top", on top of the square, 0.4 units high, centered on the midpoint of the top side of the square.
2. Draw the word "Left", 0.4 units high, centered on the left side of the square.
3. Draw the word "Right", 0.4 units high, centered on the right side of the square.
4. Draw the word "Bottom", 0.4 units high, below the square so that the top of the text is centered on the midpoint of the bottom side of the square.
5. Draw the words "This is the middle", inside the square, 0.4 units high, so that the complete text wraps around within a 2-unit width and is centered on the center point of square.

7.12   Drawing 7-1: Title Block

This title block will give you practice in using a variety of text styles and sizes. You may want to save it and use it as a title block for future drawings. In Chapter 10 we will show you how to insert one drawing into another, so you will be able to incorporate this title block into any drawing.

QTY REQ'D	D E S C R I P T I O N			P A R T N O.	ITEM NO.
	BILL OF MATERIALS				
UNLESS OTHERWISE SPECIFIED DIMENSIONS ARE IN INCHES	DRAWN BY: *B. A. Designer*	DATE		CSA INC.	
REMOVE ALL BURRS & BREAK SHARP EDGES	APPROVED BY:				
TOLERANCES FRACTIONS ± 1/64 DECIMALS ANGLES ± 0'–15' XX ± .01 XXX ± .005	ISSUED:			DRAWING TITLE:	
MATERIAL:	FINISH:		SIZE CODE IDENT NO. C 38178	DRAWING NO.	REV.
			SCALE:	DATE: SHEET OF	

DRAWING SUGGESTIONS

$$GRID = 1$$
$$SNAP = 0.0625$$

- Make ample use of TRIM as you draw the line patterns of the title block. Take your time and make sure that at least the major divisions are in place before you start entering text into the boxes.
- Set to the "text" layer before entering text.
- Use DTEXT with all the STANDARD, 0.09, left-justified text. This will allow you to do all of these in one command sequence, moving the cursor from one box to the next and entering the text as you go.
- Remember that once you have defined a style, you can make it current using the TEXT or DTEXT commands. This will save you from having to restyle more than necessary.
- Use "%%D" for the degree symbol and "%%P" for the plus or minus symbol.

TITLE BLOCK

Drawing 7-1

7.13   Drawing 7-2: Gauges

This drawing will teach you some typical uses of the SCALE and CHANGE commands. Some of the techniques used will not be obvious, so read the suggestions carefully.

DRAWING SUGGESTIONS

GRID = 0.5
SNAP = 0.125

- Draw three concentric circles at diameters of 5.0, 4.5, and 3.0. The bottom of the 3.0 circle can be trimmed later.
- Zoom in to draw the arrow-shaped tick at the top of the 3.0 circle. Then draw the 0.50 vertical line directly below it and the number "0" (middle-justified text) above it.
- These three objects can be arrayed to the left and right around the perimeter of the 3.0 circle using angles of +135 and −135 as shown.
- Use the CHANGE command to change the arrayed zeros into 10, 20, 30, etc.
- Draw the 0.25 vertical tick directly on top of the 0.50 mark at top center and array it left and right. There will be 20 marks each way.
- Draw the needle horizontally across the middle of the dial.
- Make two copies of the dial; use SCALE to scale them down as shown. Then move them into their correct positions.
- Rotate all three needles as shown.

GAUGES
Drawing 7-2

7.14   Drawing 7-3: Stamping

This drawing is trickier than it appears. There are many ways that it can be done. The way we have chosen not only works well but makes use of a number of the commands and techniques you have learned in the last two chapters. Notice that a change in limits is needed to take advantage of some of the suggestions.

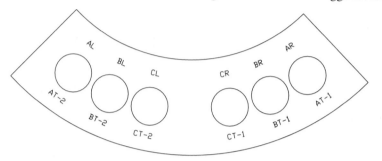

DRAWING SUGGESTIONS

$$\text{GRID} = 0.50$$
$$\text{SNAP} = 0.25$$
$$\text{LIMITS} = (0,0)\ (24,18)$$

- Draw two circles, radius 10.25 and 6.50, centered at about (13,15). These will be trimmed later.
- Draw a vertical line down from the center point to the outer circle. We will copy and rotate this line to form the ends of the stamping.
- Use the rotate, copy mode of the grip edit system to create copies of the line rotated 45 degrees and 245 degrees (coordinate display will show 315 degrees).
- Trim the lines and the circles to form the outline of the stamping.
- Draw a 1.50 diameter circle in the center of the stamping, 8.50 down from (13,15). Draw middle-justified text, "AR", 7.25 down, and "AT-1" down 9.75 from (13,15).
- Follow the procedure given in the next subsection to create offset copies of the circle and text; then CHANGE all text to agree with the drawing.

GRIP COPY MODES WITH OFFSET SNAP LOCATIONS

Here is a good opportunity to try out another grip edit feature. If you hold down the shift key while picking multiple copy points, AutoCAD will be constrained to place copies only at points offset from each other the same distance as your first two points. For example, try this:

1. Select the circle and the text.
2. Select any grip to initiate grip editing.
3. Type "ro" or select "Rotate" from the cursor menu.
4. Type "b" or select "Base pt".
5. Pick the center of the stamping (13,15) as the base point.
6. Type "c" or select "Copy".
7. Hold down Shift and move the cursor to rotate a copy 11 degrees from the original.
8. Keep holding down the shift key as you move the cursor to create other copies. All copies will be offset 11 degrees.

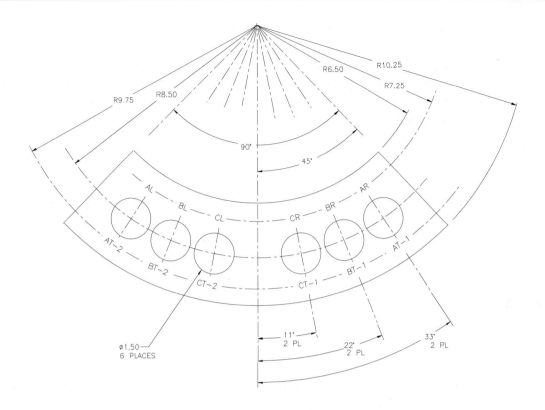

STAMPING
Drawing 7-3

7.15   Drawing 7-4: Control Panel

Done correctly, this drawing will give you a good feel for the power of the commands you now have available to you. Be sure to take advantage of combinations of ARRAY and CHANGE as described. Also, read the suggestion on moving the origin before you begin.

DRAWING SUGGESTIONS

GRID = 0.50
SNAP = 0.0625

- After drawing the outer rectangles, draw the double outline of the left button box, and fillet the corners. Notice the different fillet radii.
- Draw the "on" button with its text at the bottom left of the box. Then array it 2 × 3 for the other buttons in the box.
- CHANGE the lower right button text to "off" and draw the MACHINE # text at the top of the box.
- ARRAY the box 1 × 3 to create the other boxes.
- CHANGE text for buttons and machine numbers as shown.

MOVING THE ORIGIN WITH THE UCS COMMAND

The dimensions of this drawing are shown in ordinate form, measured from a single point of origin in the lower left-hand corner. In effect, this establishes a new coordinate origin. If we move our origin to match this point, then we will be able to read dimension values directly from the coordinate display. This may be done by setting the lower left-hand limits to (−1,−1). But it also may be done using the UCS command to establish a User Coordinate System with the origin at a point you specify. User Coordinate Systems are discussed in depth in Chapter 12. For now, here is a simple procedure:

1. Type "ucs".
2. Type "o" for the "Origin" option.
3. Point to the new origin.

That's all there is to it. Move your cursor to the new origin and watch the coordinate display. It should show "0.00,0.00,0.00", and all values will be measured from there.

CONTROL PANEL

Drawing 7–4

7.16   Drawing 7-5: Tower

This architectural drawing will take some time, and you will utilize many commands that you have learned in this and previous chapters. Notice that the settings are quite different from our standard prototype, so be sure to change them before beginning.

DRAWING SUGGESTIONS

> UNITS = architectural
> Smallest fraction = 1
> GRID = 10′
> SNAP = 1′

- This drawing can be transfered, using the proper scale, from the book to your AutoCAD. You can use the scale provided on the drawing or use an architectural scale with the setting of 1/32″ = 1′. Either transfer methods will produce similar results.
- Whatever order you choose for doing this drawing, we suggest that you make ample use of COPY, ARRAY, TRIM, and OFFSET.
- Keep ortho on, except to draw the lines at an angle.
- With snap set at 1/16, it is easy copy lines and array lines and shapes, as you will be doing frequently to reproduce the many rectangular shapes.
- You may need to turn snap off when you are selecting lines to copy, but be sure to turn it on again to specify displacements.
- Notice that you can use polar ARRAY effectively to draw the text in a circle and then use DDEDIT to change the text. Choose a text font that is similar to that shown (we used Dutch 801 Rm BT).

TOWER
DRAWING 7-5

Scale

0   10   20   30   40   50

THIS DRAWING CURTESY OF MATT ROSE

8 Dimensions

COMMANDS

DRAW	MODIFY	DIMENSIONING	
BHATCH	DIMEDIT	DDIM	DIMLINEAR
BPOLY	DIMTEDIT	DIMALIGNED	DIMOVERRIDE
		DIMANGULAR	DIMSTYLE
		DIMBASELINE	LEADER
		DIMCONTINUE	

OVERVIEW

The ability to dimension your drawings and add crosshatch patterns will greatly enhance the professional appearance and utility of your work. AutoCAD's dimensioning feature is a complex system of commands, subcommands, and variables that automatically measure objects and draw dimension text and extension lines. With AutoCAD's dimensioning tools and variables, you can create dimensions in a wide variety of formats, and these formats can be saved as styles. The time saved through not having to draw each dimension line by line is among the most significant advantages of CAD.

TASKS

8.1   Creating and Saving a Dimension Style

GENERAL PROCEDURE

1. Type "ddim", select Style... from the Dimension menu, or select the Dimension style tool from the Dimension toolbar.
2. Give your dimension style a name.
3. From the Family box, select which type of dimension you want to style first.
4. Set Geometry, Format, and Annotation styles.
5. Save settings.
6. Select other dimension types from the Family box and set these.
7. Save settings and exit.

Dimensioning in AutoCAD is highly automated and very easy compared to manual dimensioning. To achieve a high degree of automation while still allowing for the broad range of flexibility required to cover all dimension styles, the Auto-CAD dimensioning system is necessarily complex. In the exercises that follow we will guide you through the system, show you some of what is available, and give you a good foundation for understanding how to get what you want out of Auto-CAD dimensioning. We will create a basic dimension style and use it to draw standard dimensions and tolerances. We will leave it to you to explore the many variations that are possible.

In Release 14 it is best to begin by defining a dimension style. A dimension style is a set of dimension variable settings that control the text and geometry of all types of AutoCAD dimensions. Prior to Release 13, the default styles for most dimensions would use the drawing units set through the Units Control dialog box or the UNITS command. Release 13 and 14 dimensioning units, however, must be set separately. We recommend that you create the new dimension style in your template drawing and save it. Then you will not have to make these changes again when you start new drawings.

⊕ To begin this exercise, open the B template drawing.

We will make changes in dimension style settings in the template drawing so that all dimensions showing distances will be presented with two decimal places and angular dimensions will have no decimals. This will become the default dimension setting in any drawing created using the B template.

⊕ Type "ddim", select Dimension style from the Format menu, select Style from the Dimension menu, or open the Dimension toolbar and select the Dimension tool (see Figure 8-1).

Tip: Dimensioning is a good example of a case where you may want to open a toolbar and leave it open for awhile. Since dimensioning is often saved for

Figure 8-1

Figure 8-2

last in a drawing and may be done all at once, bringing up the toolbar and keeping it on your screen while you dimension may be most efficient.

Any of the preceding methods will call the Dimension Styles dialog box shown in Figure 8-2. You will see that the current dimension style is called "Standard". Among other things, the AutoCAD Standard dimension style uses four-place decimals in all dimensions, including angular dimensions.

On the left below the Dimension Style name box you will see the Family box with a set of radio buttons for the different types of dimensions. A family is a complete group of dimension settings for the different types of dimensions. The types of dimensions are shown with radio buttons: Linear, Radial, Angular, etc. You can set these individually or use the Parent radio button to set them all at once to a single format. In this exercise we will first use the Parent button to set all types of dimensions to two-place decimals. Then we will set angular dimensions individually to show no decimal places.

But first, let's give the new dimension style a name. We will use "B" to go along with our B prototype.

⊕   Double click in the Name: edit box to highlight the word "Standard".

⊕   Type "B".

⊕   Click on "Save".

This will create the new dimension style and make it current so that subsequent dimensions will be drawn using the B style.

⊕   Check to make sure that the Parent radio button is selected. It should be by default.

Before moving on, look at the three call boxes at the right. We will make changes only in the Annotation... subdialog, but you may wish to look at the others while you are here. If you do, simply open the dialog boxes and cancel them when you are through looking. Geometry... calls a subdialog that allows you to adjust aspects of the lines, arrowheads, extension lines, and center marks that make up a dimension. Format... allows for changes in the place-

Figure 8-3

ment of dimension text relative to dimension geometry. Annotation… allows changes in the text and measurements provided for AutoCAD dimensions.

⊕ Click on "Annotation…".

This will call the Annotation dialog box shown in Figure 8-3. There are areas here for adjusting Primary Units, which is what we are interested in, Tolerance, Alternate Units, and Text style. We will explore tolerances later. Alternate units are dimension units that may be automatically presented in parentheses along with primary units. Text styles you know about from the last chapter. Standard will be the default text style for dimensions, but if you have another text style defined in your drawing, you could select it here. Then all dimensions drawn with this dimension style would have the selected text style.

⊕ Click on "Units…" in the Primary Units box on the upper left of the dialog box.

This will bring up the Primary Units dialog box shown in Figure 8-4. There are adjustments available for units, dimension precision, angular units, and tolerances. The lists under Units and Angles are the same lists used by the UNITS command. The Units should show "Decimal" and the Angles box should show "Decimal Degrees". If for any reason these are not showing in your box, you should make these changes now. For our purposes all we need to change is the number of decimal places showing in the Dimension Precision box. By default it will be 0.0000. We will change it to 0.00.

⊕ Click on the arrow to the right of the Precision box.

This will open a list of precision settings ranging from 0 to 0.00000000.

⊕ Click on 0.00.

This will close the list box and show 0.00 as the selected precision. At this point we are ready to complete this part of the procedure by returning to the Dimension Style dialog box and saving our changes.

⊕ Click on "OK" to exit Primary Units.

Figure 8-4

⊕ Click on "OK" to exit Annotation.

⊕ Click on "Save" to save the change in dimension precision.

This will save the change in dimension style B. At this point dimension style B has all the AutoCAD default settings except that all dimensions, linear and angular, will be shown as two-place decimals. Next we will set the angular precision separately to 0 places.

⊕ Click on the Angular radio button.

⊕ Click on Annotation ....

⊕ Click on Units....

⊕ Change Dimension Precision to 0 decimal places.

Be sure to make the change in the same Precision box that you used before. It is the one on the left, under Dimension, not the one on the right, under Tolerance. The two boxes are identical and since the Tolerance box is directly under the Angle box, it may seem natural to make the change here. But the Tolerance box only changes the precision of tolerances, which we are not using now. The Dimension box is used to adjust the precision of all types of dimensions.

⊕ Click on "OK" to exit Primary Units.

⊕ Click on "OK" to exit Annotation.

⊕ Click on "Save" to save the changes to B.

Before leaving the Dimension Style dialog box, we recommend that you open the Format and Geometry dialog boxes. Look them over carefully to get an idea of the many ways that you can alter dimension styling. In Geometry you will find many options that affect the look of Dimension lines, arrowheads, extension lines, and center marks. In Format, you will find options that affect how dimension text is positioned in relation to dimension geometry. All of these dialog box settings alter the values of dimension variables, which are discussed in Task 8.8.

⊕ Click on "OK" to exit the Dimension Styles dialog box.

⊕   Finally, go to the File menu, save template drawing B, and use New
to open a new drawing.

If the new drawing is opened with the B prototype, the B dimension style will
be current for the next task.

8.2 Drawing Linear Dimensions

GENERAL PROCEDURE

1. Type "Dimlin", select Linear from the Dimension menu, or select the Linear Dimension tool from the Dimension toolbar.
2. Select an object or show two extension line origins.
3. Show the dimension line location.

AutoCAD Release 14 has many commands and features that aid in the drawing of dimensions, as evidenced by the fact that there is an entire pull-down menu
for dimensioning only. In this exercise you will create some basic linear dimensions
in the now-current B style.

⊕   To prepare for this exercise, draw a triangle (ours is 3.00, 4.00,
5.00) and a line (6.00) above the middle of the display, as shown in
Figure 8-5.

Exact sizes and locations are not critical. We will begin by adding dimensions
to the triangle.

The dimensioning commands are streamlined and efficient. Their full names,
however, are all rather long. They all begin with "dim" and are followed by what
used to be the name of an option (for example, DIMLINEAR, DIMALIGNED,

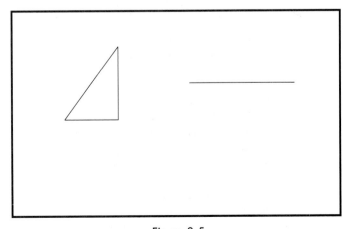

Figure 8-5

and DIMANGULAR). They do have somewhat shorter aliases, which we will show you as we go along. We encourage you to use the Dimensioning menu or the Dimensioning toolbar to avoid typing these names.

We begin by placing a linear dimension below the base of the triangle.

⊕ Type "dimlin", select Linear from the Dimension menu, or select the Linear Dimension tool from the Dimension toolbar.

This will initiate the DIMLINEAR command, with the following prompt appearing in the command area:

          First extension line origin or press ENTER to select:

There are two ways to proceed at this point. One is to show where the extension lines should begin, and the other is to select the base of the triangle itself and let AutoCAD position the extension lines. In most simple applications the latter method is faster.

⊕ Press Enter to indicate that you will select an object.

AutoCAD will replace the cross hairs with a pickbox and prompt for your selection:

                  Select object to dimension:

⊕ Select the horizontal line at the bottom of the triangle, as shown by point 1 in Figure 8-6.

AutoCAD immediately creates a dimension, including extension lines, dimension line, and text, that you can drag out away from the selected line. AutoCAD will place the dimension line and text where you indicate but will keep the text centered between the extension lines. The prompt is as follows:

          Dimension line location
          (MText/Text/Angle/Horizontal/Vertical/Rotated):

In the default sequence, you will simply show the location of the dimension. If you wish to alter the text, you can do so using the "Mtext" or "Text"

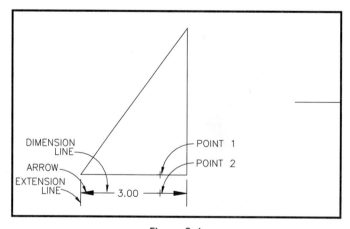

Figure 8-6

options, or you can change it later with a command called DIMEDIT. "Angle", "Horizontal", and "Vertical" allow you to specify the orientation of the text. Horizontal text is the default for linear text. "Rotated" allows you to rotate the complete dimension so that the extension lines move out at an angle from the object being dimensioned (text remains horizontal).

Note: If the dimension variable "dimsho" is set to 0 (off), you will not be given an image of the dimension to drag into place. The default setting is 1 (on), so this should not be a problem. If, however, it has been changed in your drawing, type "dimsho" and then "1" to turn it on again.

⊕ Pick a location about 0.50 below the triangle, as shown by point 2 in Figure 8-6.

Bravo! You have completed your first dimension. (Notice that our figure and others in this chapter are shown zoomed in on the relevant object for the sake of clarity. You may zoom or not as you like.)

At this point, take a good look at the dimension you have just drawn to see what it consists of. As in Figure 8-6, you should see the following components: two extension lines, two "arrows," a dimension line on each side of the text, and the text itself.

Notice also that AutoCAD has automatically placed the extension line origins a short distance away from the triangle base (you may need to zoom in to see this). This distance is controlled by a dimension variable called "dimexo", which can be changed in the Dimension Style dialog box under Geometry. It is one of many variables that control the look of AutoCAD dimensions. Another example of a dimension variable is "dimasz", which controls the size of the arrows at the end of the extension lines. Variables are discussed in Task 8.7.

Next, we will place a vertical dimension on the right side of the triangle. You will see that DIMLINEAR handles both horizontal and vertical dimensions.

⊕ Repeat the DIMLINEAR command.

You will be prompted for extension line origins as before:

        First extension line origin or press ENTER to select:

This time we will show the extension line origins manually.

⊕ Pick the right-angle corner at the lower right of the triangle, point 1 in Figure 8-7. AutoCAD will prompt for a second point:

            Second extension line origin:

Even though you are manually specifying extension line origins, it is not necessary to show the exact point where you want the line to start. AutoCAD will automatically set the dimension lines slightly away from the line as before, according to the setting of the dimexo dimension variable.

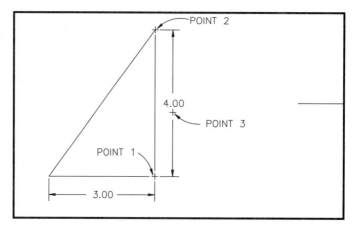

Figure 8-7

⊕ Pick the top intersection of the triangle, point 2 in Figure 8-7.

From here on, the procedure will be the same as before. You should have a dimension to drag into place, and the following prompt:

```
Dimension line location
(Mtext/Text/Angle/Horizontal/Vertical/Rotated):
```

⊕ Pick a point 0.50 to the right of the triangle, point 3 in Figure 8-7.

Your screen should now include the vertical dimension, as shown in Figure 8-7.

Now let's place a dimension on the diagonal side of the triangle. For this we will need the DIMALIGNED command.

⊕ Type "dimali" or select Aligned from the Dimension menu.

⊕ Press Enter, indicating that you will select an object.

AutoCAD will give you the pickbox and prompt you to select an object to dimension.

⊕ Select the hypotenuse of the triangle.

⊕ Pick a point approximately 0.50 above and to the left of the line.

Your screen should resemble Figure 8-8. Notice that AutoCAD retains horizontal text in aligned and vertical dimensions as the default.

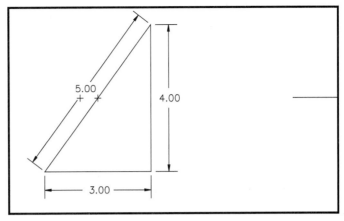

Figure 8-8

8.3 Drawing Multiple Linear Dimensions—Baseline and Continue

GENERAL PROCEDURE

1. Draw an initial linear dimension.
2. Select Baseline or Continue from the Dimension menu or the Baseline Dimension or Continue Dimension tool from the Dimension toolbar.
3. Pick a second extension line origin.
4. Pick another second extension line origin.
5. Press Enter to exit the command.

DIMBASELINE and DIMCONTINUE allow you to draw multiple linear dimensions more efficiently. In baseline format you will have a series of dimensions all measured from the same initial origin. In continued dimensions there will be a string of chained dimensions in which the second extension line for one dimension becomes the first extension for the next.

⊕ To prepare for this exercise, be sure that you have a 6.00 horizontal line, as shown in Figure 8-5 at the beginning of Task 8.2.

Although the figures in this exercise will show only the line, leave the triangle in your drawing, because we will come back to it in the next task. In this exercise we will be placing a set of baseline dimensions on top of the line and a continued series on the bottom. To use either Baseline or Continue, you must have one linear dimension already drawn on the line you wish to dimension. So we will begin with this.

⊕ Select Linear from the Dimension menu or the Linear Dimension tool from the Dimension toolbar.

⊕ Pick the left end point of the line for the origin of the first extension line.

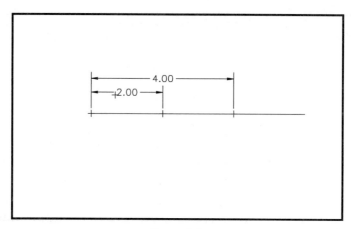

Figure 8-9

⊕ Pick a second extension origin 2.00 to the right of the first, as shown in Figure 8-9.

⊕ Pick a point 0.50 above the line for dimension text.

You should now have the initial 2.00 dimension shown in Figure 8-9. We will use DIMBASELINE to add the other dimensions above it.

⊕ Type "dimbase" or select Baseline from the Dimensioning menu or the Baseline Dimension tool from the Dimension toolbar.

AutoCAD uses the first extension line origin you picked again and prompts for a second:

```
Specify a second extension line origin or (Undo/Select):
```

⊕ Pick a point 4.00 to the right of the first extension line (in other words, 4.00 from the left end of the 6.00 line).

The second baseline dimension shown in Figure 8-9 should be added to your drawing. We will add one more. AutoCAD leaves you in the DIMBASELINE command so that you can add as many baseline dimensions as you want.

⊕ Pick the right end point of the line.

Your screen should resemble Figure 8-10. See how quickly AutoCAD draws dimensions? As long as you have your dimension style defined the way you want it, this can make dimensioning go very quickly.

AutoCAD will still be prompting for another second extension line origin. We will need to press Enter twice to exit DIMBASELINE.

⊕ Press Enter to end extension line selection.

The first time you press Enter, AutoCAD will show you a new prompt:

```
Select base dimension:
```

This prompt would allow you to begin a new series of baseline dimensions from a dimension other than the last one you drew. Bypassing this prompt will take you back to command prompt.

⊕ Press Enter to exit DIMBASELINE.

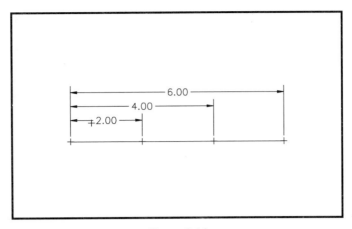

Figure 8-10

Continued Dimensions

Now we will place three continued dimensions along the bottom of the line, as shown in Figure 8-11. The process is very similar to the baseline process, so you should need little help at this point.

⊕ Begin by using DIMLINEAR to place an initial horizontal dimension 0.50 below the line, showing a length of 2.00 from the left end, as shown in Figure 8-11.

⊕ Type "dimcont" or select Continue from the Dimension menu or the Continue Dimension tool from the Dimension toolbar.

⊕ Pick a second extension line origin 2.00 to the right of the last extension line.

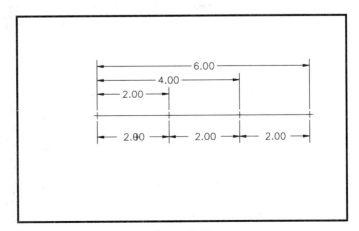

Figure 8-11

Be sure to pick this point on the 6.00 line; otherwise the extension line will be left hanging.

⊕ Pick another second extension line at the right end of the line.

⊕ Press Enter to end the continued series.

⊕ Press Enter to exit DIMCONTINUE.

Done!

8.4 Drawing Angular Dimensions

GENERAL PROCEDURE

1. Select Angular from the Dimenson menu or the Angular Dimension tool from the Dimension toolbar.
2. Select two lines that form an angle.
3. Pick a dimension location.

Angular dimensioning works much like linear dimensioning, except that you will be prompted to select objects that form an angle. AutoCAD will compute an angle based on the geometry that you select (two lines, an arc, part of a circle, or a vertex and two points) and construct extension lines, a dimension arc, and text specifying the angle.

For this exercise we will return to the triangle and add angular dimensions to two of the angles, as shown in Figure 8-12.

⊕ Type "dimang" or select Angular from the Dimension menu or the Angular Dimension tool from the Dimension toolbar.

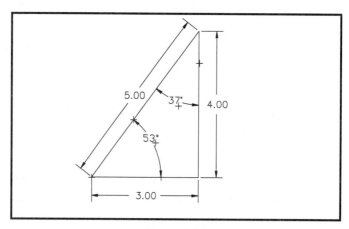

Figure 8-12

The first prompt will be

Select arc, circle, line, or press ENTER:

The prompt shows that you can use angular dimensions to specify angles formed by arcs and portions of circles as well as angles formed by lines. If you press Enter, you can specify an angle manually by picking its vertex and a point on each side of the angle. We will begin by picking lines, the most common use of angular dimensions.

⊕   Select the base of the triangle.

You will be prompted for another line:

Second line:

⊕   Select the hypotenuse.

As in linear dimensioning, AutoCAD now shows you the dimension lines and lets you drag them into place (assuming dimsho is on). The prompt asks for a dimension arc location and also allows you the option of changing the text or the text angle.

Dimension arc line location (Mtext/Text/Angle):

⊕   Move the cursor around to see how the dimension may be placed and then pick a point between the two selected lines, as shown in Figure 8-12.

The lower left angle of your triangle should now be dimensioned, as in Figure 8-12. Notice that the degree symbol is added by default in angular dimension text.

We will dimension the upper angle by showing its vertex, using the press ENTER option.

⊕   Repeat DIMANGULAR.

⊕   Press Enter.

AutoCAD prompts for an angle vertex.

⊕   Point to the vertex of the angle at the top of the triangle.

AutoCAD prompts

First angle endpoint:

⊕   Pick a point along the hypotenuse.

To be precise, this should be a snap point. The most dependable one will be the lower left corner of the triangle.

AutoCAD prompts

Second angle end point:

⊕   Pick any point along the vertical side of the triangle.

There should be many snap points on the vertical line, so you should have no problem.

⊕   Move the cursor slowly up and down within the triangle.

Figure 8-13

Notice how AutoCAD places the arrows outside the angle when you approach the vertex and things get crowded. Also notice that if you move outside the angle, AutoCAD switches to the outer angle.

⊕ Pick a location for the dimension arc, as shown in Figure 8-12.

Angular Dimensions on Arcs and Circles

You can also place angular dimensions on arcs and circles. In both cases AutoCAD will construct extension lines and a dimension arc. When you dimension an arc with an angular dimension, the center of the arc becomes the vertex of the dimension angle, and the end points of the arc become the start points of the extension lines. In a circle the same format is used, but the dimension line origins are determined by the point used to select the circle and a second point, which AutoCAD prompts you to select. These options are illustrated in Figure 8-13.

8.5 Dimensioning Arcs and Circles

GENERAL PROCEDURE

1. Select Radius or Diameter from the Dimension menu, or select the Radius Dimension or Diameter Dimension tool from the Dimension toolbar.
2. Pick the arc or circle at the point where you want the dimension line of leader to start.
3. Type text or press Enter.
4. Pikc a leader line end point locaton.

The basic process for dimensioning circles and arcs is as simple as those we have already covered. It can get tricky, however, when AutoCAD does not place the dimension where you want it. Text placement can be controlled by adjusting dimension variables. In this exercise we will create a center mark and some diameter and radius dimensions.

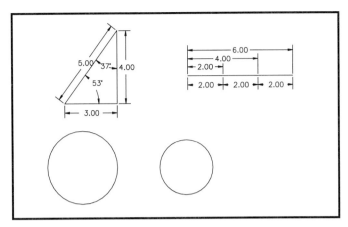

Figure 8-14

✛ To prepare for this exercise, draw two circles at the bottom of your screen, as shown in Figure 8-14.

The circles we have used have radii of 2.00 and 1.50.

Although the remaining figures in this section will show the circles only, keep the triangle and the line in your drawing, because they will be used again in Task 8.7.

✛ Select Center Mark from the Dimension menu or the Center Mark tool from the Dimension toolbar.

You cannot use "dimcen" as the command name because that is the name of the dimension variable that controls the style of the center mark. If you are typing, you will need to type the whole name "dimcenter".

Center marks resemble blips, but they are actual lines and will appear on a plotted drawing. They are the simplest of all dimension features to create and are created automatically as part of some radius and diameter dimensions.

AutoCAD prompts

Select arc or circle:

✛ Select the smaller circle.

A center mark will be drawn in the 1.50 circle, as shown in Figure 8-15.

Tip: A different type of center mark can be produced by changing the dimension variable "dimcen" from .09 to −.09. The result is shown in the dimension variables chart, Figure 8-21, later in this chapter. You may recall that this technique was introduced previously in Drawing 4-4.

Now we will add the diameter dimension shown on the larger circle in Figure 8-15.

✛ Type "dimdia" or select Diameter from the Dimension menu or the Diameter Dimension tool from the Dimension toolbar.

AutoCAD will prompt

Select arc or circle:

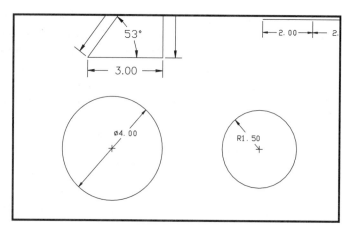

Figure 8-15

⊕   Select the larger circle.

AutoCAD will show a diameter dimension and ask for Dimension line location. The Text and Angle options allow you to change the dimension text or
put it at an angle. If you move your cursor around, you will see that you can
position the dimension line anywhere around the circle.

⊕   Pick a dimension position so that your screen resembles Figure 8-15.

Notice that the diameter symbol prefix is added automatically by default.

Radius Dimensions

The procedures for radius dimensioning are exactly the same as those for diameter dimensions. We will quickly draw a radius dimension on the smaller circle.

⊕   Type "Dimrad", select Radius from the Dimension menu or select the
Radius Dimension tool from the Dimension toolbar.

⊕   Select the 1.50 (smaller) circle.

⊕   Move the cursor outside and around the circle.

⊕   Pick a point to complete the dimension, as shown in Figure 8-15.

The "R" for radius is added automatically.

8.6   Dimensioning with Leaders

GENERAL PROCEDURE

1. Select Leader from the Dimension menu or the Leader tool from Dimension toolbar.
2. Select a start point.
3. Select an end point.
4. Select another end point.
5. Type dimension text.

Leaders are useful for attaching annotation to all kinds of objects. They may be used to dimension objects in crowded areas of a drawing and to attach text to an object. Unlike other dimension formats, in which you select an object or show a length, a leader is simply a line or series of lines with an arrow at the end to connect an object to its annotation. The LEADER command does not recognize and measure a selected object, so you will need to know the dimension text you want to use before you begin.

In this exercise we will create two leaders with associated text. One will be as simple as we can make it and the other will be more complex.

⊕ Type "lead", select Leader from the Dimension menu, or select the Leader tool from the Dimension toolbar.

AutoCAD will prompt you for a point, as in the LINE command:

> From point

Usually you will want the leader arrow to start on the object, not offset, as an extension line would be. This suggests that an object snap may be in order.

⊕ Type "nea", or select Nearest from the Object Snap cursor menu (press shift and the enter button on your mouse).

This specifies that you want to snap to the nearest point on whatever object you select. You will see that the pickbox and the Nearest snaptool will appear when an object crosses the pickbox.

⊕ Position the cross hairs so that the upper right side of the 1.50 radius circle crosses the aperture, and press the pickbutton.

The leader will be snapped to the circle and a rubber band shown extending to the cross hairs. AutoCAD will prompt for a second point, just as in the LINE command:

> To point:

⊕ Pick a second point for the leader up and to the right of the first point, as shown on the smaller circle in Figure 8-16.

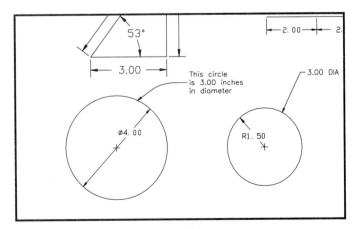

Figure 8-16

After the first point has been entered, the prompt will change:

```
To point (Format/Annotation/Undo)<Annotation>:
```

The default option "Annotation" will allow you to begin creating the text you want. We will save the other options for the next leader.

⊞ **Press Enter to indicate that you are ready to create the annotation.**

AutoCAD prompts

```
Annotation (or press ENTER for options):
```

⊞ **Type "3.00 DIA" and press Enter.**

After you have entered this text, AutoCAD will prompt you for more:

```
Mtext:
```

This indicates that if you continue entering text, it will be added beneath the first line in MTEXT paragraph form. All text created in the LEADER command is created as Mtext and can therefore be edited using all the tools available for Mtext, including the DDMODIFY command, width boundaries, attachment options, and the Edit Mtext dialog box for editing contents.

⊞ **Press Enter to complete the command.**

The annotated leader illustrated on the smaller circle in Figure 8-16 should be added to your drawing. If you look closely, you will notice that a short horizontal line segment is added automatically to "connect" the text to the leader.

Next we will create a more complex curved leader attached to three lines of Mtext.

⊞ **Repeat the "Leader" command.**

⊞ **Type "Nea" or select Nearest from the cursor menu again.**

⊞ **Pick a leader start point on the upper right side of the larger, 2.00 radius circle.**

⊞ **Pick a second point for the leader at about 45 degrees up and to the right of the first point.**

After the second point has been entered, the prompt will change to

```
To point (Format/Annotation/Undo)<Annotation>:
```

This time we will use the "Format" option to draw a curved leader. Leaders made up of a number of straight line segments or curves are often useful for maneuvering around other objects in a crowded drawing.

⊞ **Type "f".**

AutoCAD issues this prompt:

```
Spline/STraight/Arrow/None/<Exit>:
```

"Spline" is the option we want. "STraight" (you must type "st" to distinguish this option from spline) would switch us back to straight segments. "Arrow" would draw an arrow at the start point of the leader, but this is done by default. "None" would suppress the arrow.

⊕ Type "s" to create a spline curve.

⊕ Move the cursor slowly around the second point.

You will see that the line now bends and curves to the new point you are about to select.

⊕ Pick the third point slightly above and to the right of the second to create a curved leader similar to the one in Figure 8-16.

⊕ Press Enter to end the leader at this point.

AutoCAD will now prompt for an annotation:

Annotation (or press ENTER for options):

The options available if you were to press Enter here are as follows: "Tolerance" calls up a tolerance symbol dialog box so that you can add tolerancing symbols to your annotation; "Copy" lets you copy previously created text and attach it to the end of your leader; "Block" lets you attach a block to your leader (blocks are discussed in Chapter 10); "None" exits the command without adding any annotation; "Mtext" is the default. Pressing Enter here would call up the Edit Mtext dialog box.

For our purposes we can simply begin entering text.

⊕ Type "This circle" and press Enter.

⊕ Type "is 3.00 inches" and press Enter.

⊕ Type "in diameter".

⊕ Click on "OK" to complete the command.

Your screen should now resemble Figure 8-16.

8.7 Drawing Ordinate Dimensions

GENERAL PROCEDURE

1. Define a coordinate system with the origin at the corner of the object to be dimensioned.
2. Select Ordinate from the Dimension menu or the Ordinate tool from the Dimension toolbar.
3. Select a location to be dimensioned.
4. Pick a leader end point.
5. Press Enter or change dimension text.

Ordinate, or datum line, dimensions are another way to specify linear dimensions. They are used to show multiple horizontal and vertical distances from a single point or the corner of an object. Since these fall readily into a coordinate system, it is efficient to show these dimensions as the x and y displacements from a single point of origin. AutoCAD will ordinarily specify points based on the point (0,0) on your screen; therefore, it will be necessary to move the origin so that DIMORDINATE will show the appropriate dimension text. Drawing 7-4 in Chapter 7 was dimensioned in this way.

⊕ To prepare for this exercise, erase the baseline and continued dimensions created in Task 8.3. This is a good opportunity to apply the "remove" option in the ERASE command, as follows:

1. Enter the ERASE command.
2. Select all of the baseline and continued dimensions with a window or crossing box. This also will select the line.
3. Type "r" for the "Remove" option.
4. Select the line only.
5. Press Enter to carry out the command.

The dimensions will be erased, but not the line, since it has been removed from the selection set.

⊕ Now draw a 3.00 vertical line at the left end of the 6.00 horizontal line, as shown in Figure 8-17.

We will use ordinate dimensions to specify a series of horizontal and vertical distances from the intersection of the two lines. First, we need to define a temporary User Coordinate System with its origin at the intersection. User coordinate systems are crucial in 3D drawing and are explored in depth in Chapter 12.

⊕ Type "Ucs" or open the Tools menu and highlight UCS.

⊕ Type "o" or select "Origin" from the UCS submenu.

Specifying a new coordinate system by moving the point of origin is the simplest of many options in the UCS command. AutoCAD prompts

Origin point <0,0,0>:

⊕ Pick the intersection of the two lines.

If you move your cursor to the intersection and watch the coordinate display, you will see that this point is now read as (0.00,0.00,0.00).

⊕ Type "dimord", select Ordinate from the Dimension menu, or select the Ordinate Dimension tool from the Dimension toolbar.

Figure 8-17

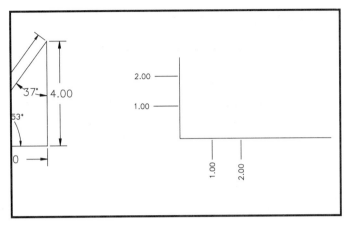

Figure 8-18

AutoCAD prompts

`Select Feature:`

In actuality, all you will do is show AutoCAD a point and then an end point for a leader. Depending on where the end point is located relative to the first point, AutoCAD will show dimension text for either an *x* or a *y* displacement from the origin of the current coordinate system.

⊕ Pick a point along the 6.00 line, 1.00 to the right of the intersection, as shown in Figure 8-18.

AutoCAD prompts

`Leader endpoint (Xdatum/Ydatum/Mtext/Text):`

You can manually indicate whether you want the *x* or *y* coordinate by typing "x" or "y". However, if you choose the end point correctly, AutoCAD will pick the right coordinate automatically. You can also provide your own text, but that would defeat the purpose of setting up a coordinate system that will give you the distances from the intersection of the two lines.

⊕ Pick an end point 0.5 below the line, as shown in Figure 8-18.

Your screen should now include the 1.00 ordinate dimension shown in Figure 8-18.

⊕ To complete this exercise, repeat the ordinate option three times and add the other ordinate dimensions shown.

When you are done, you should return to the world coordinate system. This is the default coordinate system and the one we have been using all along.

⊕ Type "Ucs" or open the Tools menu and highlight "UCS".

⊕ Type "w", or select World from the UCS submenu.

This will return the origin to its original position at the lower left of your screen.

8.8 Changing and Overriding Dimension Variables

GENERAL PROCEDURE

1. Select "Override" from the Dimension menu.
2. Type a dimension variable name.
3. Type a new value.
4. Select dimensions to alter.

Or

1. Type a variable name.
2. Type a new value.
3. Enter the DIMSTYLE command.
4. Type "a" for Apply.
5. Select dimensions to apply new variable value.

As you know from Task 8.1, you can save and restore dimension styles using the Dimension Style dialog box. When a new style is created it becomes current, and all subsequent dimensions will be drawn using the new style. Sometimes, however, you may not want to create a whole new style in order to draw one or two dimensions that are slightly different from the others in your drawing. Or you may want to create a new style and apply it to some previously drawn dimensions. The first case is handled using a dimension override, the DIMOVERRIDE command. The second is done by changing dimension variables and then using the "apply" option in the DIMSTYLE command. We will demonstrate both, beginning with an override, and then look at a complete listing of all the dimension variables and their current settings.

⊕ Select "Override" from the Dimension menu.

AutoCAD prompts

    Dimension variable to override (or Clear to remove overrides):

We can create some easily visible changes by altering the scale of a dimension using the dimscale variable.

⊕ Type "dimscale".

AutoCAD gives you the current value and prompts for a change:

                Current value <1.00> New value:

⊕ Type "2".

AutoCAD continues to prompt for variables to override so that we can change more than one at a time.

⊕ Press Enter.

Now that we have provided a new temporary dimension scale, we need to select dimensions that we want to show this scale. We can use all of our usu-

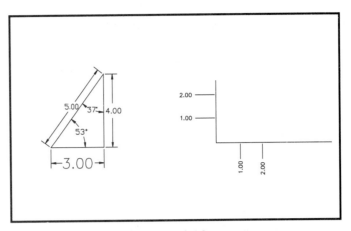

Figure 8-19

al selection methods here, including windowing and the all option. In this case we will change one dimension only.

⊕ Select the 3.00 linear dimension at the base of the triangle.

⊕ Press Enter to end object selection.

You will see that the 3.00 dimension text is redrawn twice as large, as shown in Figure 8-19. This alteration in dimension style is a one-time-only override. The change in dimscale has not been retained in memory, and any new dimensions drawn would have dimscale of 1.00. To make a more permanent change in style, we could go to the Dimension Style dialog box as before. Changes made in this way, however, will be applied to all dimensions previously drawn in the current dimension style. By changing a dimension variable at the command line, we can also gain the option of applying the change to selected dimensions only.

To change a variable at the command line, just type its name and then enter the new value.

⊕ Type "dimscale".

AutoCAD prompts

                New value for DIMSCALE <1.00>:

⊕ Type "2".

This brings you back to the command prompt. The variable has been changed in the current dimension style, as you would see by opening the Dimension Style dialog box or by creating a new dimension. To apply the change to previously drawn dimensions, you need the DIMSTYLE command.

⊕ Type "dimstyle" or select Update from the Dimension menu.

The DIMSTYLE command is not the same as the DDIM command, which calls the Dimension Style dialog box. It will list variables that have been changed and then prompt with options for other types of changes. You should see this in the command area:

```
dimension style overrides:
DIMSCALE 2.00
Dimension Style Edit
(Save/Restore/STatus/Variables/Apply/?) <Restore>:
```

Do not be confused by the use of the word "override" here. There is a difference between one-time overrides like the one we did using the DIMOVERRIDE command, and running overrides like this one which are retained in the current style until the style is restored to its original configuration.

We will use the "apply" option to apply the change in dimscale to one of our previously drawn dimensions.

⊕ Type "a".

AutoCAD needs to know which dimensions we want to apply the change to:

Select objects:

⊕ Select the 2.00 top ordinate dimension.

⊕ Press Enter to end object selection.

The 2.00 dimension text will be enlarged as shown in Figure 8-20.

While we are on the DIMSTYLE command, use it to look at a list of all the dimension variables and their current settings. Setting dimension variables is easy, but the sheer number (58 in Release 14) can be overwhelming. The dimension variable chart (Figure 8-21) will show you some of the most commonly used variables. By studying it carefully you will gain a better sense of the possibilities.

⊕ Repeat DIMSTYLE.

⊕ Type "st".

You will see 58 variables listed with their current settings and a phrase describing the effect of each setting. You will have to press Enter twice to get

Figure 8-20

COMMONLY USED DIMENSION VARIABLES

Variable	Default Value	Appearance	DESCRIPTION	New Value	Appearance
dimaso	on	All parts of dim are one entity	Associative dimensioning	off	All parts of dim are separate entities
dimscale	1.00	←—2.00—→	Changes size of text & arrows, not value	2.00	◄—2.00—►
dimasz	.18	►	Sets arrow size	.38	◄
dimcen	.09	⊕	Center mark size and appearance	−.09	⊕
dimdli	.38		Spacing between continued dimension lines	.50	
dimexe	.18		Extension above dimension line	.25	
dimexo	0.06		Extension line origin offset	.12	
dimtp	0.00	1.50	Sets plus tolerance	.01	$1.50^{+0.01}_{-0.00}$
dimtm	0.00	1.50	Sets minus tolerance	.02	$1.50^{+0.00}_{-0.02}$
dimtol	off	1.50	Generate dimension tolerances (dimtp & dimtm must be set) (dimtol & dimlim cannot both be on)	on	$1.50^{+0.01}_{-0.02}$
dimlim	off	1.50	Generate dimension limits (dimtp & dimtm must be set) (dimtol & dimlim cannot both be on)	on	1.51 1.48
dimtad	off	←— 1.50 —→	Places text above the dimension line	on	1.50
dimtxt	.18	1.50	Sets height of text	.38	1.50
dimtsz	.18	←— 1.50 —→	Sets tick marks & tick height	.25	╱— 1.50 —╱
dimtih	on	1.50	Sets angle of text When off rotates text to the angle of the dimension	off	1.50
dimtix	off	⌀0.71 +	Forces the text to inside of circles and arcs. Linear and angular dimensions are placed inside if there is sufficient room	on	⌀0.71

Figure 8-21

to the end of the list. As you may notice, these variables affect the same characteristics shown in the Dimension Style dialog box. In fact, when you make changes there you are actually changing variable settings.

Finally, before moving on, use the "restore" option to remove the change in dimscale.

⊕ Type "r", or press Enter, since Restore is the default option.

AutoCAD prompts

> ?/Enter dimension style name or press ENTER to select
> dimension:

⊕ Type "b" or the name of your current dimension style.

This will restore the original values of the B dimension style.

8.9 Changing Dimension Text with DIMEDIT

GENERAL PROCEDURE

1. Select "dimedit" or select the Dimension Edit tool from the Dimension toolbar.
2. Type "n".
3. Enter the new text.
4. Select the dimensions you want to change.

There is one more dimension command you should know about before we move on to hatching. DIMEDIT allows you to change the text of previously drawn dimensions. You can add text or change the wording or numbers in the text, alter the rotation or obliquing angle of the text, or return text to its "home" position after it has been moved.

⊕ Type "Dimedit" or select the Dimension Edit tool from the Dimension toolbar.

AutoCAD prompts with options:

> Dimension Edit (Home/New/Rotate/Oblique) <Home>:

⊕ Type "n" for New.

This indicates that you want to enter new text. Accordingly, AutoCAD opens the Multiline Text Editor and waits for you to enter text. You will see two arrows in the edit box (<>). Whatever you type will be added to the existing dimension text. If you type to the left of the arrows, you will add text to the left; if you type to the right, text will be added to the right.

We will change the 5.00 aligned dimension to read "5.00 mm".

⊕ Click on the right side of <> so that the flashing cursor moves to the right.

⊕ Type "mm".

The text will appear in the edit box.

⊕ Click on "OK" or press Enter to return to the drawing.

AutoCAD prompts for objects to receive the new text:

> Select Objects:

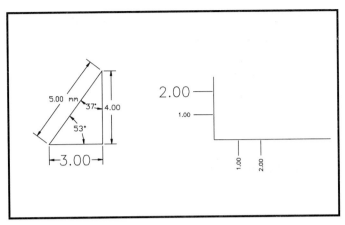

Figure 8-22

⊕ Select the 5.00 aligned dimension on the hypotenuse of the triangle.

⊕ Press Enter to end object selection.

The text will be redrawn, as shown in Figure 8-22. This command is very convenient when you want to add text to a dimension.

8.10 Using the BHATCH Command

GENERAL PROCEDURE

1. Select Hatch from the Draw menu or the Hatch tool from the Draw menu.
2. Select a pattern.
3. Define style parameters.
4. Define boundaries of object to be hatched.

Automated hatching is another immense timesaver. Release 14 includes two commands for use in crosshatching. Of the two, BHATCH and HATCH, BHATCH is more powerful and easier to use. BHATCH differs from HATCH in that it automatically defines the nearest boundary surrounding a point you have specified. The HATCH command requires you to specify manually each segment of the boundary. In other words, with BHATCH you can point to the area you want to hatch and AutoCAD will go looking for its boundaries, whereas with HATCH you select the boundaries and AutoCAD hatches what's inside.

⊕ To prepare for this exercise, clear your screen of all previously drawn objects and then draw three rectangles, one inside the other, with the word "TEXT" at the center, as shown in Figure 8-23.

⊕ Type "bh" or select Hatch from the Draw menu.

Figure 8-23

Figure 8-24

Figure 8-25

There is also a Hatch tool on the Draw toolbar, as shown in Figure 8-24, but you may have to move the toolbar into a floating position in order to access it.

All of these methods initiate the BHATCH command, which calls the Boundary Hatch dialog box shown in Figure 8-25. At the top of the box you will see the Pattern Type box. Before we can hatch anything we need to specify a pattern. Later we will show AutoCAD what we wish to hatch using the Pick Points method.

The Pattern type currently shown in the image box is a predefined pattern. There are about 68 of these patterns. But we will first use a simple user-defined pattern of straight lines on a 45-degree angle.

⊕ **Click on the arrow to the right of "Predefined".**

This opens a list including Predefined, User-defined, and Custom patterns.

⊕ **Click on "User-defined".**

When you select a user-defined pattern, there will be nothing shown in the image box. To create a user-defined pattern, you will need to specify an angle and a spacing.

⊕ **Double click in the Angle edit box, and then type "45".**

⊕ **Double click in the Spacing edit box, and then type ".5".**

The remaining box in this area is Double. Double hatching creates double hatch lines running perpendicular to each other according to the specified angle.

Next we need to show AutoCAD where to place the hatching. To the right in the dialog box is the Boundary area. The first two options are "Pick Points" and "Select Objects". Using the "Pick Points" option, you can have AutoCAD locate a boundary when you point to the area inside it. The "Select Objects" option can be used to create boundaries in the way that the older HATCH command works, by selecting entities that lie along the boundaries.

⊕ **Click on "Pick Points <".**

The dialog box will disappear temporarily and you will be prompted as follows:

```
Select internal point:
```

⊕ **Pick a point inside the largest, outer rectangle but outside the smaller rectangles.**

AutoCAD displays these messages, though you may have to press F2 to see them:

```
Selecting everything visible...
Analyzing the selected data...
Analyzing internal islands...
```

In a large drawing this process can be time consuming because the program searches all visible entities to locate the appropriate boundary. When the process is complete, all of the rectangles and the text will be highlighted. It will happen very quickly in this case.

AutoCAD continues to prompt for internal points so that you can define multiple boundaries. Let's return to the dialog box and see what we've done so far.

⊕ **Press Enter to end internal point selection.**

The dialog box will reappear. You may not have noticed, but several of the options that were "grayed out" before are now accessible. We will make use

Figure 8-26

of the "Preview Hatch" option. This allows us to preview what has been specified without leaving the command, so that we can continue to adjust the hatching until we are satisfied.

⊕ Click on "Preview Hatch <".

Your screen should resemble Figure 8-26, except that you will have to move the Boundary Hatch-Continue box away from the center of the display, as we have done. This demonstrates the "normal" style of hatching in which multiple boundaries are hatched or left clear in alternating fashion, beginning with the outermost boundary and working inward. You can see the effect of the other styles by looking at the Advanced Options dialog box. Notice that BHATCH has recognized the text as well as the other interior boundaries.

⊕ Click on Continue to return to the Boundary Hatch dialog box.

You could complete the hatching operation at this point by clicking on Apply, but let's take a look at a few more details while we are here.

⊕ Click on "Advanced...".

This calls the Advanced Options dialog box shown in Figure 8-27. In the middle you will see the hatching style area. There are three basic options that

Figure 8-27

determine how BHATCH will treat interior boundaries. "Normal" is the current style.

⊕ Click on the arrow to the right of "Normal".

You will see the other two styles listed. "Normal" hatches alternate areas moving inward, "Outer" hatches only the outer area, and "Ignore" hatches through all interior boundaries. There is an image box that shows an example of the current style, as shown in Figure 8-27.

⊕ Click on "Outer" and watch the image box.

It now shows the "Outer" style, in which only the area between the outermost boundary and the first inner boundary is hatched.

⊕ Click on the arrow again and then on "Ignore" and watch the image box.

In the "Ignore" style, all interior boundaries are ignored and the entire area including the text is hatched.

You can see the same effects in your own drawing, if you like, by clicking on "OK" and then "Preview Hatch" after changing from the "Normal" style to either of the other styles. Of course, the three styles are indistinguishable if you do not have boundaries within boundaries to hatch.

⊕ When you are done experimenting, you should select "Normal" style hatching again and return to the Boundary Hatch dialog box.

Now let's take a look at some of the fancier stored hatch patterns that AutoCAD provides.

⊕ Click on the arrow to the right of "User-Defined" and select "Predefined".

⊕ Now click on the "Pattern".

This opens a long list of AutoCAD's predefined hatch patterns along with sample images on the right. To produce the hatched image in Figure 8-28, we chose the Escher pattern.

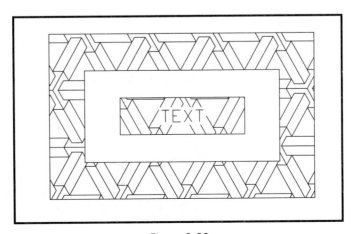

Figure 8-28

⊕   Move down the list until you come to "Escher".

⊕   Select "Escher".

⊕   Click on Okay to exit the Pattern dialog box.

To produce the figure we also used a larger scale in this hatching.

⊕   Double click in the "Scale:" edit box and type "1.5".

⊕   Double click in the "Angle:" edit box and type "0".

⊕   Click on "Preview Hatch <".

Your screen should resemble Figure 8-28, but remember this is still just the preview. When you are through adjusting hatching, you have the choice of canceling the BHATCH command, so that no hatching is added to your drawing, or completing the process by clicking on "Apply". Apply will confirm the most recent choices of boundaries, patterns, and scales, making them part of your drawing.

⊕   Click on Continue.

⊕   Click on "Apply" to exit BHATCH and confirm the hatching.

Other Advanced Options and the BPOLY Command

There are a number of worthwhile options and techniques that we have not explored in this exercise. Some of these options are available from the Advanced Options dialog box. For your information we offer the following notes:

1. When AutoCAD locates a boundary, it temporarily creates a polyline entity that completely outlines the boundaried area. A polyline (Chapter 9) is a single entity, which may be comprised of many straight and curved line segments. By default, the temporary polyline borders used by BHATCH are deleted after hatching is drawn. They may be retained for other uses, however, by checking the Retain Boundaries box in the Advanced Options dialog box.

2. Using the BPOLY command, the same procedures that are used to create polyline hatch boundaries can be used to create polyline outlines independent of any hatching operation. BPOLY calls a dialog box similar to the Advanced Options dialog, but with no intervening steps through the BHATCH dialogs.

3. In very complex drawings it may be efficient to limit the number of entities AutoCAD needs to consider when looking for boundaries. This can be done using the Make New Boundary Set option. The boundary set does not need to be precise. By including all the entities in one portion of a drawing, for example, you could still substantially reduce the magnitude of AutoCAD's task. To specify a boundary set, click on "Make New Boundary Set" in the Advanced Options dialog box.

8.11   Scaling Dimensions between Paper Space and Model Space

---

GENERAL PROCEDURE

1. Use ZOOM XP to set scale in viewports.
2. Set Dimtxt variable to a desirable text size.
3. Set Dimscale variable to 0.
4. Create dimensions in model space.

There are numerous scaling problems that arise when you are working with viewports and paper space. The ZOOM XP feature introduced in Chapter 6 allows you to create precise scale relationships between model space images and paper space units. Numerous other issues arise when you begin to use text and dimensions in paper space multiple-viewport drawings. We will begin by illustrating some of the problems.

⊕ To begin this task, you should have the multiple-view layout of Drawing 6-4 on your screen.

If this drawing is unavailable, any similar multiple-viewport drawing will do, though it may be more difficult to follow the steps given here if you are looking at a different drawing.

Note: This exercise assumes that the variable Dimscale is initially set to 1 and that Dimtxt is set to 0.18. These are default settings. If they have been changed in your drawing, you will not get the exact results shown here. Also, we assume that your current text style has a height setting of 0, meaning that it is variable. This is a default setting as well.

Draw Text in Paper Space

There are certain basic principles that are useful in adding text and dimensions to a multiple-view drawing in paper space. The first is that most text be created in paper space. To see why, try entering some text in paper space and model space as follows.

⊕ Type "ps" or double click the Model button to enter paper space.

⊕ Type "Dt" or select Text and then Single Line text from the Draw menu.

⊕ Pick a start point outside any of the viewports. Our text begins about 3 units over the center of the left viewport, as shown in Figure 8-29.

⊕ Type "1" for a text height of one unit.

This assumes that you are using the D-size paper space limits from Chapter 6. If not, you will have to adjust for your own settings.

⊕ Press Enter for 0 rotation.

Figure 8-29

⊕ Type "Drawing 6-4".

⊕ Press Enter twice.

Your screen should have text added, as shown in Figure 8-29.

⊕ Type "ms" or double click the Paper button to switch to model space.

⊕ Make the largest viewport active.

⊕ Type "Dt" or select Text and then Single Line text from the Draw menu.

⊕ Pick a start point below the two views in the viewport, as shown.

⊕ Press Enter to retain a height of 1.00 units.

⊕ Press Enter for 0 rotation.

⊕ Type "Hub".

Your screen should resemble Figure 8-29.

What has happened here? Why is the "Hub" drawn twice as big as "Drawing 6-4" (or some other size, depending on your limit and zoom factor settings)? Do you remember the zoom xp scale factor we used in this viewport? This viewport is enlarged by two times paper space. So any text you draw inside it will be enlarged by a factor of 2 as well. If you want, try drawing text in either of the other two viewports. You will find that text in the left viewport is magnified four times the paper space size and text in the uppermost viewport is magnified six times.

You could compensate for these enlargements by dividing text height by factors of 2, 4, and 6, but that would be cumbersome. Furthermore, if you decided to change the zoom factor at a later date, you would have to re-create any text drawn within the altered viewport. Otherwise, your text sizes in the overall drawing would be inconsistent. For this reason, it is recommended that text be drawn in paper space.

Dimension Model Space Objects in Model Space

When it comes to dimensions, however, the rule is just the opposite. Dimensions should be kept in model space with the objects they refer to. The main reason is that dimensions in AutoCAD are associative. They will change when the objects they document are changed. This is true if they are in the same space. It will not be true if a model space object is dimensioned in paper space.

The rule is simple, but it requires some manipulation of variables to maintain consistency in dimension text size. As we proceed, we will also encounter some layering problems.

⊕   Check to be sure that you are in model space before beginning.

⊕   Make the "dim" layer current.

⊕   Make the large, central viewport active.

⊕   Select Linear from the Dimension menu.

⊕   Pick the top of the left side view for the first extension line origin.

⊕   Pick the bottom of the same side for the second extension line origin.

⊕   Pick a dimension line location about 0.25 to the left of the object. This may seem a little close, but it will help to illustrate an important point.

⊕   Press Enter to accept the dimension text (4.00).

Your screen should resemble Figure 8-30.

There are two things to notice: The dimension looks fine in the active viewport, but it is duplicated in the enlargement on the left at twice the size and may be cut off. This illustrates our two main problems: We want all our dimensions to appear the same size, and we do not want dimensions intended for one viewport to appear in others. The first problem is a scaling issue, whereas the second involves layering. We will pursue scaling first and layer control in the next section.

To get more of a flavor of what's going on, try one more dimension.

⊕   Make the upper viewport active.

⊕   Type "Dimrad" or select Radius from the Dimension menu.

Figure 8-30

⊕ Select the circle in the upper viewport.

⊕ Pick a dimension line location that allows you to see the dimension text clearly.

⊕ Look at the size of the dimension.

Obviously, it is way too big.

⊕ Undo (U) the radial dimension.

In fact, the dimension shown in the upper viewport was three times as big as the dimension in the central viewport and twice as big as the duplicate dimension in the left viewport. As you may have guessed, the dimensions in each viewport are being magnified just as the text was previously. The default dimension text size, set to 0.18 by the dimtxt variable, is being doubled (two times paper size) to 0.36 in the central viewport. So the text "4.00" has a height of 0.36 paper space units in that viewport. But in the left viewport it has a height of 0.72 units (four times paper space). The radial dimension in the upper viewport had a height of 1.08 units, or six times the dimtxt setting.

AutoCAD has a simple fix for this problem. When the variable dimscale is set to 0 instead of the default value of 1 or some other explicit scaling factor, dimension text in viewports is adjusted according to the model space to paper space zoom factor. With this setting, dimensions in all viewports can be maintained at the same desirable size.

For our purposes, let's say we are satisfied with the 0.36 size we see in the central viewport. To achieve this size in all viewports simultaneously, we will need to set dimscale to 0 and dimtxt to 0.36.

⊕ Type "dimtxt".

AutoCAD shows you the current value and asks for a new value.

⊕ Type ".36".

⊕ Type "dimscale".

⊕ Type "0".

Now let's try drawing the radial dimension in the upper viewport again.

⊕ Select Radius from the Dimension menu.

⊕ Select the circle in the upper viewport.

⊕ Position the dimension, as shown in Figure 8-30.

Wonderful, except that now we have a tiny duplicate of the radial dimension showing in the central viewport. This is another example of the layering problem, which we will explore next.

Manipulating Layer Visibility in Multiple Viewports

The duplicate dimensions in your drawing are just one example of the need to control layer visibility separately in different viewports. This can be done using the VPLAYER command.

✦ You should be in model space to begin.

Our goal will be to make dimensions intended for the central viewport invisible in other viewports and vice versa. To accomplish this, we need at least two dimension layers. If you wanted independent dimensions in all three viewports, you would need three layers.

✦ Make the upper viewport active.

✦ Select Layer... from the Format menu.

✦ Click on "New".

✦ Type "Dim-u" (for dimensions in the upper viewport).

✦ Click in the color column of the Dim-u layer to open the Set Color dialog.

✦ Give Dim-u color number 4, cyan.

This should be the same color as your regular DIM layer.

✦ Click on OK to return to the main dialog.

✦ Click on OK to exit the dialog box.

Now that we have two dimension layers, we can freeze dimensions in the viewports where they are not wanted. But first we must move some of the previously drawn dimensions to the newly created layer.

✦ Select Properties from the Modify menu.

✦ Select the radial dimension.

✦ Press Enter to end object selection.

✦ Click on "Layer".

✦ Select "Dim-u" for the new layer.

✦ Click on Okay to exit the dialog.

Now the 4.00 vertical dimension and the 0.31 radial dimension are on different layers, although they appear the same. We need to freeze DIM in the top and left viewports and freeze DIM-U in the central viewport.

✦ If necessary, double click the Tile button to set Tilemode to 1.

✦ Type "Vplayer".

AutoCAD prompts

            ?/Freeze/Thaw/Reset/Newfrz/Vpvisdflt:

"?" will give you a list of layers currently frozen in a selected viewport. "Freeze" and "Thaw" will allow you to freeze and thaw layers in selected viewports. "Reset" sets layers in selected viewports to default visibility settings. These defaults are established using the "Vpvisdflt" option. The "New frz" option provides an efficient sequence for controlling layers in multiple viewports. With "New frz" you create a new layer that is frozen in all viewports. Then you can thaw the new layer in selected viewports where visibility is desired.

For our purposes we only need the freeze option.

⊕ Type "f".

AutoCAD prompts

Layer (s) to Freeze <>:

⊕ Type "Dim".

AutoCAD prompts

All/Select/Current<>:

⊕ Type "s".

AutoCAD temporarily switches to paper space so that you can select view-port entities.

⊕ Pick any point on the border of the left viewport.

⊕ Pick any point on the border of the top viewport.

⊕ Press Enter to end object selection.

We also need to freeze DIM-U in the central viewport.

⊕ Type "f".

⊕ Type "dim-u".

⊕ Type "s".

⊕ Select any point on the border of the central viewport.

⊕ Press Enter to end object selection.

⊕ Press Enter to exit the VPLAYER command.

Your screen will be regenerated to resemble Figure 8-31.

Turning Viewport Borders Off

We have used the borders of our viewports as part of our plotted drawing in this drawing layout. Frequently, you will want to turn them off. In a typical three-view drawing, for example, you do not draw borders around the three views.

Figure 8-31

In multiple-viewport paper space drawings the visibility of viewport borders is easily controlled by putting the viewports on a separate layer and then turning the layer off before plotting. You can make a "border" layer, for example, and make it current while you create viewports. Or you can use CHPROP to place viewports on the border layer later.

8.12   Review Material

Questions

1. You are working in a drawing with units set to architectural, but when you begin dimensioning, AutoCAD provides four-place decimal units. What is the problem? What do you need to do so that your dimensioning units match your drawing units?
2. Describe at least one way to change the size of the arrowheads in the dimensions of a drawing.
3. What must you do before you can create either baseline or continued dimensions?
4. Describe an efficient method for moving dimension text away from the center of a dimensioned circle.
5. What is a "nearest" object snap, and why is it important when dimensioning with leaders?
6. Why is it usually necessary to move the origin of the coordinate system in order to make good use of ordinate dimensioning?
7. You have created a number of dimensions in a drawing and wish to change some of them to a new dimension style. Assuming you have already created the new dimension style, what command and what option will allow you to update some of your previously drawn dimensions? What item on the Dimension menu executes this command?
8. What is the difference between HATCH and BHATCH?
9. Why is it important to dimension in model space?
10. In what circumstances would it be necessary to use VPLAYER rather than just turning layers on and off?

Drawing Problems

1. Create a new dimension style called "Dim-2". Dim-2 will use architectural units with 1/2″ precision for all units except angles, which will use two-place decimals. Text in Dim-2 will be 0.5 units high.
2. Draw an isoceles triangle with vertexes at (4,3), (14,3), and (9,11). Draw a 2″ circle centered at the center of the triangle.
3. Dimension the base and one side of the triangle using the Dim-2 dimenson style.
4. Add a diameter dimension to the circle.
5. Add an angle dimension to one of the base angles of the triangle. Make sure that the dimension is placed outside of the triangle.
6. Hatch the area inside the triangle and outside the circle using the predefined crosshatch pattern.

8.13   Drawing 8-1: Tool Block

In this drawing the dimensions should work well without editing. The hatch is a simple user-defined pattern used to indicate that the front and right views are sectioned views.

DRAWING SUGGESTIONS

GRID = 1.0
SNAP = 0.125
HATCH line spacing = 0.125

- As a general rule, complete the drawing first, including all crosshatching, and then add dimensions and text at the end.

- Place all hatching on the hatch layer. When hatching is complete, set to the dim layer and turn the hatch layer off so that hatch lines will not interfere when you select lines for dimensioning.

- The section lines in this drawing can be easily drawn as leaders. Set the "dimasz" variable to 0.38 first. Check to see that ortho is on; then begin the leader at the tip of the arrow, and make a right angle as shown. After picking the other end point of the leader, press Enter to bring up the "Annotation (or press ENTER for options)" prompt. Then press Enter to call up options. Type "n" for None so that you will have no text.

- You will need to set the dimtix variable to "on" in order to place the 3.25 diameter dimension at the center of the circle in the top view, and "off" to create the leader style diameter dimension in the front section.

- Remember, multiple lines of text can be drawn with the LEADER command and will be centered on the Leader.

TOOL BLOCK

Drawing 8-1

8.14   Drawing 8-2: Flanged Wheel

Most of the objects in this drawing are straightforward. The keyway is easily done using the TRIM command. Use DIMTEDIT or grips to move the diameter dimension, as shown in the reference.

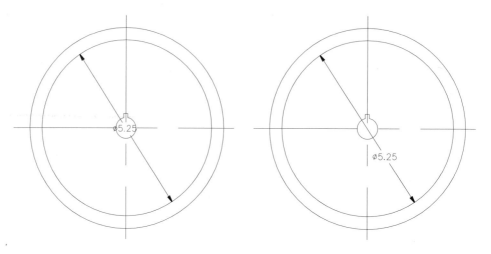

DRAWING SUGGESTIONS

GRID = 0.25
SNAP = 0.0625
HATCH line spacing = 0.50

- You will need a 0.0625 snap to draw the keyway. Draw a 0.125 × 0.125 square at the top of the 0.63 diameter circle. Drop the vertical lines down into the circle so they may be used to TRIM the circle. TRIM the circle and the vertical lines, using a window to select both as cutting edges.
- Remember to set to layer "hatch" before hatching, layer "text" before adding text, and layer "dim" before dimensioning.

FLANGED WHEEL

Drawing 8-2

8.15   Drawing 8-3: Shower Head

This drawing makes use of the procedures for hatching and dimensioning you learned in the last two drawings. In addition, it uses an angular dimension, baseline dimensions, leaders, and "%%c" for the diameter symbol.

DRAWING SUGGESTIONS

$$GRID = 0.50$$
$$SNAP = 0.125$$
$$HATCH \text{ line spacing} = 0.25$$

- You can save some time on this drawing by using MIRROR to create half of the right side view. Notice, however, that you cannot hatch before mirroring, because the mirror command will reverse the angle of the hatch lines.
- To achieve the angular dimension at the bottom of the right side view, you will need to draw the vertical line coming down on the right. Select this line and the angular line at the right end of the shower head, and the angular extension will be drawn automatically. Add the text "2 PL" using the DIMEDIT command.
- Notice that the diameter symbols in the vertical dimensions at each end of the right side view are not automatic. Use %%c to add the diameter symbol to the text.

SHOWER HEAD

Drawing 8-3

8.16   Drawing 8-4: Nose Adaptor

Make ample use of ZOOM to work on the details of this drawing. Notice that the limits are set larger than usual, and the snap is rather fine by comparison.

DRAWING SUGGESTIONS

> LIMITS = (0,0) (36,24)
> GRID = 0.50
> SNAP = 0.125
> HATCH line spacing = 0.25

- You will need a 0.125 snap to draw the thread representation shown in the reference. Understand that this is nothing more than a standard representation for screw threads; it does not show actual dimensions. Zoom in close to draw it, and you should have no trouble.

- This drawing includes two examples of "simplified drafting" practice. The thread representation is one, and the other is the way in which the counterbores are drawn in the front view. A precise rendering of these holes would show an ellipse, since the slant of the object dictates that they break through on an angle. However, to show these ellipses in the front view would make the drawing more confusing and less useful. Simplified representation is preferable in such cases.

NOSE ADAPTOR
Drawing 8-4

8.17   Drawing 8-5: Plot Plan

This architectural drawing makes use of three hatch patterns and several dimension variable changes. Be sure to make these settings as shown. Notice that we have simplified the format of the drawing page for this drawing. This is because the drawings are becoming more involved and because you should need less information to complete them at this point. We will continue to show drawings this way for the remainder of the book.

DRAWING SUGGESTIONS

GRID = 10′

SNAP = 1′

LIMITS = 180′,120′

LTSCALE = 2′

- The "trees" shown here are symbols for oaks, willows, and evergreens.
- BHATCH will open a space around text inside a defined boundary; however, sometimes you will want more white space than BHATCH leaves. The simple solution is to draw a box around the text area as an inner boundary. If the BHATCH style is set to "Normal" it will stop hatching at the inner boundary. Later you can erase the box, leaving an island of white space around the text.

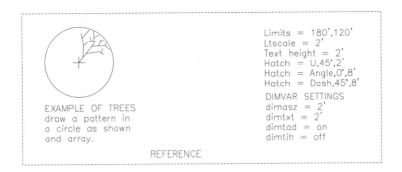

EXAMPLE OF TREES
draw a pattern in
a circle as shown
and array.

Limits = 180',120'
Ltscale = 2'
Text height = 2'
Hatch = U,45',2'
Hatch = Angle,0°,8'
Hatch = Dash,45°,8'
DIMVAR SETTINGS
dimasz = 2'
dimtxt = 2'
dimtad = on
dimtih = off

REFERENCE

PLOT PLAN

Drawing 8-5

8.18   Drawing 8-6: Panel

This drawing is primarily an exercise in using ordinate dimensions. Both the drawing of the objects and the adding of dimensions will be facilitated dramatically by this powerful feature.

DRAWING SUGGESTIONS

GRID = 0.50
SNAP = 0.125
UNITS = three-place decimal

- After setting grid, snap, and units, create a new user coordinate system with the origin moved in and up about one unit each way. This technique was introduced in Task 8.6. For reference, here is the procedure:
  1. Type or select "UCS".
  2. Type "o" for "Origin".
  3. Pick a new origin point.

- From here on all of the objects in the drawing can be easily placed using the *x* and *y* displacements exactly as they are shown in the drawing.

- When objects have been placed, switch to the dim layer and begin dimensioning using the ordinate dimension feature. You should be able to move along quickly, but be careful to keep dimensions on each side of the panel lined up. That is, the leader end points should end along the same vertical or horizontal line.

PANEL
DRAWING 8-6

8.19   Drawing 8-7:Angle Support

In this drawing you are expected to use the 3D view to create three orthographic views. Draw a Front View, Top View, and Side View. The Front and Top Views will be drawn showing all necessary hidden lines, and the Right Side View will be drawn in full section. The finished multiview drawing should be fully dimensioned.

Top View

Front View   Right Side View

DRAWING SUGGESTIONS

- Start this drawing by laying out the top view. Use the top view to line up the front view and side view.
- Use the illustration of the Right Side View when planning out the full section. Convert the hidden lines to solid lines, and use BHATCH to create crosshatching.
- Complete the Right Side View in full section using the ANSI31 hatch pattern.
- Be sure to include all the necessary hidden lines and center lines in each view.

Right Side View

ANGLE SUPPORT
Drawing 8-7

9

Polylines

COMMANDS

<u>TOOLS</u>	<u>DRAW</u>		<u>FORMAT</u>	<u>MODIFY</u>
FILL	DONUT	POLYGON	MLSTYLE	MLEDIT
	MLINE	SKETCH		PEDIT
	PLINE	SOLID		OFFSET
	POINT			

OVERVIEW

This chapter should be fun. As you can see by the preceding list, you will be learning a large number of new commands. You will see new things happening on your screen with each command. The commands in this chapter are used to create special entities, some of which cannot be drawn any other way. All of them are complex objects made up of lines, circles, and arcs (like the text, dimensions, and hatch patterns discussed in the previous chapter), but they are stored and treated as singular entities. Some of them, such as polygons and donuts, are familiar geometric figures, while others, like polylines, are peculiar to CAD.

TASKS

9.1 Drawing POLYGONs

GENERAL PROCEDURE

1. Type "Pol", select the Polygon tool from the Draw toolbar, or select Polygon from the Draw menu.
2. Type the number of sides.
3. Pick a center point.
4. Indicate "Inscribed" or "Circumscribed".
5. Show the radius of the circle.

Among the most interesting and flexible of the entities you can create in Auto-CAD is the polyline. In this chapter we will begin with two regularly shaped polyline entities, polygons and donuts. These entities have their own special commands, separate from the general PLINE command (Tasks 9.4 and 9.5), but are created as polylines and can be edited just as any other polyline would be.

Polygons with any number of sides can be drawn using the POLYGON command. (Rectangles can be drawn by showing two corners using the RECTANG command, which draws polyline rectangles.) In the default sequence, AutoCAD will construct a polygon based on the number of sides, the center point, and a radius. Optionally, the "edge" method allows you to specify the number of sides and the length and position of one side (see Figure 9-1).

⊕ Type "pol", select Polygon from the Draw menu, or select the Polygon tool from the Draw toolbar, as shown in Figure 9-2.

AutoCAD's first prompt will be for the number of sides:

Number of sides <4>:

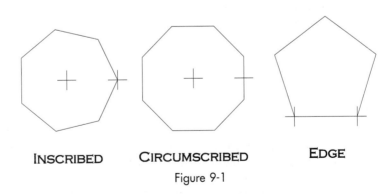

INSCRIBED   CIRCUMSCRIBED   EDGE

Figure 9-1

Figure 9-2

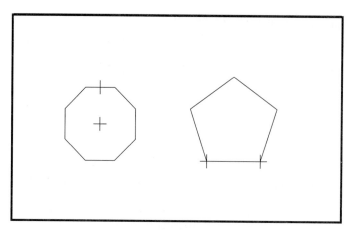

Figure 9-3

⊕ Type "8".

Now you are prompted to show either a center point or the first point of one edge:

Edge/<Center of polygon>:

⊕ Pick a center point, as shown by the blip on the left in Figure 9-3.

From here the size of the polygon can be specified in one of two ways, as shown in Figure 9-1. The radius of a circle will be given and the polygon drawn either inside or outside the imaginary circle. Notice that in the case of the "inscribed" polygon, the radius is measured from the center to a vertex, while in the "circumscribed" polygon it is measured from the center to the midpoint of a side. You can tell AutoCAD which you want by typing "i" or "c" or selecting from the screen.

Inscribed in circle/Circumscribed about circle (I/C) <I>:

The default is currently "inscribed". We will use the "circumscribed" method instead.

⊕ Type "c".

Now you will be prompted to show a radius of this imaginary circle (that is, a line from the center to a midpoint of a side).

Radius of circle:

⊕ Show a radius similar to the one in Figure 9-3.

We leave it to you to try out the "inscribed" option. We will draw one more polygon, using the "edge" method.

⊕ Press Enter to repeat the POLYGON command.

⊕ Type "5" for the number of sides.

⊕ Type "e".

AutoCAD will issue a different series of prompts:

First endpoint of edge:

⊕ Pick a point, as shown on the right in Figure 9-3.

AutoCAD prompts

Second endpoint of edge:

⊕ Pick a second point as shown.

Your screen should resemble Figure 9-3.

9.2 Drawing DONUTs

GENERAL PROCEDURE

1. Type "do" or select Donut from the Draw menu.
2. Type or show an inside diameter.
3. Type or show an outside diameter.
4. Pick a center point.
5. Pick another center point.
6. Press Enter to exit the command.

The DONUT command is logical and easy to use. You show inside and outside diameters and then draw as many donut-shaped objects of the specified size as you like.

⊕ Clear your display of polygons before continuing.

⊕ Type "do" or select Donut from the Draw menu.

AutoCAD prompts

Inside diameter <0.50>:

We will change the inside diameter to 1.00.

⊕ Type "1".

AutoCAD prompts

Outside diameter <1.00>:

We will change the outside diameter to 2.00.

⊕ Type "2".

AutoCAD gives you a donut to drag into place and prompts

Center of doughnut:

⊕ Pick any point.

A donut will be drawn around the point you chose, as shown by the "fat" donuts in Figure 9-4. (If your donut is not filled, see Task 9.3.)

AutoCAD stays in the DONUT command, allowing you to continue drawing donuts.

⊕ Pick a second center point.

⊕ Pick a third center point.

You should now have three "fat" donuts on your screen as shown.

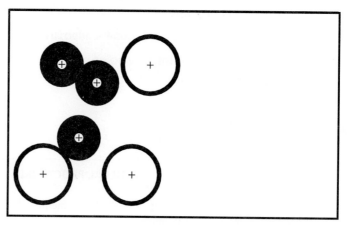

Figure 9-4

⊕ Press Enter to exit the DONUT command.

Now reenter the donut command, change the inside diameter to 3.00 and the outer diameter to 3.25, and draw three or four "thin" donuts, as shown in Figure 9-4. When you are done, leave the donuts on the screen so that you can see how they are affected by the FILL command.

9.3 Using the FILL command

GENERAL PROCEDURE

1. Type "Fill".
2. Type "on" or "off".
3. Type or select "regen".

Donuts, wide polylines (Tasks 9.4 and 9.5), and 2D solids (Task 9.8) are all affected by FILL. With FILL on, these entities are displayed and plotted as solid filled objects. With FILL off, only the outer boundaries are displayed (donuts are shown with radial lines between the inner and outer circles). Since filled objects are slower to regenerate than outlined ones, you may want to set FILL off as you are working on a drawing and turn it on when you are ready to print or plot.

⊕ For this exercise you should have at least one donut on your screen from Task 9.2.

⊕ Type "fill".

AutoCAD prompts

ON/OFF <ON>:

⊕ Type "off".

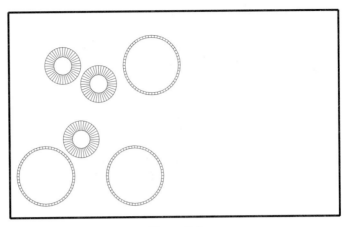

Figure 9-5

You will not see any immediate change in your display when you do this. To see the effect, you will have to regenerate your drawing.

⊕ **Type "re" or select Regen from the View menu.**

Your screen will be regenerated with FILL off and will resemble Figure 9-5. Many of the special entities that we will be discussing in the remainder of this chapter can be filled, so we encourage you to continue to experiment with FILL as you go along.

Note: You can also turn FILL on and off by clicking in the Solid Fill check box in the Drawing Aids dialog box.

9.4 Drawing Straight Polyline Segments

GENERAL PROCEDURE

1. Type "pl" , select Polyline from the Draw menu, or select the Polyline tool from the Draw toolbar.
2. Pick a start point.
3. Type or select width, halfwidth, or other options.
4. Pick other points.

In AutoCAD there are several ways in which collections of entities can be treated as one unit. In the last two chapters you saw how text, dimensions, and hatch patterns are all created as complex entities that can be selected and treated as single objects. In the next chapter you will see how to create groups and blocks from separate entities. In this chapter you will see another kind of conglomerate entity, the polyline. You have already drawn several polylines without going through the PLINE command. Donuts and polygons both are drawn as polylines and therefore can be edited using the same edit commands that work on other polylines. You can, for instance, fillet all the corners of a polygon at once. Using the PLINE command itself, you can draw anything from a simple line to a series of lines and arcs with varying widths. Most important, polylines can be edited using many of the ordinary edit commands as well as a set of specialized editing procedures found in the PEDIT command.

We will begin by creating a simple polyline rectangle. The process will be much like drawing a rectangular outline with the LINE command, but the result will be a single object rather than four distinct line segments.

⊕ Clear your display of donuts before continuing.

⊕ Type "pl", select Polyline from the Draw menu, or select the Polyline tool from the Draw toolbar, as shown in Figure 9-6.

AutoCAD begins with a prompt for a starting point:

From point:

⊕ Pick a start point, such as P1 in Figure 9-7.

From here the PLINE prompt sequence becomes more complicated:

```
Current line width is 0.00
Arc/Close/Halfwidth/Length/Undo/Width/<Endpoint of line>:
```

The prompt begins by giving you the current line width, left from any previous use of the PLINE command.

Then the prompt offers options in the usual format. "Arc" will lead you into to another set of options that deal with drawing polyline arcs. We will save polyline arcs for Task 9.5. "Close" works as in the LINE command to con-

Figure 9-6

Figure 9-7

nect the last end point in a sequence to the original starting point. We will get to the other options momentarily.

This time around we will draw a series of 0 width segments, just as we would in the LINE command.

⊕ Pick an end point, such as P2 in Figure 9-7.

AutoCAD will draw the segment and repeat the prompt.

⊕ Pick another end point, P3 in Figure 9-7.

⊕ Pick another end point, P4 in Figure 9-7.

⊕ Type "c" for "Close" to complete the rectangle, as shown in Figure 9-7.

⊕ Now select the rectangle by pointing to any of its sides.

You will see that the entire rectangle is selected, rather than just the side you pointed to. This means, for example, that you can FILLET or CHAMFER all four corners of the rectangle at once. Try it if you like, using the following procedure:

1. Type "Fillet" or select Fillet from the Modify menu.
2. Type "r".
3. Specify a radius.
4. Repeat the FILLET command.
5. Type "p" or select "Polyline" to indicate that you want to fillet an entire polyline.
6. Select the rectangle.

Note: If a corner is left without a fillet, it is probably because you did not use the close option when you completed the rectangle.

Now let's create a rectangle with wider lines.

⊕ Enter the PLINE command.

⊕ Pick a starting point, as shown by P1 in Figure 9-8.

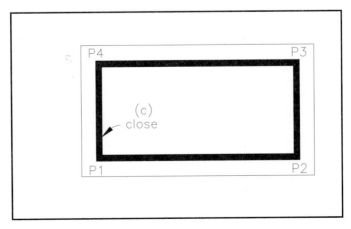

Figure 9-8

AutoCAD prompts

```
Arc/Close/Halfwidth/Length/Undo/Width/<Endpoint of line>:
```

This time we need to make use of the "Width" option.

⊕ Type "w".

AutoCAD will respond with

```
Starting width <0.00>:
```

You will be prompted for two widths, a starting width and an ending width. This makes it possible to draw tapered lines. For this exercise, our lines will have the same starting and ending width.

Note: The "halfwidth" option differs from "width" only in that the width of the line to be drawn is measured from the center out. With either option you can specify by showing rather than typing a value.

⊕ Type ".25".

AutoCAD prompts

```
Ending width <0.25>
```

Notice that the starting width has become the default for the ending width. To draw a polyline of uniform width, we accept this default.

⊕ Press Enter to keep the starting width and ending width the same.

AutoCAD now returns to the previous prompt:

```
Arc/Close/Halfwidth/Length/Undo/Width/<Endpoint of line>:
```

⊕ Pick an end point, as shown by P2 in Figure 9-8.

⊕ Continue picking points to draw a second rectangle, as shown in Figure 9-8.

Be sure to use the close option to draw the last side; otherwise, the last two sides will overlap rather than join.

The only options we have not discussed in this exercise are "Length" and "Undo". "Length" allows you to type or show a value and then draws a segment of that length starting from the end point of the previous segment and continuing in the same direction (if the last segment was an arc, the length will be drawn tangent to the arc). "Undo" undoes the last segment, just as in LINE.

In the next task we will draw some pline arc segments.

9.5 Drawing Polyline Arc Segments

GENERAL PROCEDURE

1. Enter the PLINE command.
2. Pick a start point.
3. Specify a width.
4. Type "a" or select "arc".
5. Type or select options or pick an end point.

A word of caution: Because of the flexibility and power of the PLINE command, it is tempting to think of polylines as always having weird shapes, tapered lines, and strange sequences of lines and arcs. Most books perpetuate this by consistently giving peculiar examples to show the range of what is possible with polylines. This is useful but misleading. Remember, polylines are practical entities even for relatively simple applications such as the rectangles drawn in Task 9.4.

Having said that, we will proceed to add our own bit of strangeness to the lore of the polyline. We will draw a polyline with three arc segments and one tapered straight line segment, as shown in Figure 9-9. We call this thing a "goosenecked funnel." You may have seen something like it at your local garage.

⊕ Type "pl", select Polyline from the Draw menu, or select the Polyline tool from the Draw toolbar.

⊕ Pick a new start point, as shown by P1 in Figure 9-9.

⊕ Type "w" or select "width" to set new widths.

⊕ Type "0" for the starting width.

⊕ Type ".5" for the ending width.

⊕ Type "a".

This will bring up the arc prompt, which looks like this:

```
Angle/CEnter/CLose/Direction/Halfwidth/Line/Radius/Second
pt/Undo/Width/<Endpoint of arc>:
```

Let's look at this prompt for a moment. To begin with, there are four options that are familiar from the previous prompt. "CLose", "Halfwidth", "Undo", and "Width" all function exactly as they would in drawing straight polyline segments. The "Line" option returns you to the previous prompt so that you can continue drawing straight line segments after drawing arc segments.

The other options, "Angle", "CEnter", "Direction", "Radius", "Second pt", and "Endpoint of arc", allow you to specify arcs in ways similar to the ARC command. One difference is that AutoCAD assumes that the arc you want will be tangent to the last polyline segment entered. This is often not the

Figure 9-9

case. The "center" and "direction" options let you override this assumption where necessary, or you can begin with a short line segment to establish direction before entering the arc prompt.

⊕ Pick an end point to the right, as shown by P2 in Figure 9-9, to complete the first arc segment.

Tip: If you did not follow the order shown in the figures and drew your previous rectangle clockwise, or if you have drawn other polylines in the meantime, you will find that the arc does not curve downward, as shown in Figure 9-9. Fix this by using the Direction option. Type "d" and then point straight down. Now you can pick an end point to the right as shown.

AutoCAD prompts again:

```
Angle/CEnter/CLose/Direction/Halfwidth/Line/Radius/Second
pt/Undo/Width/<Endpoint of arc>:
```

For the remaining two arc segments, retain a uniform width of 0.50.

⊕ Enter points P3 and P4 to draw the remaining two arc segments as shown.

Now we will draw two straight line segments to complete the polyline.

⊕ Type "L" (this takes you back to the original prompt).
⊕ Pick P5 straight up about 1.00 as shown.
⊕ Type "w" or select "width".
⊕ Press Enter to retain 0.50 as the starting width.
⊕ Type "3" for the ending width.
⊕ Pick an end point up about 2.00 as shown.

Your screen should resemble Figure 9-9.

9.6 Editing Polylines with PEDIT

GENERAL PROCEDURE

1. Type "Pe" or open the Modify menu, highlight Object, and then select Polyline.
2. Select a polyline.
3. Type or select a PEDIT option.
4. Follow the prompts.

The PEDIT command provides a subsystem of special editing capabilities that work only on polylines. We will not attempt to have you use all of them; some you may never need. Most important is that you be aware of the possibilities so that when you find yourself in a situation calling for a PEDIT procedure you will know what to look for. After executing the following task, study Figure 9-12, the PEDIT chart. For further information see the *AutoCAD User's Guide*.

We will perform two edits on the polylines already drawn.

⊕ Type "Pe" or select Object and then Polyline from the Modify menu.
You will be prompted to select a polyline:

<code>Select polyline:</code>

⊕ Select the outer 0-width polyline rectangle drawn in Task 9.4.
Notice that PEDIT works on only one object at a time and that selected poly-lines do not become dotted. You are prompted as follows:

<code>Open/Join/Width/Edit vertex/Fit/Spline/Decurve/Ltype
gen/Undo/eXit/ <X>:</code>

"Open" will be replaced by "Close" if your polyline has not been closed. "Undo" and "eXit" are self-explanatory. Other options are illustrated in Figure 9-12. "Edit vertex" brings up the subset of options shown on the right side of the chart. When you do vertex editing, AutoCAD will mark one vertex at a time with an x. You can move the x to other vertices by pressing Enter, typing "n", or selecting "Next".

Now we will edit the selected polyline by changing its width.

⊕ Type "w" for the Width option.
This option allows you to set a new uniform width for an entire polyline. All tapering and variation is removed when this edit is performed.

AutoCAD prompts

<code>Enter new width for all segments:</code>

⊕ Type ".25".
Your screen will be redrawn to resemble Figure 9-10.

You should be at the "Close/Join/Width/Edit vertex..." prompt before continuing. The last polyline is still selected so that you can continue shaping it with other PEDIT options.

⊕ Press Enter to exit PEDIT.

Figure 9-10

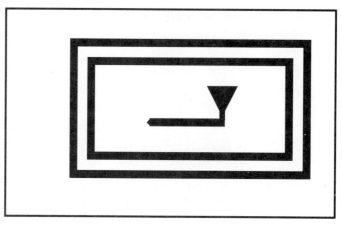

Figure 9-11

⊕ Press Enter to repeat PEDIT.

This exiting and reentering is necessary in order to select another poly-line to edit.

⊕ Select the "gooseneck funnel" polyline.

This time we'll try out the "Decurve" option. Decurve straightens all curves within the selected polyline.

⊕ Type "d" or select "Decurve".

Your screen will resemble Figure 9-11.

To complete this exercise, we suggest that you try some of the other editing op-tions. In particular, you will get interesting results from "Fit" and "Spline". Be sure to study the PEDIT chart (Figure 9-12) before going on to the next task.

9.7 Creating Parallel Objects with OFFSET

GENERAL PROCEDURE

1. Type "Offset," select Offset from the Modify menu, or select the Offset tool from the Modify toolbar.
2. Type or show an offset distance.
3. Select object to offset.
4. Show which side to offset.

Offset creates parallel copies of lines, circles, arcs, or polylines. You will find a number of typical applications in the drawings at the end of this chapter. In this brief exercise we will perform an offset operation to add a third border, as shown in Figure 9-13.

⊕ Type "Offset", select Offset from the Modify menu, or select the Off-set tool from the Modify toolbar, as shown in Figure 9-14.

PEDIT				
(EDITING POLYLINES)				

ENTIRE POLYLINE		VERTEX EDITING	
BEFORE	AFTER	BEFORE	AFTER
CLOSE		BREAK	
CREATES CLOSING SEGMENT		REMOVES SECTIONS BETWEEN TWO SPECIFIED VERTICES	
OPEN		INSERT	
REMOVES CLOSING SEGMENT		NEW VERTEX IS ADDED AFTER THE CURRENTLY MARKED VERTEX	
JOIN		MOVE	
TWO OBJECTS WILL BE JOINED MAKING ONE POLYLINE. OBJECTS MUST BE EXACT MATCH. POLYLINE MUST BE OPEN		MOVES THE CURRENTLY MARKED VERTEX TO A NEW LOCATION	
WIDTH		STRAIGHTEN	
CHANGES THE ENTIRE WIDTH UNIFORMLY		STRAIGHTENS THE SEGMENT FOLLOWING THE CURRENTLY MARKED VERTEX	
FIT		TANGENT	
COMPUTES A SMOOTH CURVE		MARKS THE TANGENT DIRECTION OF THE CURRENTLY MARKED VERTEX FOR LATER USE IN FITTING CURVES	
SPLINE		WIDTH	
COMPUTES A CUBIC B-SPLINE CURVE		CHANGES THE STARTING AND ENDING WIDTHS OF THE INDIVIDUAL SEGMENTS FOLLOWING THE CURRENTLY MARKED VERTEX	
LTYPE GEN			
SET TO ON GENERATES LTYPE IN CONTINUOUS PATTERN	SET TO OFF GENERATES LTYLE TO START AND END DASHED AT VERTEX		

Figure 9-12

Figure 9-13

Figure 9-14

AutoCAD prompts

Offset distance or Through <Through>:

There are two methods. You can type or show a distance, or you can show a point that you want the new copy to run through. We will use the distance method. Then if you like you can undo the command and try it again using the "through point" system.

⊕ Type ".75".

AutoCAD prompts for an object:

Select object to offset:

⊕ Point to the outer rectangle.

AutoCAD now needs to know whether to create the offset image to the inside or outside of the rectangle:

Side to offset:

⊕ Pick a point anywhere outside the rectangle.

Your screen should now resemble Figure 9-14. AutoCAD continues to prompt for objects to offset, so you will need to press Enter when you are done.

⊕ Press Enter to exit the OFFSET command.

To create the same border using the through point method, follow this procedure:

1. Enter the OFFSET command.
2. Type "t".
3. Select the rectangle.
4. Pick a "through point" 0.75 out from any of the sides of the rectangle.

9.8 Drawing SOLIDs

GENERAL PROCEDURE

1. Type "So" or open the Draw toolbar, highlight surfaces, and select 2D Solid.
2. Pick a first point.
3. Pick a second point.
4. Pick a third point.
5. Pick a fourth point or press Enter to draw a triangular section.
6. Pick another third point or press Enter to exit the command.

SOLID allows you to draw rectangular and triangular solid-filled shapes in two dimensions by specifying points that become corners or vertices. There is no rela-

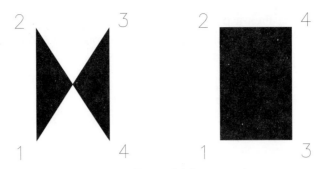

Figure 9-15

tion between the 2D solid command and 3D solid modeling, which is the subject of Chapter 14.

There is a trick to using SOLID for rectangular sections involving the order in which you enter points. If you enter them in the wrong order, you will get the bow tie effect shown in Figure 9-15. It is natural to enter points in a rectangle by moving around the perimeter. However, AutoCAD solids are drawn with edges between point 1 and point 3 and between point 2 and point 4, so you need to be careful about the order in which you pick points.

⊕ To begin this task, clear the screen of polylines left over from Task 9.7.

⊕ FILL and ORTHO should be on for this exercise. We will begin with a rectangular solid.

⊕ Type "So".

There is also a Solid tool on the Surfaces toolbar.

AutoCAD will prompt for a series of points, beginning with

First point:

⊕ Pick a point similar to P1 in Figure 9-16.

AutoCAD prompts

Second point:

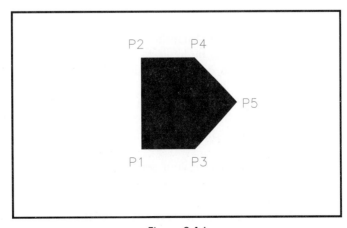

Figure 9-16

⊕ Pick a point similar to P2.

These first two points will become the end points of one side of a rectangular solid. AutoCAD prompts

Third point:

⊕ Pick a point similar to P3.

Remember that an edge will be drawn between point 1 and point 3. AutoCAD prompts

Fourth point:

⊕ Pick a point similar to P4 in Figure 9-16.

When the fourth point is entered, AutoCAD will draw a solid rectangle and continue to prompt for points.

Third point:

If you continue entering points, the previous points 3 and 4 will become points 1 and 2 of the new section. You can draw a triangular section by picking a third point and then pressing Enter in response to the prompt for a fourth point. This also means that you will need to press Enter twice when you want to exit SOLID. We will draw a triangular solid before exiting.

⊕ Turn ortho off and pick a point similar to P5 in Figure 9-16.
⊕ Press Enter in response to the "Fourth point:" prompt.

Your screen should resemble Figure 9-16.

⊕ Press Enter again to exit the command.

9.9 Making and Viewing Slides

GENERAL PROCEDURE

1. Type "Mslide" or "Vslide".
2. Type or select the name of a .sld file.

Slides are simply "snapshots" of AutoCAD displays that are saved in a reduced format so they can be loaded quickly. They cannot be plotted or edited, but they are often used in developing business presentations that can be shown on a computer screen.

Slides are easily created using MSLIDE. Once created they can be displayed using the VSLIDE command. Since slides resemble drawings, it is important to understand the primary difference: Slides cannot be edited, added to, or changed in any way.

To create a slide of your present display, follow this procedure:

⊕ Type "Mslide".

MSLIDE stands for "make slide." It creates a slide from your current screen display. When the command is entered, you will see a Create Slide File dialog box. This is a standard file list box, listing files that have a .sld extension. When the box opens, the cursor will be blinking in the File: edit box so that you can type in a name for the slide you want to create.

⊕ Type a name for the file, like "9-1" or "solid."

⊕ Press Enter or Click on "OK".

It's that simple. Your display will be saved as a file with a .sld extension. To see that it is really there, you must first alter your screen in some way and then load the file using VSLIDE.

⊕ Erase the solid from your screen.

⊕ Type "Vslide".

You will see another standard file list dialog box. This one will be titled "Select Slide File".

⊕ Type or select the name of the file you just created with MSLIDE.

⊕ Press Enter or click on "OK".

Your slide will appear.

⊕ Try to select the solid or any other objects that appear in your slide.

You will find that you cannot. It is possible to draw new objects while a slide is showing on your screen. These are not part of the slide but are part of your current drawing. If you REDRAW the screen, the newly drawn objects will remain and the slide will disappear.

⊕ To clear the slide from your screen, type "r" or select "Redraw" from the View menu.

Most slide applications use a series of slides, exactly as you would in a photographic slide show. This process can be automated and timed using a special kind of file called a script file. There are a number of commands used in the making of a script file, including SCRIPT, DELAY, RESUME, and RSCRIPT, in addition to MSLIDE and VSLIDE. See the *AutoCAD User's Guide* for further information if your goals include the use of slide presentations.

9.10 Drawing and Editing Multilines

GENERAL PROCEDURE

1. Type "ml," select Multiline from the Draw menu, or select the Multiline tool from the Draw toolbar.
2. Pick a from point.
3. Pick a to point.
4. Pick another to point, or press Enter to exit the command.

Multilines are groups of parallel lines with various forms of intersections and end caps. Each individual line is called an element, and you can have up to 16 elements in a single multiline style. Drawing multilines is about as simple as drawing lines. The complexity comes in defining multiline styles and in editing intersections.

Figure 9-17

In this task we will draw standard multilines, create a new style, and edit the intersection of two multilines.

⊕ To begin this exercise, clear the screen of solids or other objects left from previous exercises.

First, we will draw some standard multilines.

⊕ Type "ml", select Multiline from the Draw menu, or select the Multiline tool from the Draw toolbar, as shown in Figure 9-17.

AutoCAD will issue the following prompt:

Justification/Scale/Style/<From point>:

If you stick with the default option, you will see that the MLINE sequence is exactly like drawing a line. "Justification" refers to the way elements are positioned in relation to the points you pick on the screen. The default justification is "Top". This means that the top element of the multiline will be positioned at the cross hairs when you pick points. Try it, and we will discuss the other options later.

⊕ Pick a "from point" similar to P1 in Figure 9-18.

AutoCAD gives you a standard, two-element multiline to drag and prompts for another point:

To Point:

Move the cursor and notice how the cross hairs continue to connect with the top element. The other two options for justification are "Zero" and "Bottom". Zero lines up in the middle of the elements, at the zero point or ori-

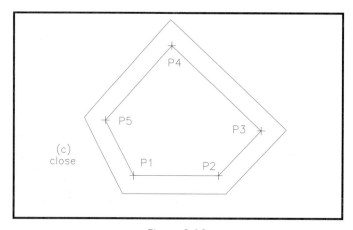

Figure 9-18

gin. You will understand this better after we create a new style. Bottom lines up on the bottom element.

⊕ Pick a "to point" similar to P2 in Figure 9-18.

Exact lengths and angles are not important. Move the cursor around and notice how AutoCAD adjusts the corner to maintain parallel line elements.

AutoCAD has added an undo option now that you have one multiline segment complete.

Undo/<To point>:

⊕ Pick P3, as in Figure 9-18.

Once you have two complete multiline segments, AutoCAD adds a close option:

Close/Undo/<To point>:

⊕ Pick P4, as in Figure 9-18.
⊕ Pick P5, as in Figure 9-18.
⊕ Type "c" to close and complete the figure.

Creating Multiline Styles

The real power of multilines comes when you learn to create your own multiline style. This is done through the Multiline Styles dialog box, called by the ML-STYLE command.

⊕ Type "mlstyle" or select "Multiline Style..." from the Format menu.

This will call the dialog box shown in Figure 9-19. Standard is the name of the current multiline style, which, as we have seen, includes two continuous line elements. A word of caution here: The Multiline Styles dialog box is not as user friendly as some. It will not respond well if you do not do things in the prescribed order. In particular, you must first establish element and multiline

Figure 9-19

properties, then give the style a name, save it, and add it to the list of available styles. Any variation in this order will cause problems.

We will begin by adding a new style to the list of multiline styles and then adding a third element to the new style.

⊕ Double click in the Name edit box.

Standard should be highlighted.

⊕ Type "new".

⊕ Click on "add" to add New to the style list.

New should now be showing in the Current style box.

⊕ Select "Element Properties…".

This calls the Element Properties dialog box shown in Figure 9-20. First look at the elements box. It shows that there are now only two elements, one is offset 0.5 above the origin point of the multiline (0.0) and the other is offset −0.5, or 0.5 below the origin. Standard multilines have a zero point between the two lines, but since the default justification is top, the cross hairs line up on the top element. With zero justification they would line up at 0.0. With Bottom justification they would line up on the −0.5 element.

⊕ Click on "Add".

This is how we begin to add a new element. As soon as you click "Add", a third element is added to the box. Notice that it is offset 0.0. In other words, it is right on the zero line between the two offset lines. For this style we will leave it there. If we needed to offset it, we would type a new offset number in the offset box.

Next, notice that all three elements are listed as having BYLAYER color and linetype. This means that the color and linetype will be determined by whatever layer the multiline is drawn on. We will change the linetype of our newly added middle element. This element should be highlighted in blue. If it is not, click on it to highlight it before proceeding.

⊕ Click on "Linetype…".

This calls the "Select Linetype" dialog box shown in Figure 9-21. This box contains all the loaded linetypes in your drawing. From past exercises, you should at least have the hidden and center linetypes loaded, so we will use one of these. (If for any reason your template drawing does not have the

Figure 9-20

Figure 9-21

HIDDEN linetype or if you want to use a linetype that is not loaded, select "Load…" from this dialog box and load them now.)

⊕ Run down the list until you see "HIDDEN".

⊕ Select "HIDDEN".

⊕ Click on "OK".

Notice that the element at 0.0 now has the HIDDEN linetype style.

⊕ Click on "OK" again.

When you return to the Multiline Styles dialog box, you should see that the middle element has been added to the image box but is shown as a continuous line. The image box shows elements by position but does not show color or linetype.

Now let's look at the Multiline Properties dialog box.

⊕ Click on "Multiline Properties…".

This calls up the dialog box shown in Figure 9-22. This box controls the way joints and ends of multilines are treated. The variety of options is shown in

Figure 9-22

Figure 9-23

Figure 9-23. For our purposes it will not be necessary to add joints or end caps at this point.

⊕ Click on "OK" or "Cancel" to exit the Multiline Properties box.

⊕ Click on "Save" to save the new style.

This will call a Save Multiline Style dialog box.

⊕ Click on "Save" to save the new style in the "ACAD" file.

Once your style has been named, defined, and saved and is the current style, you are ready to leave the box and draw some new multilines.

⊕ Click on "OK" to exit the dialog box.

⊕ Type "ml"or select the Multiline tool from the Draw toolbar.

⊕ Pick two points to draw the horizontal multiline shown in Figure 9-24.

⊕ Press Enter to exit the MLINE command.

⊕ Repeat MLINE and pick two more points to draw the vertical multiline shown in Figure 9-24.

Editing Multiline Intersections

Multilines can be modified using many of the same edit commands that are used with other entities. In addition, there is a special MLEDIT command for editing the

Figure 9-24

Figure 9-25

intersection of two multilines. The possibilities will be easy to see since the dialog box illustrates the options using a figure similar to the one you have just drawn.

⊕ Type "mledit" or select Object and then Multiline from Modify menu.
This calls the Multiline Edit Tools dialog box shown in Figure 9-25. When you select any of the 12 images in the box, the name of that type of edit will be shown at the lower left corner of the box. Since the figure on your screen is similar to the one used in these image boxes, what you see is pretty much what you will get when you perform any of these edits.

⊕ Click on the top left image box.
As you see, this choice is called a Closed Cross.

⊕ Click on "OK".
Now select the two multilines to edit.

⊕ Pick the vertical multiline.
The order in which you pick is clearly significant with this and many other of the multiline edits. In this case the second multiline selected does not change and will appear to "cross over" the first.

⊕ Pick the horizontal multiline.
Your screen should resemble Figure 9-26.

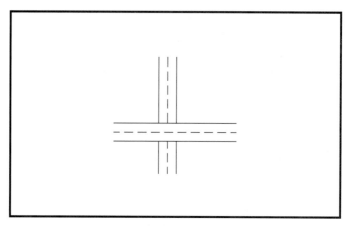

Figure 9-26

With up to 16 elements, 256 colors, 58 standard linetypes, plus the different end-cap forms and the various types of intersection edits, the possibilities for creating multiline styles are substantial. We encourage you to experiment before going on.

9.11 Drawing POINTs (Optional)

GENERAL PROCEDURE

1. Type "Point" or select the Point tool from the Draw toolbar.
2. Pick a point.

On the surface this is the simplest DRAW command in AutoCAD. However, if you look at Figure 9-27, you will see figures that were drawn with the POINT command that do not look like ordinary points. This capability adds a bit of power and complexity to the otherwise simple POINT command.

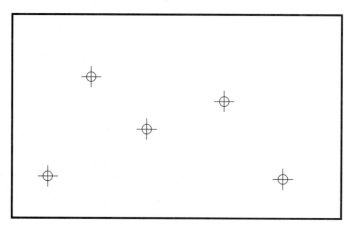

Figure 9-27

⊕ Erase objects from previous exercises.

⊕ Turn off the grid (F7).

⊕ Type "Po".

There is a Point tool on the Draw toolbar, but you may have to move the toolbar to a floating position to access it.

⊕ Pick a point anywhere on the screen.

AutoCAD will place a point at the specified location and return you to the "Command:" prompt. Look closely and you will see the point you have drawn. Besides those odd instances in which you may need to draw tiny dots like this, points can also serve as object snap "nodes." See the OSNAP chart, Figure 6-8 in Chapter 6.

But what about those circles and crosses in Figure 9-27? AutoCAD has 18 other simple forms that can be drawn as points. Before we change the point form, we need to see our options.

⊕ Select Point Style from the Format menu.

AutoCAD displays a Point Style dialog box with an icon menu, as shown in Figure 9-28. It shows you graphic images of your choices. You can pick any of the point styles shown by pointing. You can also change the size of points using the Point Size edit box.

⊕ Pick the style in the middle of the second row.

⊕ Click on "OK" to exit the dialog box.

⊕ Type "Po" or select the Point tool from the Draw toolbar.

⊕ Pick a point anywhere on your screen.

AutoCAD will draw a point in the chosen style, as shown in Figure 9-28.

If you have selected the POINT command from the toolbar, AutoCAD will continue to draw points wherever you pick them until you exit the command. If you have entered POINT from the command line, you will have to repeat it to draw more points.

⊕ Repeat POINT, if necessary, and pick another point.

Figure 9-28

Draw a few more points, or return to the dialog box to try another style.

⊕ If necessary, cancel the POINT command.

9.12 Using the SKETCH Command (Optional)

GENERAL PROCEDURE

1. Type "Sketch" or select the Sketch tool from the Miscellaneous toolbar.
2. Type an increment.
3. Pick a start point (pen down).
4. Move cursor to sketch lines.
5. Pick an end point (pen up).
6. Record, exit, quit, or erase.

The SKETCH command allows you to draw freehand lines. We include it here as an optional task. It is not used in any of the drawings that follow.

The key to SKETCH is becoming familiar with its pen-up, pen-down action. Also, get used to the idea that SKETCHed lines are not part of the drawing until you "record" them or exit the SKETCH command.

⊕ Type "Sketch".

AutoCAD prompts

> SKETCH record increment <0.10>:

This will allow you to decide how fine or coarse you want your lines to be. Remember also that AutoCAD will continue to observe your snap. If you want a small record increment, turn snap off.

⊕ Press Enter to accept .10 as the record increment.

You will see the following prompt:

> Sketch. Pen eXit Quit Record Erase Connect.

We will discuss these options in a moment. They will make more sense after you have done some sketching.

⊕ To begin sketching, choose any point on your screen and press the pickbutton once.

This puts your imaginary sketching pen down.

⊕ Move the cursor and watch the lines that appear on the screen.

⊕ Press the pickbutton again.

This picks your imaginary pen up again, resulting in an end point. If you move the cursor again, no new lines will be drawn.

⊕ Press the pickbutton once again and move the cursor. The pen is down and you can continue sketching from a new start point.

Now look at the other options:

Sketch. Pen eXit Quit Record Erase Connect.

"P" picks the imaginary pen up and down, but the pickbutton is more convenient. "X" records the lines you have drawn and exits the command. "Q" exits without recording. "R" records without exiting. "E" allows you to erase some of the lines you have sketched in the last sequence. The action of this erase option is interesting, and you should try it. "C" connects you to the point where you last picked up your pen. "." draws a straight line from the point where you left off to the current position of the cross hairs.

Note: Since SKETCHed objects are made up of large numbers of very small lines, they take up a great deal of memory.

9.13   Review Material

Questions

1. If you wanted to draw a polygon around the outside of a circle so that its sides were tangent to the circle, what option of the POLYGON command would you use?
2. Halfwidth is to width as radius is to diameter. Explain.
3. Why does PLINE prompt for two different widths?
4. Why is it important to use the Close option when drawing closed polygons using the PLINE command?
5. How does AutoCAD decide in which direction to draw a polyline arc?
6. You are drawing a rectangular 2D Solid 2 units high by 4 units wide. Your first point is at (2,2) and your second point is at (2,4). Assuming you want to move to the right, where should points 3 and 4 be? List them in order.
7. What is an AutoCAD slide? How is it different from a drawing?
8. Where is the zero point in a standard AutoCAD multiline?
9. What properties make up a multiline style definition?
10. When is it necessary to use the MLEDIT command?

Drawing Problems

1. Draw a regular six-sided polygon centered at (9,6) with a circumscribed radius of 3.0 units. The top and bottom sides should be horizontal.
2. Fillet all corners of the hexagon with a single execution of the FILLET command, giving a radius of 0.25 units.
3. Give the sides of the hexagon a uniform width of 0.25 units.
4. Draw a STANDARD two-element multiline justified to its zero point from the midpoint of one angled side of the hexagon to the midpoint of the diagonally opposite side.
5. Draw a second multiline in the same manner, using the other two angled sides so that the two multilines cross.
6. Edit the intersection of the two multilines to create an "Open Cross" intersection.

9.14 Drawing 9-1: Backgammon Board

This drawing should go very quickly. It is a good warm-up and will give you practice with MLINE, PLINE, and SOLID. Remember that the dimensions are always part of your drawing now, unless otherwise indicated.

DRAWING SUGGESTIONS

GRID = 1.00
SNAP = 0.125

- First create the multiline line style for the frame with three elements 0.25, 0.00, and −0.50 and joints on as shown. Then draw the 15.50 × 17.50 multiline frame.
- Draw a 0-width 15.50 × 13.50 polyline rectangle and then OFFSET it 0.125 to the inside. The inner polyline is actually 0.25 wide; but it is drawn on center, so the offset must be half the width.
- Enter the PEDIT command and change the width of the inner polyline to 0.25. This will give you your wide filled border.
- Draw the four triangles at the left of the board and then array them across. The filled triangles are drawn with the SOLID command; the others are just outlines drawn with LINE or PLINE. (Notice that you cannot draw some solids filled and others not filled.)
- The dimensions in this drawing are straightforward and should give you no trouble. Remember to set to layer "dim" before dimensioning.

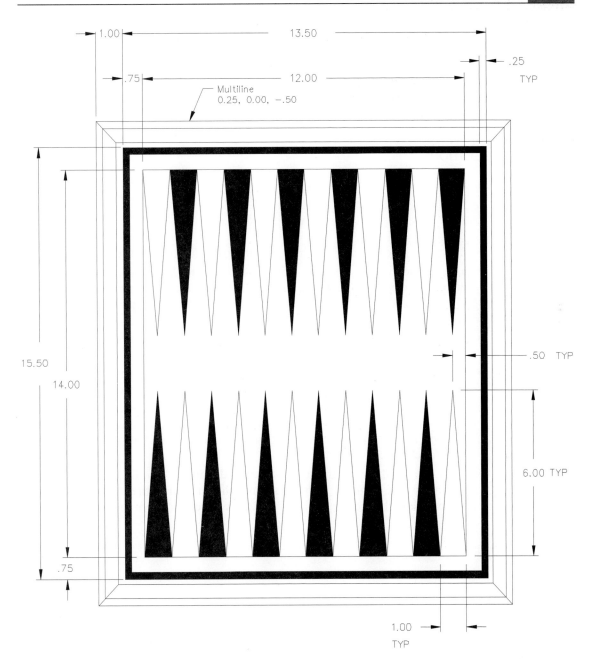

BACKGAMMON BOARD
Drawing 9–1

9.15   Drawing 9-2: Dart Board

Although this drawing may seem to resemble the previous one, it is quite a bit more complex and is drawn in an entirely different way. Using SOLID to create the filled areas here would be impractical because of the arc-shaped edges. We suggest you use DONUTs and TRIM them along the radial lines.

DRAWING SUGGESTIONS

LIMITS = (0,0) (24,18)
GRID = 1.00
SNAP = 0.125

- The filled inner circle is a donut with 0 inner and 0.62 outer diameters.
- The second circle is a simple 1.50 diameter circle. From here, draw a series of donuts. The outside diameter of one will become the inside diameter of the next. The 13.00 and 17.00 diameter outer circles must be drawn as circles rather than donuts so they will not be filled.
- Draw a radius line from the center to one of the quadrants of the outer circle and array it around the circle.
- You may find it easier and quicker to turn fill off before trimming the donuts. Also, use layers to keep the donuts separated visually by color.
- To TRIM the donuts, select the radial lines as cutting edges. This is easily done using a very small crossing box around the center point of the board. Otherwise you will have to pick each line individually in the area between the 13.00 and 17.00 circle.
- Draw the number 5 at the top of the board using a "middle" text position and a rotation of 2 degrees. Array it around the circle and then use the DDEDIT command to change the copied fives to the other numbers shown.

CIRCLE DIAMETERS

Ø.62
Ø1.50
Ø7.50
Ø8.25
Ø13.00
Ø17.00

DART BOARD

Drawing 9–2

9.16 Drawing 9-3: Printed Circuit Board

This drawing uses donuts, solids, and polylines. Also notice the ordinate dimensions.

DRAWING SUGGESTIONS

> UNITS = 4-place decimal
> LIMITS = (0,0) (18,12)
> GRID = 0.5000
> SNAP = 0.1250

- Because this drawing uses ordinate dimensions, moving the 0 point of the grid using the UCS command will make the placement of figures very easy.
- The 26 rectangular tabs at the bottom can be drawn as polylines or solids.
- After placing the donuts according to the dimensions, draw the connections to them using polyline arcs and line segments. These will be simple polylines of uniform 0.03125 halfwidth. The triangular tabs will be added later.
- Remember, AutoCAD begins all polyline arcs tangent to the last segment drawn. Often this is not what you want. One way to correct this is to begin with a line segment that establishes the direction for the arc. The line segment can be extremely short and still accomplish your purpose. Thus many of these polylines will consist of a line segment, followed by an arc, followed by another line segment.
- There are two sizes of the triangular tabs, one on top of the rectangular tabs and one at each donut. Draw one of each size in place and then use multiple COPY, MOVE, and ROTATE commands to create all the others.

PRINTED CIRCUIT BOARD
DRAWING 9-3

9.17   Drawing 9-4: Carbide Tip Saw Blade

This is a nice drawing that will give you some good experience with the OFF-SET command. How would you draw the sides of the carbide tip if you could not use OFFSET?

DRAWING SUGGESTIONS

$$GRID = 1.00$$
$$SNAP = 0.125$$

- After drawing the 7.25 diameter circle, draw a vertical line 1.50 over from the center line. This line will become the left side of the detailed "cut."
- Use DIST with an object snap to the intersection of the circle and the vertical line to locate the 0.58 vertical distance.
- Draw the horizontal center line through the 0.58 point and the vertical center line 0.16 to the right.
- Use the center lines in drawing the 0.16 radius arc.
- From the right end point of the arc, draw a line extending out of the circle at 80 degrees. The dimension is given as 10 degrees from the vertical, but the coordinate display will show 80 degrees from the horizontal instead.
- OFFSET this line 0.06 to the right and left to create the lines for the left and right sides of the carbide tip.
- Draw a horizontal line 0.12 up from the center line. TRIM it with the sides of the carbide tip and create 0.06 radius fillets right and left.
- Draw the 3.68 radius circle to locate the outside of the tip.
- BREAK and TRIM the three 80-degree lines, leaving three extension lines for use in dimensioning. Then copy the whole area out to the right for the detail. When you start working on the detail, SCALE it up 2.00.
- In the original view, erase the extension lines and then array the cut and carbide tip around the circle. TRIM the circle out of the new cuts and tips.
- You can use a "Rotated" dimension at 10 degrees to create the 0.12 and 0.06 dimensions in the detail.
- Be sure to type in your own values as you dimension the detail, since it has been scaled.

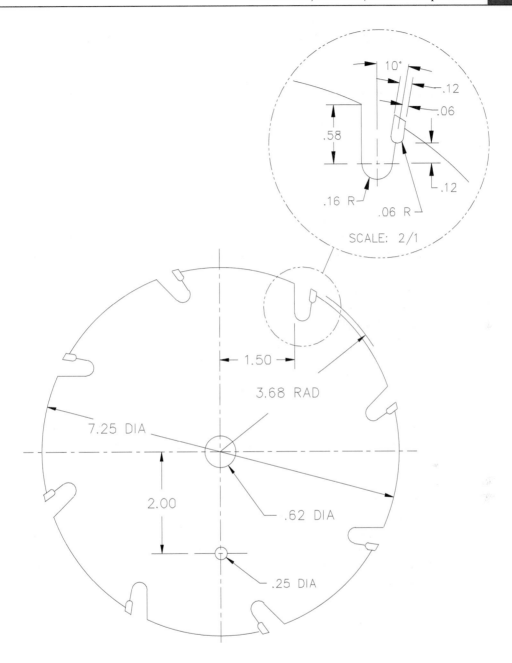

10°

.12

.06

.58

.16 R

.06 R

.12

SCALE: 2/1

1.50

3.68 RAD

7.25 DIA

2.00

.62 DIA

.25 DIA

CARBIDE TIP SAW BLADE

Drawing 9−4

9.18   Drawing 9-5: Gazebo

This architectural drawing makes extensive use of both the POLYGON command and the OFFSET command.

Drawing Suggestions

> UNITS = Architectural
> GRID = 19
> SNAP = 20
> LIMITS = (0′,0′) (48′,36′)

- All radii except the 6″ polygon are given from the center point to the midpoint of a side. In other words, the 6″ polygon will be "inscribed," while all the others will be "circumscribed."
- Notice that all polygon radii dimensions are given to the outside of the 2″ X 4″. OFFSET to the inside to create the parallel polygon for the inside of the board.
- Create radial studs by drawing a line from the midpoint of one side of a polygon to the midpoint of the side of another, or the midpoint of one to the vertex of another as shown; then offset 1″ each side and erase the original. Array around the center point.
- TRIM lines and polygons at vertices.
- You can make effective use of MIRROR in the elevation.

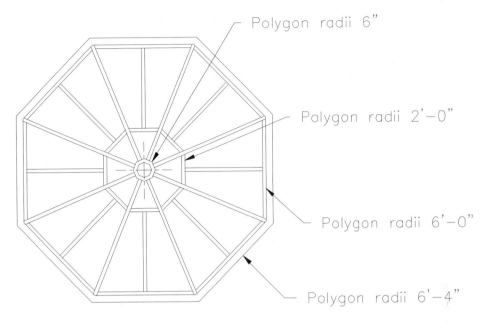

Polygon radii 6"

Polygon radii 2'-0"

Polygon radii 6'-0"

Polygon radii 6'-4"

ROOF FRAMING

4'

4"

1'-2"

4"
(TYP)

8'

8"
(TYP)

6"

2'-4"

2'-6"

4"

4"

4" THK CONCRETE SLAB

All lumber 2" x 4" unless otherwise noted

FRONT ELEVATION

GAZEBO
Drawing 9-5

9.19 Drawing 9-6: Frame

This drawing will give you practice using the MULTILINE command. The object is to draw the Front, Left Side, and Top Views. Position the views as indicated in the reference drawing. Although at first glance this drawing appears to be easy, it is somewhat complex, so proceed with caution. There are numerous ways in which the drawing can be done, but we suggest you take advantage of the MULTILINE command to draw each view. The drawing will be fully dimensioned, and all hidden lines will be shown.

Drawing Suggestions

- Begin by setting the MULTILINE command to a spacing of 1/2″.
- Draw the Left Side view first using the MULTILINE command and use the "C" to close the lines. Notice that the hidden lines are not shown in the reference drawing. You are to provide all hidden lines.
- Use the Left Side view to line up the front view, making sure you use the MULTILINE command.
- Finally, draw the Top View using the Front View for alignment.

FRAME

Drawing 9-6

10

Groups and Blocks

COMMANDS

DRAW	**MODIFY**	**INSERT**	**VIEW**	**STANDARD**
BLOCK	ATTEDIT	XBIND	ATTDISP	GROUP
INSERT		XREF		COPYCLIP
WBLOCK				
ATTEXT				
DDATTDEF				
DDATTE				
ATTDEF				

OVERVIEW

You have seen several ways in which AutoCAD can treat a complex object as a single entity. In this chapter you will learn to create "groups" and "blocks." A group is simply a set of objects that can be selected, named, and manipulated collectively. A block is a set of objects more permanently defined as a single entity. Blocks can be inserted repeatedly in many drawings also can be given attributes. An attribute is an item of information about a block, such as a part number or price, that is stored along with the block definition. All the information stored in attributes can be extracted from a drawing and used to produce itemized reports. This is a powerful feature of CAD that has no direct counterpart in manual drafting.

Blocks may be stored within individual drawings or saved as complete drawings in themselves. In the latter case they can then be inserted into other drawings as blocks or linked to other drawings as "external references," using the XREF command. These features allow you to create symbol libraries made up of commonly used objects.

TASKS

10.1 Creating GROUPs

GENERAL PROCEDURE

1. Type "G" or select Object Group… from the Tools menu.
2. Type a name.
3. Click on "New".
4. Select objects to be included in the group definition.
5. Press Enter to end object selection.
6. Click on OK to exit the dialog.

The simplest way to create a complex entity from previously drawn entities is to group them into a unit with the GROUP command. Groups are given names and can be selected for all editing processes if they are defined as selectable.

In this exercise we will form groups from objects that also will be used later to define blocks. In this way you will get a feel for the different functions of these two methods of creating collections of objects. You will be creating simple symbols for a computer, monitor, digitizer, and keyboard as seen from above, looking down. Once created, these may also be used in Drawing 10–1.

⊕ Begin by making the following changes in the drawing setup:

1. Set to layer 0 (the reason for doing this is discussed in the Note following this list).
2. Change to architectural units, with smallest fraction = 1.
3. Set GRID = 1'.
4. Set SNAP = 1".
5. Set LIMITS = (0',0') (48',36').

Note: Blocks created on layer 0 will be inserted on the current layer. Blocks created on any other layer will stay on the layer on which they are created. Inserting blocks is discussed in Task 10.3.

⊕ Zoom into an area approximately 12' × 9'

⊕ Draw the four objects in Figure 10-1.

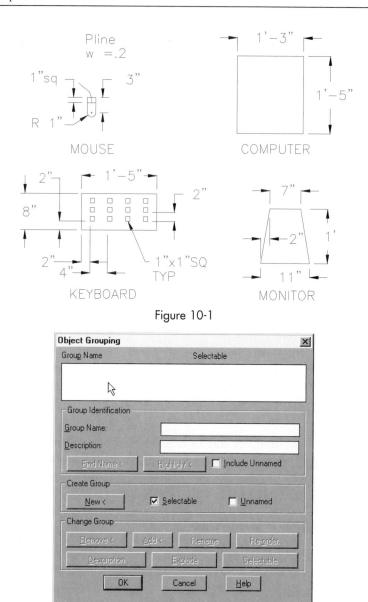

Figure 10-1

Figure 10-2

Draw the geometry only; the text and dimensions in the figure are for your reference only and should not be on your screen.

We will define the "keyboard" as a group.

⊕ Type "G" or select Object Group… from the Tools menu.

Either method will call the Object Grouping dialog box shown in Figure 10-2. At the top of the box is the Group Name list box. It will be empty now since there are no groups defined in this drawing. Below that is the Group Identification area, with edit boxes for entering a group name (up to 31 characters) and a group description (up to 64 characters). The flashing cursor bar should be in the group name box so that you can enter a name. Our first group will be the set of rectangles you have drawn as a symbol for a keyboard.

⊕ Type "keyboard" in the Group Name edit box.

Now look at the Create Group area. The three boxes here are "New <", "Selectable", and "Unnamed". To create a group, you must indicate that it is a new group. But first, you need to be sure that the group will be defined as selectable, if that is your intention, as it most often will be. Unnamed groups are usually groups that have been created by copying named groups. In these cases AutoCAD assigns names beginning with *A and followed by a number.

⊕ Be sure that "Selectable" is checked.

⊕ Click on "New <" in the Create Group area.

At this point the dialog box will disappear to give you access to objects in your drawing. You will see a "Select Objects:" prompt at the command line.

⊕ Select the keyboard outer rectangles and small rectangles using a window.

⊕ Press Enter to end object selection.

This will bring back the dialog box. "KEYBOARD" should now be in the list box, with a "Yes" to the right indicating that it is a selectable group.

⊕ Click on "OK" to exit the dialog box.

The keyboard is now defined in the drawing as a selectable group. To see that this is so, try selecting it.

⊕ Position the pickbox anywhere on the "Keyboard" and press the pickbutton.

You will see from the highlights and blue grip boxes that the complete group is selected. That is all you need to do with groups at this point. Groups are useful for copying and manipulating groups of objects that tend to stay together. The following notes will help you to go further with groups if you wish.

1. If you click on "Find Name" and then select any object that is part of group, AutoCAD will show you the name (or names) of the group (or groups) that the object belongs to.
2. Unnamed groups are only included in the Group Name list if Include Unnamed is checked.
3. In editing commands you can select a group by pointing or by typing "group" at the Select Objects prompt and then typing the name of the group.
4. If the PICKSTYLE variable is set to 0 (default value is 1), you will only be able to select groups by typing their names, not by pointing.

Concerning the Change Group area of the dialog box:

1. Remove and Add allow you to remove or add individual objects of a previously defined group.
2. The objects in a group have a defined order, which can be changed using the Group Order dialog box. Select "Re-order..." in the Object Grouping dialog box.
3. You can change the description of a previously defined group by highlighting the name on the group list, typing or editing the description, and then clicking on Description.
4. You can delete a group definition by highlighting its name on the group list and then clicking on Explode.

5. To switch the selectability status of a defined group between yes and no, use the Selectable box at the bottom right of the dialog box.

10.2 Creating BLOCKs

GENERAL PROCEDURE

1. Type "B", select the Make Block tool from the Draw toolbar, or open the Draw menu, highlight Block, and then select Make.
2. Type a name.
3. Pick an insertion point.
4. Select objects to be included in the block definition.

Blocks are more permanent than groups. Blocks can be stored as part of an individual drawing or as separate drawings and can be inserted into any drawing. In general, the most useful blocks are those that will be used repeatedly in many drawings and therefore can become part of a library of predrawn objects used by you and others in your work group. In mechanical drawing, for instance, you may want a set of screws drawn to standard sizes that can be called out anytime. Or, if you are doing architectural drawing, you might find a library of doors and windows useful.

In this chapter we are creating a set of simple symbols for some of the tools we know you will be using no matter what kind of CAD you are doing—namely, computers, monitors, keyboards, digitizers, plotters, and printers. We define them as blocks and then assemble them into a workstation. Later we will insert workstations into an architectural drawing called "CAD ROOM."

⊕ Type "B", select the Make Block tool from the Draw toolbar, as shown in Figure 10-3, or open the Draw menu, highlight Block, and then select Make.

These methods execute the BMAKE command and open the Block Definition dialog box shown in Figure 10-4. BMAKE is a new command. BLOCK, the older command, serves the same purpose but operates from the command line.

⊕ Type "computer" in the Block name box.

Next, choose object to define the block.

⊕ Click on "Select Objects<".

The dialog box disappears, giving access to objects in the drawing.

Figure 10-3

Figure 10-4

⊕ Use a window to select the whole computer box.

AutoCAD continues to prompt for object selection.

⊕ Press Enter to end object selection.

This brings you back to the dialog box.

Blocks are intended to be inserted into drawings, so any block definition needs to include an insertion base point. Insertion points and insertion base points are critical in the whole matter of using blocks. The insertion base point is the point on the block that will be at the intersection of the cross hairs when you insert the block. Therefore, when defining a block, try to anticipate the point on the block you would most likely use to position the block on the screen. If you do not define a base point, AutoCAD will use the origin of the coordinate system, which may be quite inconvenient.

⊕ Click on "Select point<".

⊕ Use a midpoint object snap to pick the middle of the bottom line of the computer as the insertion point, as shown in Figure 10-5.

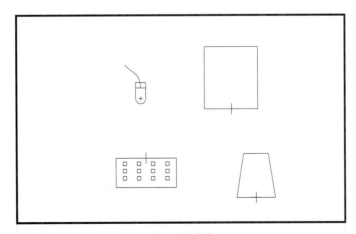

Figure 10-5

A common practise is to create a number of blocks, one after the other, and then assemble them at the end. To facilitate this method, remove the check from the box that says "Retain objects". With this setting, newly defined blocks will be erased from the screen automatically. They can be retrieved using OOPS if necessary (but not U, as this would undo the block definition).

⊕ Click in the "Retain objects" box to remove the check.

The block definition is complete.

⊕ Click on OK to exit the dialog.

You have created a "computer" block definition. The computer has vanished from your screen but may be inserted using the INSERT command, which we will turn to momentarily. Now repeat the BMAKE process to make a "keyboard" block.

⊕ Repeat BMAKE.

⊕ Type "keyboard" in the Block name box.

⊕ Click on "Select Objects<".

⊕ Select the keyboard.

Since you have already defined the keyboard as a selectable group, one pick should select the whole thing. In the command area AutoCAD will show how many individual objects are in the selection set, and also that there is one group in the set. The group definition of the keyboard will now become part of the block definition.

⊕ Press Enter to end selection.

⊕ Click on "Select point<".

⊕ Pick the midpoint of the top line of the keyboard as the insertion base point.

Repeat the blocking process two more times to create "monitor" and "mouse" blocks, with insertion base points as shown in Figure 10-5. When you are done, your screen should be blank.

WBLOCK

The WBLOCK command is very similar to BLOCK, except that it writes a block out to a separate file so that it may be inserted in other drawings. You can WBLOCK a previously defined block or create a new block definition as you write the block out. You can also WBLOCK an entire drawing. This can be quite useful since a WBLOCKed drawing takes up less memory than a SAVEd one. We will be using WBLOCK as well as BLOCK extensively in the drawings at the end of this chapter.

10.3 INSERTing Previously Defined Blocks

GENERAL PROCEDURE
1. Type "i" , select Block from the Insert menu, or select the Insert Block tool from the Draw toolbar.
2. Type a block name.
3. Pick an insertion point.
4. Answer prompts for horizontal and vertical scale and for rotation angle.

The INSERT and DDINSERT commands are used to bring blocks into a drawing. The four block definitions you created in Task 10.1 are now part of the drawing database and can be inserted in this drawing anywhere you like. INSERT or DDINSERT, the dialog box version, also can be used to insert complete drawings into other drawings. Among other things, these procedures are useful in creating assembly drawings. You will find that assembling blocks can be done efficiently using appropriate OSNAP modes to place objects in precise relation to one another. Assembly drawing will be the focus of the drawing tasks at the end of this chapter.

In this task we will insert the computer, monitor, keyboard, and digitizer back into the drawing to create the "workstation" assembly shown in Figure 10-6. We will also discuss other options for drawing file management, including the use of complete drawings as blocks or as "external references."

⊕   If you are still on layer 0, switch to layer 1.

⊕   Type "1", select "Block" from the Insert menu, or select the Insert Block tool from the Draw toolbar, as shown in Figure 10-7.

This will bring up the Insert dialog box shown in Figure 10-8. Now is a good time to see that your block definitions are still in your database, even though they are no longer on the screen.

⊕   Click on "Block..." in the dialog box.

You should see a Defined Blocks dialog box with a list like this:

> COMPUTER
> KEYBOARD
> MONITOR
> MOUSE

Figure 10-6

Figure 10-7

Figure 10-8

⊕ Select "COMPUTER" from the list, and then click on "OK" to return to the Insert dialog.

⊕ Click on "OK" again to begin the insertion.

From here on you will follow prompts from the command line. AutoCAD now needs to know where to insert the computer, and you will see this prompt:

Insertion point:

Notice that AutoCAD gives you a block to drag into place and that it is positioned with the block's insertion base point at the intersection of the cross hairs.

⊕ Pick a point near the middle of the screen, as shown in Figure 10-6.

What comes next is a set of prompts that allow you to scale and rotate the block as you insert it. This vastly increases the flexibility and power of the blocking system, although in many instances, including this one, you will accept all the defaults.

The first prompt asks for a scale factor:

X scale factor <1> / Corner / XYZ:

Unlike the SCALE command, which automatically scales both horizontally and vertically, blocks can be stretched or shrunk in either direction independently as you insert them. You can type an X scale factor or specify both an X and a Y factor at once by showing two corners of a window using the Corner option. The third option, XYZ, is reserved for 3D applications. Pressing Enter will retain the block's present length.

⊕ Press Enter to retain an X scale factor of 1.

AutoCAD follows with a prompt for vertical scale:

Y scale factor (default=X):

⊕ Press Enter to retain a Y factor of 1.

You now have the opportunity to rotate the object:

```
Rotation angle <0>:
```

⊕ Press Enter to retain 0 degrees of rotation.

Notice that the block is inserted on layer 1 even though it was created on layer 0. Remember that *this only works with blocks drawn on layer 0.* Blocks drawn on other layers stay on the layer they were drawn on when they are inserted.

Now let's add a monitor.

⊕ Repeat the DDINSERT command.

Notice that the last block inserted becomes the default block name in the Block name box. This facilitates procedures in which you insert the same block in several different places in a drawing.

⊕ Select "Block..." in the Insert dialog box.

⊕ Select "MONITOR" in the Defined Blocks dialog box.

⊕ Click on "OK" in both dialog boxes.

⊕ Pick an insertion point 2 or 3 inches above the insertion point of the computer, as shown in Figure 10-6.

⊕ Press Enter three additional times to retain X and Y scale factors of 1, and a rotation of 0.

You should have the monitor sitting on top of the computer and be back at the "command" prompt. We will insert the keyboard, as shown in Figure 10-6.

⊕ Repeat DDINSERT.

⊕ Click on "Block...".

⊕ Click on "KEYBOARD".

⊕ Exit both dialog boxes.

⊕ Pick an insertion point 1 or 2 inches below the computer, as shown in Figure 10-6.

⊕ Press Enter three additional times to retain X and Y scale factors of 1 and a rotation of 0.

You should now have the keyboard in place.

⊕ Repeat DDINSERT once more and place the mouse block to the right of the other blocks as shown in Figure 10-6.

Congratulations, you have completed your first assembly. Now that you are familiar with BMAKE and DDINSERT, you have the primary tools needed to create and utilize a symbol library. Tasks 10.5 and 10.6 introduce you to attributes. We will create attributes to hold information about CAD workstations and include them in the definition of a new "ws" block. Then we will insert several workstations into our drawing and edit some of the attribute information. But before going on, let's look at "external references" and the Windows clipboard, two other ways to import information from one drawing into another.

External References

An external reference is a drawing that is "attached" to another drawing through the use of the XREF command. External references are similar to blocks and can be used for many of the same purposes. They are particularly important in network environments.

In the previous exercise we inserted blocks that were defined within our current drawing. We can use exactly the same procedure with the DDINSERT command to insert a complete drawing file into our current drawing. The inserted drawing would then become a block within the current drawing, although its original drawing file would still exist separately. The XREF command is an alternative to inserting complete drawings. The principal difference between inserted drawings and externally referenced drawings is that inserted drawings are actually merged with the current drawing database, whereas externally referenced drawings are only linked. You cannot edit an external reference from within the current drawing. However, if the XREFed drawing is changed, the changes will be reflected in the current drawing the next time it is loaded or when the Reload option of the XREF command is executed. This allows several people at separate workstations to work on different aspects of a single master drawing, which is updated automatically as changes are made in the various referenced drawings.

Since XREF only loads enough information to "point to" the externally referenced drawing, it does not increase the size of the current drawing file as significantly as INSERT does. The options of the XREF command are as follows:

Bind:	Merges an external reference completely into the current drawing. The end result is the same as INSERTing a drawing, but binding does not have to occur until the final version of the drawing is complete. There is also an XBIND command that allows you to exclude certain types of information when you bind an external reference. The dimensions, for example, can be left out if they are drawn on a separate layer.
Detach:	Removes the link between the current drawing and specified external references. Detached objects are no longer seen in your drawing.
Path:	Tells AutoCAD where to locate an external reference. This option is used to update a link when file structure is changed or the externally referenced drawing is moved. Otherwise, the link cannot be maintained.
Reload:	Reloads an external reference without leaving the current drawing. This is most useful in networked environments in which one person may be working on a drawing that is referenced in another person's drawing. Using this option, the most recent changes can be brought into the current drawing.
Attach:	Creates a link between the current drawing and another drawing.

Management of Named Objects

What happens when an externally referenced or inserted drawing has layers, linetypes, text styles, dimension styles, blocks, or views with names that conflict with those in the current drawing? Good question. In the case of INSERTed drawings, name definitions in the current drawing override those in the inserted block. In the case of XREFed drawings, named objects are given special designations that eliminate the confusion. For example, if drawing A is attached to drawing B and both have a layer called FLOOR, a new layer is created in B called A|FLOOR.

Raster Images

A raster image is an image such as a picture or photograph that has been encoded as computer information. Any ordinary computer graphic image is an example. Such images can be brought into a Release 14 drawing much as an external reference would be. Raster images are attached and linked to AutoCAD drawings but do not actually become part of the drawing database so that they do not take up large amounts of memory. Once attached, raster images can be inserted repeatedly in the same drawing just like blocks. To insert a raster image, select Raster Image... from the Insert menu.

10.4 Using the Windows Clipboard

GENERAL PROCEDURE

1. Select the Cut to Clipboard or Copy to Clipboard tool from the Standard toolbar.
2. Select objects (steps 1 and 2 can be reversed).
3. Move to another Windows 95 application.
4. Type Ctrl-V or select "Paste" in that application.

The Windows 95 clipboard makes it very easy to copy objects from an Auto-CAD drawing into other Windows applications. You will use the Copy to Clipboard and Cut to Clipboard tools from the Standard toolbar, which activate the COPYCLIP and COPYCUT commands. Cut will remove the selected objects from your AutoCAD drawing, while Copy will leave them. When you send objects to the Clipboard, using COPYCLIP or CUTCLIP, the objects will be defined as a block and given a random name. This is not the best procedure for creating blocks within AutoCAD, however, since you have no control over the name.

In this task we will go through the steps to copy part of an AutoCAD drawing to another Windows application. We have used Microsoft Word for the example, but the procedure is very simple and will work with any Windows application that supports Windows OLE (Object Linking and Embedding).

⊕ To begin this task you should be in an AutoCAD drawing with some objects on your screen.

We will use the computer workstation from the last task, but any objects will do.

⊕ Select the Copy to Clipboard tool from the Standard toolbar, as shown in Figure 10-9.

Figure 10-9

AutoCAD prompts for object selection.

⊕ Using a window selection, select all of the objects in the computer workstation assembled in the last task.

⊕ Press Enter to end object selection.

AutoCAD will save the selected objects to the clipboard. Nothing will happen on your screen, but the selected objects are stored as a block entity and could be pasted back into this drawing or another AutoCAD drawing. Most important, they can now be pasted into another Windows application. The following steps assume that a word processing application is open in the background.

⊕ Click on the Windows 95 minimize button at the top right of the AutoCAD window.

⊕ Open another Windows 95 application.

⊕ Move the cursor wherever you wish in the new application.

⊕ Type Ctrl-V or select "Paste" from the Edit menu in your application.

Voila!... We hope. This procedure will work very smoothly if your application accepts AutoCAD drawing formats, and very poorly otherwise.

Now that you have pasted AutoCAD objects into your application, any further manipulation will require you to learn about that application.

⊕ When you are ready to return to AutoCAD, close the current application and click on the AutoCAD program button on the Windows 95 taskbar.

That's all there is to it. It is equally simple to paste text and images from other compatible Windows applications into AutoCAD. Just reverse the process, cutting or copying from the other application and pasting into AutoCAD.

10.5 Defining Attributes with DDATTDEF

GENERAL PROCEDURE

1. Select Block and then Define Attributes... from the Draw menu.
2. Specify attribute modes.
3. Type an attribute tag.
4. Type an attribute prompt.
5. If desired, type a default attribute value.
6. Include the attribute in a block definition.

Attributes can be confusing, and you should not spend too much time worrying over their details unless you are currently involved in an application that requires their use. On the other hand, they are a powerful tool, and if you have a basic understanding of what they can do, you could be the one in your work setting to recognize when to use them.

One of the difficulties of learning about attributes is that you have to define them before you see them in action. It is therefore a little hard to comprehend what your definitions mean the first time around. Bear with us and follow instructions closely; it will be worth your effort.

In this task we will define attributes that will hold information about CAD workstations. The attributes will be defined in a flexible manner so that the workstation block can represent any number of hardware configurations.

When we have defined our attributes, we will create a block called "ws" that includes the whole workstation assembly and its attributes.

⊕   **To begin this task, you should have the assembled workstation from Task 10.2 on your screen.**

First we will define an attribute that will allow us to specify the type of computer in any individual occurrence of the "ws" block. As is often the case, you have a choice between a command sequence and a dialog box. We will show you the DDATTDEF dialog box. The older ATTDEF command covers exactly the same specifications but works in a step-by-step sequence at the command line.

⊕   **Open the Draw menu, highlight Block, and select Define Attributes....**

This will open the Attribute Definition dialog box shown in Figure 10-10.

Look first at the check boxes at the top left under "Mode". We will be using all the default modes in this first attribute definition. This means that when our workstation block is inserted, the computer attribute value will be visible in the drawing (because "Invisible" is not checked), variable with each insertion of the block (because "Constant" is not checked), verified only once ("Verify" is not checked), and not preset to a value ("Preset" is not checked).

Next look at the box to the right under "Attribute". The cursor should be blinking in the Tag edit box. Like a field name in a database file, a tag identifies the kind of information this particular attribute is meant to hold. The tag appears in the block definition as a field name. In occurrences of the block, the tag is replaced by a specific value. "Computer," for example, could be replaced by "IBM."

Figure 10-10

⊕　Type "Computer" in the Tag edit box.

⊕　Move the cursor to the "Prompt" edit box.

As with the tag, the key to understanding the attribute prompt is to be clear about the difference between block definitions and actual occurrences of blocks in a drawing. Right now we are defining an attribute. The attribute definition will become part of the definition of the "ws" block and will be used whenever ws is inserted. Attribute definitions function as containers for information. Each time we insert ws we can specify some or all of the information that its attributes hold. This is what will allow us to use our ws block to represent different hardware configurations. With the definition we are creating, there will be a prompt whenever we insert ws that asks us to enter information about the computer in a given configuration.

⊕　Type "Enter computer type:".

We also have the opportunity to specify a default attribute value, if we wish, by typing in the Value edit box. This time, we will use no default in our attribute definition.

The box labeled "Text Options" allows you to specify text parameters as you would in DTEXT. Visible attributes appear as text on the screen. Therefore, the appearance of the text needs to be specified. The only change we will make is to specify a height.

⊕　Click in the edit box to the right of "Height <" and then type "4".

If you click on the "Height <" box itself, the dialog box will disappear so that you can indicate a height by pointing.

Finally, AutoCAD needs to know where to place the visible attribute information in the drawing. You can type in x, y, and z coordinate values, but you are much more likely to show a point.

⊕　Click on "Pick Point <".

The dialog box will disappear temporarily to allow access to the screen. You will also see a "Start point:" prompt in the command area.

We will place our attributes 8 inches below the keyboard, as shown in Figure 10-11.

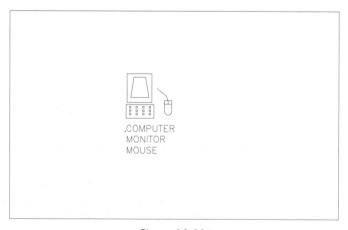

Figure 10-11

⊕ Pick a start point 8 inches below the left side of the keyboard, as shown in Figure 10-11.

The dialog box will reappear.

⊕ Click on "OK" to complete the dialog.

The dialog box will disappear and the attribute tag "Computer" will be drawn as shown. Remember, this is an attribute definition, not an occurrence of the attribute. "Computer" is our attribute tag. After we define the workstation as a block and the block is inserted, you will answer the "Enter computer type:" prompt with the name of a computer type, and the name itself will be in the drawing rather than this tag.

Now we will proceed to define three more attributes, using some different options.

⊕ Repeat DDATTDEF by pressing enter or selecting Block and then Define Attributes... from the Draw menu.

We will use all the default modes again, but we will provide a default monitor value in this attribute definition.

⊕ Type "Monitor" for the attribute tag.

⊕ Type "Enter monitor type:" for the attribute prompt.

⊕ Type "Super VGA" for the default attribute value.

Now when AutoCAD shows the prompt for a monitor type, it will also show Super VGA as the default.

You can align a series of attributes by checking the Align below previous attribute box at the lower right of the dialog box.

⊕ Click in the check box labeled "Align below previous attribute".

⊕ Click on "OK" to complete the dialog.

The attribute tag "Monitor" should be added to the workstation below the "Computer" tag.

Next, we will add an "invisible, preset" attribute for the mouse. "Invisible" means that the attribute text will not be visible when the block is inserted, although the information will be in the database and can be extracted. "Preset" means that the attribute has a default value and does not issue a prompt to change it. However, unlike "constant" attributes, you can change preset attributes using the DDATTE command, which we will explore in Task 10.5.

⊕ Repeat DDATTDEF.

⊕ Click in the check box next to "Invisible".

⊕ Click in the check box next to "Preset".

⊕ Type "Mouse" for the attribute tag.

You will not need a prompt, since the preset attribute is automatically set to the default value.

⊕ Type "Microsoft" for the default attribute value.

⊕ Click in the Align below previous attribute check box to position the attribute below "Monitor" in the drawing.

⊕ Click on "OK" to complete the dialog.

The "Mouse" attribute tag should be added to your screen, as shown in Figure 10-11. Once again, remember that this is the attribute definition. When ws is inserted the attribute value, "Microsoft" will be written into the database, but nothing will appear on the screen since the attribute is defined as invisible.

Finally, the most important step of all: We must define the workstation as a block that includes all our attribute definitions.

⊕ Type "b" or select the Make Block tool from the Draw toolbar.

⊕ Type "ws" for the block name.

⊕ Click on "Select Objects<".

⊕ Window the workstation assembly and all three attribute tags.

⊕ Press Enter to end object selection.

⊕ Click on "Select Point <".

⊕ Pick an insertion point at the midpoint of the bottom of the keyboard.

⊕ Remove the check from "Retain Objects".

⊕ Click on "OK" to end the dialog.

The newly defined block will disappear from the screen. In the next task we will insert several workstations back into your drawing and then use DDATTE to change an attribute value.

10.6   Editing Attributes with DDATTE and ATTEDIT

GENERAL PROCEDURE

1. Open the Modify menu, highlight Object, and select Attribute.
2. Select Single or Global editing.
3. Specify blocks and attributes to include in the editing process.
4. In one-by-one editing, specify the property to be edited and edit it.
5. In global editing, specify the string to change and new string.

The DDATTE and ATTEDIT commands provide the capacity to change values and text properties of attributes in blocks that have been inserted. They do not allow you to edit attribute definitions. Block definitions and attribute definitions can be changed only by re-creating them.

There are two ways to edit attributes. One-by-one editing allows you to change individual attribute values, text position, height, angle, style, layer, and color. Global editing allows you to change values only.

⊕ To begin this task, you should have a clear screen, but the ws block with its attributes as defined in the previous task must be stored in your current drawing.

⊕ Insert three workstations, using the following procedure (note the attribute prompts):

1. Type "i" or select the Insert Block tool from the Draw toolbar.

2. Type or select "ws" for the block name.
3. Pick an insertion point.
4. Press Enter for X and Y scale factors and rotation angle.
5. Answer the attribute prompts for monitors and computers.

We specified one 486 and two Pentium computers for this exercise and retained all the monitor defaults (Super VGA). Your hardware information may be entirely different, but this exercise will be simpler if you use ours. Notice that you are not prompted for mouse specifications because that attribute is preset.

When you are done, your screen should resemble Figure 10-12.

The first thing we will do with the inserted blocks is use ATTDISP ("attribute display") to turn invisible attributes on.

Displaying Invisible Attributes

The ATTDISP command allows control of the visibility of all attribute values, regardless of their defined visibility mode.

⊕ Open the View menu, highlight Display, and select Attribute Display.
   The submenu shows you three options. "Normal" means that visible attributes are visible and invisible attributes are invisible. "On" turns all attributes on. "Off" turns all attributes off.

⊕ Select "on".
   Your screen will be regenerated with invisible attributes on, as shown in Figure 10-13. You can leave ATTDISP on in this exercise or turn it back to "normal".

Now we will do an edit. Imagine that these three workstations represent part of a small worksite and that we just purchased a new Super VGA 20" monitor. We could erase one of the workstations and reinsert it with new attribute information, but it will be simpler to edit just the one attribute that needs to change.

Figure 10-12

Figure 10-13

Figure 10-14

⊕   Open the Modify menu, highlight Object, and then Attribute, and then select "Single".

This enters the DDATTE command. AutoCAD will prompt you to select a block.

⊕   Select the middle workstation.

You will see the Edit Attributes dialog box shown in Figure 10-14. Notice that all defined attributes are available, including the preset digitizer attribute.

⊕   Click in the Monitor edit box and add "20"" to the text.

⊕   Click on "OK" to end the dialog.

The attribute text will be changed as shown in Figure 10-15.

Now let's perform a global edit.

⊕   Open the Modify menu, highlight Object, and then Attribute, and then select Global.

Figure 10-15

This enters the ATTEDIT command. In what appears to be a glitch in our version of Release 14, AutoCAD prompts

> Edit attributes one at a time? <Y>:

You will have to enter "n" to move on to global editing, a step that should be automated at this point. Perhaps this has been fixed by the time you are reading this.

⊕ If necessary, type "n".

AutoCAD prompts

> Edit only attributes visible on the screen? <Y>

If you left ATTDISP "on", all attributes are visible.

⊕ Press Enter to edit only visible attributes.

AutoCAD issues a series of three prompts that allow you to narrow down the field of attributes to be edited.

> Block name specification <*>:

If we had more than one type of block on the screen, we could limit editing to occurrences of whatever block we wished to name. But we have only the ws block.

⊕ Press Enter.

AutoCAD prompts

> Attribute tag specification <*>:

This allows us to narrow the field to a single tag—all the computers, for example.

⊕ Type "computer".

AutoCAD now prompts for an attribute value:

> Attribute value specification <*>:

This allows us to specify only computers with the value—"Pentium", for example.

⊕ Press Enter.

Now AutoCAD asks us to select attributes by pointing or windowing:

Select Attributes:

⊕ Select the two Pentium computer attributes.

Now AutoCAD knows which attributes to edit. It will allow you to change the entire text of the two attributes, or only part. It does this by requesting a string:

String to change:

A string is simply a text sequence. It may be part or all of the text.

⊕ Type "Pentium".

Now AutoCAD prompts

New string:

⊕ Type "Pentium 166".

The two selected attributes will be changed, as shown in Figure 10-16.

Extracting Attribute Information from Drawings

Although there are many good reasons to use attributes, the most impressive is the ability to create extract files (the ATTEXT and DDATTEXT commands), which can be processed by other programs to generate reports, bills of materials, inventories, parts lists, and quotations. This means, for example, that with a well-managed CAD system you can do a drawing of a construction project and get a complete price breakdown and supply list directly from the drawing database, all processed by computer. To accomplish this, you need a complete library of parts with carefully defined attributes and a program such as dBASE IV or LOTUS 1-2-3 that is capable of receiving the extract information and formatting it into a useful report.

Unfortunately, since we have no way of knowing what programs are available to you and since we want to keep the focus of this book on drawing rather than programming, it is beyond our scope to create the files and formats necessary for extracting attributes. With a little imagination, however, you should be able to see the possibilities. With a database program, for example, we could match the computer, monitor, and digitizer names in our block references to a price list contained in

Figure 10-16

a database file, calculate totals and subtotals, and format an elaborate report. This is a matter worthy of a whole book of its own, and we have only scratched the surface here. If you want additional information, see the *AutoCAD User's Guide*.

10.7 EXPLODEing Blocks

GENERAL PROCEDURE

1. Type "Explode", select Explode from the Modify menu, or select the Explode tool from the Modify toolbar.
2. Select objects.
3. Press Enter to carry out the command.

The EXPLODE command undoes the work of the BLOCK or GROUP command. It takes a set of objects that have been defined as a block or group and re-creates them as independent entities. EXPLODE works on dimensions and hatch patterns as well as on blocks created in the BMAKE or BLOCK commands. It does not work on XREF drawings until they have been attached permanently through the bind option.

⊕ To begin this task, you should have at least one ws block on your screen.

⊕ To see why you need this command, select a ws block by pointing.

You will see grips at the insertion point of the block and at the start point of the two visible attributes.

⊕ Try selecting the monitor independently.

You will be unable to do this. Since the monitor, computer, keyboard, and digitizer are all part of a single entity, the ws block, they cannot be selected or edited except as a unit. The attributes are an exception. They can be edited with DDATTE and DDATTEDIT and can be moved independently using the stretch feature of grip editing, if they have been defined as visible. However, in most applications you will not want to explode block references that contain attribute information, because EXPLODE replaces the information with attribute tags.

Let's try exploding a workstation.

⊕ Type "Explode", select Explode from the Modify menu, or select the Explode tool from the Modify toolbar, as shown in Figure 10-17.

You will have to move the Modify toolbar into a floating position to access the Explode tool.

You will be prompted to select objects.

Figure 10-17

Figure 10-18

⊕ Select a ws block.

⊕ Press Enter to carry out the command.

Notice that the attribute information is replaced by tags, as shown in Figure 10-18.

⊕ Now try selecting the monitor again.

⊕ Try selecting other parts of the workstation.

All of the component parts of the previously blocked workstation can now be edited separately. However, notice that there are still blocks within this configuration. Try selecting one of the buttons on the keyboard, for example. You will see that the keyboard is still considered a single entity. This is an example of a nested block. The keyboard block is one component of the former workstation block. Since EXPLODE moves through levels of nesting one at a time, blocks that were included in the definition of the ws block are still blocks when it is exploded.

Before going on, take a look at the following chart, Other Commands to Use with Blocks. It is a list and description of other commands that are frequently used in conjunction with blocks.

Other Commands to Use with Blocks

Command	Usage
BASE	Allows you to specify a base insertion point for an entire drawing. The base point will be used when the drawing is inserted in other drawings.
DBLIST	Displays information for all entities in the current drawing database. Information includes type of entity and layer. Additional information depends on the type of entity. For blocks, it includes insertion point, X scale, Y scale, rotation, and attribute values.
LIST	Lists information about a single block or entity. Information listed is the same as that in DBLIST, but for the selected entity only.
MINSERT	Multiple Insert. Allows you to insert arrays of blocks. MINSERT arrays take up less memory than ARRAYs of INSERTed blocks.
PURGE	Deletes unused blocks, layers, linetypes, shapes, or text styles from a drawing.
WBLOCK	Saves a block to a separate file so that it can be inserted in other drawings. Does not save unused blocks or layers, and therefore can be used to reduce drawing file size.

10.8   Review Material

Questions

1. Why is it often a good idea to create blocks on layer 0?
2. What is the difference between a group and a block?
3. What is an insertion base point, as used in the BLOCK command? What is an insertion point, as used in the INSERT command?
4. Blocks, external references, and raster images are all inserted with a scale factor. Why?
5. Explain how you could, in theory, create a complete drawing using the INSERT command only.
6. What is the difference between COPY and COPYCLIP?
7. What is an attribute tag? What is an attribute prompt? What is an attribute value?
8. What are the three settings of ATTDISP?
9. Explain the value of attribute extraction.
10. What other complex entities can be EXPLODEd besides blocks?
11. What happens to attribute values when a block is exploded?

Drawing Problems

1. Save the current drawing so that you can use the settings for Drawing 10-1. Open a new drawing using the B prototype and create a hexagon circumscribed around a circle so that both have a 1.0 unit radius. These objects should be created so that when they are defined as a block, they will be inserted on layer 2 regardless of what layer is current at the time.
2. Define an attribute to go with the hexagon and circle. The tag should identify the two as a hex bolt; the prompt should ask for a hex bolt diameter. The attribute should be visible in the drawing, center justified 0.5 units below the block, with text 0.3 units high.
3. Create a block with the bolt and its attribute. Leave a clear screen when you are done.
4. Draw a rectangle on layer 1, with lower left corner at (0,4) and upper right corner at (18,8).
5. Insert 0.5 diameter hex bolts at (2,6) and (16,6). Insert a 1.0 unit hex bolt at (9,6). The sizes of each hex bolt should appear beneath the bolt.

10.9   Drawing 10-1: Cad Room

This architectural drawing is primarily an exercise in using blocks and attributes. Use your ws block and its attributes to fill in the workstations and text after you draw the walls and countertop. New blocks should be created for the plotters and printers, as described following. The drawing setup is the same as that used in the chapter.

DRAWING SUGGESTIONS

UNITS = Architectural, smallest fraction = 1
GRID = 19
SNAP = 10
LIMITS = (0',0') (48',36')

- The "plotter" block is a 1×3 rectangle, with two visible, variable attributes (all the default attribute modes). The first attribute is for a manufacturer and the second for a model. The "printers" are 2×2.5 with the same type of attributes. Draw the rectangles, define their attributes 8 inches below them, create the BLOCK definitions, and then INSERT plotters and printers as shown.

    Note: Do not include the labels "plotter" or "laser printer" in the block, because text in a block will be rotated with the block. This would give you inverted text on the front countertop. Insert the blocks and add the text afterward. The attribute text can be handled differently, as described following.

- The "8 pen plotter" was inserted with a Y scale factor of 1.25.

THE MIRRTEXT SYSTEM VARIABLE

The two workstations on the front counter could be inserted with a rotation angle of 180 degrees, but then the attribute text would be inverted also and would have to be turned around using ATTEDIT. Instead, we have reset the "mirrtext" system variable so that we could mirror blocks without attribute text being inverted:

1. Type "mirrtext".
2. Type "0".

Now you can mirror objects on the back counter to create those on the front. With the "mirrtext" system variable set to "0", text included in a MIRROR procedure is not inverted as it would be with mirrtext set to "1" (the default). This applies to attribute text as well as ordinary text. However, it does not apply to ordinary text included in a block definition.

CAD ROOM
Drawing 10-1

10.10   Drawing 10-2: Base Assembly

This is a good exercise in assembly drawing procedures. You will be drawing each of the numbered part details and then assembling them into the "Base Assembly."

DRAWING SUGGESTIONS

We will no longer provide you with units, grid, snap, and limit settings. You can determine what you need by looking over the drawing and its dimensions. Remember that you can always change a setting later if it becomes necessary.

- You can create your own title block from scratch or develop one from "Title Block," Drawing 7-1, if you have saved it. Once created and SAVEd or WBLOCKed, a title block can be inserted and scaled to fit any drawing. Auto-CAD also comes with drawing templates that have borders and title blocks.

USING MINSERT TO CREATE A TABLE

The parts list should also be defined as a block. Since many drawings include parts lists, you will want to be able to create a table quickly with any given number of rows. Try this:

1. Define a block that represents one row of the parts list.
2. WBLOCK it so it can be used in any drawing.
3. When you insert it, use either ARRAY or MINSERT to create the number of rows in the table (MINSERT creates an array of a block as part of the insertion process).

MANAGING PARTS BLOCKS FOR MULTIPLE USE

You will be drawing each of the numbered parts (B101-1, B101-2, etc.) and then assembling them. In an industrial application the individual part details would be sent to different manufacturers or manufacturing departments, so they must exist as separate, completely dimensioned drawings as well as blocks that can be used in creating the assembly. An efficient method is to create three separate blocks for each part detail: one for dimensions and one for each view in the assembly. The dimensioned part drawings will include both views. The blocks of the two views will have dimensions, hidden lines, and center lines erased.

Think carefully about the way you name blocks. You might want to adopt a naming system like this: "B101-1D" for the dimensioned drawing, "B101-1T" for a top view without dimensions, and "B101-1F" for a front view without dimensions. Such a system will make it easy to call out all the top view parts for the top view assembly, for example. A more detailed procedure is outlined for Drawings 10-3 and 10-4.

- Notice that the assembly requires you to do a considerable amount of trimming away of lines from the blocks you insert. This can be done easily, but you must remember to EXPLODE the inserted blocks first.

ITEM NO.	PART NO.	DESCRIPTION		QTY
6	B101-6	FLAT WASHER	1/2	8
5	B101-5	NUT	1/2-13 UNC	4
4	B101-4	HEX HEAD BOLT	1/2-13 UNC x 3.50 LG	4
3	B101-3	SHOULDER PIN		1
2	B101-2	SPACER		1
1	B101-1	BASE		1

CAD Support Associates

DRAWING TITLE: **BASE ASSEMBLY**

DRAWING NO. Drawing 10-2

SIZE C   SCALE: DATE: SHEET: REV

BASE ASSEMBLY

B101-1

B101-2

B101-3

B101-4

B101-5

B101-6

12 x 45° CHAMFER
BOTH ENDS

KNURL

⌀1.25   ⌀1.00   ⌀2.00

4.75   4.00   3.50

⌀1.00 THRU
C'BORE ⌀1.25
x .50 DEEP

6.25 SQ   3.12   ⌀2.00

⌀.50 THRU
4 HOLES EQ SP
ON ⌀3.50 B.C.

⌀2.00   4.25   1.50

⌀2.00 THRU   ⌀4.50   1.50

⌀.50 THRU
4 HOLES EQ SP
ON ⌀3.50 B.C.

0.75   0.52   1/2-13 unc

0.12   1.25   ⌀.62

4.00   2.00   0.52   0.75   1/2-13 unc   .06 x 45° CHAMFER

10.11   Drawings 10-3 and 10-4:
Double Bearing Assembly
and Scooter Assembly

All of the specific drawing techniques required to do the individual part details in these two drawings are ones that you have encountered in previous chapters. What is new is the blocking and assembly process. The procedure outlined here is a step-by-step elaboration of the kind of block management system we introduced in the last drawing.

DRAWING SUGGESTIONS

1. Draw each part detail in whatever two- or three-view form is given. Make the drawing complete with hidden lines, center lines, and dimensions.
2. SAVE or WBLOCK the part, giving it a file name that identifies it as a complete, dimensioned drawing for example, "CAPD").
3. ERASE dimensions, hidden lines, and center lines. If you have kept your layers separated, you can turn off layer 0 and then erase everything left using a window or crossing box. Then turn 0 on again.
4. BLOCK the views separately, giving each a name that will identify it with its view (for example, "CAPT" for the top view of the cap, "CAPF" for cap front, and "CAPR" for cap right). It is essential that your naming system keep these BLOCKed views distinct from the dimensioned drawing of step 2.
5. Insert blocks from step 4 to create the assembly. EXPLODE and TRIM where necessary.

ASSEMBLY DRAWING

ITEM NO.	DESCRIPTION	PART NO.	QTY
4	HEX HEAD BOLT 1/2-13 UNC x 2.25 LG	DB1-4	6
3	BUSHING	DB1-3	2
2	CAP	DB1-2	1
1	BASE	DB1-1	1

DRAWN BY: _____ DATE: _____

DRAWING TITLE:
Double Bearing

DRAWING NO.
Drawing10-3

SIZE | REV

SCALE: DATE: SHEET OF

NOTE: FILLETS AND ROUNDS 1/8 RADIUS
EXCEPT AS NOTED

DRAWING COMPLIMENTS OF DAVID SUMNER

BUSHING

HEX HEAD BOLT

1/2-13 x 2 1/4 UNC-2A

CAP

BASE

WHEEL DETAIL

ITEM NO.	DESCRIPTION		PART NO.	QTY
13	HEX NUT	1/4-20 UNC	S100-13	8
12	TRUSS HEAD SCREW	1/4-20 UNC x 1.50 LG	S100-12	8
11	HEX NUT	3/8-16 UNC	S100-11	4
10	HEX HEAD BOLT	3/8-16 UNC x 5.00 LG	S100-10	1
9	HEX HEAD BOLT	3/8-16 UNC x 4.00 LG	S100-9	1
8	HEX HEAD BOLT	3/8-16 UNC x 3.25 LG	S100-8	2
7	BRACE		S100-7	1
6	SPACER		S100-6	3
5	KICK STAND		S100-5	1
4	FOOT REST		S100-4	1
3	FRAME		S100-3	1
2	HANDLE BAR		S100-2	2
1	WHEEL		S100-1	2

CAD Support Associates

DRAWING TITLE:

SCOOTER ASSEMBLY

SIZE	DRAWING NO.	REV.
	Drawing 10-4	
SCALE:	DATE:	SHEET OF

DRAWN BY: DATE:

11 Isometric Drawing

COMMANDS

TOOLS	**DRAW**	**VIEW**
SNAP (isometric)	ELLIPSE	VIEW
		DDVIEW

OVERVIEW

Learning to use AutoCAD's isometric drawing features should be a pleasure at this point. There are very few new commands to learn, and anything you know about manual isometric drawing will translate easily to the computer. In fact, the isometric snap, grid, and cross hairs make isometric drawing considerably easier on a CAD system than on the drafting board. Once you know how to get into the isometric mode and to change from plane to plane, you will be on your way. You will find that many of the commands you have learned previously will continue to work for you and that using the isometric drawing planes is a good warmup for 3D wireframe drawing, which is the topic of the next chapter.

TASKS

11.1   Using Isometric SNAP

GENERAL PROCEDURE

1. Open the Drawing Aids dialog box from the Tools menu.
2. Click "On" under "Isometric Snap/Grid".
3. Click OK.

To begin drawing isometrically you need to switch to the isometric snap style. You will find the grid and cross hairs behaving in ways that may seem odd at first, but you will quickly get used to them.

⊕   Select "Drawing Aids..." from the Tools menu.

   You will see the Drawing Aids dialog box.

⊕   Click the "On" box under "Isometric Snap/Grid".

⊕   Click on "OK".

   At this point your grid and cross hairs will be reoriented so that they resemble Figure 11-1. This is the isometric grid. Grid points are placed at 30-, 90-, and 150-degree angles from the horizontal. The cross hairs are initially turned to define the left isometric plane. The three isoplanes will be discussed in Task 11.2.

⊕   To get a feeling for how this snap style works, enter the LINE command and draw some boxes, as shown in Figure 11-2.

   Make sure that ortho is off and snap is on, or you will be unable to draw the lines shown.

Figure 11-1

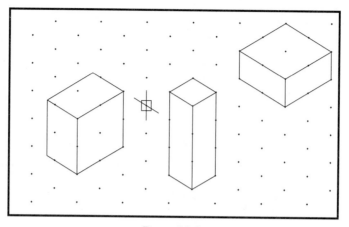

Figure 11-2

11.2 Switching Isometric Planes

GENERAL PROCEDURE

1. Press Ctrl-E or F5 once to switch to the "top" plane.
2. Press Ctrl-E or F5 again to switch to the "right" plane.
3. Press Ctrl-E or F5 again to return to the "left" plane.

If you tried to draw the boxes in Task 11.1 with ortho on, you have discovered that it is impossible. Without changing the orientation of the cross hairs, you can draw in only one of the three isometric planes. We need to be able to switch planes so that we can leave ortho on for accuracy and speed. There are several ways to do this, but the simplest, quickest, and most convenient way is to use F5 or Ctrl-E.

Before beginning, take a look at Figure 11-3. It shows the three planes of a standard isometric drawing. These planes are often referred to as top, front, and right.

Figure 11-3

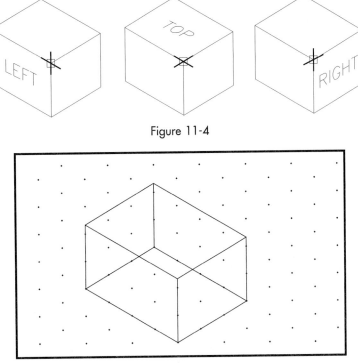

Figure 11-4

Figure 11-5

However, AutoCAD's terminology is top, left, and right. We will stick with Auto-CAD's labels in this chapter.

Now look at Figure 11-4 and you will see how the isometric cross hairs are oriented to draw in each of the planes.

⊕ Press F5 to switch from "left" to "top."

⊕ Press F5 again to switch from "top" to "right."

⊕ Press F5 once more to switch back to "left."

⊕ Now turn ortho on and draw a box outline like the one in Figure 11-5.
You will need to switch planes several times to accomplish this. Notice that you can switch planes using F5 without interrupting the LINE command. If you find that you are in the wrong plane to construct a line, switch planes. Since every plane allows movement in two of the three directions, you will always be able to move in the direction you want with one switch. However, you may not be able to hit the snap point you want. If you cannot, switch planes again.

11.3 Using COPY and Other Edit Commands

Most commands work in the isometric planes just as they do in standard orthographic views. In this exercise we will construct an isometric view of a bracket using the LINE, COPY, and ERASE commands. Then we will draw angled corners

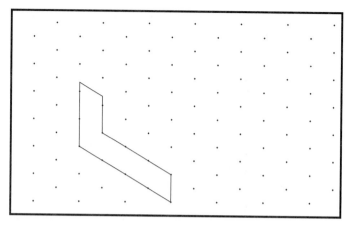

Figure 11-6

using CHAMFER. In the next task we will draw a hole in the bracket with EL-LIPSE, COPY, and TRIM.

⊞ To begin this exercise, clear your screen of boxes and check to see that ortho is on.

⊞ Draw the L-shaped object shown in Figure 11-6.

Notice that this is drawn in the left isoplane and that it is 1.00 unit wide.

Next, we will copy this object 4.00 units back to the right to create the back surface of the bracket.

⊞ Type "Co" or select the Copy Object tool from the Modify toolbar.

⊞ Use a window or crossing box to select all the lines in the L.

⊞ Press Enter to end object selection.

⊞ Pick a base point at the inside corner of the L.

It is a good exercise to turn ortho on, switch planes, and move the object around in each plane. You will see that you can move in two directions in each plane and that in order to move the object back to the right, as shown in Figure 11-7, you must be in either the top or the right plane.

Figure 11-7

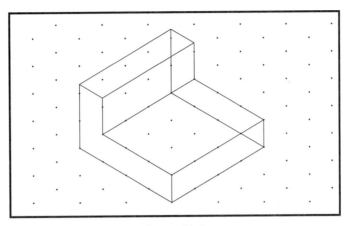

Figure 11-8

⊕ Pick a second point of displacement four units back to the right, as shown in Figure 11-7.

⊕ Enter the LINE command and draw the connecting lines in the right plane, as shown in Figure 11-8.

If you wish, you can draw only one of the lines and use the COPY command with the multiple option to create the others.

Creating Chamfers in an Isometric View

Keep in mind that angular lines in an isometric view do not show true lengths. Angular lines must be drawn between end points located along paths that are vertical or horizontal in one of the three drawing planes. In our exercise we will create angled lines by using the CHAMFER command to cut the corners of the bracket. This will be no different from using CHAMFER in orthographic views.

⊕ Select Chamfer from the Modify menu or the Chamfer tool from the Modify toolbar.

⊕ Type "d".

AutoCAD will prompt for a first chamfer distance.

⊕ Type "1".

⊕ Press Enter to accept 1.00 as the second chamfer distance.

⊕ Repeat the CHAMFER command.

⊕ Pick two edges of the bracket to create a chamfer, as shown in Figure 11-9.

⊕ Repeat CHAMFER.

Chamfer the other three corners so that your drawing resembles Figure 11-9.

⊕ ERASE the two small lines left hanging at the previous corners.

⊕ To complete the bracket, enter the LINE command and draw lines between the new chamfer end points.

Figure 11-9

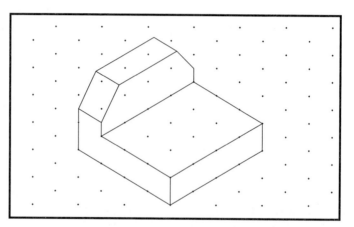

Figure 11-10

⊞ Finally, ERASE the two unseen lines on the back surface to produce Figure 11-10.

11.4 Drawing Isometric Circles with ELLIPSE

GENERAL PROCEDURE

1. Locate the center point.
2. Type "el" or select the Ellipse tool from the Draw toolbar.
3. Type "I".
4. Pick the center point.
5. Type or show the radius or diameter.

The ELLIPSE command can be used to draw true ellipses in orthographic views or ellipses that appear to be circles in isometric views (called "isocircles" in AutoCAD). In this task we will use the latter capability to construct a hole in the bracket.

⊕ To begin this task you should have the bracket shown in Figure 11-10 on your display.

The first thing you will need in order to draw an isocircle is a center point. Often it will be necessary to locate this point carefully using DIST, temporary lines, or point filters (Chapter 12). You must be sure that you can locate the center point before entering the ELLIPSE command.

In our case it will be easy since the center point will be on a snap point.

⊕ Type "el," select Ellipse from the Draw menu, or select the Ellipse tool from the Draw toolbar, as shown in Figure 11-11.

AutoCAD will prompt

        Arc/Center/Isocircle<Axis endpoint 1>:

The option we want is "Isocircle". We will ignore the others for the time being.

⊕ Type "i".

AutoCAD prompts

                Center of circle:

If you could not locate the center point, you would have to exit the command now and start over.

⊕ Use the snap and grid to pick the center of the surface, as shown in Figure 11-12.

Figure 11-11

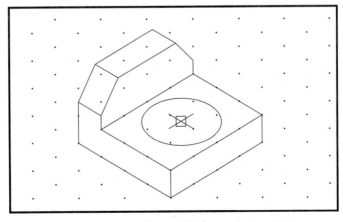

Figure 11-12

AutoCAD gives you an isocircle to drag, as in the CIRCLE command. The isocircle you see will depend on the isoplane you are in. To understand this try switching planes to see how the image changes.

⊕ Stretch the isocircle image out and then press F5 to switch iso-planes. Observe the isocircle. Try this two or three times.

⊕ Switch to the top isoplane before moving on.

AutoCAD is prompting for a radius or diameter:

<Circle radius>/Diameter:

A radius specification is the default here, as it is in the CIRCLE command.

⊕ Type a value or pick a point so that your isocircle resembles the one in Figure 11-12.

Next, we use the COPY and TRIM commands to create the bottom of the hole.

⊕ Type "Co" or select the Copy tool from the Modify toolbar.

⊕ Select the isocircle by pointing, or type "l" for "last".

⊕ End object selection.

⊕ Pick a base point.

Any point could be used as the base point. A good choice would be the top of the front corner. If you do this, then choosing the bottom of the front corner as a second point will give you the exact thickness of the bracket.

⊕ Pick a second point 1.00 unit below the base point.

Your screen should now resemble Figure 11-13. The last thing we must do is TRIM the hidden portion of the bottom of the hole.

⊕ Type "tr" or select the Trim tool from the Modify toolbar.

⊕ Pick the first isocircle as a cutting edge.

⊕ Press Enter to end cutting edge selection.

⊕ Select the hidden section of the lower isocircle.

⊕ Press Enter to exit TRIM.

The bracket is now complete and your screen should resemble Figure 11-14.

Figure 11-13

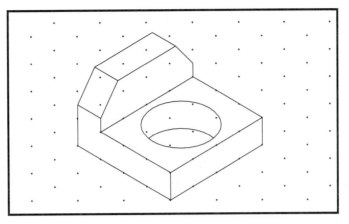

Figure 11-14

Note: Sometimes you will not get the results you expect when using TRIM in an isometric view. It may be necessary to use BREAK and ERASE as an alternative.

This completes the present discussion of isometric drawing. You will find more in the drawing suggestions at the end of this chapter.

Now we will go on to explore the nonisometric use of the ELLIPSE command and then to show you two new tricks for controlling your display.

11.5 Drawing Ellipses in Orthographic Views

GENERAL PROCEDURE

1. Type "el" or select the Ellipse tool from the Draw toolbar.
2. Pick one end point of an axis.
3. Pick the second end point.
4. Pick a third point showing the length of the other axis.

The ELLIPSE command is important for drawing isocircles but also for drawing true ellipses in orthographic views. There is also a new option to create elliptical arcs.

An ellipse is determined by a center point and two mutually perpendicular axes. In AutoCAD, these specifications can be shown in two nearly identical ways, each requiring you to show three points (see Figure 11-15). In the default method you will show two end points of an axis and then show half the length of the other axis, from the midpoint of the first axis out (the midpoint of an axis is also the center of the ellipse). The other method allows you to pick the center point of the ellipse first, then the end point of one axis, followed by half the length of the other axis.

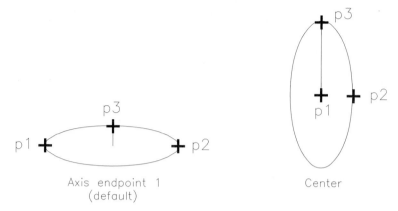

Figure 11-15

✦ In preparation for this exercise, return to the standard snap mode using the following procedure:
   1. Open the Drawing Aids dialog box from the Tools menu.
   2. Click the "On" box under "Isometric Snap/Grid" so that the *x* is removed.
   3. Press Enter or click on OK.

You will see that your grid is returned to the standard pattern and the cross hairs are horizontal and vertical again. Notice that this does not affect the isometric bracket you have just drawn.

We will briefly explore the ELLIPSE command and draw some standard ellipses.

✦ Type "el" or select the Ellipse tool from the Draw toolbar or Ellipse from the Draw menu.

AutoCAD prompts

Arc/Center/<Axis endpoint 1>:

✦ Pick an axis end point as shown by p1 on the ellipse at the lower left of the display in Figure 11-16.

Figure 11-16

AutoCAD prompts for the other end point:

Axis endpoint 2:

⊕ Pick a second end point as shown by p2.

AutoCAD gives you an ellipse to drag and a rubber band so that you can show the length of the other axis. Only the length of the rubber band is significant; the angle is already determined to be perpendicular to the first axis. Because of this the third point will only fall on the ellipse if the rubber band is perpendicular to the first axis.

The prompt that follows allows you to show the second axis distance as before, or a rotation around the first axis:

<Other axis distance>/Rotation:

The rotation option is awkward to use, and we will not explore it here; see the *AutoCAD Command Reference* for more information.

⊕ Pick p3 as shown.

This point will show half the length of the other axis.

The first ellipse should now be complete. Now we will draw one showing the center point first.

⊕ Repeat the ELLIPSE command.

⊕ At the "Arc/Center/<Axis endpoint 1>:" prompt, type "c".

AutoCAD will give you a prompt for a center point:

Center of Ellipse:

⊕ Pick a center point (p1), as shown at the middle left of Figure 11-16.

Now you will have a rubber band stretching from the center to the end of an axis and the following prompt:

Axis endpoint:

⊕ Pick an end point, as shown in Figure 11-16 (p2).

The prompt that follows allows you to show the second axis distance as before, or a rotation around the first axis:

<Other axis distance>/Rotation:

⊕ Pick an axis distance, as shown by p3.

Here again the rubber band is significant for distance only. The point you pick will fall on the ellipse only if the rubber band is stretched perpendicular to the first axis. Notice that it is not in Figure 11-16.

Drawing Elliptical Arcs

Elliptical arcs can be drawn by trimming complete arcs or by using the arc option of the ELLIPSE command. Using the arc option, you will first construct an ellipse in one of the two methods shown previously and then show the arc of that ellipse that you want to keep. Determining arcs can be quite complicated because of the many different parameters available. You will remember this from Chapter 4, which you learned the arc command. In this exercise we will stick to a simple procedure; you should have no difficulty pursuing the more complex options on your own.

⊕ Enter the ELLIPSE command.

⊕ Pick a first axis end point, as shown by p1 at the upper left in Figure 11-16.

⊕ Pick a second end point, p2 in the figure.

⊕ Pick p3 to show the second axis distance.

AutoCAD will draw an ellipse as you have specified, but the image is only temporary. Now you need to show the arc you want drawn. The two options are "Parameter" and "start angle". Parameter will take you into more options that allow you to specify your arc in different ways, similar to the options of the ARC command. We will stick with the default option.

⊕ Pick p4 to show the angle at which the elliptical arc will begin.

Move the cursor slowly now and you will see all the arcs that are possible starting from this angle.

⊕ Pick p5 to indicate the end angle and complete the command.

11.6 Saving and Restoring Displays with DDVIEW

GENERAL PROCEDURE

1. Select "Named View..." from the View menu.
2. Select New to create a new view.
3. Type a view name.
4. Define the view.
5. Click on "Save View".
6. Click on OK.

The word "view" in connection with the DDVIEW command has a special significance in AutoCAD. It refers to any set of display boundaries that have been named and "saved" using the DDVIEW command. Views that have been saved can be restored rapidly and by direct reference rather than by redefining the location and size of the area to be displayed. DDVIEW can be useful in creating drawing layouts and anytime you know that you will be returning frequently to a certain area of a large drawing. It saves having to zoom out to look at the complete drawing and then zoom back in again on the area you want.

Imagine that we have to do some extensive detail work on the area around the hole in the bracket and also on the top corner. We can define each of these as a view and jump back and forth at will.

⊕ To begin this exercise, you should have the bracket on your screen, as shown in Figure 11-17.

⊕ Select "Named views..." from the View menu.

Figure 11-17

Figure 11-18

Figure 11-19

This opens the View Control dialog box shown in Figure 11-18. The first thing we need to do is define some views. Then we will see how to switch from one view to another. The first view to define is the current view. We will give it a new name and save it so that we can return quickly.

⊞ Click on "New...".

This takes you to the Define New View dialog box shown in Figure 11-19. Notice that the Current Display radio button is selected. All we have to do is give the current display a name and then save it as a view.

⊕ Type "A" in the "New Name" edit box.

Views are designed for speed, so it makes sense to assign them short names.

⊕ Click on "Save View".

The View Control dialog box reappears, with A showing on the list of defined views. Next we will use a window to define a smaller view.

⊕ Click on "New..." to return to the Define New View dialog box.

⊕ Type "H" in the "New Name" edit box.

⊕ Select the Define Window radio button.

Notice that several previously grayed out items are now accessible.

⊕ Click on "Window<".

The dialog box disappears, giving you access to the screen.

⊕ Pick first and second corners to define a window around the hole in the bracket, as shown in Figure 11-17.

⊕ Click on "Save view".

You are now back in the View Control dialog box with A and H on the list of views. Define one more view to show the upper left corner of the bracket, as shown in Figure 11-17.

⊕ Click on "New...".

⊕ Type "C" for the view name.

⊕ Click on "Window<".

⊕ Define a window, as shown in Figure 11-17.

⊕ Click on "Save view".

You have now defined three views. To see the views in action we must restore them.

⊕ Highlight "H".

⊕ Click on "Restore".

⊕ Click on "OK".

Your screen should resemble Figure 11-20.

Now switch to the corner view.

Figure 11-20

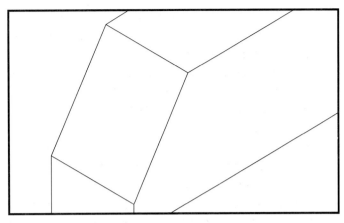

Figure 11-21

⊕   Repeat the DDVIEW command.
⊕   Highlight "C".
⊕   Select "Restore".
⊕   Click on "OK".

Your screen should resemble Figure 11-21.

11.7   Review Material

Questions

1. What are the angles of the cross hairs and grid points in an isometric grid?
2. What function key is used to switch from one isometric plane to another?
3. What are the names for the isometric planes in AutoCAD?
4. What is an isocircle? Why are isocircles drawn in the ELLIPSE command?
5. How many different isocircles can you draw that have the same radius and the same center?
6. How many points does it take to define an ellipse?
7. What do these points define in each of the two basic methods of drawing an orthographic ellipse?
8. What must you do before you can use the DDVIEW command to restore a view?
9. What are the two basic ways to define a view?

Drawing Problems

1. Using the isometric grid, draw a 4-by-4 square in the right isoplane.
2. Copy the square back 4 units along the left isoplane.
3. Connect the corners of the two squares to form an isometric cube. Erase any lines that would be hidden in this object.
4. Use text rotation and obliquing to draw the word "Top" in the Top plane of the cube so that the text is centered on the face and aligned with its edges. The text should be 0.5 units high.
5. In a similar manner, draw the word "Left" at the center of the left side and the word "Right" at the center of the right side. All text should align with the face that it is on.

11.8 Drawing 11-1: Mounting Bracket

This drawing is a direct extension of the exercises in the chapter. It will give you practice in basic AutoCAD isometrics and in transferring dimensions from orthographic to isometric views.

DRAWING SUGGESTIONS

- When the center point of an isocircle is not on snap, as in this drawing, you will need to create a specifiable point and snap onto it. Draw intersecting lines from the midpoints of the sides so that you can snap to that intersection, or use DIST and draw a point there. Then use a "node" snap.
- Often when you try to select a group of objects to copy, there will be many crossing lines that you do not want to include in the copy. This is an ideal time to use the "remove" option in object selection. First window the objects you want along with those nearby that are unavoidable, and then remove the unwanted objects one by one.
- Frequently you will get unexpected results when you try to TRIM an object in an isometric view. AutoCAD will divide an ellipse into a series of arcs, for example, and only trim a portion. If you do not get the results you want, use the BREAK command to control how the object is broken, and then erase what you do not want.
- There is no arc option when you use ELLIPSE to draw isocircles, so semicircles like those at the top and bottom of the slots must be constructed by first drawing isocircles and then trimming or erasing unwanted portions.
- Use COPY frequently to avoid duplicating your work. Since it may take a considerable amount of editing to create holes and fillets, do not COPY until edits have been done on the original.
- The row of small arcs that show the curve in the middle of the bracket are multiple copies of the fillet at the corner.

.50 DIA
2 PLACES

Ø2.50

R 1.75
REF

1.50

2.00

.25

2.25

.25 RAD
FILLET TYP

3.50

4.00

2.00

2.50

1.25

1.50

1.00

.25 RAD
4 PLACES

DATE

DRAWN BY:

CAD Support Associates, Inc.

DRAWING TITLE:

MOUNTING BRACKET

DRAWING NO
DRAWING 11-1

REV

SIZE
C

SCALE

DATE

SHEET   OF

11.9 Drawing 11-2: Radio

This drawing introduces text and will be greatly simplified by the use of the rectangular ARRAY command. Placing objects on different layers so they can be turned on and off during TRIM, BREAK, and ERASE procedures will make things considerably less messy.

DRAWING SUGGESTIONS

- Use the "box method" to do this drawing. That is, begin with an isometric box according to the overall outside dimensions of the radio. Then go back and cut away the excess as you form the details of the drawing.
- The horizontal "grill" can be done with a rectangular array since it runs straight on the vertical. Look carefully at the pattern to see where it repeats. Draw one set and then array it. Later you can go back and trim away the dial and speaker areas.
- Draw isocircles over the grill and break away the lines over the speaker. When you are ready to hatch the speaker, draw another trimmed isocircle to define the hatch boundary, create the hatch, and then erase the boundary.
- The knobs are isocircles with copies to show thickness. You can use tangent-to-tangent osnaps to draw the front-to-back connecting lines.
- The text is created on two different angles that line up with the left and right isoplanes. We leave it to you to discover the correct angles.

9V BATTERY

3.12

1.50

.75

8.00

4.38

.12 TYP

5.00

1.00

.25

FM 80 90 100 110 90

AM 50 60 70 80

R1.62

2.38

VOLUME ON OFF

TUNING

AM FM

3.00

1.25

.25

.12

Ø1.00 ELLIPSE
3 PLACES

TEXT SIZE = .12

CAD Support Associates, Inc.

DRAWING TITLE: RADIO

DRAWING NO.   DRAWING 11-2

DRAWN BY   DATE

SIZE   SCALE: DATE   SHEET   OF

REV

11.10   Drawing 11-3: Fixture Assembly

This is a difficult drawing. It will take time and patience but will teach you a great deal about isometric drawing in AutoCAD.

DRAWING SUGGESTIONS

- This drawing can be done either by drawing everything in place as you see it, or by drawing the parts and moving them into place along the common center line that runs through the middle of all the items. If you use the former method, draw the center line first and use it to locate the center points of isocircles and as base points for other measures.

- As you go, look for pieces of objects that can be copied to form other objects. Avoid duplicating efforts by editing before copying. In particular, where one object covers part of another, be sure to copy it before you trim or erase the covered sections.

- To create the chamfered end of item 4, begin by drawing the 1.00 diameter cylinder 3.00 long with no chamfer. Then copy the isocircle at the end forward 0.125. The smaller isocircle is 0.875 (7/8), since 0.0625 (1/16) is cut away from the 1.00 circle all around. Draw this smaller isocircle and TRIM away everything that is hidden. Then draw the slanted chamfer lines using LINE, not CHAMFER. Use the same method for item 5.

- In both the screw and the nut you will need to create hexes around isocircles. Use the dimensions from a standard bolt chart.

- Use three-point arcs to approximate the curves on the screw bolt and the nut. You are after a representation that looks correct. It is impractical and unnecessary to achieve exact measures on these objects in the isometric view.

TOLERANCE FOR HOLES AND PINS

ITEM 4   CLASS RC2 FIT
ITEM 5   CLASS LT4 FIT
ITEM 1   CLASS RC2 FIT FOR CORNER PIN HOLES
ITEM 1   CLASS LT4 FIT FOR CENTER HOLE
ITEM 2   CLASS RC2 FIT FOR CENTER HOLE
ITEM 2   CLASS RC1 FIT FOR CORNER PIN HOLES
ITEM 3   CLASS RC2 FIT FOR CENTER HOLE

ITEM NO.	DESCRIPTION		PART NO.	QTY
7	NUT	1/4–20 UNC	F113-7	4
6	HEX HEAD BOLT	1/4–20 UNC x 3.00 LG	F113-6	4
5	CORNER PIN		F113-5	4
4	CENTER PIN		F113-4	1
3	SPACER	1.25 O.D. x 1.00 I.D. x 1.25 THK	F113-3	1
2	DISK	2.00 O.D. x 1.00 I.D. x .12 THK	F113-2	2
1	END PLATE	4.00 SQUARE x .50 THK	F113-1	2

CAM Support Associates, Inc.

DRAWING TITLE
FIXTURE ASSEMBLY

SIZE **D**   DRAWING NO.   DRAWING 11-3   REV

SCALE   DATE: SHEET   OF

DRAWN BY:

11.11   Drawing 11-4: Flanged Coupling

The isometric view in this three-view drawing must be done working off the center line.

DRAWING SUGGESTIONS

- Draw the major center line first. Then draw vertical center lines at every point where an isocircle will be drawn. Make sure to draw these lines extra long so that they can be used to trim the isocircles in half. By starting at the back of the object and working forward, you can take dimensions directly from the right side view.
- Draw the isocircles at each center line and then trim them to represent semicircles.
- Use end point, intersection, and tangent to tangent osnaps to draw horizontal lines.
- Trim away all obstructed lines and parts of isocircles.
- Draw the four slanted lines in the middle as vertical lines first. Then, with ortho off, CHANGE their end points, moving them in 0.125.
- Remember, MIRROR will not work in the isometric view, although it can be used effectively in the right side view.
- Use BHATCH to create the crosshatching.
- If you have made a mistake in measuring along the major center line, STRETCH can be used to correct it. Make sure that ortho is on and that you are in an isoplane that lets you move the way you want.

FLANGED COUPLING
Drawing 11—4

THIS DRAWING COURTESY OF RICHARD F. ROSS

11.12   Drawing 11-5: Garage Framing

This is a fairly complex drawing that will take lots of trimming and careful work. Changing the "snapang" (snap angle) variable so that you can draw slanted arrays is a method that can be used frequently in isometric drawing.

DRAWING SUGGESTIONS

- You will find yourself using COPY, ZOOM, and TRIM a great deal. OFFSET also will work well. This is a good place to use dynamic zoom.

- You may want to create some new layers of different colors if you have a color monitor. Keeping different parts of the construction walls, rafters, and joists on different layers will allow you to have more control over them and add a lot of clarity to what you see on the screen. Turning layers on and off can considerably simplify trimming operations.

- You can cut down on repetition in this drawing by using arrays on various angles. For example, if the snapang variable is set to 150 degrees, the 22″ wall in the left isoplane can be created as a rectangular array of studs with 1 row and 17 columns set 16 inches apart. To do so, follow this procedure:
    1. Type "snapang".
    2. Enter a new value so that rectangular arrays will be built on isometric angles (30 or 150).
    3. Enter the ARRAY command and create the array. Use negative values where necessary.
    4. Trim the opening for the window.

- One alternative to this array method is to set your snap to 16″ temporarily and use multiple COPY to create the columns of studs, rafters, and joists. Another alternative is to use the grip edit offset snap method beginning with an offset snap of 16″ (i.e., press Shift when you show the first copy displacement and continue to hold down Shift as you make other copies).

- The cutaway in the roof that shows the joists and the back door is drawn using the standard nonisometric ELLIPSE command. Then the rafters are trimmed to the ellipse and the ellipse is erased. Do this procedure before you draw the joists and the back wall. Otherwise you will be trimming these as well.

- Use CHAMFER to create the chamfered corners on the joists.

2"X4" STUD
16" O.C.

9'-1"

2"X10" RAFTER
16" O.C.

(2)2"X4" TOP PLATE

(2)2"X4" HEADER

30

GARAGE FRAMING
Drawing 11-5

THIS DRAWING COURTESY OF TOM CASEY

ROUGH OPENING
7'X10'-6"
2 PLACES

ROUGH OPENING
6'-8"X3'

2"X10" JOIST
16" O.C

2"X12" RIDGE

12
6

ROUGH
OPENING
4'X3'
2 PL.

22'-0"

2"X4" STUD
16" O.C.

2"X4" SHOE

11.13   Drawing 11-6: Cast Iron Tee

The objective of this exercise is to complete the isometric view of the tee using dimensions from the three-view drawing. Begin this isometric by working off the center line.

DRAWING SUGGESTIONS

- Be sure that ortho is on and that you are in an isoplane that is correct for the lines you want to draw. Take full advantage of OBJECT SNAP as you lay out this drawing.
- Draw the two major center lines as shown in isometric first. Draw them to exact length. Then draw vertical center lines at every point where an isocircle will be drawn. These center lines should be drawn longer so the isocircles will trim more easily. You will notice that OFFSET and MIRROR will not work very well in the isometric mode.
- After establishing the centers, draw the isocircles for the three flanges.
- When you have completed the flanges, draw the isocircles for the wall of the tee.
- Draw all horizontal and vertical lines and trim away all nonvisible lines and parts of isocircles. Fillet the required intersections.
- After completing the outline of the tee, use BHATCH to create the crosshatching.

5 1/2

9/16 DRILL
12 HOLES

2 1/2

11/16

7

4 3/8

7/16

7 1/2 6 3

4 1/2

7/16

3/4   3/4

9

FILLET &
ROUNDS 1/8 R

3" CAST IORN TEE
Drawing 11-6

12 Wireframe Models

COMMANDS

VIEW		DRAW
UCS	DDVPOINT	RULESURF
VPOINT	UCSICON	

OVERVIEW

It is now time to begin thinking in three dimensions. 3D drawing in AutoCAD is logical and efficient. You can create wireframe models, surface models, or solid models and display them from multiple points of view. In this chapter we will focus on User Coordinate Systems, 3D viewpoints, and wireframe modeling. These are the primary tools you will need to understand how AutoCAD allows you to work in three dimensions on a two-dimensional screen. Tasks 12.1 through 12.5 will take you through a complete 3D wireframe modeling exercise using four different coordinate systems that we will define.

If you have completed Chapter 11, you will find that working on isometric drawings has prepared you well for 3D drawing. There will be a similar process of switching from plane to plane, but there are two primary differences. First, you will not be restricted to three isometric planes: You can define a User Coordinate System aligned with any specifiable plane. Second, and most important, the model you draw will have true 3D characteristics. You will be able to view it, edit it, and plot it from any definable point in space.

TASKS

12.1 Creating and Viewing a 3D Wireframe Box

In this task we will create a simple 3D box that we can edit in later tasks to form a more complex object. In Chapter 1 we showed how to turn the coordinate system icon (see Figure 12-1) off and on. For drawing in 3D you will definitely want it on. If your icon is not visible, follow this procedure to turn it on:

1. Open the View menu and highlight "Display" and then "UCS", as shown in Figure 12-2.
2. Select "on" from the sub menu.

Figure 12-1

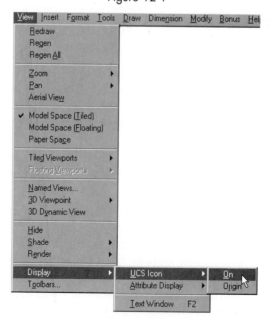

Figure 12-2

For now, simply observe the icon as you go through the process of creating the box, and be aware that you are currently working in the same coordinate system that you have always used in AutoCAD. It is called the World Coordinate System (WCS), to distinguish it from others you will create yourself beginning in Task 12.2.

Currently, the origin of the WCS is at the lower left of your screen. This is the point (0,0,0) when you are thinking 3D, or simply (0,0) when you are in 2D. The x coordinates increase to the right horizontally across the screen, and y coordinates increase vertically up the screen as usual. The z axis, which we have ignored until now, currently extends out of the screen toward you and perpendicular to the x and y axes. This orientation of the three planes is also called a plan view. Soon we will switch to a "front, right, top" or "southeast isometric" view.

Let's begin.

⊕ Draw a 2.00 by 4.00 rectangle near the middle of your screen, as shown in Figure 12-1. Do not use the RECTANG command to draw this figure because we will want to select individual line segments later on.

Changing Viewpoints

To move immediately into a 3D mode of drawing and thinking, our first step will be to change our viewpoint on this object. There are two commands that allow you to create 3D points of view, VPOINT and DVIEW. DVIEW, which is discussed at the end of Chapter 13, is complex and best suited for creating carefully adjusted presentation images, including perspective views. The VPOINT command is somewhat simpler and best used for setting up basic views during the drawing and editing process. A good understanding of all the VPOINT options will increase your understanding of AutoCAD's 3D space. For this reason we have included at the end of this chapter an optional discussion of the different options available in the VPOINT command. There are three or four different methods, developed over time as Autodesk has tried to simplify the viewpoint definition process with each new release of AutoCAD.

In Release 14 the simplest and most efficient method is to use the 3D Viewpoints Presets submenu from the View pull-down menu. For our purposes, this is the only method you will need.

⊕ Open the View menu and highlight "3D Viewpoint".

This will open a submenu beginning with "Plan View", as shown in Figure 12-3. Using this method, AutoCAD will take you directly into 1 of 11 preset viewpoints. In all of the nonisometric views in the submenu (Plan View, Top, Bottom, Left, Right, Front, Back) the x and y axes will be rotated 90 degrees or not at all. You will see the drawing from directly above (Plan and Top) or directly below (Bottom), or you will look in along the x axis (Left and Right) or along the y axis (Front and Back).

We will use a Southeast Isometric view. The isometric views all rotate the xy axes plus or minus 45 degrees and take you up 30 degrees out of the XY plane. It is simple if you imagine a compass. The lower right quadrant is the southeast. In a southeast isometric view you will be looking in from this quadrant and down at a 30 degree angle. Try it.

Figure 12-3

Figure 12-4

⊞ Select "SE Isometric" from the submenu.

The menu will disappear and the screen will be redrawn to show the view shown in Figure 12-4. Notice how the grid and the coordinate system icon have altered to show our current orientation. These visual aids are extreme-

ICON	DESCRIPTION
	WCS (World Coordinate System) "W" appears on "Y" arm
	UCS (User Coordinate System) NO "W" appears on "Y" arm
	+ Appears in box and "W" appears on the "Y" arm if the current UCS is the same as the WCS
	Box appears at the base of ICON if viewing UCS from above its X–Y plane
	Box is missing if viewing UCS from below its X–Y plane
	Broken pencil ICON appears if viewing direction is "EDGE ON" or near "EDGE ON" X–Y plane of current UCS

Figure 12-5

ly helpful in viewing 3D objects on the flat screen and imagining them as if they were positioned in space.

At this point you may wish to experiment with the other views in the 3D Viewpoint submenu. You will probably find the isometric views most interesting at this point. Pay attention to the grid and the icon as you switch views. Variations of the icon you may encounter here and later on are shown in Figure 12-5. With some views you will have to think carefully and watch the icon to understand which way the object is being presented.

When you are done experimenting, be sure to return to the southeast isometric view shown in Figure 12-4. We will use this view frequently throughout this chapter and the next.

Whenever you change viewpoints, AutoCAD displays the drawing extents, so that the object fills the screen and is as large as possible. Often you will need to zoom out a bit to get some space to work in. This is easily done using the "Scale(X)" option of the ZOOM command.

⊕   Open the View menu, highlight Zoom, and select Scale, or select the Zoom Scale tool from the Zoom flyout on the Standard toolbar, as shown in Figure 12-6.

⊕   Type ".5".

This tells AutoCAD to adjust and redraw the display so that objects appear half as large as before.

Figure 12-6

Your screen will be redrawn with the rectangle at half its previous magnification.

Entering 3D Coordinates

Next we will create a copy of the rectangle placed 1.25 above it. This brings up a basic 3D problem: AutoCAD interprets all pointer device point selections as being in the *XY* plane, so how does one indicate a point or a displacement in the *Z* direction? There are three possibilities: typed 3D coordinates, *X/Y/Z* point filters, and object snaps. Object snap requires an object already drawn above or below the *XY* plane, so it will be of no use right now. We will use typed coordinates first and then discuss how point filters could be used as an alternative. Later we will be using object snap as well.

3D coordinates can be entered from the keyboard in the same manner as 2D coordinates. Often this is an impractical way to enter individual points in a drawing. However, within COPY or MOVE it provides a simple method for specifying a displacement in the *Z* direction.

⊕ Type "co", select Copy from the Modify menu, or select the Copy tool from the Modify toolbar.

AutoCAD will prompt for object selection.

⊕ Select the complete rectangle.

⊕ Press Enter, the space bar, or the enter equivalent button on your pointing device to end object selection.

AutoCAD now prompts for the base point of a vector or a displacement value:

<Base point or displacement>/Multiple:

Typically, you would respond to this prompt and the next by showing the two end points of a vector. However, we cannot show a displacement in the *Z* direction by pointing. This is important for understanding AutoCAD coordinate systems. Unless an object snap is used, all points picked on the screen with the pointing device will be interpreted as being in the *XY* plane of the current UCS. Without an entity outside the *XY* plane to use in an object snap, there is no way to point to a displacement in the *Z* direction.

⊕ Type "0,0,1.25".

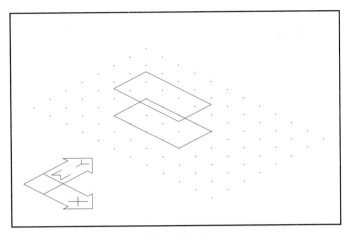

Figure 12-7

AutoCAD now prompts

Second point of displacement:

You can type the coordinates of another point, or press Enter to tell Auto-CAD to use the first entry as a displacement from (0,0,0). In this case, pressing Enter will indicate a displacement of 1.25 in the Z direction, and no change in X or Y.

⊕   Press Enter.

AutoCAD will create a copy of the rectangle 1.25 directly above the original. Your screen should resemble Figure 12-7.

X/Y/Z Point Filters (Optional)

Point filters can be very useful in 3D, although they may seem odd until you get a feel for when to use them. In a point filter we filter out coordinates from one point and use them to create a new point. Notice that in the displacement we just entered, the only thing that changes is the Z value. Note also that we could specify the same displacement using any point in the XY plane as a base point. For example, (3,6,0) to (3,6,1.25) would show the same displacement as (0,0,0) to (0,0,1.25). In fact, we don't even need to know what X and Y are as long as we know that they don't change.

That is how an ".XY" point filter works. We borrow, or "filter", the X and Y values from a point, without pausing to find out what the values actually are, and then specify a new Z value. Other types of filters are possible, of course, such as ".Z" or ".YZ".

You can use a point filter, like an object snap, anytime AutoCAD asks for a point. After a point filter is specified, AutoCAD will always prompt with an "of". In our case you are being asked, "You want the X and Y values of what point?" In response, you pick a point, and then AutoCAD will ask you to fill in Z. Notice that point filters can be "chained" so that, for example, you can filter the X value from one point and combine it with the filtered Y value from another point.

To use an *.XY* filter in the COPY command instead of typing coordinates, for example, you could follow this procedure:

1. Enter the COPY command.
2. Select the rectangle.
3. For the displacement base point, pick any point in the *XY* plane.
4. At the prompt for a second point, type ".xy".
5. At the "of" prompt, type "@" or pick the same point again.
6. At the "(need Z):" prompt, type "1.25". The result would be Figure 12-7, as before.

Using Object Snap

We now have two rectangles floating in space. Our next job is to connect the corners to form a wireframe box. This is done easily using "Endpoint" object snaps. This is a good example of how object snaps allow us to construct entities not in the *XY* plane of the current coordinate system.

⊕ Hold down the shift key and press the enter button on your mouse.
⊕ Select "Osnap Settings..." from the cursor menu.
⊕ Click the check box next to "Endpoint."
⊕ Click on OK.

The running Endpoint object snap is now on and will affect all point selection. You will find that object snaps are very useful in 3D drawing and that Endpoint mode can be used frequently.

Now we will draw some lines.

⊕ Enter the LINE command and connect the upper and lower corners of the two rectangles, as shown in Figure 12-8.

(We have removed the grid for clarity, but you will probably want to leave yours on.)

Before going on, pause a moment to be aware of what you have drawn. The box on your screen is a true wireframe model. Unlike an isometric drawing, it is a 3D

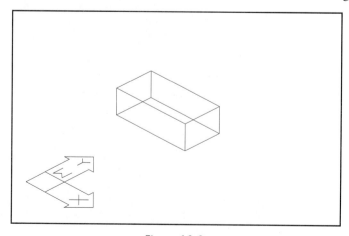

Figure 12-8

model that can be turned, viewed, and plotted from any point in space. It is not, however, a solid model or a surface model. It is only a set of lines in 3D space. Removing hidden lines or shading would have no effect on this model.

In the next task you will begin to define your own coordinate systems that will allow you to perform drawing and editing functions in any plane you choose.

12.2   Defining and Saving User Coordinate Systems

GENERAL PROCEDURE

1. Type "UCS" or select UCS from the Tools menu.
2. Choose an option.
3. Specify a coordinate system.
4. Name and save the new coordinate system.

In this task you will begin to develop new vocabulary and techniques for working with objects in 3D space. The primary tool will be the UCS or DDUCS command. You will also learn to use the UCSICON command to control the placement of the coordinate system icon.

Until now we have had only one coordinate system to work with. All coordinates and displacements have been defined relative to a single point of origin. In Task 12.1 we changed our point of view, but the UCS icon changed along with it, so that the orientations of the x, y, and z axes relative to the object were retained. With the UCS command you can define new coordinate systems at any point and any angle in space. When you do, you can use the coordinate system icon and the grid to help you visualize the planes you are working in, and all commands and drawing aids will function relative to the new system.

The coordinate system we are currently using is unique. It is called the World Coordinate System and is the one we always begin with. The "W" at the base of the coordinate system icon indicates that we are working in the world system. A User Coordinate System is nothing more than a new point of origin and a new orientation for the x, y, and z axes.

We will begin by defining a User Coordinate System in the plane of the top of the box, as shown in Figure 12-9.

⊕   Leave the Endpoint osnap mode on for this exercise.

⊕   Open the Tools menu and highlight "UCS".

There is also a UCS tool on the UCS toolbar shown in Figure 12-10, but you will have to open the toolbar before you can access it. If you type "ucs" or select the tool from the toolbar, you will work with prompts at the command line. Here we will begin using the pull-down menu options and later use the command line as well.

On the pull-down menu, you will see options on a submenu, as illustrated in Figure 12-11. We will begin by using "Origin" to create a UCS that is parallel to the WCS.

⊕   Select "Origin" from the submenu.

Figure 12-9

Figure 12-10

Figure 12-11

AutoCAD will prompt for a new origin:

Origin point <0,0,0>:

This option does not change the orientation of the three axes. It simply shifts their intersection to a different point in space. We will use this simple procedure to define a UCS in the plane of the top of the box.

⊕ Use the Endpoint object snap to select the top left front corner of the box, as shown by the location of the icon in Figure 12-9.

You will notice that the "W" is gone from the icon. However, the icon has not moved. It is still at the lower left of the screen. It is visually helpful to place it at the origin of the new UCS, as in the figure. To do this we need the UCSICON command.

⊕ Open the View menu and highlight "Display" and then "UCS Icon".

⊕ Select "Origin".

The icon will move to the origin of the new current UCS, as in Figure 12-9. With UCSICON set to origin, the icon will shift to the new origin whenever we define a new UCS. The only exception would be if the origin were not on the screen or too close to an edge for the icon to fit. In these cases the icon would be displayed in the lower left corner again.

The "top" UCS we have just defined will make it easy to draw and edit entities that are in the plane of the top of the box and to perform editing in planes that are parallel to it, such as the bottom. In the next task we will begin drawing and editing using different coordinate systems, and you will see how this works. For now, we will spend a little more time on the UCS command itself. We will define two more user coordinate systems, but first let's save this one so that we can recall it quickly when we need it later.

⊕ Open the Tools menu and highlight "UCS".

This time we will use the "Save" option.

⊕ Select "Save".

AutoCAD will ask you to name the current UCS so that it can be called out later:

?/Desired UCS name:

We will name our coordinate system "top." It will be the UCS we use to draw and edit in the top plane. This UCS would also make it easy for us to create an orthographic top view later on.

⊕ Type "top".

The top UCS is now saved and can be recalled using the "Restore" option or by making it "current" using the UCS Control dialog box (select "Named UCS..." from the UCS submenu).

Strictly speaking, it is not necessary to save every UCS. However, it often saves time, since it is unlikely that you will have all your work done in any given plane or UCS the first time around. More likely, you will want to move back and forth between major planes of the object as you draw. Be aware also that you can return to the last defined UCS with the "Previous" option.

Next we will define a "front" UCS using the "3point" option.

✛ Open the Tools menu, highlight 'UCS", and select "3 point" from the submenu.

AutoCAD prompts

`Origin point <0,0,0>:`

In this option you will show AutoCAD a new origin point, as before, and then a new orientation for the axes as well. Notice that the default origin is the current one. If we retained this origin, we could define a UCS with the same origin and a different axis orientation.

Instead, we will define a new origin at the lower left corner of the front of the box, as shown in Figure 12-12.

✛ With the Endpoint osnap on, pick P1, as shown in Figure 12-12.

AutoCAD now prompts you to indicate the orientation of the *x* axis:

`Point on positive portion of the X axis <1.00,0.00,-1.25>:`

✛ Pick the right front corner of the box, P2, as shown.

The object snap ensures that the new x axis will now align with the front of the object. AutoCAD prompts for the *y* axis orientation:

`Point on positive-Y portion of the UCS XY plane
<0.00,1.00,-1.25>:`

By definition, the *y* axis will be perpendicular to the *x* axis; therefore, Auto-CAD needs only a point that shows the plane of the *y* axis and its positive direction. Because of this, any point on the positive side of the *y* plane will specify the *y* axis correctly. We have chosen a point that is on the *y* axis itself.

✛ Pick P3, as shown.

When this sequence is complete, you will notice that the coordinate system icon has rotated along with the grid and moved to the new origin as well. This UCS will be convenient for drawing and editing in the front plane of the box, or editing in any plane parallel to the front, such as the back.

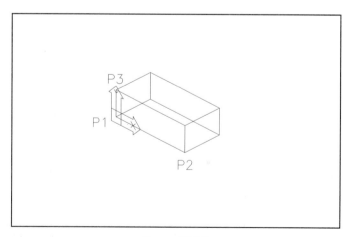

Figure 12-12

Now save the "front" UCS, using the command line this time.

⊕ Press Enter to repeat the UCS command.

⊕ Type "s" to save.

⊕ Type "front" to name the UCS.

Finally, we will use the "Origin" and "Y" axis rotation options together to create a right-side UCS.

⊕ Open the Tools menu and highlight "UCS".

⊕ Select "Origin".

⊕ Pick the lower front corner of the box for the origin, as shown in Figure 12-13.

The UCS icon will move to the selected point.

⊕ Repeat the UCS command.

We will rotate the UCS icon around its y axis to align it with the right side of the box.

In using any of the rotation options ("X axis", "Y axis", and "Z axis"), the first thing you have to decide is which axis is the axis of rotation. If you look at the current position of the icon and think about how it will look when it aligns with the right side of the box, you will see that the y axis retains its position and orientation while the x axis turns through 90 degrees. In other words, since x rotates around y, y is the axis of rotation.

⊕ Type "y".

Now AutoCAD prompts for a rotation:

```
Rotation angle around Y axis <0.0>:
```

It takes some practice to differentiate positive and negative rotation in 3D. If you like, you can use AutoCAD's right-hand rule, which can be stated as follows: If you are hitchhiking (pointing your thumb) in a positive direction along the axis of rotation, your fingers will curl in the direction of positive rotation for the other axis. In our case, align your right thumb with the positive y axis, and you will see that your fingers curl in the direction we want the x axis to rotate. Therefore, the rotation of x around y is positive.

Figure 12-13

⊕ Type "90".

You should now have the UCS icon aligned with the right side of the box, as shown in Figure 12-13. Save this UCS before going on to Task 12.3.

⊕ Press enter to repeat UCS command.

⊕ Type "s".

⊕ Type "right".

12.3 Using Draw and Edit Commands in a UCS

Now the fun begins. Using our three new coordinate systems and one more we will define later, we will give the box a more interesting "slotted wedge" shape. In this task we will cut away a slanted surface on the right side of the box. Since the planes we will be working in are parallel to the front of the box, we will begin by making the "front" UCS current. All our work in this task will be done in this UCS.

⊕ Open the Tools menu and highlight "UCS".

⊕ Select "Named UCS...".

This will open the UCS control dialog box, shown in Figure 12-14. Now that we have three new coordinate systems defined, you will find this dialog box a simple way to switch between them.

⊕ Highlight "Front" in the dialog box

⊕ Click on "Current".

⊕ Click on "OK".

The UCS icon should return to the front plane.

In this case we also could have used the "Previous" option since "front" was the previous UCS.

Look at Figure 12-15. We will draw a line down the middle of the front (line 1) and use it to trim another line coming in at an angle from the right (line 2).

Figure 12-14

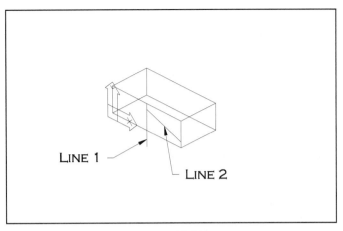

Figure 12-15

    ⊕   Type "L" or select the Line tool from the Draw toolbar.

    ⊕   Open the object snap cursor menu.

    ⊕   Select Midpoint.

        This will temporarily override the Endpoint object snap.

    ⊕   Point to the top front edge of the box.

        AutoCAD will snap to the midpoint of the line.

    ⊕   Make sure that ortho is on (F8).

        Notice how ortho works as usual, but relative to the current UCS.

    ⊕   Pick a second point anywhere below the box.

    ⊕   Exit the LINE command.

        This line will be trimmed later, so the exact length does not matter.

    Next we will draw Line 2 on an angle across the front. This line will become one edge of a slanted surface. Your snap setting will need to be at 0.25 or smaller, and ortho will need to be off. The grid, snap, and coordinate display all work relative to the current UCS, so it is a simple matter to draw in this plane.

    ⊕   Check your snap setting and change it to .25 if necessary.

    ⊕   Turn ortho off (F8).

    ⊕   Enter the LINE command.

    ⊕   Press F3 to override the Endpoint object snap.

    ⊕   Use incremental snap (F9) to pick a point .25 down from the top edge of the box on line 1, as shown in Figure 12-15.

    ⊕   Press F3 again.

        Remember that F3 is the same as a "None" object snap selection.

⊕ Pick a second point 0.25 up along the right front edge of the box, as shown.

⊕ Exit the LINE command.

Now trim line 1.

⊕ Type "tr" or select the Trim tool from the Modify toolbar.

You will see the following message in the command area:

`View is not plan to UCS. Command results may not be obvious.`

In the language of AutoCAD 3D, a view is plan to the current UCS if the *XY* plane is in the plane of the monitor display and its axes are parallel to the sides of the screen. This is the usual 2D view, in which the *y* axis aligns with the left side of the display and the *x* axis aligns with the bottom of the display. In previous chapters we always worked in plan view. In this chapter we have not been in plan view since the beginning of Task 12.1.

With this message, AutoCAD is warning us that boundaries, edges, and intersections may not be obvious as we look at a 3D view of an object. For example, lines that appear to cross may be in different planes.

Having read the warning, we continue.

⊕ Select line 2 as a cutting edge.

⊕ Press Enter to end cutting edge selection.

⊕ Point to the lower end of line 1.

⊕ Press Enter to exit TRIM.

Your screen should resemble Figure 12-16.

Now we will copy our two lines to the back of the box. Since we will be moving out of the front plane, which is also the *XY* plane in the current UCS, we will require the use of the running Endpoint object snaps to specify the displacement vector.

⊕ Type "co" or select the Copy tool from the Modify toolbar.

⊕ Pick lines 1 and 2. (You may need to zoom in on the box at this point to pick Line 1.)

⊕ Press Enter to end object selection.

Figure 12-16

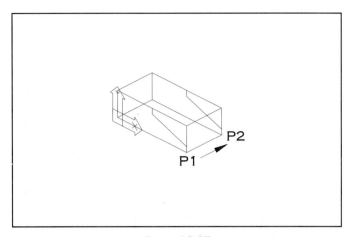

Figure 12-17

⊕ Use the Endpoint osnap to pick the lower front corner of the box, P1 as shown in Figure 12-17.

⊕ At the prompt for a second point of displacement, use the Endpoint osnap to pick the lower right back corner of the box, P2 as shown.

Your screen should now resemble Figure 12-17.

What remains is to connect the front and back of the surfaces we have just outlined and then trim away the top of the box. We will continue to work in the front UCS and to use Endpoint osnaps.

We will use a multiple COPY to copy one of the front-to-back edges in three places.

⊕ Enter the COPY command.

⊕ Pick the bottom right edge for copying.

⊕ Press Enter to end object selection.

⊕ Type "m".

⊕ Pick the front end point of the selected edge to serve as a base point of displacement.

⊕ Pick the top end point of line 1 (P1 in Figure 12-18).

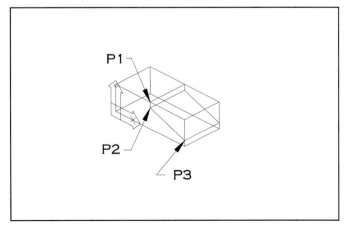

Figure 12-18

⊕ Pick the lower end point of line 1 (P2) as another second point.

⊕ Pick the right end point of line 2 (P3) as another second point.

⊕ Press Enter to exit the COPY command.

Finally, we need to do some trimming.

⊕ Type "Tr" or select the Trim tool from the Modify toolbar.

For cutting edges, we want to select lines 1 and 2 and their copies in the back plane (lines 3 and 4 in Figure 12-18). Since this can be difficult, a quick alternative to selecting these four separate lines is to use a crossing box to select the whole area. As long as your selection includes the four lines, it will be effective.

⊕ Select the area around lines 1 and 2 with a crossing box.

Note: Trimming in 3D can be tricky. Remember where you are. Edges that do not run parallel to the current UCS may not be recognized at all.

⊕ Press Enter to end cutting edge selection.

⊕ One by one, pick the top front and top back edges to the right of the cut, and the right front and right back edges above the cut, as shown by the x's in Figure 12-19.

⊕ Press Enter to exit the TRIM command.

⊕ Enter the ERASE command and erase the top edge that is left hanging in space.

We use ERASE here because this line does not intersect any edges.

Your screen should now resemble Figure 12-20.

12.4 Working on an Angled Surface

In this task we will take our 3D drawing a step further by constructing a slot through the new slanted surface and the bottom of the object. This will require the creation of a new UCS. In completing this task, you will also use the OFFSET command and continue to develop a feel for working with multiple coordinate systems.

Begin by defining a UCS along the angled surface.

Figure 12-19

Figure 12-20

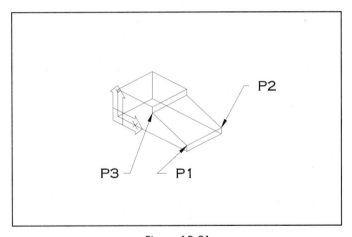

Figure 12-21

⊞   Open the Tools menu, highlight UCS, and select "3 point".

⊞   Using the Endpoint osnap, pick P1, as shown in Figure 12-21.

⊞   Using an Endpoint osnap, pick P2, as shown.

⊞   Using an Endpoint osnap, pick P3, as shown.

⊞   Press Enter to repeat the UCS command.

⊞   Type "s" or select "Save".

⊞   Type "angle" for the name of the UCS.

Now we are ready to work in the plane of the angled surface.

From here on, we have moved our UCS icon back to the lower left of the screen for the sake of clarity in our illustrations. You may leave it at its origin on your screen, if you like, or move it by entering the UCSICON command again and typing "no" or opening the View menu, highlighting Display and then UCS Icon, and then deselecting "Origin".

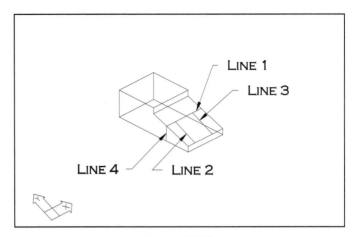

Figure 12-22

⊕   Open the object snap cursor menu.

⊕   Select "Osnap Settings…".

⊕   Click on Clear All.

⊕   Click "OK".

⊕   If ortho is off, turn it on (F8).

We will create line 1 across the angled surface, as shown in Figure 12-22, by offsetting the right front edge of the wedge.

⊕   Select the Offset tool from the Modify toolbar.

⊕   Type or show a distance of 1.50.

⊕   Pick the top right front edge.

⊕   Point anywhere above and to the left of the edge.

⊕   Exit the OFFSET command.

⊕   Draw lines 2 and 3 perpendicular to the first, as shown. They will be over 0.50 and 1.50 from the current y axis.

Watch the coordinate display and notice how the coordinates work in this UCS as in any other.

⊕   Turn ortho off.

⊕   Using snap for the top point and a Perpendicular object snap for the lower point, drop line 4 down to the bottom front edge.

Notice again how object snap modes work for you, especially to locate points that are not in the *XY* plane of the current UCS.

⊕   Create lines 5 and 6, as shown in Figure 12-23, by making two copies of line 4, extending down from the ends of lines 2 and 3, as shown.

⊕   ERASE line 4 from the front plane.

⊕   Using Endpoint osnaps, connect lines 5 and 6 to each other in the plane of the bottom of the object.

⊕   Using Endpoint and Perpendicular osnaps, connect lines 5 and 6 to the bottom edge of the right side.

Figure 12-23

Figure 12-24

⊕ Using Endpoint osnaps, draw two short vertical lines on the right side, connecting to lines 2 and 3.

⊕ TRIM line 1 and the two lines on the right side across the opening of the slot to create Figure 12-24.

12.5 Using RULESURF to Create 3D Fillets

GENERAL PROCEDURE

1. Create fillets in two planes.
2. Open the Draw menu, highlight Surfaces, and select Ruled Surface.
3. Pick a fillet.
4. Pick the corresponding side of the fillet in the other plane.

There are two parts to completing this task. First, we will fillet the top and bottom corners of the slot drawn in Task 12.4. Then we will use the RULESURF command to create filleted surfaces between the top and bottom of the slot.

⊕ To begin this task you should be in the angle UCS, as in Task 12.4, and your screen should resemble Figure 12-24.

⊕ Select the Fillet tool from the Modify menu.

AutoCAD will prompt as usual:

```
(TRIM mode) Current fillet radius = 0.50
Polyline/Radius/<Select first object>:
```

⊕ Type "r".

⊕ Type ".25" for the radius value.

⊕ Press Enter to repeat the FILLET command.

⊕ Pick two lines that meet at one of the upper corners of the slot.

Look at Figure 12-25 to see where we are headed.

⊕ Press Enter to repeat the FILLET command.

⊕ Pick two lines that meet at the other upper corner of the slot.

⊕ Repeat FILLET.

⊕ Pick two lines that meet at one of the lower corners of the slot.

⊕ Press Enter to repeat the FILLET command.

⊕ Pick two lines that meet at the other lower corner of the slot.

⊕ Erase the two vertical lines left outside the fillets.

Your screen should resemble Figure 12-25.

Now we will use a new command to connect the upper and lower fillets with 3D surfaces. RULESURF is one of several commands that create 3D surfaces. These commands create entities called "3D polygon meshes," which are discussed in detail in Chapter 13. This will serve as a quick introduction and will allow you to create 3D fillets in the drawings at the end of this chapter.

The RULESURF command creates a 3D surface between two lines or curves in 3D space. Our two curves will be the upper and lower fillets at each of the two corners.

Figure 12-25

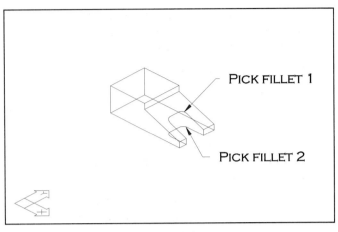

Figure 12-26

✦ Open the Draw menu, highlight "Surfaces", and select Ruled Surface. AutoCAD will prompt

Select first defining curve:

✦ Pick one of the top fillets, as shown by pick 1 in Figure 12-26. AutoCAD will prompt for a second curve:

Select second defining curve:

✦ Pick the corresponding fillet in the bottom plane, with a pickpoint on the corresponding side, as shown by pick 2 in Figure 12-26.

AutoCAD will draw a set of faces to represent the surface curving around the fillet radius, as shown in Figure 12-27.

The trick in using RULESURF is to be sure that you show a pickpoint toward one side of the curve and that you pick the next curve with a point on the corresponding side. Otherwise you will get an hourglass effect, as shown in Figure 12-28. We'll work more with 3D surfaces in the next chapter.

Figure 12-27

PICK 1

PICK 2

PICKING OPPOSITE SIDES OF FILLETS
WILL CAUSE UNDESIRABLE HOURGLASS
EFFECT (NOT RECOMMENDED)

Figure 12-28

⊕ To complete this task, repeat the RULESURF command and draw the fillet at the other corner of the groove.

When you are done, your screen should resemble Figure 12-27. This completes the introduction to drawing 3D wireframe models and using User Coordinate Systems. What follows is a more detailed examination of the VPOINT command.

12.6 Exploring Other Methods of Using the VPOINT Command (Optional)

This discussion of other methods of using VPOINT and DDVPOINT is intended as a reference. The information presented here is not necessary to complete the drawings in this chapter, and no specific exercise is intended. However, if you are interested in gaining a full understanding of the VPOINT and DDVPOINT commands, try creating the views described and outlined in the charts and figures in this section. In Chapter 13 you will also find a complete discussion of the DVIEW command for fine tuning and creating perspective and cutaway views.

Entering 3D Coordinates of a Viewpoint (Vector)

From the initial "Rotate/<View point>" prompt of the VPOINT command, the default method is to type in 3D coordinates. This is the same as the Vector option on the pull-down menu (open the View menu, highlight "3D Viewpoints" and then select "Vector" from the submenu). When you first enter the VPOINT command from the WCS plan view, the default viewpoint is given as (0,0,1). This means that you are viewing the object from a point somewhere along the positive z axis. You are at 0 in the x and y directions and at 11 in the z direction. In other words, you are directly above the XY plane looking straight down, a plan view. Think of the x coordinate as controlling right–left orientation, the y coordinate as controlling back–front, and the z coordinate as controlling up–down.

By changing the x coordinate to 1 (right) and leaving y at 0 (neither front nor back) and z at 1 (above), you can create a viewpoint above and to the right of the object $(1,0,1)$. Similarly, $(1,-1,1)$ would move you to the right $(x = 1)$, back you up a bit $(y = -1)$ so that you are in front of the object, and raise your point of view $(z = 1)$ so that you are above the object looking down. This common $(1,-1,1)$ viewpoint is the same as the southeast isometric or right, front, top viewpoint used throughout this chapter.

We will explore other methods of specifying viewpoints in a moment, but first look at the following chart. It summarizes the effects of the x, y, and z coordinates and gives you coordinates for some standard views. You should have a good understanding of why each view appears as it does.

X Right-Left	Y Back-Front	Z Up-Down	View Description
0	0	1	Plan
0	0	−1	"Worm's eye"
1	0	0	Right side
−1	0	0	Left side
0	1	0	Back
0	−1	0	Front
1	1	1	Northeast Isometric
1	−1	1	Southeast Isometric

We suggest that you try some of these viewpoints and experiment with others not listed. Your goal should be to get a feel for how different coordinate combinations move your point of view in relation to objects on the screen. You can use numbers other than one, but precise distance relationships are difficult to follow in viewpoint definition.

Rotation

The other option shown in the prompt is "Rotation". This option works the same whether typed or selected from the 3D Viewpoint submenu. AutoCAD will prompt for two angles. The first is an angle in the XY plane. It is measured from the x axis, with 0 being straight out to the right, as usual.

The second angle goes up or down from the XY plane, with 0 being ground level. Thus an angle of 90 degrees from the XY plane would define the plan view.

The following chart will give you the rotation versions of some of the same major views shown on the pull-down menu and the previous chart.

From X	From XY	View Description
0	0	Right side
0	90	Plan
90	0	Back side
180	0	Left side
270	0	Front
45	30	Northeast Isometric
−45 (or +315)	30	Southeast Isometric
45	−30	Back, Right, Bottom
etc.	etc.	

Figure 12-29

Rotated views are also accessible through the DDVPOINT command, which calls the Viewpoint Presets dialog box ("Select…" on the 3D Viewpoint submenu). This Viewpoint Presets dialog box is shown in Figure 12-29. DDVPOINT can also be initiated by typing "vp" at the command line. We will use this method to create a Northeast isometric or back, right, top view.

⊕ Open the View menu, highlight 3D Viewpoint, and click on Select….

This will call up the Viewpoint Presets dialog box, as shown in Figure 12-29.

Using this method, AutoCAD lets you choose the two angles it needs to create a new viewpoint from the two "dials" on the left and right. The angle from the x axis can be specified by selecting a point in the circle on the right or by typing a number in the edit box at the bottom. The angle from the XY plane can be typed or shown using the semicircle at the right of the dialog box. As you make selections by pointing in the circle or semicircle, the white "needle" will move and the angle value will be entered in the edit box.

⊕ Set the angle from the x axis by picking the top right box, "45" as shown in Figure 12-29.

Notice that selecting this box enters the value 45.0 in the From: X Axis edit box and moves the white pointer to 45. The angle of 45 moves us into the "back, right" viewpoint area, the northeast quadrant.

The second angle specification (the angle from the XY plane) can be shown in a similar manner by picking a point on the semicircle at the right or by typing a value in the edit box at the bottom. The angle you specify will be the z dimension viewing position, a viewing height above or below the object. We will choose to look down at an angle of 30 degrees.

⊕ Pick the area labeled +30.

This will move the white pointer and enter the value 30 in the XY Plane edit box.

⊕ When your dialog box shows 45.0 and 30.0 as the two viewing angles, pick OK to create the new viewpoint.

Your screen should be redrawn to show a back, right, top view.

Using the two angles in the dialog box to set rotation in the XY plane and the viewing height, you can create a large variety of points of view. We encourage you to experiment with these. Try changing the first angle to 225 to create a left, front, top view. What two angles will give you a front view at ground level? What will a view from below the object look like? As you experiment, pay attention to the UCS icon. With some views you will have to think carefully and watch the icon to understand which way the object is being presented.

The Compass and Axes System

If you enter the VPOINT command and then press Enter in response to the "Rotate/<View point>" prompt, or select "Tripod" from the 3D Viewpoint submenu, you will see a display that resembles Figure 12-30.

The triple axes represent the orientation of the object. When you move your cursor, you will see these rotating. Some users may find this visualization easier to comprehend because it represents the object itself rather than your point of view in relation to the object. However, this effect is much more clearly realized in the DVIEW command, discussed in Chapter 13.

The other part of the display is a rather unusual representation of a globe. The horizontal and vertical axes show the X and Y dimensions, as you would expect, and the circles show the Z dimension. This actually shows a globe transformed into a cone and then flattened. The "north pole" of the globe has become a point at the center of the compass, while the "south pole" has been widened into a circle at the outside of the compass. In between is another circle representing the "equator," or ground 0 region.

This simply means that anywhere inside the first circle will give you a top-down view; outside the first circle will give you a bottom-up view. Anywhere on the middle circle will give you a ground-level view.

Notice that the small cross that moves as you move your cursor. This represents your point of view in the coordinate system.

Figure 12-30

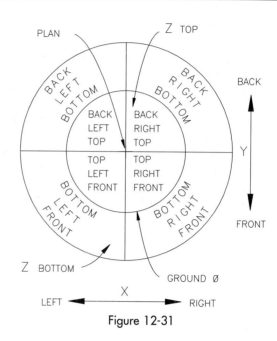

Figure 12-31

Figure 12-31 gives you a summary of the compass points and how they relate to standard views. Try them out if you like.

12.7   Review Material

Questions

1. It is possible to create a 3D view in which the grid is indistinguishable from an isometric snap grid. How is this grid and objects drawn on it different from the isometric grid and objects drawn on it?
2. What is a wireframe model?
3. What is the significance of the W on the UCS icon?
4. What coordinates indicate a displacement of −5 in the z direction from the point (6,6,6)?
5. Why is it usually necessary to utilize object snap to select a point on an object outside of the XY plane of the current UCS?
6. What information defines a User Coordinate System?
7. What is the right-hand rule?
8. What command did you use in this chapter that drew a surface rather than a wire entity?
9. You were apparently able to draw a line from a point in the xy plane to a point above the plane without using object snap because both points appeared to be on grid snap points. What will happen when you view this line from another viewpoint?
10. What angle from the xy plane defines a plan view?
11. What angle in the xy plane defines a front view?

Drawing Problems

1. Set up a southeast isometric 3D viewpoint in the World Coordinate System and draw a regular hexagon with a circumscribed radius of 4.0 units.
2. Create a half-sized scaled copy of the hexagon centered at the same center as the original hexagon; then move the smaller hexagon 5.0 units up in the z direction.
3. Connect corresponding corners of the two hexagons to create a tapered hexagonal prism in three dimensions.
4. Create a UCS aligned with any of the faces of the hexagonal prism.
5. Use this UCS to draw the text "Lamp Shade", at 0.3 units high, on the face that aligns with the new UCS.
6. View the object from the world plan view, the plan view of the current UCS, and a northwest isometric view.

12.8   Drawing 12-1: Clamp

This drawing is similar to the one you did in the chapter. Two major differences are that it is drawn from a different viewpoint and that it includes dimensions in the 3D view. This will give you additional practice in defining and using User Coordinate Systems. Your drawing should include dimensions, border, and title.

DRAWING SUGGESTIONS

- We drew the outline of the clamp in a horizontal position and then worked from a northeast isometric or back, left, top point of view.
- Begin in WCS plan view drawing the horseshoe-shaped outline of the clamp. This will include fillets on the inside and outside of the clamp. The more you can do in plan view before copying to the top plane, the less duplicate editing you will need to do later.
- When the outline is drawn, switch to a northeast isometric view.
- COPY the clamp outline up 1.50.
- Define User Coordinate Systems as needed, and save them whenever you are ready to switch to another UCS. You will need to use them in your dimensioning.
- The angled face, the slots, and the filleted surfaces can be drawn just as in the chapter.

DIMENSIONING IN 3D

The trick to dimensioning a 3D object is that you will need to restore the appropriate UCS for each set of dimensions. Think about how you want the text to appear. If text is to be aligned with the top of the clamp (i.e., the 5.75 overall length), you will need to draw that dimension in a "top" UCS; if it is to align with the front of the object (the 17 degree angle and the 1.50 height), draw it in a "front" UCS, and so forth.

- Define a UCS with the "View" option in order to add the border and title. Type "UCS", and then "v". This creates a UCS aligned with your current viewing angle.

SETTING SURFTAB1

Notice that there are 8 lines defining the RULESURF fillets in this drawing, compared to 6 in the chapter. This number of lines is controlled by the setting of the variable Surftab1, which is discussed in Chapter 13. You can change it by typing "Surftab1" and entering "8" for the new value.

R2.25

R1.00

5.75

3.38

2.65

1.50

0.25

0.75

17° (REF)

2.54

.25 RAD
4 PLACES

CLAMP

DRAWING 12-1

12.9 Drawing 12-2: Guide Block

In this drawing you will be working from dimensioned views to create a wireframe model. This brings up some new questions: Which view should you start with? How do you translate the views into the 3D image? A good general rule is this: Draw the top or bottom in the *XY* plane of the WCS: otherwise, you will have trouble using the VPOINT command.

DRAWING SUGGESTIONS

- In this drawing it is tempting to draw the right side in WCS plan view first, because that is where most of the detail is. If you do this, however, you will have difficulty creating the view as shown. Instead, we suggest that you keep the bottom of the object in the WCS *XY* plane and work up from there, as has been the practice throughout this chapter. The reason for this is that the VPOINT command works relative to the WCS. Therefore, front–back, left–right, and top–bottom orientations will make sense only if the top and bottom are drawn plan to the WCS.
- Draw the 12.50 × 8.00 rectangle shown in the top view and then copy it up 4.38 to form the top of the guide's base.
- Change over to the same southeast isometric or front, right, top 3D viewpoint we used in the chapter.
- Connect the four corners to create a block outline of the base of the object.
- Now you can define a new UCS on the right side and do most of your work in that coordinate system, since that is where the detail is. Once you have defined the right-side UCS, you may want to go into its plan view to draw the right-side outline, including the arc and circle of the guide. Then come back to the 3D view to copy back to the left side.

    Tip: You can save some time switching viewpoints by using the save and restore options of the VIEW command. When a view is saved, it includes the 3D orientation along with the zoom factor that was current at the time of the save. Also, ZOOM previous can be used to restore a previous 3D point of view. It will not, however, restore a UCS.

- Use RULESURF with Surftab1 set to 16 to fill in surfaces between the arcs and circles.

THESE VIEWS & DIMENSIONS
ARE FOR REFERENCE ONLY

GUIDE BLOCK
DRAWING 12-2

3D WIRE FRAME MODEL

12.10 Drawing 12-3: Slide Mount

This drawing continues to use the same views, coordinate systems, and techniques as the previous drawings, but it has more detail and is a bit trickier.

DRAWING SUGGESTIONS

- Draw the H-shaped outline of the top view in WCS plan.
- Copy up in the z direction.
- Connect the corners to create a 3D shape.
- Define a right-side view and create the slot and holes.
- Copy back to the left side, connect the corners, and trim inside the slot.
- Return to WCS (bottom plane).
- Use RULESURF between circles to create mounting holes.
- Draw filleted cutout and countersunk holes. Each countersunk hole will require three circles, two small and one larger.
- Use RULESURF to create inner surfaces of countersunk holes.

∅.1875 × .75 DP
4 HOLES

3.500

.25
.25

2.56

.72

.44

.31

THESE VIEWS & DIMENSIONS
ARE FOR REFERENCE ONLY

.63

∅.170 THRU
C'SINK ∅.343 × 82°
2 HOLES

4.00

.812

1.59

.500

2.19

.34

369

1.25

.75

R.12
4 PL

2.00

1.50

1.00

.50

**3D WIRE FRAME
MODEL**

SLIDE MOUNT

DRAWING 12-3

12.11   Drawing 12-4: Stair Layout

This wireframe architectural detail will give you a chance to use architectural units and limits in 3D. It will require the use of a variety of edit commands.

DRAWING SUGGESTIONS

- In the WCS plan view, begin with a $2'' \times 12'$ rectangle that will become the bottom of a floor joist. This will keep the bottom floor in the plan view, consistent with our practice in this chapter.
- COPY the rectangle up $8''$ and connect lines to form the complete joist.
- ARRAY $16''$ on center to form the first floor.
- COPY all joists up $9'$-$6''$ to form the second floor.
- Create the stairwell opening in the second floor with double headers at each end.
- Add the $\frac{3}{4}''$ subfloor to the first floor.
- The outline of the stair stringers can be constructed in a number of ways. One possibility is as follows: Draw a guideline down from the front of the left double header and then another over $10'$-$10''$ to locate the end of the run; from the right end of the run, draw one $7\frac{1}{2}''$ riser and one $9\frac{1}{2}''$ tread, beginning from the top surface of the subflooring; use a multiple copy and End point osnaps to create the other steps; when you get to the top, you will find you need to TRIM the top tread slightly to bring it flush with the header.
- We leave it to you to construct the back line of the stringer. It needs to be parallel with the stringer line and down $1'$ from the top tread, as shown.

2×8
(16"o.c.)

STAIRWELL
OPNG 9'-6"

9 1/2"
TREAD

7 1/2"
RISER

9'-6"

3/4"
SUB-FLOOR

10'-10"
RUN

2×4 (2)

2×8
(16"o.c.)

STAIR LAYOUT
DRAWING 12-4

12.12   Drawing 12-5: Housing

The objective for this drawing is to create a 3D wireframe model of the housing. The RULESURF command is used extensively. If you use Section B-B as your front view, you will find it easier to create the 3D wireframe.

DRAWING SUGGESTIONS

- Draw the rectangular outline of the top view in WCS plan.
- Copy up in the z direction to the appropriate levels.
- Change the origin of the UCS in the z direction to the proper height; then create the inner rectangle.
- Fillet all corners and rulesurf as necessary to create a 3D shape.
- Use RULESURF between circles to create cylindrical pads and semicircular cutouts. Be sure to change the UCS to the appropriate position when adding detail to a particular view.
- Each counterbore hole will require three circles, two small and one larger.
- Use RULESURF to create inner surfaces of counterbore holes.

SECTION A—A

R1.125
3 pl

B

R.50

ø1.500
2 PL

ø .625 THRU
C'BORE FAR SIDE
ø 1.000 × .625 DP
3 PLACES

2.750

7.500

7.000

0.500

3.500

A

A

1.000

2.250

R 75
4 PLACES

B

4.000

0.750

ø1.000

2.000

1.250

4.500

0.750

10.500

SECTION B—B

HOUSING
Drawing 12—5

13 Surface Models

COMMANDS

SURFACES	VIEW	RENDER	VARIABLES
3DFACE	DVIEW	HIDE	Surftab1
3DMESH	MVSETUP		Surftab2
EDGESURF	REDRAWALL		
REVSURF	REGENALL		
RULESURF	VPORTS		
TABSURF			

OVERVIEW

In this chapter we will continue to explore Release 14 3D drawing features, with a focus on surface modeling. The VPORTS (or VIEWPORTS) command will allow the creation of multiple tiled viewports so that an object may be viewed from several points of view simultaneously. The 3DFACE command will be introduced to draw three- and four-sided surfaces. In addition, you will create "polygon meshes" to represent complex three-dimensional surfaces.

TASKS

13.1 Using Multiple Tiled Viewports

GENERAL PROCEDURE

1. Highlight "Tiled Viewports" on the View menu.
2. Select the number of viewports desired.
3. Enter orientation of viewports.
4. Define views in each viewport.

A major feature needed to draw effectively in 3D is the ability to view an object from several different points of view simultaneously as you work on it. The VPORTS, or VIEWPORTS, command is easy to use and can save you from having to jump back and forth between different views of an object. Viewports can be used in 2D to place several zoom magnifications on the screen at once, as shown in Chapter 3. More important, viewports can be used to place several 3D viewpoints on the screen at once. This can be a significant drawing aid. If you do not continually view an object from different points of view, it is easy to create entities that appear correct in the current view but that are clearly incorrect from other points of view.

In this task we will divide your screen in half and define two views so that you can visualize an object in plan view and a 3D view at the same time. As you work, remember that this is only a display command. The viewports we use in this chapter will be simple "tiled" viewports. Tiled viewports cover the complete drawing area, do not overlap, and cannot be plotted simultaneously. Plotting multiple viewports can be accomplished, but only in paper space with nontiled viewports.

⊞ **Highlight "Tiled Viewports" on the View menu.**

This will open the submenu shown in Figure 13-1. If you type the command you will see the same options at the command line prompt.

The "Layout..." option will call the Tiled Viewport Layout dialog box shown in Figure 13-2. Notice that the list on the left simply names the 12 layout options on the right. Any of these could also be specified by selecting a number of viewports from the submenu and then following the sequence of command prompts.

For our purposes we will create a simple two-way vertical split, the "Two: Vertical" option in the dialog box.

⊞ **Select "Two: Vertical" or the box on the left end of the second row on the icon menu.**

⊞ **Click on "OK" to complete the dialog.**

Your screen will be regenerated to resemble Figure 13-3.

You will notice that the grid is rather small and confined to the lower part of the window and that the grid may be off in the left viewport. The shape of the viewports necessitates the reduction in drawing area. You can enlarge details as usual using the ZOOM command. Zooming and panning in one viewport will have no effect on other viewports. However, you can have only one

Figure 13-1

Figure 13-2

UCS in effect at any time, so a change in the coordinate system in one viewport will be reflected in all viewports.

If you move your pointing device back and forth between the windows, you will see an arrow when you are on the left and the cross hairs when you are on the right. This indicates that the right window is currently active. Drawing and editing can be done only in the active window. To work in an-

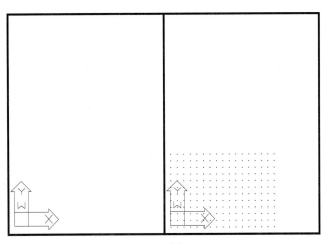

Figure 13-3

other window, you need to make it current by picking it with your pointing device. Often this can be done while a command is in progress.

⊕ **Move the cursor into the left window and press the pickbutton on your pointing device.**

Now the cross hairs will appear in the left viewport, and you will see the arrow when you move into the right viewport.

⊕ **If the grid is off in your left viewport, you may want to turn it on at this point.**

⊕ **Move the cursor back to the right and press the pickbutton again.**

This will make the right window active again.

There is no value in having two viewports if each is showing the same thing, so our next job will be to change the viewpoint in one of the windows. We will leave the window on the left in plan view and switch the right window to a 3D view. For consistency, we will use the familiar southeast isometric view used in the last chapter.

⊕ **From the View menu highlight "3D Viewpoint" and then select "SE Isometric".**

Your screen should now be redrawn with a southeast isometric view in the right viewport as shown in Figure 13-4.

Once you have defined viewports, any drawing or editing done in the active viewport will appear in all the viewports. As you draw, watch what happens in both viewports.

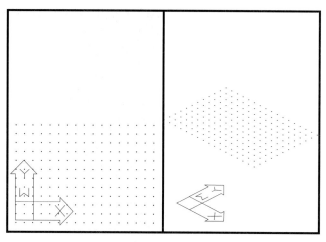

Figure 13-4

13.2   Creating Surfaces with 3DFACE

GENERAL PROCEDURE

1. Type "3DFace" or open the Draw menu, highlight Surfaces, and select 3D Face.
2. Pick three or four points going around the face.
3. Continue defining edges or press Enter to exit the command.

3DFACE creates triangular and quadrilateral surfaces. 3D faces are built by entering points in groups of three or four to define the outlines of triangles or quadrilaterals, similar to objects formed by the 2D SOLID command. The surface of a 3D face is not shown on the screen, but it is recognized by the HIDE command and by the RENDER command and other rendering programs, such as RenderMan or 3D Studio.

Layering is critical in surface modeling. Surfaces quickly complicate a drawing so that object selection and object snap become difficult or impossible. Also, you may want to be able to turn layers off or freeze them to achieve the results you want from the HIDE command. You may eventually want a number of layers specifically defined for faces and surfaces, but this will not be necessary for the current exercise.

⊕   Open the Draw menu and highlight Surfaces.

This calls the submenu shown in Figure 13-5. There is also a Surface toolbar with a 3D face tool, as shown in Figure 13-6.

⊕   Select "3D Face".

AutoCAD will prompt

First point:

Figure 13-5

Figure 13-6

You can define points in either of the two viewports. In fact, you can even switch viewports in the middle of the command.

⊕ Pick a point similar to P1, as shown in Figure 13-7.
AutoCAD prompts

> Second point:

⊕ Pick a second point, moving around the perimeter of the face, as shown.
Be aware that the correct order for defining 3D faces is different from the 2D SOLID command (Chapter 9). It is important to pick points in order around the face; otherwise you will get a bow tie or hourglass effect.

AutoCAD prompts

> Third point:

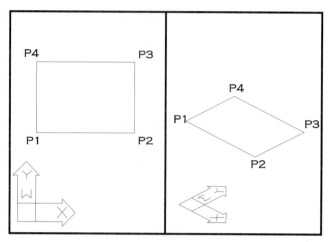

Figure 13-7

⊕ Pick a third point, as shown.
AutoCAD prompts

Fourth point:

Note: If you pressed Enter now, AutoCAD would draw the outline of a triangular face, using the three points already given.

⊕ Pick the fourth point of the face.
AutoCAD draws the fourth edge of the face automatically when four points have been given, so it is not necessary to complete or close the rectangle.

AutoCAD will continue to prompt for third and fourth points so that you can draw a series of surfaces to cover an area with more than four edges. Keep in mind, however, that drawing faces in series is only a convenience. The result is a collection of independent three- and four-sided faces.

⊕ Press Enter to exit the 3DFACE command.
In the next task we will copy this face in order to demonstrate the HIDE command. But first, a word about invisible edges.

Invisible Edges in 3Dfaces

The edges of a 3Dface can be visible or invisible as desired. To define an invisible edge, type "i" before entering the first point of the edge. You can even define "phantom" 3D faces in which no edges are visible. In Release 14 there is also an EDGE command that allows you to change the visibility of edges after they have been drawn. It may be easier to draw all edges visible and then make some invisible with this command.

Take a look at Figure 13-8. This figure illustrates the need for invisible edges in 3Dfaces. Since 3DFACE only draws triangles or quadrilaterals, objects with more

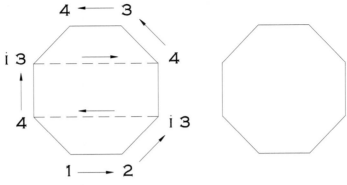

Figure 13-8

than four edges must be drawn as combinations of three- and four-sided shapes. An octagon, for example, can be drawn as two trapezoids and a rectangle, as shown. However, you would not want the two horizontal edges across the middle showing, so the command allows you to make them invisible by typing "i" or selecting "Invisible" from the screen menu before picking the point that begins the invisible edge. This takes forethought and planning. You must remember that the end point of a visible edge also may be the starting point of the next invisible edge.

In Release 14, it may be easier to draw edges visible and then go back and make some invisible using the EDGE command. You can access EDGE by opening the Draw menu, highlighting surfaces, and selecting Edge. The command will ask you to select edges and then will reverse the visibility of any edge you select. It includes a Display option, which will display all edges so that they may be selected.

> **Note:** Invisible edges will be hidden if the "Splframe" system variable is set to 0, the default setting. If the variable is set to 1, invisible edges will be displayed. To change this setting, type "Splframe" and then "1".

13.3   Removing Hidden Lines with HIDE

GENERAL PROCEDURE

1. Type "hi," or open the View menu and select Hide.
2. Wait....

The HIDE command is easy to execute. However, execution may be slow in large drawings, and careful work may be required to create a drawing that hides the way you want it to. This is a primary objective of surface modeling. When you've got everything right, HIDE will temporarily remove all lines and objects that would be obstructed in the current view, resulting in a more realistic representation of the object in space. A correctly surfaced model can also be used to create a shaded rendering. Hiding has no effect on wireframe drawings, since there are no surfaces to obstruct lines behind them.

✢   To begin this exercise, you should have the 3Dface from the previous task on your screen.

✢   COPY the face up 2 units in the *z* direction, using the following procedure:

1. Type "co" or select the Copy tool from the Modify menu.
2. Select the face.
3. Press Enter to end object selection.
4. Type and enter "0,0,2".
5. Press Enter at the prompt for a second point.

You now have two 3Dfaces in your drawing. Since the second is directly over the first, you cannot see both in the plan view. From the viewpoint in the right viewport, however, the second face only partially covers the first. Since these are surfaces, rather than wireframes, the top face should hide part of the lower face.

✢   Make the right viewport active.

✢   Type "hi" or open the View menu and select "Hide".

Your screen should be regenerated to resemble Figure 13-9.

In the command area, AutoCAD gives you a message that says

```
Regenerating drawing.
Hidden lines: done 100%
```

In this case the hiding and regeneration will happen very quickly. In a larger drawing you will have to wait.

Following are some important points about hidden line removal that you should read before continuing:

1. Hidden line removal can be done from the plot configuration dialog box. However, due to the time involved and the difficulty of getting a hidden view just

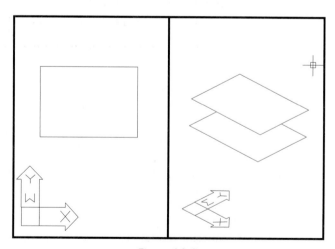

Figure 13-9

right, it is usually better to experiment on the screen first and then plot with hidden lines removed when you know you will get the image you want.

2. Whenever the screen is regenerated, hidden lines are returned to the screen.

3. The image created through hidden line removal is *not* retained in BLOCKing, WBLOCKing, GROUPing, or saving VIEWs.

4. Hidden line removal can be captured in slides (the MSLIDE and VSLIDE commands, Chapter 9). But remember, slides cannot be plotted.

5. Layer control is important in hidden line removal. Layers that are frozen are ignored by the HIDE command, but layers that are off are treated like layers that are visible. This can, for example, create peculiar blank spaces in your display if you have left surfaces or solids on a layer that is off at the time of hidden line removal.

13.4   Using 3D Polygon Mesh Commands

GENERAL PROCEDURE

1. Create geometry to be used in defining the surface.
2. If necessary, set Surftab1 and Surftab2.
3. Enter a 3D polygon mesh command.
4. Use existing geometry to define the surface.

3DFACE can be used to create simple surfaces. However, most surface models require large numbers of faces to approximate the surfaces of real objects. Consider the number of faces in Figure 13-10, the globe you will be creating when you do Drawing 13-3. Obviously, you would not want to draw such an image one face at a time.

AutoCAD includes a number of commands that make the creation of some types of surfaces very easy. These powerful commands create 3D polygon meshes.

Figure 13-10

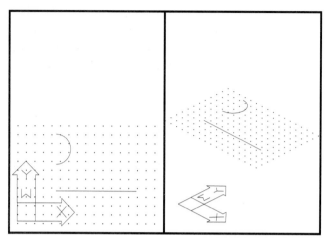

Figure 13-11

Polygon meshes are made up of 3D faces and are defined by a matrix of vertices. They can be treated as single entities and edited with the PEDIT command or exploded into individual 3D faces.

⊕ To begin this task, ERASE the two faces from the last task and draw an arc and a line below it, as shown in Figure 13-11. Exact sizes and locations are not important.

The entities may be drawn in either viewport.

Now we will define some 3D surfaces using the arc and line you have just drawn.

TABSURF

The first surface we will draw is called a "tabulated surface." To use the TABSURF command, you need a line or curve to define the shape of the surface and a vector to show its size and direction. The result is a surface generated by repeating the shape of the original curve at every point along the path specified by the vector.

⊕ Type "Tabsurf" or open the Draw menu, highlight Surfaces, and select Tabulated Surface.

There is also a Surface toolbar with a Tabulated Surface tool, as shown in *Figure 13-6*. AutoCAD will prompt

Select path curve:

The path curve is the line or curve that will determine the shape of the surface. In our case it will be the arc.

⊕ Pick the arc.

AutoCAD will prompt for a vector:

Select direction vector:

We will use the line. Notice that the vector does not need to be connected to the path curve. Its location is not significant, only its direction and length.

There is an oddity here to watch out for as you pick the vector. If you pick a point near the left end of the line, AutoCAD will interpret the vector as extending from left to right. Accordingly, the surface will be drawn to the right. By the same token, if your point is near the right end of the line, the surface will be drawn to the left. Most of the time you will avoid confusion by picking a point on the side of the vector nearest the curve itself.

⊕ Pick a point on the left side of the line.

Your screen will be redrawn to resemble Figure 13-12. Notice that this is a flat surface even though it may look 3D. If this is not obvious in the plan view, it should be more apparent in the 3D view.

Tabulated surfaces can be fully 3D, depending on the path and vector chosen to define them. In this case we have an arc and a vector that are both entirely in the *XY* plane, so the resulting surface is also in that plane.

Surftab1

You will also notice that the surface is defined by long, narrow faces that run parallel to the vector. If you zoom up on either end of the surface, you will see that the arc is only approximated by the shorter edges of these six faces. Unlike the polygons or broken curves AutoCAD often uses to display arcs and circles in order to speed regeneration time, this mesh of quadrilateral faces is the actual current definition of this surface. To achieve a more accurate approximation, we can increase the number of faces. This is done by changing the setting of a variable called "Surftab1" and drawing the object again.

Let's undo the tabulated surface so that we can draw it again with a new Surftab1 setting.

⊕ Type "u" or select the Undo tool from the Standard toolbar.

Figure 13-12

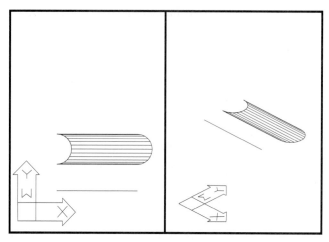

Figure 13-13

⊕ Type "Surftab1".
AutoCAD prompts:

New value for SURFTAB1 <6>:

The default value shows why we see six lines in the tabulated surface. When we change the setting, we will get a different number of lines and degree of accuracy.

⊕ Type "12".
⊕ Open the Draw menu, highlight Surfaces, and select Tabulated Surfaces.
⊕ Pick the arc for the path curve.
⊕ Pick the line for the direction vector.

Your screen should now resemble Figure 13-13.

RULESURF

TABSURF is useful in defining surfaces that are the same on both ends, assuming you have one end and a vector. Often, however, you have no vector, or you need to draw a surface between two different paths. In these cases you will need the RULESURF command.

For example, what if we need to define a surface between the line and the arc? Let's try it.

⊕ Type "u" to undo the last tabulated surface.
⊕ Open the Draw menu, highlight Surfaces, and select Ruled Surface.

You are familiar with this command sequence from Chapter 12. The first prompt is

Select first defining curve:

⊕ Pick the arc, using a point near the bottom.

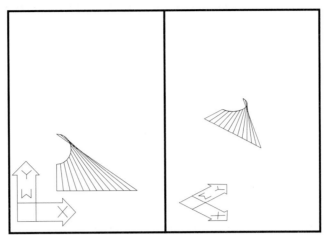

Figure 13-14

Remember that you must pick points on corresponding sides of the two defining curves in order to avoid an hourglass effect.

AutoCAD prompts

Select second defining curve:

⊕ Pick the line, using a point near the left end.

Your screen should resemble Figure 13-14. Again, notice that this surface is within the *XY* plane even though it may look 3D. Ruled surfaces may be drawn just as easily between curves that are not coplanar.

If you look closely, you will notice that this ruled surface is drawn with 12 lines, the result of our Surftab1 setting.

Some other typical examples of ruled surfaces are shown in the chart in Figure 13-20 at the end of this task.

EDGESURF

TABSURF creates surfaces that are the same at both ends and move along a straight line vector. RULESURF draws surfaces between any two boundaries. There is a third command, EDGESURF, which draws surfaces that are bounded by four curves. Edge-defined surfaces have a lot of geometric flexibility. The only restriction is that they must be bounded on all four sides. That is, they must have four edges that touch.

To create an EDGESURF, we need to undo our last ruled surface and add two more edges.

⊕ Type "u".
⊕ Add a line and an arc to your screen, as shown in Figure 13-15.
Remember, you can draw in either viewport.
⊕ Open the Draw menu, highlight Surfaces, and select Edge Surface.

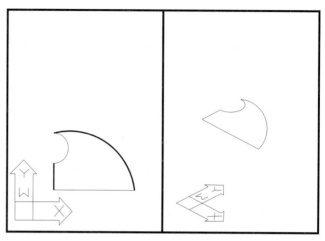

Figure 13-15

AutoCAD will prompt for the four edges of the surface, one at a time:

Select edge 1:

⊕ Pick the smaller arc.

AutoCAD prompts

Select edge 2:

⊕ Pick the larger arc.

AutoCAD prompts

Select edge 3:

⊕ Pick the longer line.

AutoCAD prompts

Select edge 4:

⊕ Pick the smaller line.

Your screen should now resemble Figure 13-16.

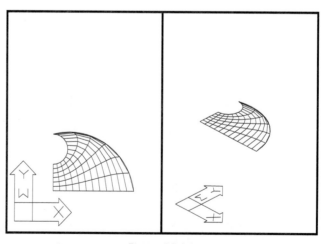

Figure 13-16

Surftab2

There is something new to be aware of here. With TABSURF and RULESURF, surfaces were defined by edges moving in only one direction. With EDGESURF, you have a matrix of faces and edges going two ways. You will notice that there are 12 edges going one way and 6 going the other, as shown in Figure 13-16. This brings us to the variable Surftab2. If we change its setting to 12 also, we will see 12 edges in each direction.

Try it.

⊕ Type "u" to undo the EDGESURF command.

⊕ Type "Surftab2".

⊕ Type "12".

⊕ Enter the EDGESURF command and select the four edges again.

The result should resemble Figure 13-17.

REVSURF

We have one more 3D polygon mesh command to explore, and this one is probably the most impressive of all. REVSURF creates surfaces by spinning a curve through a given angle around an axis of revolution. Just as tabulated surfaces are spread along a linear path, surfaces of revolution follow a circular or arc-shaped path. As a result, surfaces of revolution are always fully three dimensional, even if their defining geometry is in a single plane, as it will be here.

⊕ In preparation for this exercise, undo the EDGESURF, so that your screen resembles Figure 13-15 again.

We will create two surfaces of revolution. The first will be a complete 360-degree surface using the smaller arc and the smaller line for definition. The second will be a 270-degree surface using the larger arc and the larger line.

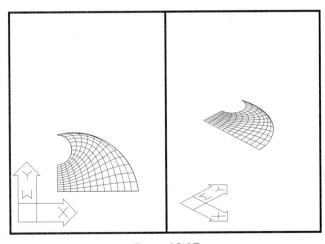

Figure 13-17

⊕ Open the Draw menu, highlight Surfaces, and select Revolved Surface.

AutoCAD needs a path curve and an axis of revolution to define the surface. The first prompt is

> Select path curve:

⊕ Pick the smaller arc.

AutoCAD prompts

> Select axis of revolution:

⊕ Pick the smaller line.

AutoCAD now needs to know whether you want the surface to begin at the curve itself or somewhere else around the circle of revolution:

> Start angle <0>:

The default is to start at the curve.

⊕ Press Enter to begin the surface at the curve itself.

AutoCAD prompts

> Included angle (+=ccw, -=cw) <Full circle>:

Entering a positive or negative degree measure will cause the surface to be drawn around an arc rather than a full circle. The default will give us a complete circle.

⊕ Press Enter.

Your screen should be drawn to resemble Figure 13-18. If you look closely, you will see that this globe has 12 lines in each direction. REVSURF, like EDGESURF, uses both Surftab1 and Surftab2. Also notice that this command gives us a way to create spheres. If the path curve is a true semicircle and the axis is along the diameter of the semicircle, then the result will be a sphere. There is another way to create a sphere, which we will discuss in Task 13.5.

Figure 13-18

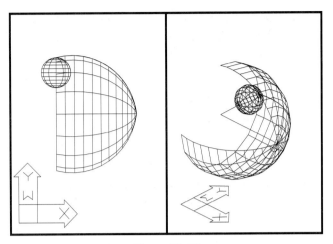

Figure 13-19

Now we will create a larger surface that does not start at 0 degrees and does not include a full circle.

⊕   Press Enter to repeat the REVSURF command.
⊕   Pick the larger arc for the curve path.
⊕   Pick the left end of the longer line for the axis of revolution.
      If you pick the right end, the positive and negative angles will be reversed in the two steps following.
⊕   Type "90" for the start angle.
      This will cause the surface to begin 90 degrees up from the *XY* plane.
⊕   Type "−270" for the included angle.
      This will cause the surface to revolve 270 degrees clockwise around the axis. The result should resemble Figure 13-19. You may have to use PAN in one or both viewports to position the objects on the screen as we have shown them.

Next, we will demonstrate the use of the 3D Objects dialog box, which contains AutoLISP routines to create nine more basic surface models. Take a look at the polygon mesh examples in Figure 13-20 before proceeding.

13.5   Creating Surface Models Using the "3D Objects" AutoLISP Routines

---

GENERAL PROCEDURE

1. Type "3D" or open the Draw menu, highlight Surfaces, and select 3D surfaces....
2. Choose an object and follow the prompts.

POLYGON MESH COMMANDS			
COMMAND	BEFORE	SETVAR SETTINGS	AFTER
TABSURF		SURFTAB1 = 6	
RULESURF		SURFTAB1 = 12	
		SURFTAB1 = 6	
		SURFTAB1 = 6	
		SURFTAB1 = 6	
EDGESURF		SURFTAB1 = 6 SURFTAB2 = 8	
		SURFTAB1 = 6 SURFTAB2 = 8	
		SURFTAB1 = 6 SURFTAB2 = 8	
		SURFTAB1 = 12 SURFTAB2 = 10	
REVSURF		SURFTAB1 = 16 SURFTAB2 = 8	

Figure 13-20

AutoCAD provides nine AutoLISP routines that create three-dimensional surface models of basic shapes. AutoLISP routines act just like commands, except that they take a moment to load before they execute. Also note that these routines will only work if AutoLISP is loaded with appropriate memory allocation. If you have a problem, see the *AutoCAD Installation Guide*.

Like the 3D meshes explored in Task 13.4, the 3D surface models created this way can be treated as single entities or EXPLODEd and edited as collections of 3D faces. Each of the objects has its own set of prompts, depending on its geometry. We will demonstrate one object in this task and leave the rest for you to explore on your own.

⊕ To begin this task, clear your screen of objects left from Task 13.3.

⊕ Open the Draw menu, highlight Surfaces, and select 3D surfaces....
This will open the 3D objects dialog box shown in Figure 13-21. You can also select object tools from the Surface toolbar, shown in Figure 13-6.

Note: To create 3D surface models, you must use the 3D command, the Surfaces toolbar, or the 3D objects dialog box. Typing "sphere", "cone", "torus",

Figure 13-21

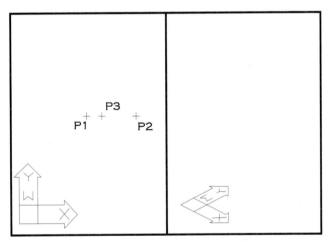

Figure 13-22

etc. directly at the command line will create solid models instead of surface models. We will use these commands in Chapter 14.

✥ Select the torus, as shown, by picking on the torus image or the word torus on the list.

This will bring you to the first Torus prompt:

`Center of torus:`

✥ Pick a center point as shown by P1 in Figure 13-22.

AutoCAD prompts

`Diameter/<radius> of torus:`

The next point we pick will show the overall radius of the torus.

⊕ Show a radius distance of about 6.00 units, as shown by P2 in Figure 13-22.

AutoCAD prompts

```
Diameter/<radius> of tube:
```

This will be the diameter or radius of the torus tube. If you specify the tube size by pointing, remember that the distance is being shown from the center point of the torus, at P1, to P3, though the tube actually will be constructed from its own center line at P2.

⊕ Show a radius of about 2.00 units, as shown by P3 in Figure 13-22.

AutoCAD prompts

```
Segments around tube circumference <16>:
```

You will be prompted for segment numbers around the tube and around the torus. These specify mesh density just like Surftab1 and Surftab2.

⊕ Press Enter to accept the default of 16 segments.

AutoCAD prompts

```
Segments around torus circumference <16>:
```

⊕ Press Enter to accept the default of 16 segments.

Your screen should resemble Figure 13-23. As in the case of the 3D polygon mesh commands, notice how much surface modeling this AutoLISP routine accomplishes through a few simple prompts.

To appreciate the nature of surface models once again, we recommend that you make the right viewport active at this point and execute the HIDE command. You will see an image of the torus with hidden lines removed.

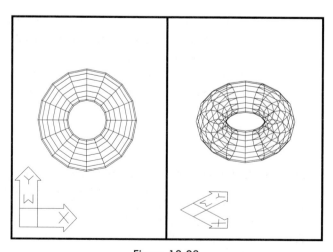

Figure 13-23

13.6   Creating Approximated Surfaces Using PEDIT (Optional)

GENERAL PROCEDURE

1. Draw a 3DMESH in three dimensions.
2. Type "pedit" or select the Pedit tool from the Special Edit flyout on the Modify toolbar.
3. Select the mesh.
4. Specify a surface type.
5. Type "s" or select "smooth".
6. Exit PEDIT.

Within the PEDIT command there are some very impressive design features, which we introduce in this task and the next as optional exercises. These techniques will not be needed in the drawings that follow, but your knowledge of AutoCAD and surface modeling will be incomplete without them.

The techniques of curve and surface approximation are most useful when you have a curved object in mind but have not derived exact specifications for it, or when an irregular curved object passes through many different planes and would be very hard to draw face by face. You may be able to draw an outline and specify some key points, but beyond that what you conceive may be simply a smooth curve that follows the basic shape of your outline. AutoCAD provides mathematical algorithms that can translate outlines into smooth curves. This can be accomplished with 2D and 3D polylines and with 3D meshes.

3D meshes can be curved according to three different formulas, controlled by the variable "Surftype" (not to be confused with Surftab1 and Surftab2). Surftype can be set to 5 for a quadratic approximation, 6 for cubic approximation, and 8 for bezier.

In this exercise we will create a simple rectangular 3D mesh in one plane, move two of its vertices to make it three dimensional, and then use the Smooth option of the PEDIT command to create approximated surfaces.

⊕ To begin this task, clear your screen of all objects left from the last task, and return to a single viewport using the following procedure:

1. Make the right viewport active.
2. Open the View menu, highlight Tiled Viewports, and select 1 Viewport.

The screen will be redrawn with a single viewport resembling the currently active viewport.

3DMESH

The 3DMESH command allows you to create 3D polygon meshes "manually," vertex by vertex. Because of the time involved, the complete command is best used as a programmer's tool. However, there is an AutoLISP program that provides a very simple version of the 3DMESH command, which we will demonstrate here. Those interested in the full command sequence should see the *AutoCAD Command Reference.*

The AutoLISP version of the 3DMESH command is initiated through the 3D command. You must type the 3D command to ensure that you get a simple mesh rather than the complete 3DMESH command.

⊕ Zoom in so that the grid covers most of the screen.

⊕ Type "3D".

⊕ Type "m" to initiate the Mesh option.

AutoCAD prompts

First corner:

We will be prompted for four corners to define the outer boundaries of the mesh, and then for two numbers to specify the number of vertices.

⊕ Pick a corner, as shown by P1 in Figure 13-24.

AutoCAD will prompt for another corner:

Second corner:

⊕ Pick a second corner 4.00 to the right of P1.

⊕ Pick a third corner 3.00 in the y direction from P2.

⊕ Pick P4 as shown.

When you have picked four corners, your mesh should be outlined and one side highlighted. AutoCAD is asking for the number of vertices to be defined in the "M" direction:

Mesh M size:

The letters M and N are used to designate the two directions in which the mesh will be defined. The highlighted side shows the M direction. The M size is equivalent to the Surftab1 setting. The highlighted side will be divided equally by the number of vertices we specify.

⊕ Type "5".

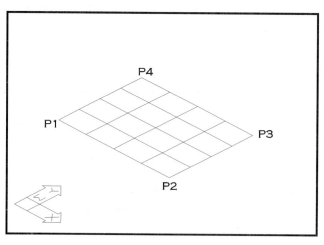

Figure 13-24

AutoCAD highlights a side perpendicular to the first and prompts

Mesh N size:

Like Surftab2, the "N" specification will determine the number of vertices in this direction.

⊕ Type "5" again.

    Your screen will be redrawn to resemble Figure 13-24.

The mesh will be drawn with five vertices in each direction. Later we will copy it twice so that we can produce three different types of smooth surfaces, but first we need to move some vertices up and down in the z direction to give it three-dimensionality. This can be done using XY filters and the grip edit stretch mode.

⊕ Select the mesh.

    The mesh will be highlighted and grips will appear at each vertex.

⊕ Pick the grip at the back right corner of the mesh.

    The stretch mode works the same as in previous chapters, except that now we will be moving vertices up and down out of the XY plane. If you have not previously used point filters, here is an opportunity to become familiar with this useful 3D tool.

⊕ Type ".xy" or open the cursor menu (shift-cursor enter button), select Point Filters, and then select .XY.

    AutoCAD prompts

.XY of

We are going to move the vertex straight up into the z dimension, so we want the same x and y coordinates with a new z. The XY filter will take the x and y values from whatever point we specify and combine them with a new z value. We can pick the same vertex again to show x and y, or we can type "@", indicating the last point entered. The z value will need to be typed since there are no objects outside of the XY plane to snap onto.

⊕ Type "@" or pick the highlighted vertex grip again.

    AutoCAD responds

(need Z):

⊕ Type "2".

    This will move the corner vertex up 2.00, as shown in Figure 13-25.

Now we will move the opposite corner down −3.00.

⊕ Pick the grip at the front left corner, opposite the corner you just edited.

⊕ Type ".xy" or open the cursor menu, select Point filters, and select .XY.

⊕ Type "@" or pick the same grip again.

⊕ Type "−3".

    We are now ready to create a cubic-style smoothed surface from our 3D mesh.

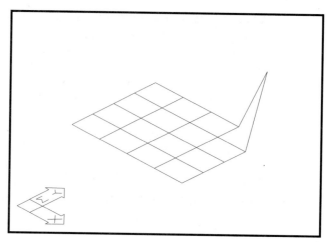

Figure 13-25

⊕ Type "pedit" or open the Modify menu, highlight Object, and se-
    lect Polyline.

    AutoCAD will prompt for a polyline, but 3D polygon meshes may also
    be selected.

⊕ Pick any point on the mesh.

    The mesh will not be highlighted when you pick it, but you will see the fol-
    lowing command prompt:

    `Edit Vertex/Smooth surface/Desmooth/Mclose/Nclose/Undo/eXit<X>:`

    The option we will be using is "Smooth surface".

⊕ Type "s".

    Your screen will be redrawn to resemble Figure 13-26.

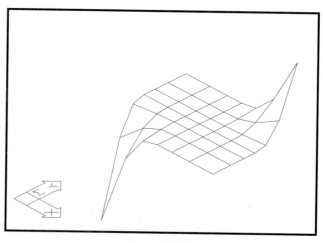

Figure 13-26

Note: If the variable "Splframe" is set to 1, your screen will show no change. Splframe shows the frame or outline used in defining an approximated curve. Because of the complexity of meshes, AutoCAD does not show a curved surface and its "frame" at the same time. With Splframe set to the default of 0, you will see the smoothed version with no frame. With a setting of 1 you see the original frame without the approximation.

Next we will make copies of the mesh and smooth the copies with the variable "surftype" set to create quadratic and bezier surfaces.

⊕ Press Enter to exit the PEDIT command.

⊕ Zoom all and make two copies of the mesh.

⊕ Type "Surftype".

⊕ Type "5".

Surftype is 6 for cubic (the default), 5 for quadratic, and 8 for Bezier.

⊕ Open the Modify menu, highlight Object, and select Polyline.

⊕ Select the first copy of the mesh.

⊕ Type "s" or select "Smooth".

Watch carefully. The differences between cubic and quadratic surfaces in this object will be slight. In fact, you will have to look hard to see them. We have indicated them with arrows in Figure 13-27 for your convenience. To show a more dramatic difference, you would need to create a more dramatic 3D figure by moving more vertices up or down. If you have the time, be our guest. Also consider changing the density of surface approximation through the variables "Surfu" and Surfv". For more information, see the *AutoCAD Command Reference.*

⊕ Exit the PEDIT command.

⊕ Type "Surftype".

⊕ Type "8" for a Bezier surface.

⊕ Open the Modify menu, highlight Object, and select Polyline.

⊕ Select the remaining copy of the mesh.

⊕ Type "s" to smooth the mesh.

Your meshes will resemble those in Figure 13-27.

Now that you know how to create smoothed surfaces, creating two-dimensional curve approximations should be easy. We include the following discussion as a reference.

Curve Approximation

Creating approximated curves in two dimensions is analogous to smoothing surfaces in three dimensions. The process is the same, with a few changes in variable

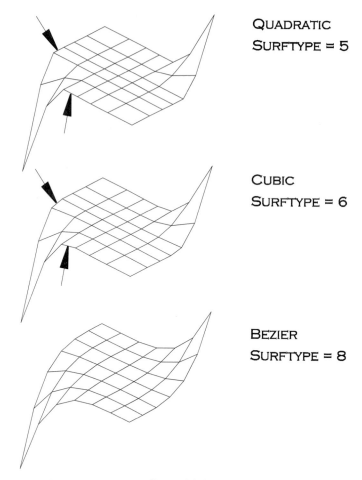

QUADRATIC
SURFTYPE = 5

CUBIC
SURFTYPE = 6

BEZIER
SURFTYPE = 8

Figure 13-27

names. Instead of beginning with a 3D mesh, you begin with a polyline. Polyline frames can be curved through the "Fit" or "Spline" options of the PEDIT command. Fit replaces all straight segments of a polyline with pairs of arc segments. The resulting curve passes through all existing vertices, and new vertices are created to join the arcs. Spline curves follow the shape of their frames, but they do not necessarily pass through all vertices. Instead they pass through the first and last points and tend toward the ones between according to either the quadratic or cubic formula. (There is no Bezier option for spline curves.)

If the variable "Splineframe" is set to 1 instead of the default 0, AutoCAD will display the defining frame along with the curve. Also, the degree of accuracy of curve approximation can be varied by changing the setting of the variable "Splinesegs". This variable controls the number of segments a polyline will be considered to have in the calculations of the spline formulas.

Examples of fit, cubic, and quadratic curves are shown in Figure 13-28.

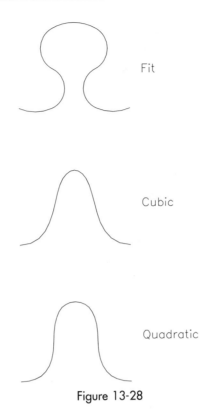

Fit

Cubic

Quadratic

Figure 13-28

13.7 Using MVSETUP to Create Multiple Viewport Layouts

GENERAL PROCEDURE

1. Create objects in model space.
2. Type "mvsetup".
3. Enable paper space.
4. Insert a title block.
5. Create viewports.
6. Scale viewports.
7. Align viewports.
8. Set paper space limits to extents.
9. Plot.

The MVSETUP command has a number of useful features, as evidenced by items 4 through 7 in the preceding procedure list.

In this task we will create a simple 3D surface model and then go through the steps involved in using MVSETUP to plot a multiple-view layout of the object in paper space.

Figure 13-29

✛ To begin this task you should be in model space with a blank screen.

✛ For demonstration purposes, draw a 3D surface model of a wine glass, about 6.00 units high, using the following procedure.

    1. Daw a 2D polyline outline and axis of revolution, as shown in Figure 13-29.

    2. Enter the REVSURF command.

    3. Select the outline as the path curve.

    4. Select the line segment as the axis of revolution.

    5. Press Enter twice to accept the defaults and create a complete revolution.

    6. ERASE the axis.

✛ Type "Mvsetup".

If tilemode is set to on, AutoCAD will prompt

                     `Enable Paperspace? (No/Yes):`

You must be in paperspace to create multiple nontiled viewports.

✛ Press Enter to enable paper space.

Your screen will go blank and the paper space icon will appear, as in the MVIEW command. You will see the following prompt:

    `Align/Create/Scale viewports/Options/Title block/Undo:`

We will be using all of these options to create a drawing layout of the wine glass. First, we will insert a title block and set up paper space to reflect a B-size drawing sheet.

✛ Type "t", for the "Title block" option.

MVSETUP prompts

           `Delete objects/Origin/Undo/<Insert title block>:`

✛ Press Enter to insert a title block at the current origin.

MVSETUP switches to the text window and shows a list of paper sizes. An ANSI-B sheet is designated by the number 8.

⊕   Type "8".

Now we need to create some viewports.

⊕   Type "c" for the "Create" option.

MVSETUP prompts

```
Delete objects/Undo/<Create Viewports>:
```

⊕   Press Enter to create viewports.

The text window returns again, showing a list of available viewport layout options. We will use a standard four-view engineering layout.

⊕   Type "2".

The text window disappears and MVSETUP prompts with two options for specifying the boundary area of the viewports:

```
Bounding area for viewports. Default/<First point>:
```

The first point option will allow you to create a window within which the four viewports will be drawn. The default option will choose an area based on your title block. In some cases you will not be offered a default. If this happens, window the area where you want the viewports to be drawn.

⊕   Type "d" for the "Default" option.

MVSETUP prompts for a distance between viewports in the x direction. This is similar to defining an array.

⊕   Type "1".

⊕   Press Enter to create the same distance in the y direction.

Be prepared for some fireworks. MVSETUP will draw four viewports and then create three 2D projections and a 3D view within them. When this is done your screen should resemble Figure 13-30, though the size of objects may be different.

MVSETUP also has its own scaling option, which sets zoom scale factors between paper space and viewports. We will use this feature to scale down the three orthographic views and leave the 3D view as is.

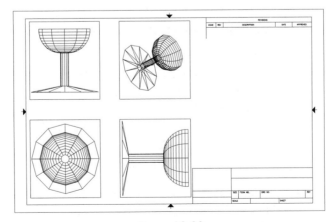

Figure 13-30

⊕   Type "s" for the "Scale viewports" option.

MVSETUP puts you into paper space, regardless of where you were before, so that you can select viewports.

⊕   Select the three projections (top left, bottom left, and bottom right viewports) one at a time by pointing to the borders.

⊕   Press Enter to end object selection.

MVSETUP prompts

```
Set zoom scale factors for viewports. Interactively/<Uniform>:
```

The interactive mode lets you establish different zoom factors in each selected viewport independently. The Uniform option will set them all to the same factor.

⊕   Press Enter for a uniform zoom factor.

The next options will allow you to specify a ratio of paper space units to model space units. We will use a ratio of one paper space unit to two model space units.

⊕   Press Enter to specify one paper space unit.

⊕   Type "2" to specify two model space units.

Your screen will be redrawn as shown in Figure 13-31.

We have one more layout operation to perform before we are ready to plot. You may notice that the three projections are not lined up with each other. This can be readily fixed using the Align option.

⊕   If the image in your lower left viewport does not appear to be centered, first exit the MVSETUP command, go into model space, and PAN in this viewport to center the image.

⊕   If necessary, reenter the MVSETUP command.

⊕   Type "a" for the "Align" option.

MVSETUP prompts

```
Angled/Horizontal/Vertical alignment/Rotate view/Undo:
```

Figure 13-31

⊕ Type "h" to perform a horizontal alignment.

MVSETUP prompts for a base point. This should be a point of alignment in the viewport that will remain unchanged by the alignment.

⊕ Pick the center of the glass in the lower left viewport.

MVSETUP prompts for another point. This should be the corresponding point in another viewport. When we are done, this point will align with the base point selected in the first viewport.

⊕ Pick any point along the center line of the glass in the bottom right viewport.

The command will bring the two views in line, as shown in Figure 13-32.

Now do a vertical alignment on the remaining view.

⊕ Type "v".

⊕ Pick the same base point at the center of the glass in the lower left viewport.

⊕ Pick any point along the center line of the glass in the top left viewport for the other point.

At this point the three views should align and your drawing should resemble Figure 13-32.

Before you proceed to a plot preview, set limits equal to extents in your drawing. This will make the plot configuration easier to manage.

⊕ Press Enter to return to the first MVSETUP prompt.

⊕ Type "o" for the "Options" option.

MVSETUP prompts

```
       Choose option to set—Layer/LImits/Units/Xref:
```

⊕ Type "Li" for "Limits".

⊕ Type "y" to set drawing limits equal to drawing extents.

⊕ Press Enter twice to exit MVSETUP.

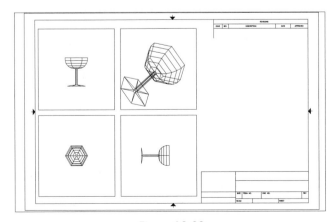

Figure 13-32

⊕ Check to be sure that you are in paper space (look for the paper space icon). If not, type "ps".

⊕ Type "Plot" or select the Print tool from the Standard toolbar.

We are, of course, ignoring the step of adding documentation to the title block.

⊕ Select either "Extents" or "Limits" from "Additional Parameters".

⊕ Assuming you are actually using B-size paper, make this selection from the Size subdialog box.

⊕ If "Scaled to Fit" is not checked, click in the box to check it.

⊕ Click on "Full" and then "Preview".

If you like what you see, then you are ready to plot.

13.8 Creating Perspective and Clipped 3D Views with DVIEW

GENERAL PROCEDURE

1. Type "dv" or select "3D Dynamic View" from the View menu.
2. Select objects to view.
3. Specify a DVIEW option.
4. Specify a view.
5. Specify another option or exit the command.
6. Use VIEW to save 3D views.

For most drawing purposes, using the VPOINT command or preset views from the pull-down menu is adequate and efficient for creating 3D views of objects. However, the DVIEW ("Dynamic View") command has several capabilities that do not exist in VPOINT. DVIEW allows you to "drag" the object or portions of it as you define the view. In addition, it has the capability of creating perspective views and allows you to "clip" the object at specified planes to temporarily remove all objects in front of or behind a specified plane.

Within the DVIEW command there are also options to zoom, pan, and rotate ("Twist") to achieve the exact display you want and to remove hidden lines to better visualize the view you are creating. As a general rule, DVIEW is best used when your drawing is complete and you want to create a plot or display that shows it to best advantage. Perspective views, for example, are strictly for presentation. Many draw and edit commands will not work at all in a perspective view.

In this task we will test some of the DVIEW options on a simple mesh in one plane. In particular, this mesh will demonstrate clearly the effect of the perspective view feature.

⊕ To begin this task, you should be in model space with a blank screen.

First, create a 3D mesh using the 3D surfaces program. If you need assistance beyond the instructions that follow, see Task 13.5 in this chapter.

⊕ Type "3D".

⊕ Type "m" for the "Mesh" option.

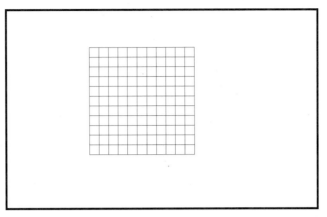

Figure 13-33

⊕ Pick the four corners of a square, approximately 6.00 × 6.00, as illustrated in Figure 13-33. Exact size and location are insignificant.

⊕ Type "12" for the "M size".

⊕ Type "12" for the "N size".

Before entering DVIEW it will be useful to have a smaller snap increment. This will become apparent when we use the "Camera" option to establish a viewpoint dynamically.

⊕ Set your Snap to .05.

⊕ Type "dv" or select "3D Dynamic View" from the View pull-down menu.

AutoCAD prompts for object selection:

Select objects:

One of the advantages of DVIEW is that it lets you adjust your view of objects in 3D space dynamically. To do this effectively, however, the number of objects on the screen may need to be limited. If you have ever tried to drag a complex object across the screen, you are familiar with the problem. The object is drawn and redrawn so slowly as you move your pointing device that the dragging process becomes too cumbersome to be useful. In the DVIEW command, you select a portion of your drawing to serve as a "preview image" for the process of dynamic view adjustment. The rest of the drawing is temporarily invisible and ignored. When you have defined the view you want by manipulating the preview image, exit DVIEW and the complete drawing will be restored in the newly defined view.

For our purposes, there is only the mesh to select.

Note: AutoCAD also provides a default preview image. If you press Enter at the "Select objects:" prompt, DVIEW will show a simple wireframe house for your preview image. Or if you prefer, you can even create your own default image. (See the *AutoCAD Command Reference*.) For most purposes, however, you will want to see at least a portion of the drawing you are working on.

⊕ Select the mesh.

⊕ Press Enter to end object selection.

AutoCAD will prompt with the following DVIEW options:

```
CAmera/TArget/Distance/POints/PAn/Zoom/TWist/CLip/Hide/Off/
                    Undo/<eXit>:
```

These options vary considerably in their effect and ease of use. We will begin with a "Zoom".

Note: To avoid confusion, AutoCAD switches to the WCS whenever you enter DVIEW. DVIEW proceeds with the WCS in effect and then returns you to your UCS when you exit the command. We are working in the WCS in this exercise anyway, so this will not be noticeable.

"Pan" and "Zoom"

Panning in the DVIEW command is easy. After specifying a base point, you can drag objects around the screen in any direction.

⊕ Type "pa".

⊕ Pick a point near the middle of the mesh for a base point.

⊕ Move the cursor slowly and observe the preview image moving along with it.

⊕ Center the image on the display.

Zooming in DVIEW is a little different from the regular ZOOM command.

⊕ Type "z".

AutoCAD places a "slider bar" at the top of the screen, as shown in Figure 13-34, and prompts

```
            Adjust zoom scale factor <1>:
```

The slider bar consists of a scale with numbered divisions (0x,1x,4x,9x,16x), a diamond-shaped "cursor" that is controlled by your pointing device, and two rubber bands that connect you to a short line marking the current magnifica-

Figure 13-34

tion. The current value is always "1x." If you move the cursor to the right, objects on the screen will be enlarged by the factors shown on the scale; if you move to the left, they will be reduced by fractional factors.

⊕ Move the cursor so that the diamond is on the short vertical line at the "1x."

"1x" is the current magnification, so the preview image will appear as it did before you entered the zoom option, except that any color will be gone.

⊕ Now stretch the rubber bands to the right and left and watch the mesh expand and shrink.

Notice that it doesn't take much movement to produce a significant change. If snap is on you may want to turn it off to see the full range of magnification.

⊕ Pick a zoom factor of about 2.00.

Your mesh will be enlarged, and AutoCAD will return to the DVIEW options prompt:

```
CAmera/TArget/Distance/POints/PAn/Zoom/TWist/CLip/Hide/Off/
Undo/<eXit>:
```

⊕ If necessary, use the PAn option to center the mesh on the screen.

"Camera" and "Target"

Next we will change our view of the image using the "CAmera" option. "Camera" and "Target" refer to two aspects of a point of view relative to a 3D object. ("Distance" is a third we will discuss shortly.)

Photographic metaphors are used extensively in AutoCAD rendering procedures as well as in DVIEW. When you sight through an actual camera, what you see is dependent on the location of the camera and the direction its lens is pointed. In the metaphor, "Camera" refers to your point of view in space, and "Target" refers to the point at which the camera is aimed. In the DVIEW command you change views by moving the point of view (Camera), by aiming it toward a new point (Target), or both.

In practice, setting the "Camera" placement is very similar to using the rotation option of the VPOINT command. If you recall, in using "VPOINT Rotate" you define an angle of rotation within the *XY* plane and a viewing angle above or below the plane. Viewpoints we have used typically in this book are 315 degrees in the plane and 30 degrees up from the plane.

To demonstrate the perspective feature, we are going to use a longer, flatter viewing angle. Notice that this view would be impractical for drawing purposes but will create a dramatic perspective effect.

⊕ Type "ca".

The appearance of your preview image will depend on the placement of your pointing device. The prompt will be

```
Toggle angle in/Enter angle from XY plane <90.0000>:
```

- You can enter angles by typing or by picking a point on the screen. Picking may seem easier and has the advantage of allowing you to drag the preview image into place. However, it is difficult to conceptualize exactly what the cursor and image are doing. If you type, AutoCAD will ask for an angle from the *XY* plane and then an angle in the *XY* plane. But first watch how the cursor works.

⊕ Move the cursor slowly and watch how the preview image and the coordinate display react.

The behavior of the cursor will be unfamiliar. In effect, vertical movement of the cursor controls the angle from the *XY* plane, while horizontal movement controls the angle in the *XY* plane. If you move the cursor freely, you are seeing both angles adjusted simultaneously.

You will have better control if snap is on. This is where a small snap increment is useful in this exercise.

⊕ If snap is off, turn it on.

⊕ Move several snap points horizontally and then several vertically.

Continue moving horizontally and vertically to get a feel for the camera position system. As the camera moves up and down from the plane, the preview image appears to tip forward and back. It may be difficult to visualize what is happening as you pass below 0 degrees. As you pass zero, the front of the object begins to tip away from you so that you are looking up from underneath. If you move the camera back and forth in the plane, the image will appear to turn.

For a good perspective view, we want an angle of about 9 degrees from the *XY* plane and 0 degrees in the *XY* plane. The reason for using the number 9 is this: The range of angles is from -90 to $+90$, a total of 180 degrees; 9 degrees is the angular equivalent of one snap point since 0.05×180 is 9. To ensure that you get the results presented here, we suggest that you type in the angles.

⊕ Type "9" for the angle from XY.

⊕ Type "0" for the angle in XY.

Your screen will resemble Figure 13-35. Though it appears that your mesh has been flattened, in fact this is a three-dimensional parallel projection. The

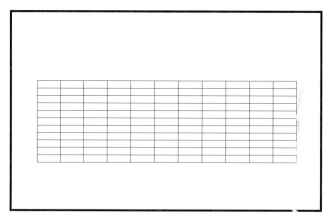

Figure 13-35

flattening is a result of foreshortening. When we switch to a perspective view, the appearance will be quite different. Notice that it would be extremely difficult to draw in this foreshortened image.

Note: If you find that your mesh has turned into a horizontal line on the screen, it is because you have reversed angles. With 0 as the angle from the *XY* plane, you will be looking edge on and the mesh will appear as a line regardless of what angle in the *XY* plane is specified. Type "t" to toggle between angle in and angle from in the prompt.

Target

We will not use the TArget option in this exercise. The process is exactly the same as the Camera option. Vertical and horizontal movement of the cursor controls the rotation of the target point from and in the *XY* plane. The camera location does not change. Instead, we change the direction in which the camera is aimed. It is like panning with a movie camera. The camera pans up and down with the vertical motion of the cursor, left and right with horizontal motion. You will notice that the image on the screen shifts more radically than in the Camera option and that it is easy to "pan" away from the image so that it flies off the screen entirely.

"Distance" and Perspective

Another aspect of any camera-to-target relationship is the distance between the two. The "Distance" option moves the camera position in or out along the line of sight. It differs from "Zoom" in that it automatically creates a perspective view.

⊕ Type "d".
  The distance option uses a slider bar just like the zoom option. However, since Distance turns perspective on and distances are interpreted differently in perspective viewing, your preview image will look very different from the way it appeared before you entered the option.
⊕ Move the cursor left and right and watch the image move along the lines of perspective.
⊕ Move the slider to about 1.5x and press the pickbutton.
  Your screen will resemble Figure 13-36. Notice the perspective effect and the perspective icon that replaces the UCS icon.

Note: If you enter the "Zoom" option while in a perspective view, you will see AutoCAD prompt for a "Lens length" rather than a zoom factor. In perspective, "DVIEW Zoom" operates like adjusting a lense on a camera to enlarge or reduce the field of vision. This is consistent with the photographic metaphor. We suggest you try it.

Saving 3D Views with VIEW

Once you are in perspective, you will find that your drawing capabilities are severely limited. Many commands will not work at all. If you wish to do more drawing and editing, you will need to leave the perspective view and go back to the

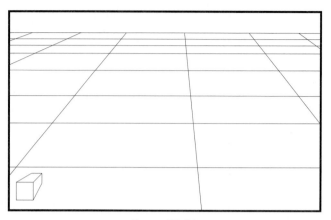

Figure 13-36

usual parallel projection. However, by using the VIEW command you can save all the view adjustment work you have done so that you can come back to it at any time without going through DVIEW again. When you do, any editing or drawing done in the meantime will be included and adjusted to the defined view. For reference, here is the procedure for saving a view:

1. Type "view".
2. Type "s" for "Save".
3. Type a name for the view.

Clipping Planes

We will explore one last feature of the DVIEW command. By using a "clipping" plane, we will temporarily remove part of the drawing.

⊕   Type "cl".

This option allows you temporarily to remove everything in front of or behind a specified plane. In a full 3D model of a house, for example, you can use this option to remove a wall and display the inside of a room.

AutoCAD prompts

Back/Front/<Off>:

If "back" is chosen, everything behind the specified plane will be removed; if "front" is chosen, objects in front will be removed. We will use a front clipping plane.

⊕   Type "f".

AutoCAD places a horizontal slider bar at the top of the screen.

⊕   Move the cursor all the way to the right.

This places the clipping plane completely behind the mesh so that the entire image is clipped, leaving nothing but the horizon.

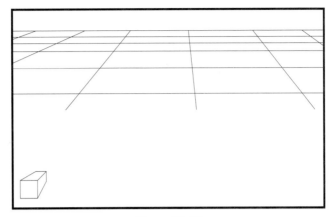

Figure 13-37

⊕ Move the cursor slowly to the left.

Watch the image gradually appear as the clipping plane covers up less and less. Keep moving to the left until the whole image is visible. Notice that the clipping plane is perpendicular to the line of sight, parallel to the plane of the screen.

⊕ Now move the cursor back to the right until you have an image similar to the one in Figure 13-37.

⊕ Press the pickbutton to register the clipping plane position.

⊕ Press Enter to exit the DVIEW command.

Your screen will be redrawn as shown in Figure 13-37.

Clipped images, like perspective views, can be saved using the VIEW command.

The Dview Hide Option

There is a "Hide" option within the DVIEW command that allows you to remove hidden lines from your preview image. This can help in visualizing the 3D object and as a preview of the HIDE command itself. Hidden lines are only removed temporarily. They will return as soon as you exit DVIEW.

Turning Off Perspective and Clipping Planes

It is extremely important to turn off perspective and clipping when you are through with them. With perspective on, you will be unable to execute most drawing functions. Try zooming, for example, and you will get a standard message:

```
** That command may not be invoked in a perspective view **
```

Clipping planes are somewhat less inhibiting but remain in effect even as you change viewpoints. When you switch viewpoints, the line of sight and viewing angle may change dramatically. However, the clipping plane will remain parallel to the plane of the screen and at the same "distance". This can yield some pretty strange results.

Both effects may be turned off by reentering the DVIEW command. The "Off" option of the first prompt will turn perspective off, while "CLip" has its own "Off" option. In either case, you can speed up the process by pressing Enter at the "Select objects:" prompt and ignoring AutoCAD's default preview image.

There are still quicker methods, however. For example, you usually will leave a perspective view in order to work in another 3D view or a plan view. You can go directly into these by entering the VPOINT or PLAN commands and specifying a new view.

VPOINT and PLAN will turn perspective off but not clipping planes. However, if you have saved any views, you can restore them using the VIEW command. VIEW will remove clipping planes as well as perspective if they were not in effect when the view was defined.

In summary, you can use VIEW or DVIEW to remove clipping planes and perspective, and VPOINT or PLAN to remove perspective only.

13.9   Review Material

Questions

1. Why is it important to keep two or more different views of an object on the screen as you are drawing and editing it?
2. What two basic geometric shapes can be drawn as a 3DFACE?
3. How does the HIDE command treat objects on layers that are turned off?
4. What geometry is needed to define a tabulated surface? a ruled surface? an edge surface? a revolved surface?
5. What one basic surface entity makes up all AutoCAD surfaces?
6. What is the function of the Align option in the MVSETUP command?
7. Why does the DVIEW command ask you to select objects to view? What happens if you do not select objects?
8. Explain the photographic metaphor as used by the camera option of the DVIEW command.
9. What option of the DVIEW command will take you into a perspective view?
10. Why is it important to use the VIEW command in conjunction with the DVIEW command?

Drawing Problems

1. Begining with a blank drawing using the B template, create a three-tiled viewport screen configuration with two viewports on the left and one viewport on the right.

2. Create a world plan view in the top left viewport, a front view in the bottom left viewport, and a southeast isometric view in the large right viewport.
3. Draw a line from (9,9,0) to (11,9,0). Draw a polyline from (9,9,0), to (7,9,0), to (7,7,0), to (6,5,0), to (4,4,0).
4. Modify the polyline so that it takes the shape of spline curve.
5. Create a 360-degree surface of revolution by revolving the spline curve around the original 2.00 unit line.
6. Make the right viewport active and remove hidden lines.

13.10   Drawing 13-1: REVSURF Designs

The REVSURF command is fascinating and powerful. As you get familiar with it, you may find yourself identifying objects in the world that can be conceived as surfaces of revolution. To encourage this process, we have provided this page of 12 REVSURF objects and designs.

To complete the exercise, you will need only the PLINE and REVSURF commands. In the first six designs we have shown the path curves and axes of rotation used to create the design. In the other six you will be on your own.

Exact shapes and dimensions are not important in this exercise. Imagination is. When you have completed our designs, we encourage you to invent a number of your own.

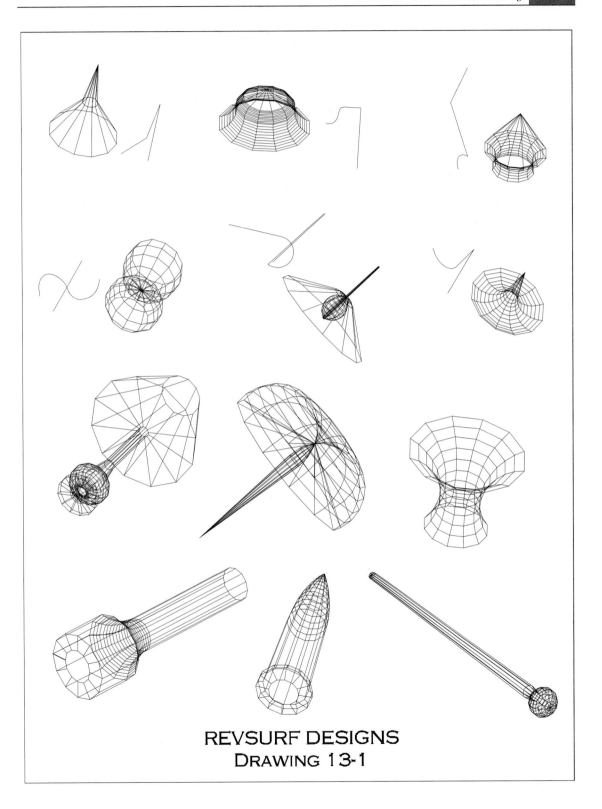

REVSURF DESIGNS
DRAWING 13-1

13.11   Drawing 13-2: Picnic Table

This is a tricky drawing that must be done carefully. It requires efficient use of the UCS command along with a number of edit commands. To create an image that hides as shown in the reference, you must cover all surfaces with 3D faces.

DRAWING SUGGESTIONS

- Use a three-viewport configuration, with top (plan) and front views on the left and a 3D view on the right. Be sure to keep an eye on all viewports as you go, since it is quite likely that you will create some lines that look correct in one view but not in others.
- Use a separate layer for 3D faces and add the faces as you go. This will save you from retracing your steps. Notice that the faces on the chamfered braces are drawn with one invisible line across the middle.
- We recommend that you start with the top of the table and work down. Placing the legs directly behind the chamfered braces can be tricky. One way to do this is to draw the legs even with the side of the table first (in a UCS with its *XY* plane flush with a side of the table) and then MOVE them back.
- Save the angled braces for last. Once the leg braces are drawn, you can locate the angled braces by drawing a line from the midpoint of the small brace in the middle of the table top to the midpoint of the bottom of a leg brace. Then OFFSET this line 1″ each way to create the two lower edges of one angled brace.

PICNIC TABLE

DRAWING NO.
DRAWING 13-2

CAD Support Associates

ALL CHAMFERS 2" X 2"

2" X 6"

2" X 6"

2" X 4"

5'

6'

3'

1'

8'

1'-0 1/2"

2'-8"

4'-3"

30°

1'-0"

1'-4"

13.12   Drawing 13-3: Globe

This drawing uses several of the 3D mesh commands. Some of the 3D construction is a little tricky, but you may be pleasantly surprised. Follow the suggestions and you will find that this one is easier than it looks.

DRAWING SUGGESTIONS

- Use a three-viewport configuration with top and front views on the left and a 3D view on the right.
- Begin with the base circles, drawing in the plan (top) view, and then MOVE the circles into place along the z axis.
- MOVE the small inner circle up 12.25 to locate the top of the shaft. Draw the center line from the center of this circle to the top center of the base. Then COPY this line on itself and ROTATE the line and circle 23.5 degrees around the midpoint of the line to position the center of the shaft.
- OFFSET the shaft center line 0.125. Later, you will TRIM a 4.00-diameter circle to this line. Then using the center line of the shaft as the axis of rotation for a REVSURF will leave a hole in the middle of the globe for the shaft.
- Draw the 4.00, 4.75, and 5.38 circles and TRIM them to the vertical, 23.5-degree, and 46-degree lines as shown.
- With your UCS parallel to the front view, COPY the 4.75 and 5.38 circles 1.25 and 2.25 in the z direction to form the two sides of the globe support. ERASE the original circles.
- TABSURF the shaft.
- RULESURF the base circles. There will be three ruled surfaces to complete the base.
- REVSURF the top of the base, using a single line from a quadrant to the center for a path curve and the vertical centerline for the axis.
- RULESURF the globe support. This will require four ruled surfaces.
- REVSURF the globe.
- Freeze all nonsurface lines before HIDEing.

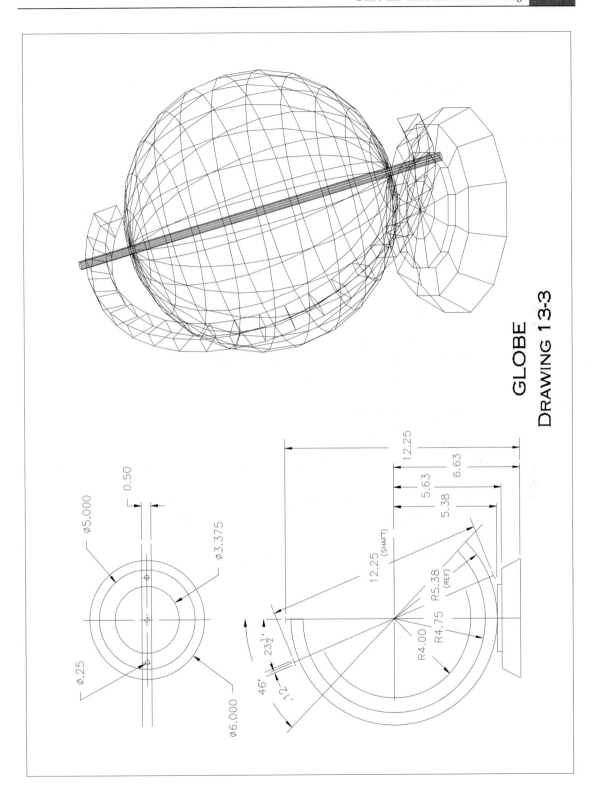

GLOBE
DRAWING 13-3

13.13   Drawing 13-4: Nozzle

This is a tough drawing that will give you a real 3D workout. You will need to define numerous UCSs as you go. Your goal should be to create the two views A and B. Dimensioning is not part of the exercise. The dimensioned figure is not a complete wireframe, but a guide to show you the abstract relationships necessary to complete the surface model.

DRAWING SUGGESTIONS

- We began in a front, right, top view. This puts the main center line of the nozzle in the *XY* plane of the WCS, while the circles that show the outlines of the nozzle would be perpendicular to it. When we were done, we rotated the objects slightly to show them more clearly.

- Make ample use of COPY and OFFSET in drawing the circles and center lines of the nozzle, the hexes and circles of the knob, and the polyline curve path of the nozzle.

- The circle and center line at the right end of the 45-degree angle can be constructed using a COPY and ROTATE of the circle and center line just in front of the angle. This must be done in a UCS parallel to the WCS.

- The curve in the nozzle is a −45-degree REVSURF around the center line 1.00 to the right of the turn.

- The two darkened lines show the path curves used with REVSURF to draw the nozzle and the knob. Construct lines first and then go over them with PLINE or 3DPOLY. 3DPOLY is similar to PLINE, but it uses 3D points instead of 2D points and has no option to draw arcs. In general, 3D polylines are more flexible and can be drawn at times when the current UCS would not allow the construction of a 2D polyline.

- The center line through the knob (along the arrow) runs perpendicular to the polyline outline of the nozzle. Use a PERpendicular osnap to construct the center line and then define UCSs in relation to the center line to construct the knob.

Ø1.00
Ø1.25
.25
Ø.25
.32
.32 ACROSS FLATS
.12

A

.12
.32
0.13
0.13
.50
0.83
R1.00
1.38
45°
3.58
Ø.38
Ø1.75
Ø2.25

B

DRAWN BY:	DATE	**CAD Support Associates, Inc.**		
		DRAWING TITLE: **NOZZLE**		
		SIZE **B**	DRAWING NO. **DRAWING 13-4**	REV.
		SCALE:	DATE:	SHEET: OF

14 Solid Models

COMMANDS

SOLIDS		MODIFY	RENDER	
BOX	SECTION	INTERSECT	LIGHT	SCENE
CYLINDER	SLICE	SUBTRACT	MATLIB	SHADE
EXTRUDE	SPHERE	UNION	RENDER	
REVOLVE	WEDGE		RMAT	

OVERVIEW

Solid modeling is a built-in component of AutoCAD Release 14. Solid modeling is in many ways easier than either wireframe or surface modeling. In solid modeling you can draw a complete solid object by picking a few points, in a fraction of the time it would take to draw line by line, surface by surface. Furthermore, once the object is drawn it contains far more information than a wireframe or surface model. In this chapter you will draw a simple solid model using several solid drawing and editing commands.

TASKS

14.1   Creating Solid BOXes and WEDGEs

GENERAL PROCEDURE

1. Enter BOX or WEDGE.
2. Specify corner point and distances in the *XY* plane of the current UCS (or define a base plane first and then specify points).
3. Specify a height.

Solid modeling requires a somewhat different type of thinking from any of the drawings you have done so far. Instead of focusing on lines and arcs, edges and surfaces, you will need to imagine how 3D objects might be pieced together by combining or subtracting basic solid shapes. This building block process is called constructive solid geometry and includes joining, subtracting, and intersecting operations. A simple washer, for example, could be made by cutting a small cylinder out of the middle of a larger cylinder. In AutoCAD solid modeling you can begin with a flat outer cylinder, then draw an inner cylinder with a smaller radius centered at the same point, and then subtract the inner cylinder from the outer, as illustrated in Figure 14-1.

This operation, which uses the SUBTRACT command, is the equivalent of cutting a hole and is one of three Boolean operations (after the mathematician George Booles) used to create composite solids. UNION joins two solids to make

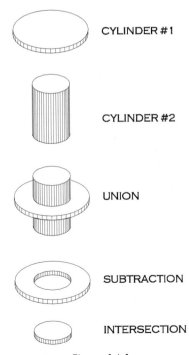

CYLINDER #1

CYLINDER #2

UNION

SUBTRACTION

INTERSECTION

Figure 14-1

a new solid, and INTERSECT creates a composite solid in the space where two solids overlap (see Figure 14-1).

In this chapter you will create a composite solid from the union and subtraction of several solid primitives. Primitives are 3D solid building blocks—boxes, cones, cylinders, spheres, wedges, and torus. They all are regularly shaped and can be defined by specifying a few points and distances.

⊕ To begin this task, go into a right front top view (315 degrees from x and 45 degrees from *XY*).

Notice that this is a slightly higher viewing angle than the southeast isometric view we used in the previous two chapters. If you are unfamiliar with the use of the Viewpoint Preset dialog box, use the following procedure:

1. Type "vpoint".
2. Type "r" for "Rotate".
3. Type "315" for the angle in the *XY* plane from the x axis.
4. Type "45" for the angle from the *XY* plane.

⊕ Type "box" or open the Draw menu, highlight Solids, and select Box.

There is also a Solids toolbar with a Box tool, as illustrated in Figure 14-2.

In the command area you will see the following prompt:

Center/<Corner of box> <0,0,0>:

"Center" allows you to begin defining a box by specifying its center point. Here we will use the "Corner of box" option to begin drawing a box in the baseplane of the current UCS. We will draw a box with a length of 4, width of 3, and height of 1.5.

⊕ Pick a corner point similar to point 1 in Figure 14-3.

Figure 14-2

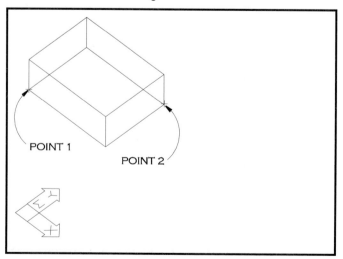

Figure 14-3

AutoCAD will prompt

Cube/Length/<Other corner>:

With the "Cube" option you can draw a box with equal length, width, and height simply by specifying one distance. The "Length" option will allow you to specify length, width, and height separately. If you have simple measurements that fall on snap points, as we do, you can show the length and width at the same time by picking the other corner of the base of the box (the default method).

⊕ Move the cross hairs over 4 in the x direction and up 3 in the y direction to point 2, as shown in Figure 14-3.

Notice that "length" is measured along the x axis, and "width" is measured along the y axis.

⊕ Pick point 2 as shown.

Now AutoCAD prompts for a height. "Height" is measured along the z axis. As usual, you cannot pick points in the z direction unless you have objects to snap to. Instead, you can type a value or show a value by picking two points in the XY plane.

⊕ Type "1.5" or pick two points 1.5 units apart.

Your screen should resemble Figure 14-3.

Next we will create a solid wedge. The process will be exactly the same, but there will be no "Cube" option.

⊕ Type "we" or open the Draw menu, highlight Solids, and select Wedge.

AutoCAD prompts

Center/<Corner of wedge> <0,0,0>:

⊕ Pick the front corner point of the box, as shown in Figure 14-4.

As in the BOX command, AutoCAD prompts for a cube, length, or the other corner:

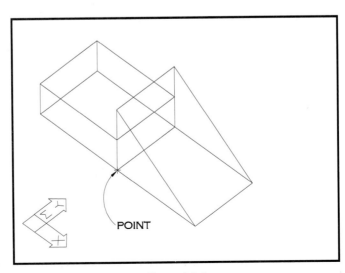

Figure 14-4

Cube/Length/<other corner>:

This time let's use the length and width option.

⊕ Type "L".

The rubber band will disappear and AutoCAD will prompt for a length, which you can define by typing a number or showing two points.

⊕ Type "4" or show a length of 4.00 units.

AutoCAD now prompts for a width. Remember, length is measured in the x direction, and width is measured in the y direction.

⊕ Type "3" or show a width of 3 units.

AutoCAD prompts for a height.

⊕ Type "3" or show a distance of 3 units.

AutoCAD will draw the wedge you have specified. Notice that a wedge is simply half a box, cut along a diagonal plane.

Your screen should resemble Figure 14-4. Although the box and the wedge appear as wireframe objects, they are really quite different, as you will find. In Task 14.2 we will join the box and the wedge to form a new composite solid.

14.2 Creating the UNION of Two Solids

GENERAL PROCEDURE

1. Type "Union" or open the Modify menu, highlight Boolean, and select Union.
2. Select solid objects to join. (Steps 1 and 2 may be reversed if noun/verb selection is enabled.)

Unions are simple to create and usually easy to visualize. The union of two objects is an object that includes all points that are on either of the objects. Unions can be performed just as easily on more than two objects. The union of objects can be created even if the objects have no points in common (i.e., they do not touch or overlap).

Right now we have two distinct solids on the screen; with UNION we can join them.

⊕ Type "Union" or open the Modify menu, highlight Boolean, and select Union.

There is also a Union tool on the Modify II toolbar, as shown in Figure 14-5.

Figure 14-5

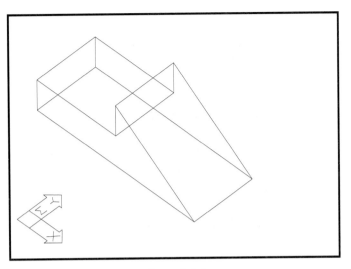

Figure 14-6

AutoCAD will prompt you to select objects.

⊕ Point or use a crossing box to select both objects.

⊕ Press Enter to end object selection.

Your screen should resemble Figure 14-6.

14.3 Working Above the *XY* Plane Using Elevation

GENERAL PROCEDURE

1. Type "Elev".
2. Enter elevation and thickness values.

In this task we will draw two more solid boxes while demonstrating the use of elevation to position objects above the *XY* plane of the current UCS. Changing elevations simply adds a single *Z* value to all new objects as they are drawn and can be used as an alternative to creating a new UCS. With an elevation of 1.00, for example, new objects would be drawn 1.00 above the *XY* plane of the current UCS. You can also use a thickness setting to create 3D objects, but these will be created as surface models, not solids.

⊕ To begin this task you should have the union of a wedge and a box on your screen, as shown in Figure 14-6.

We will begin by drawing a second box positioned on top of the first box. Later we will move it, copy it, and subtract it to form a slot in the composite object.

⊕ Type "Elev".

AutoCAD prompts

> New current elevation <0.00>:

The elevation is always set at 0 unless you specify otherwise.

⊹ Type "1.5"

This will bring the elevation up 1.5 out of the *XY* plane, putting it even with the top of the first box you drew.

AutoCAD now prompts for a new current thickness. Thickness does not apply to solid objects because they have their own thickness.

⊹ Press Enter to retain 0.00 thickness.

This brings us back to the command prompt. If you watch closely you will see that the grid has also moved up into the new plane of elevation.

⊹ Type "Box" or open the Draw menu, highlight Solids, and select Box.
⊹ Pick the upper left corner of the box, point 1 in Figure 14-7.
⊹ Type "L" to initiate the "length" option.
⊹ Type "4" or pick two points (points 1 and 2 in Figure 14-7) to show a length of 4 units.
⊹ Type ".5" or pick two points (points 1 and 3) to show a width of 0.5 units.
⊹ Type "2" or pick two points to show a height of 2 units.

Your screen should resemble Figure 14-7. Notice how you were able to pick points on top of the box because of the change in elevation just as if we had changed coordinate systems. Before going on, return to 0.00 elevation.

⊹ Type "elev".
⊹ Type "0".
⊹ Press Enter to retain 0.00 thickness.

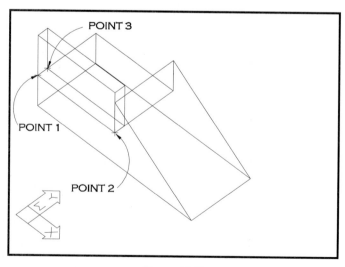

Figure 14-7

14.4 Creating Composite Solids with SUBTRACT

GENERAL PROCEDURE

1. Create solid objects to subtract and objects to be subtracted from.
2. Position objects relative to each other.
3. Type "su" or open the Modify menu, highlight Boolean, and select Subtract.
4. Select objects to be subtracted from.
5. Select objects to subtract.

SUBTRACT is the logical opposite of UNION. In a union operation, all the points contained in one solid are added to the points contained in other solids to form a new composite solid. In a subtraction, all points in the solids to be subtracted are removed from the source solid. A new composite solid is defined by what is left.

In this exercise, we will use the objects already on your screen to create a slotted wedge. First we need to move the thin upper box into place, then we will copy it to create a longer slot, and finally we will subtract it from the union of the box and wedge.

⊕   To begin this task, you should have the composite box and wedge solid and the thin box on your screen, as shown in Figure 14-7.

Before subtracting, we will move the box to the position shown in Figure 14-8.

⊕   Type "m" or select the Move tool from the Modify toolbar.

⊕   Select the narrow box drawn in the last task.

⊕   Press Enter to end object selection.

⊕   At the "Base point or displacement" prompt use a midpoint object snap to pick the midpoint of the top right edge of the narrow box.

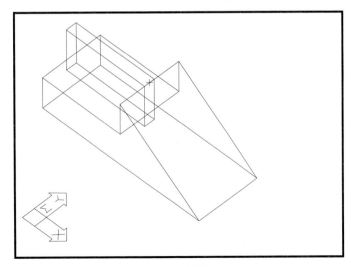

Figure 14-8

⊕ At the "Second point of displacement" prompt use another mid-point object snap to pick the top edge of the wedge, as shown in Figure 14-8.

This will move the narrow box over and down. If you were to perform the subtraction now, you would create a slot but it would only run through the box, not the wedge. We can create a longer slot by copying the narrow box over to the right using grips.

⊕ Select the narrow box.

⊕ Pick any of the eight grips.

⊕ If ortho is off, turn it on.

Now if you move the cursor in the *x* direction you will see a copy of the box moving with you. Solids cannot be stretched, so we must make a copy to lengthen the slot.

⊕ Type "c".

⊕ Move the cursor between 2.00 and 4.00 units to the right and press the pickbutton.

If you don't go far enough the slot will be too short. If you go past 4.00, the slot will be interrupted by the space between the box and the copy.

⊕ Press Enter to leave the grip edit mode.

Your screen will resemble Figure 14-9.

⊕ Type "su" or open the Modify menu, highlight Boolean, and select Subtract.

There is also a Subtract tool on the Modify II toolbar, as shown in Figure 14-6.

AutoCAD asks you to select objects to subtract from first:

```
Select solids and regions to subtract from ...
                Select objects:
```

⊕ Pick the composite of the box and the wedge.

Figure 14-9

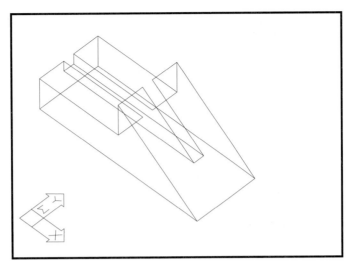

Figure 14-10

⊕ **Press Enter to end selection of source objects.**

AutoCAD prompts for objects to be subtracted:

```
Select solids and regions to subtract...
Select objects:
```

⊕ **Pick the two narrow boxes.**

⊕ **Press Enter to end selection.**

Your screen will resemble Figure 14-10.

Next we will draw a solid cylinder, move it into place, and subtract it to form a hole at the right end of the slot.

⊕ **Type "Cylinder" or open the Draw menu, highlight Solids, and select Cylinder.**

There is also a Cylinder tool on the Solids toolbar, shown in Figure 14-2.

AutoCAD prompts

```
Elliptical/<center point> <0,0,0>:
```

⊕ **Pick any convenient center point away from the composite solid.**

It does not matter where the cylinder is drawn since we are going to move it to the end of the slot using a midpoint object snap.

To create a hole the same width as the slot, we need a diameter of 0.5 or a radius of 0.25.

⊕ **Type ".25" for the radius value.**

The cylinder must be made high enough to reach through the slot. Any height over 1.00 will do.

⊕ **Type "1" for the height.**

The cylinder will be drawn as shown in Figure 14-11 except that your cylinder will probably have only four vertical lines (they will actually look like two

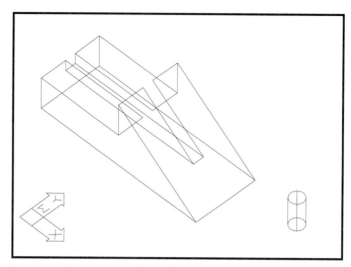

Figure 14-11

lines because they hide each other). The density of lines displayed by Auto-CAD to represent curved solid surfaces is controlled by a variable called "Isolines". We will change ours to show eight lines.

⊕ Type "isolines".

AutoCAD prompts

        New value for ISOLINES <4>:

⊕ Type "8".

⊕ Type "Regen".

Next we will move the cylinder to the end of the slot using a grip edit and a midpoint object snap.

⊕ Select the cylinder.

There will be a grip at the top and bottom centers of the cylinder. We want to move the top center to the midpoint of the end of the wedge.

⊕ Select the top center grip on the cylinder.

⊕ Use a midpoint object snap to move the cylinder to the end of the slot, as shown in Figure 14-12.

Now it's time to subtract.

⊕ Type "su" or open the Modify menu, highlight Boolean, and select Subtract.

⊕ Select the composite object.

⊕ Press Enter to end object selection.

⊕ Select the cylinder.

⊕ Press Enter to end object selection.

Your screen will resemble Figure 14-13.

Figure 14-12

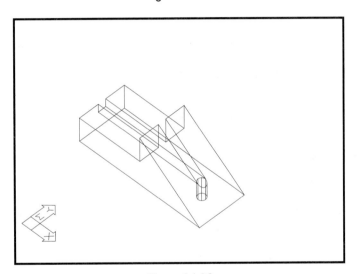

Figure 14-13

14.5 Creating Chamfers and Fillets on Solid Objects

GENERAL PROCEDURE

1. Type "cha", select Chamfer from the Modify menu, or select the Chamfer tool from the Modify toolbar.
2. Pick a base surface.
3. Press Enter or type "n" to select the next surface.
4. Enter chamfer distances.
5. Pick edges to be chamfered.
6. Press Enter to end object selection.

Constructing chamfers and fillets on solids is simple, but the language of the prompts can cause confusion due to some ambiguity in the designation of edges and surfaces to be modified. We will begin by putting a chamfer on the top left of the model.

⊕ To begin this task you should have the solid model shown in Figure 14-13 on your screen.

⊕ Type "cha", select Chamfer from the Modify menu, or select the Chamfer tool from the Modify toolbar.

The first chamfer prompt is the same as always:

```
(TRIM mode) Current chamfer Dist1 = 0.00, Dist2 = 0.00
Polyline/Distance/Angel/Trim/Method/<Select first line>:
```

⊕ Select point 1, as shown in Figure 14-14.

AutoCAD highlights the left surface and prompts

```
                        Select base surface:
                        Next/<OK>:
```

We are constructing a chamfer on the left surface of the object. However, chamfers and fillets happen along edges that are common to two surfaces. What is a "base surface" in relation to a chamfered edge? Actually, it refers to either of the two faces that meet at the edge where the chamfer will be. As long as you pick this edge, you are bound to select one of these two surfaces, and either will do. Which of the two surfaces is the "base surface" and which is the "adjacent surface" will not matter until you enter the chamfer distances, and then only if the distances are unequal. However, AutoCAD allows you to switch to the other surface that shares this edge, by typing "n" for the "Next" option.

Figure 14-14

⊕ Press Enter.

AutoCAD prompts

> `Enter base surface distance <0.00>:`

⊕ Type ".5" for the base surface distance.

Now AutoCAD prompts

> `Enter other surface distance <0.50>:`

Now you can see the significance of "base surface." The chamfer will be created with the first distance on the base surface side and the second distance on the other surface side. If the chamfer is symmetrical, it will not matter which is which.

⊕ Type ".25" for the other base surface distance.

This will construct a chamfer that cuts 0.5 down into the left side and 0.25 back along the top side.

Now AutoCAD prompts for the edge or edges to be chamfered.

> `Loop/<Select edge>:`

"Loop" will construct chamfers on all edges of the chosen base surface. Selecting edges will allow you to place them only on the selected edges. You will have no difficulty selecting edges if you pick the edge you wish to chamfer again. The only difference is that you will need to pick twice, once on each side of the slot.

⊕ Pick the top left edge of the model, to one side of the slot (point 1 in Figure 14-14 again).

⊕ Pick the same edge again, but on the other side of the slot (point 2 in Figure 14-14).

⊕ Press Enter to end edge selection.

Your screen will resemble Figure 14-15.

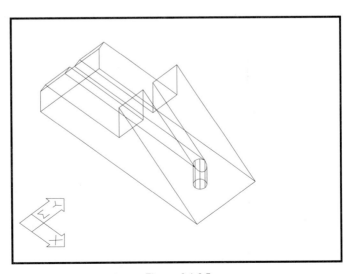

Figure 14-15

Creating Fillets

The procedure for creating solid fillets is simpler. There is one less step since there is no need to differentiate between base and other surfaces in a fillet.

⊕ Type "Fillet" and select Fillet from the Modify menu or the Fillet tool from the Modify toolbar.

AutoCAD prompts

    Polyline/Radius/Trim/<Select first object>:

⊕ Pick the edge where the box and the wedge meet, point 1 in Figure 14-16.

AutoCAD prompts

    Enter radius <0.50>:

⊕ Press enter or type ".5".

The next prompt looks like this:

    Chain/Radius/<Select edge>:

"Chain" will allow you to fillet around all the edges of one side of a solid object at once. For our purposes we do not want a chain. Instead we want to select the two edges on either side of the slot.

⊕ Pick the same edge on the other side of the slot, point 2 in Figure 14-16.

You will see this prompt again:

    Chain/Radius/<Select edge>:

The prompt repeats in order to allow you to select more edges to fillet.

⊕ Press Enter to end selection of edges.

Figure 14-16

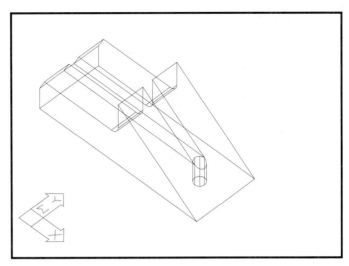

Figure 14-17

Your screen will resemble Figure 14-17.

Important: Before proceeding, save the composite wedge as a block so that you can insert it later when we use it to explore shading and rendering.

⊕ Type "b" or select the Make Block tool from the Draw toolbar.
⊕ Type "w" for the block name.
⊕ Click on "Select Objects<".
⊕ Select the composite wedge.
⊕ Press Enter to end object selection.
⊕ Click on "Select Point<".
⊕ Select an insertion base point; any corner will do.
⊕ Click to remove the check from "Retain objects".
⊕ Click on "OK".

When the block definition is complete, the wedge will disappear from the screen.

14.6 Creating Solid Objects with EXTRUDE

GENERAL PROCEDURE

1. Create a polyline, circle, or region shape in two dimensions.
2. Type "ext", or open the Draw menu, highlight Solids, and select Extrude.
3. Select objects.
4. Specify an extrusion height.
5. Specify an extrusion taper angle.

Release 14 includes two additional ways to create solid objects. First, using the EXTRUDE command, simple 2D polylines and regions can be built up or repeated along a linear path stretching up or down from the plane in which they are drawn. Second, using REVOLVE, 2D polylines and regions can be revolved around an axis along a circular or semicircular path. The REVOLVE command is very similar to REVSURF, but it creates a solid rather than a surface model.

In this task we will draw a simple polyline shape and extrude it to create a solid. In the next task we will begin working with regions.

⊕ To begin this task, your screen should be clear of all objects left from the previous task.

⊕ Draw a 2.00 by 4.00 polyline rectangle, as shown in Figure 14-18.

Be sure to use PLINE or RECTANG to create this 2D polyline. 3DPOLY, which draws 3D polylines, will not work with EXTRUDE.

⊕ Type "ext", or open the Draw menu, highlight Solids, and select Extrude.

There is also an Extrude tool on the Solids toolbar, as shown in Figure 14-6.

AutoCAD will prompt you to select objects. Only regions, polylines, and circles can be extruded.

⊕ Select the rectangle.

⊕ Press Enter to end object selection.

AutoCAD prompts

Path/<Height of extrusion>:

The "Path" option is a powerful feature that allows you to create an extrusion along any pathway in the *z* direction. As in the TABSURF command, you need a line or polyline to serve as a pathway. A solid may then be cre-

Figure 14-18

ated by essentially repeating the 2D object(s) at every point along the selected path.

If you use the default "Height of extrusion" option, the extrusion will be measured straight up into the *z* direction (or down if you enter a negative number).

⊕ Type "3" or show a distance of 3.00 units (distance may be shown in the *XY* plane).

AutoCAD prompts:

Extrusion taper angle <0>:

This prompt gives you the opportunity to create a tapered extrusion by specifying an angle. This will be an angle between the *z* axis and the edge of the extruded object.

⊕ Type "10".

Your screen should resemble Figure 14-19. Be aware that if your taper angle is too large, edges may meet before the specified height is reached. In the case of an extrusion with a rectangular base, this would result in a prism, with a ridge at the top rather than a smaller rectangle.

The extruded solid you have just created will function exactly like the solid objects created earlier. It can be used in union, subtraction, and intersection with other solids to create complex solid objects.

In the next task we will explore solid regions.

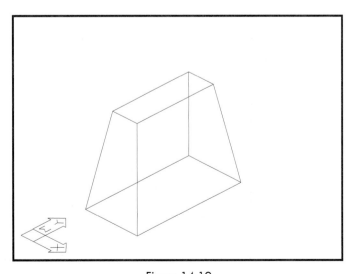

Figure 14-19

14.7 Creating 2D Region Entities

GENERAL PROCEDURE

1. Draw 2D polyline shapes.
2. Type "Region" or select the Region tool from the Polygon flyout on the Draw toolbar.

Regions are the 2D equivalent of 3D solids. They can be combined through union, subtraction, and intersection using the same commands used with solids. Regions are similar to faces in that they cover 2D spaces. Like polylines, they can be extruded to form 3D solids.

In this task we will create a simple composite region from two polyline rectangles. Individual regions are created using the REGION command on previously drawn polylines.

⊕ To begin this task, undo the last extrusion, so that you are left with the 2.00 × 4.00 polyline rectangle shown previously in Figure 14-18.

⊕ Draw a second complete polyline rectangle, 1.00 × 2.00, centered on the midpoint of the edge of the first, as shown in Figure 14-20.

Note: You must draw all four sides of this rectangle, even though you will not see the side that lies along the left side of the larger rectangle. Regions can only be constructed from closed polyline figures.

Next we will convert the two rectangles into 2D regions.

⊕ Type "reg", select Region from the Draw menu or select the Region tool from the Draw toolbar.

Figure 14-20

AutoCAD prompts you to select objects.

⊕ Pick both rectangles with a window or crossing window.

⊕ Press Enter to end object selection.

You will see no change, although there will be a message in the command area that says that two regions have been created.

Now if you subtract the smaller rectangle from the larger, you will see that these regions behave just like 3D solids.

⊕ Type "sub", or open the Modify menu, highlight Boolean, and select Subtract.

⊕ Select the larger rectangle as the region to subtract from.

⊕ Press Enter to end object selection.

⊕ Select the smaller rectangle as the region to subtract.

⊕ Press Enter to end object selection.

Your screen will resemble Figure 14-21.

14.8 Creating Solids by Revolving 2D Entities Using REVOLVE

GENERAL PROCEDURE

1. Draw regions or 2D polyline shapes.
2. Type "rev" or open the Draw menu, highlight Solids, and select Revolve.
3. Select objects.
4. Specify an axis of revolution.
5. Specify an angle of revolution.

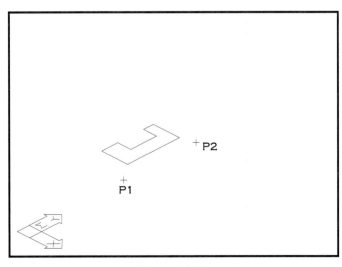

Figure 14-21

REVOLVE is a powerful solid modeling command that creates solid objects by revolving 2D polyline shapes and regions around an axis. It functions in ways very similar to the REVSURF surface modeling command.

In this task we will create a spool-shaped 3D solid by revolving the composite region from the last task around an axis in the *XY* plane.

⊕ To begin this task, you should have the composite region shown in Figure 14-21 on your screen.

⊕ Type "rev" or open the Draw menu, highlight Solids, and select Revolve.

There is also a Revolve tool on the Solids toolbar, as shown in Figure 14-6.

⊕ Select the composite region.

⊕ Press Enter to end selection.

AutoCAD prompts

```
Axis of revolution - Object/X/Y/<Start point of axis>:
```

"Object" allows you to select a line or a one-segment polyline as the axis of revolution. "X" and "Y" allow you to specify one of the axes of the current UCS. We will specify an axis by pointing.

⊕ Pick a start point 1.00 unit to the right of the region, as shown in Figure 14-21.

AutoCAD prompts for an end point of the axis.

⊕ Pick an end point like P2 in Figure 14-21.

AutoCAD prompts

```
Angle of revolution <full circle>:
```

Like REVSURF, REVOLVE gives you the option of creating only a portion of the circle of revolution. Unlike REVSURF, there is no option to begin the object somewhere other than in the plane of the region itself.

⊕ Press Enter to create the full circle.

Your screen will resemble Figure 14-22.

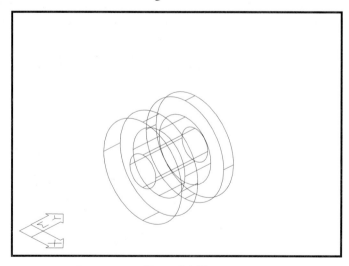

Figure 14-22

In the remaining tasks we will create a cutaway view and a section; then we will introduce shading and rendering.

14.9 Creating Solid Cutaway Views with SLICE

GENERAL PROCEDURE

1. Type "Slice" or select the Slice tool from the Solids toolbar.
2. Select objects.
3. Specify a cutting plane.
4. Specify a point on the plane.
5. Pick a side to retain.

A single solid or composite solid may be sliced along its intersection with a specifiable plane. The plane is specified in terms common to several solid commands.

In this task we will cut the object created in the last task along a plane parallel to the current z and y axes and retain the left portion so that we can view the inside of the "spool."

⊕ **Type "sl" or open the Draw menu, highlight Solids, and select Slice. There is also a Slice tool on the Solids toolbar, as shown in Figure 14-6.**

AutoCAD will prompt you to select objects.

⊕ **Select the spool.**

⊕ **Press Enter to end object selection.**

AutoCAD now prompts for plane specification:

        Slicing plane by Object/Zaxis/View/XY/YZ/ZX/<3points>:

A similar prompt is used in the SECTION command, which we will explore next. The slicing plane requested here can be determined by an object, a point on the z axis, or one of the current UCS planes, or by showing three points. In this task we will use a *YZ* plane.

Take a look at Figure 14-23. It should help you visualize the *XY*, *YZ*, and *ZX* planes. The actual slicing plane will be parallel to a plane of origin in the current

Figure 14-23

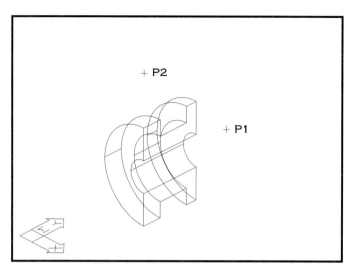

Figure 14-24

UCS. In other words, it does not have to have the same origin. Once you have determined which plane you want to use, the next step will be to specify a point on the plane.

⊕ Type "YZ".

AutoCAD will prompt for a point on the *YZ* plane. The default point is (0,0,0), which will specify the *YZ* plane of the current UCS. Any other point will specify a plane parallel to the current *YZ* plane.

⊕ Pick a point so that the *y* axis of the cross hairs runs through the center of the spool.

This will cause the spool to be cut along its center line.

AutoCAD prompts

    Both sides/<Point on the desired side of the plane>:

⊕ Pick any point to the left of the previous point (that is, left in the *x* direction).

This will show that you want to retain the portion of the spool that lies along the left side of the cutting plane. Your screen should resemble Figure 14-24.

Next we will create a cross section of the remaining half.

14.10 Creating Sections with SECTION

GENERAL PROCEDURE

1. Type "sec" or open the Draw menu, highlight Solids, and select Section .
2. Select objects.
3. Specify a sectioning plane.

Figure 14-25

Sectioning works just like slicing, but the outcome is a 2D region taken from the solid along the specified plane. In this task we will create a region section of the spool by sectioning it along the *XY* plane. The result will be a U-shaped block. It will look exactly like the region we used to create the revolved solid in the first place.

⊕ Type "sec" or open the Draw menu, highlight Solids, and select Section.

There is also a Section tool on the Solids toolbar, as shown in Figure 14-6.

⊕ Select the cut spool.

⊕ Press Enter to end object selection.

AutoCAD prompts

    Section plane by Object/Last/Zaxis/View/XY/YZ/ZX/<3points>:

This is the same prompt as the slicing plane prompt, except for the first word. This time we will cut along the current *XY* plane.

⊕ Type "XY".

AutoCAD will prompt for a point on the *XY* plane. Any point will do.

⊕ Press Enter for the point (0,0,0) or pick any point.

AutoCAD will create the section. To see it well, you will need to move it or move the spool. When you are done your screen should resemble Figure 14-25.

14.11 SHADEing Solid Models

GENERAL PROCEDURE

1. Adjust layers, colors, and variables to create desired effects.
2. Type "Shade" or select the Shade tool from the Render toolbar.

Shaded images are simple to create. There are relatively few variables to manipulate. For more dramatic and realistic images you will need to delve into the realm of rendering, introduced in the next task. Unlike shading, rendering involves a large number of variables and will require a great deal of practice before you become proficient.

In working with shaded images your only options concern the color of objects in the image, the manner in which edges are shown, and the relative amounts of diffuse and ambient light. In this exercise we will create a shaded image of the composite wedge from earlier in the chapter. In the next task we will use the same object for rendering.

⊕ Erase all objects from your screen.

⊕ Type "i" or select the Insert Block tool from the Draw toolbar.

⊕ Click on Block... to see the list of defined blocks.

⊕ Select the W block.

⊕ Click on "OK".

⊕ Click on "OK" again.

⊕ Insert the wedge near the middle of your grid.

⊕ Press Enter to accept all the default scale values.

Since this book does not contain color illustrations, we have moved our wedge to layer 0 so that the image is shaded in gray and white. If you do the same, your screen images will more closely match our illustrations. The following procedure is provided if you wish to work with gray and white rather than color images.

1. Make layer 0 current by opening the layer list on the Standard toolbar and double clicking on layer 0.

2. Explode the W block.

3. Draw a line anywhere on layer 0.

4. Use the Match Properties tool from the Standard toolbar to move the wedge to layer 0.

⊕ Turn off the grid.

You will not want the grid in your shaded or rendered images, and turning it off afterward will cause the screen to be redrawn (you will have to repeat the rendering).

⊕ Open the View menu and highlight Shade.

This will open the submenu shown in Figure 14-26. The four options provided correspond to the four settings of the SHADEDGE variable. SHADEDGE determines whether edges of shaded objects are outlined and the complexity of color values used.

⊕ Select 256 Color Edge Highlight.

This will produce shaded image similar to Figure 14-27. We suggest that you try the other three settings to see how they appear on your screen before going on to the next task.

Figure 14-26

Figure 14-27

14.12 RENDERing Solid Models

GENERAL PROCEDURE

1. Position lights.
2. Attach materials.
3. Adjust light intensity.
4. Render.
5. Save scene.

Rendering goes far beyond shading by creating the effect of light falling on the various surfaces of a solid or surface model. Rendering is a complex craft whose mastery requires many hours of experimentation. Most of the techniques involved concern the placement and setting of lights. There are four types of lights, and each light has its own set of variables and settings, which will dramatically affect the end result. Knowing the various lights, how to position them, and how to understand their respective settings is a good place to begin. But this knowledge alone will not take you very far. You will need to accumulate many hours of experience in order to know what you want and how to achieve it.

In this task we will show you how to position lights and how to use some of the most critical settings. We will continue to use the wedge shaded in the last task and to work on layer 0.

⊕ To begin this task you should have the wedge on your screen in a southeast isometric viewpoint, as in the last task.

Ambient Light

First, we will simply render the object as is without any change in lighting. What you will see will be entirely dependent on the default ambient light setting. Ambient light is background light that fills space and is the same everywhere. It has no direction and can only be varied as to color and intensity.

⊕ Type "Render" or Open the View menu, highlight Render, and select Render....

There is also a Render tool on the Render toolbar, shown in Figure 14-28. AutoCAD will display the Render dialog box shown in Figure 14-29. Ignore the options in the dialog box for now.

Figure 14-28

Figure 14-29

Figure 14-30

⊕ Click on "Render Scene".

After a few moments you will see an image similar to the one in Figure 14-30. As you can see, this image is only a slight advancement over the shaded images in the last task. To enhance the lighting, we need the LIGHT command.

The Lights Dialog Box

Lights are created, placed, and modified using the Lights dialog box.

⊕ Type "Light" or open the View menu, highlight Render, and select Lights....

There is also a Lights tool on the Render toolbar, shown in Figure 14-28.

The LIGHT command opens the Lights dialog box, shown in Figure 14-31. Look at the Ambient Light area on the right. Ambient light has only color and intensity. With the scroll bar at the top you can vary the intensity from 0 to 1.00. The default setting is 0.30. Try changing the intensity using the following procedure:

1. Using the scroll bar, select greater ambient light intensity. Increase it to 1.00 to see the effect clearly.
2. Click on "OK".

Figure 14-31

3. Open the Vew menu, highlight Render, and select Render....
4. Click on "Render Scene" in the Render dialog box.

Also in the Ambient Light box are three scroll bars for mixing the amounts of red, green, and blue light. All types of lights have these scroll bars so that you can vary the color quality of the light coming from individual light sources as well as ambient light color. Feel free to experiment with color settings at this time. The effect of the color mix is especially clear on a gray and white object like ours. For example, if you set the green and blue on 0 and leave the red at 1.00, you will see that what remains of the ambient light is shown as small red dots on the surfaces of the object. With all three set at 1.00, the default, the effect is that of white light.

Changing the background color

You may find that rendered images are too dark against the AutoCAD background screen color. This is particularly true if you are creating gray and white images against a black screen. You can remedy this by changing to a white background through the Preferences dialog box. Or you can add a backgound to your rendering through the Background dialog box, which is part of the Rendering system. The difference is that the rendered background becomes part of the rendering, whereas the AutoCAD window background does not. The procedure for changing the AutoCAD window background is as follows:

1. Open the Tools menu and select Preferences... from the bottom of the menu.
2. Click on the Display tab.
3. Click on Colors....
4. Select Graphic Windows Background from the Window element list.
5. Click on the White or another light color.
6. Click "OK" twice.

To introduce rendering backgrounds we will add a gradient background. Because of the colors involved, we will not be able to illustrate the results.

⊞ Open the View menu, highlight Render, and select Background....
This will call the Background dialog box illustrated in Figure 14-32. There are many possibilities available, which we will not explore here. Notice that the Solid radio button is selected and the AutoCAD background box is checked. With these two settings many options are inaccessible, and we will continue to use the AutoCAD window background color.

⊞ Click on the Gradient radio button.
Notice that the AutoCAD background check box becomes inaccessible automatically, because it is solid and incompatible with a gradient color scheme. You will also see that the color adjustment area and the horizon, height, and rotation area are now accessible. To see what the current gradient looks like, use the Preview box.

⊞ Click on Preview.
The Preview image will appear, showing a background that grades from red to green to blue. Notice that these are the colors shown on the left next to

Figure 14-32

top, middle, and bottom. One of these three will be highlighted with a dark border. The selected color can be adjusted with the three color scroll bars in the middle. These scrolls can be used like a palette to mix the amounts of red, green, and blue in the top, middle, and bottom colors. Finally, the horizon, height, and rotation scroll bars can be used to vary the proportions and orientation of color lines in the gradient.

You should experiment with these settings to get a feel for how they work.

⊕ When you are done experimenting, click on OK to retain your background.

⊕ Open the View menu, highlight Render, and select Render....

⊕ In the Render dialog box, select "Render Scene...".

In a few moments you should see your ambient light rendering with a color gradient background. Next we will add some more focused lighting.

We will be exploring three types of light placement. To define light position, it will be helpful to create a three-viewport configuration so that you can see what is happening from different viewpoints.

⊕ Open the View menu, highlight Tiled Viewports, and select "3 Viewports".

⊕ Press Enter to accept the default "Right" configuration.

Your screen will be redrawn with three viewports.

⊕ Click in the top left viewport to make it active.

⊕ Type "Plan" to create a plan view.

⊕ Press Enter to accept the default, current UCS.

⊕ Type "z" and then ".5x" to zoom out.

⊕ Click in the bottom left viewport to make it active.

Figure 14-33

⊕ Open the View menu, highlight 3D Viewpoint, and select "Front" to create a front view.

⊕ Type "z" and then ".5x" to zoom out.

⊕ Click in the right viewport to make the 3D viewport active.

⊕ Zoom in on the 3D image using a window selection.

Your screen should now resemble Figure 14-33.

Spotlight

We are going to add a spotlight on the right side of the object, aimed in along the slot. Light placement is probably the most important consideration in rendering. If you have used point filters previously, then you have already learned all you need to know in order to position lights. Keep in mind that lights will usually be positioned above the XY plane and will probably be alone in space. Point filters can be very helpful in this situation since there is nothing to snap them on to.

Before we can add a light, we must designate the light type, specify that it is new, and give it a name.

⊕ Type "lights", open the View menu, highlight Render, and select Lights…

⊕ Click the arrow next to "Point Light" at the lower left of the Lights dialog box.

The options will be shown as Point Light, Distant Light, and Spotlight. We begin with a spotlight because its focus and directionality make it easy to understand.

⊕ Click on "Spotlight".

⊕ Click on "New".

This will call up the New Spotlight dialog box shown in Figure 14-34. Notice first that there is a place for a name, a scroll bar for intensity, and three scroll bars for color, just as in the ambient light box. There are also areas for position, hotspot and falloff, and attenuation. We will discuss these areas in a moment, but first let's give the light a name and a position.

⊕ Type "Spot" in the Light Name edit box.

Figure 14-34

⊕ Click on "Modify <" under "Position".

This closes the dialog box temporarily and gives you access to your drawing. On the command line you will see the following prompt:

Enter light target <current>:

Spotlights have a target and a source position. As is the case with real spotlights, AutoCAD rendering spotlights are carefully placed and aimed at a particular point in the drawing. The light falls in a cone shape and diminishes away from the center of the cone. You can vary the size of the focal beam using the Hotspot scroll bar, and the size of the surrounding falloff area using the Falloff scroll bar.

For this exercise we will place a light above and to the right of the wedge, aimed directly into the slot. If you look at the plan and front views in your drawing, you will see that RENDER has already placed a temporary spotlight symbol in your drawing. This is a default position, which you can ignore. We will be using point selection and XY filters to place the target and the light source where we want them.

⊕ At the prompt for a light target, type ".xy" or open the cursor menu, highlight Point Filters, and select ".XY".

AutoCAD prompts ".xy of" and waits for you to choose a point in the *XY* plane.

⊕ Click in the upper left window to make the plan view active.

⊕ Pick a point about 1.0 units to the left of the cylindrical hole, as shown in Figure 14-35.

Ortho should be off to do this.

AutoCAD now prompts for a *Z* value:

(need Z):

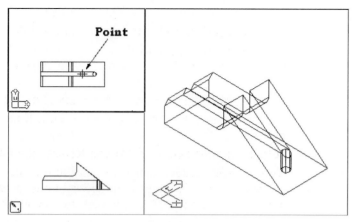

Figure 14-35

To place the target point right in the slot, we will need to have a *Z* value of 1.00 (the bottom of the slot is 1.00 above the *XY* plane).

⊕ Type "1".

The target point has been specified. Now AutoCAD prompts for the spotlight location:

Enter light location <current>:

We will use an .xy filter to place the light source to the right and above the wedge.

⊕ Type ".xy" or open the cursor menu, highlight Point Filter, and select ".XY".

⊕ In response to the "of" prompt, select a point about 2.00 units to the right of the wedge, as shown in Figure 14-36.

⊕ In response to the "need Z" prompt, type "5" to position the spotlight 5.00 above the *XY* plane.

This will bring back the New Spotlight dialog box.

Figure 14-36

⊕ Click on "OK" to exit the New Spotlight dialog box.

⊕ Click on "OK" to exit the Lights dialog box.

You will now see a spotlight icon in your drawing. The three-view configuration will show clearly how it is positioned and directed. Let's render the scene again to see the spotlight in action.

⊕ Click on the right viewport to make it active.

⊕ Type "Render" or open the View menu, highlight Render, and select Render....

⊕ Select "Render Scene" from the Render dialog box.

You will see a rendered image similar to the one in Figure 14-37. In this image you can clearly see how the spotlight hits the wedge just behind the hole and falls off in waves along the back on the object.

To achieve a more precise light cone, you can change from a Gouraud style rendering to a Phong rendering.

⊕ Press enter to repeat RENDER.

⊕ Select "More Options...".

⊕ Click on the "Phong" radio button in the Render quality box.

⊕ Click on "OK".

⊕ Click on "Render Scene".

Your new rendered image will resemble Figure 14-38.

Next we will be adding a point light, but before going on you may want to experiment with some of the other features of spotlighting (available in the New Spotlight or Modify Spotlight subdialog of the Lights dialog box). Try varying the

Figure 14-37

Figure 14-38

hotspot and falloff. Notice that the hotspot must always be smaller than the falloff. You will also see significant differences when you vary the attenuation. Attenuation is the rate at which light intensity diminishes relative to distance from the light source. In the default Inverse Linear setting, light two units away from its source will appear half as bright. If you switch to Inverse Square attenuation, light at two units will be only a fourth as bright as at the source. So switching to inverse square will cause the light from a spotlight to diminish more quickly over a shorter distance.

When you are done experimenting, we suggest that you return to our settings so that your images continue to resemble ours. These include the following: Ambient light is at 1.00 intensity and all colors are at 1.00. The spotlight is at 4.47 intensity, all colors are at 1.00, hotspot is at 44 degrees with falloff at 45 degrees, and attenuation is inverse linear.

Point Light

Point light works like a light bulb with no shade. It radiates outward equally in all directions. Like spotlighting, the light from a point light attenuates over distance.

In this exercise we will place a point light right inside the slot of the wedge. This will clearly show the light bulb effect of a small point of light radiating outward.

⊕   Type "Light" or open the View menu, highlight Render, and select Lights....

⊕   Click on the arrow to the right of "Spotlight" and switch to "Point Light".

⊕   Click on "New...".

⊕   Type "Point" in the Light Name edit box.

⊕   Click on "Modify <".

For a point light you only need to specify a location, since point light has no direction other than outward from the source. The prompt is

Enter light location <current>:

We will use the same point filtering system to locate this light.

⊕   At the prompt type ".xy" or open the cursor menu, highlight Point Filters, and select .XY.

⊕   At the "of" prompt, pick a point in the plan view at the center of the slot and about 1.00 unit behind the plane where the box and the wedge join, as shown in Figure 14-39.

⊕   Type "1.25" for a Z value.

Since the slot is at 1.00 from the XY plane, this will put the point light just above the bottom of the slot.

⊕   Click on "OK".

⊕   Click on "OK" again to exit the Lights dialog box.

⊕   Click on the right viewport to make it active.

⊕   Type "Render" or open the View menu, highlight Render, and select Render....

⊕   Select "Render Scene" from the Render dialog box.

Figure 14-39

Figure 14-40

Your rendered object will resemble Figure 14-40. In this image you can clearly see the effect of the point light within the slot along with the spotlight falling on the right side of the object.

Distant Light

The last type of light is called distant light and is often used to achieve the effect of direct sunlight. In AutoCAD rendering, a distant light source emits beams of light that are parallel and travel in one direction only. Distant light does not attenuate. It is the same at any distance from the source. Distant light placement is defined by a directional vector; the command line prompt will ask for a "to" point and a "from" point. You can define this vector precisely using point filters, as we have done previously. The to point will probably be on an object or in the XY plane. The from point will be above the XY plane. Most important is the angle and direction between the two points. You can define these points using point filters, as we have done previously, or you can use the sunlight-oriented Azimuth and Altitude dials shown in the Distant Light dialog box. Since you have already used point filters, we will introduce the dial system here for variety.

⊕   Type "Light" or open the View menu, highlight Render, and select Lights....

Figure 14-41

⊕ Click on the arrow to the right of "Point Light" and switch to "Distant Light".

⊕ Click on "New...".

This brings up the New Distant Light dialog box shown in Figure 14-41. You will see scroll bars for intensity and color on the left. On the right you will see the Azimuth and Altitude dials and scroll bars above a light source vector modification area. By selecting "Modify <" you could proceed to place the distant light source with to and from points using point selection and point filters. The Azimuth and Altitude system may help you to think more specifically in terms of sunlight. The Azimuth setting will determine the position of sunlight relative to the east–west horizon. In other words, it will simulate the variations of sunlight depending on your position on the planet and the time of year. The Altitude setting will simulate time-of-day variations. In the northern hemisphere in late morning, for example, the sun is coming from the south (180 degrees on the azimuth dial) from an altitude of, let's say, 65 degrees. You can use the scroll bars, points on the dials, or typing in the edit boxes to achieve these settings. You can also use the Sun Angle Calculator to find appropriate settings for different times and places.

⊕ Type "Dist" in the Light Name edit box.

⊕ Using the scroll bar, move the Azimuth setting all the way to the right so that the edit box reads 180 degrees.

⊕ Using the scroll bar, move the Altitude setting partway to the right so that the edit box shows 65 degrees.

Changes in these settings will also cause changes in the Light Source Vector box and in the dials above the scroll bars.

⊕ Click on "OK".

Figure 14-42

⊕ Click on "OK" in the Lights dialog box.

⊕ Type "Render" or select the Render tool from the Render toolbar.

⊕ Select "Render Scene" from the Render dialog box.

Your image will resemble the rendering in Figure 14-42. By comparing this image with the one in Figure 14-40, you can see the effect of adding distant "sunlight" to this rendering.

The Render Window

To get a full view of a rendered image, it is often desirable to send the rendering to the Render Window rather than view the rendering within a single viewport. This will be most apparent when there are several small viewports on the screen. To use the render window, you have to make one change in the Render dialog box.

⊕ Press Enter to repeat Render.

⊕ In the dialog box, click the arrow to the right of the box that says "Viewport".

This will be on the right in the Destination section of the dialog box. The arrow will open a list that shows Viewport, Render Window, and File as Destination options. Rendering to a viewport you have already done; rendering to a file will send the rendering information directly to a file without displaying the image on your screen. Render files can be created in TGA, TIFF, GIF, PostScript, X11, PBM, PGM, PPM, BMP, PCX, SUN FITS, FAX G III, and IFF formats and may then be displayed in other graphics systems.

⊕ Click on Render Window.

The list will close and Render Window will be shown in the Destination box.

⊕ Click on Render Scene.

In a moment the rendered wedge will be shown in the Render Window. This window has standard Windows 95 features and can be moved, maximized, or minimized. Once it is opened there will be a label for it on the Windows 95 taskbar. You can switch between the Drawing Window and the Render Window, as you would with other open applications.

⊕ Click on the maximize button to see a full-screen rendered image.

⊕ Click on the AutoCAD drawing name label on the Windows 95 taskbar to return to the drawing window.

Scenes

A rendered scene is made up of a view and a set of lights. Once you have positioned lights, you may want to present the image from different points of view and use different configurations of lights. Defined scenes can be saved so that you can re-create them easily and even switch from one to another. For example, let's create a scene without the spotlight to see the effect of the distant light and the point light together.

⊕ Type "Scene" or open the View menu, highlight Render, and select Scene....

There is also a Scene tool on the Render toolbar, as shown in Figure 14-28. This will bring up the Scenes dialog box shown in Figure 14-43.

⊕ Select "New...".

⊕ Type "NoSpot" for a scene name (spaces not allowed in names).

⊕ Highlight "Point" and "Dist" in the Lights area (hold down the shift key to highlight both names).

Make sure that "Spot" is not highlighted.

⊕ Click on "OK".

⊕ In the Scenes dialog box, make sure that "NOSPOT" is highlighted and then click on "OK".

Now that the new scene is defined, you can create a new rendering.

⊕ Type "render" or open the View menu, highlight Render, and select Render....

⊕ In the Render dialog box, make sure that "NOSPOT" is highlighted under "Scene to Render".

⊕ Click on "Render Scene".

Your "Nospot" scene will resemble Figure 14-44 and will be rendered to the Render window.

⊕ Click on the AutoCAD drawing name label on the Windows 95 taskbar to return to the drawing window.

Notice that the image in the viewport is not the new rendering but the previous image with the spotlight included. The rendered image in the Render window does not affect the image in the viewport.

Figure 14-43

Figure 14-44

Attaching Materials

Materials can be created or selected from AutoCAD's materials library. Each material definition has its own characteristic color, ambient light color, reflection color, and roughness value. Materials can also be created or modified. Changing an object's material will dramatically affect the way it is rendered, so it will usually make sense to attach materials before adjusting light intensity and color. In this exercise we will simply take you through the procedure of loading materials from the AutoCAD library and attaching them to an object. When you experiment on your own, you will see color effects that we cannot show in this book.

⊕ Type "rmat" or open the View menu, highlight Render, and select Materials....

There is also a Materials tool on the Render toolbar, as shown in Figure 14-45.

Notice that there is a Materials Library option as well as a Materials option. These two options refer to the MATLIB and RMAT commands. MATLIB opens the Materials Library dialog box and RMAT opens the Materials dialog. Materials Library is used to load Materials into a drawing, while Materials is used to attach, modify, and create materials. Since you can access the Materials library through the Materials dialog box, it is often more efficient to go this way. RMAT will call the Materials dialog box shown in Figure 14-46. Before we can attach a material, we must load at least one from the Materials Library. To use this box, select a material or materials on the right and then select Import to bring them into your drawing.

⊕ Click on Materials Library....

This will open the Materials Library dialog box shown in Figure 14-47. To load materials, they must be selected on the right and then imported.

⊕ Select "Beige Matte".

⊕ While "Beige Matte" is highlighted, select "<-Import".

The Beige Matte material definition will be loaded and you will see it on the Materials List at the left.

Figure 14-45

Figure 14-46

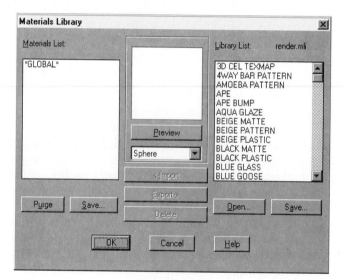

Figure 14-47

⊕ Click on "OK".

Now you must attach the material to the object you are rendering. When there is more than one object, you can attach different materials to different objects.

⊕ Click on "Attach <".

The dialog box disappears and you will see this prompt:

        Select objects to attach "BEIGE MATTE" to:

⊕ Select the wedge.

⊕   Press Enter to end object selection.

⊕   Click on "OK."

You are now ready to render.

⊕   Open the View menu, highlight Render, and select the Render....

⊕   Select "Render Scene" from the Render dialog box.

Your rendered image will be similar to the last image, but it will appear in beige tones.

14.13   Review Material

Questions

1. What 3D solid objects and commands would you use to create a square nut with a bolt hole in the middle?
2. What command allows you to draw outside the *xy* plane of the current UCS without the use of typed coordinates, object snap, or point filters?
3. Why is there a prompt for a base surface in CHAMFER but not in FILLET?
4. What is the difference between a REGION and a 2D SOLID? What is the difference between a REGION and a 3DFACE?
5. What options are available for the creation of different effects in shaded images?
6. What is the major additional effect available in rendered images that is not available in shaded images?
7. How would you use a point filter to place a spotlight 5.0 units above the point (3,5,0)?
8. What is ambient light?
9. What are the shapes and qualities of spotlights, point lights, and distant lights? What is attenuation, and how does it affect each type of lighting?
10. What four qualities make up a material definition?

Drawing Problems

1. Open a new drawing with the B prototype, switch to a southeast isometric view, and draw a solid cylinder, centered at (9,6,0), with a radius of 3.0 units and a height of 5.0 units.
2. On layer 1, draw a solid box 2.0 × 2.0 units at the base, with a height of 5.0 units, centered at (9,6,0).
3. Subtract the box from the cylinder.
4. Create a section view of the composite object cut along the diagonal of the rectangular hole.
5. Create a rendered image with a solid blue background, a spotlight with target at (9,6,3) and source at (14,8,6), and a distant light at the default position. Ambient light should be set to full 1.00 intensity.

14.14   Drawings 14-1 through 14-5:
Bushing Mount, Link Mount, 3D Assembly,
Tapered Bushing, Pivot Mount

We offer the following drawing suggestions for Drawing 14-1. The principles demonstrated here will carry over into drawings 14-2 through 14-5, and you should be capable of handling them on your own at this point. In all cases you are encouraged to experiment with renderings when the model is complete.

Use an efficient sequence in the construction of composite solids. In general, this will mean saving union, subtraction, and intersection operations until most of the solid objects have been drawn and positioned. This approach allows you to continue to use the geometry of the parts for snap points as you position other parts.

DRAWING SUGGESTIONS

- Use at least two views, one plan and one 3D, as you work.
- Begin with the bottom of the mount in the *XY* plane. This will mean drawing a $6.00 \times 4.00 \times 0.50$ solid box sitting on the *XY* plane.
- Draw a second box, $1.50 \times 4.00 \times 3.50$, in the *XY* plane. This will become the upright section at the middle of the mount. Move it so that its own midpoint is at the midpoint of the base.
- Draw a third box, $1.75 \times 0.75 \times 0.50$, in the *XY* plane. This will be copied and become one of the two slots in the base. Move it so that the midpoint of its long side is at the midpoint of the short side of the base. Then MOVE it 1.125 along the *x* axis.
- Add a 0.375 radius cylinder with 0.50 height at each end of the slot.
- Copy the box and cylinders 3.75 to the other side of the base to form the other slot.
- Create a new UCS 2.00 up in the *z* direction. You can use the origin option and give (0,0,2) as the new origin. This puts the *XY* plane of the UCS directly at the middle of the upright block, where you can easily draw the bushing.
- Move out to the right of the mount and draw the polyline outline of the bushing, as shown in the drawing. Use REVOLVE to create the solid bushing.
- Create a cylinder in the center of the mount, where it can be subtracted to create the hole in the mount upright.
- Union the first and second boxes.
- Subtract the boxes and cylinders to form the slots in the base and the bushing-sized cylinder to form the hole in the mount.

A

Ø1.250
LN 3 FIT

4.00
2.00
1.50
3.50
1.50
2.25
0.50
3.75
6.00
1.12
1.12
1.75

.375 R (TYP)

Ø1.250
LN 3 FIT

Ø2.00

Ø.375 THRU
RC 1 FIT

1.50
1.75

B

DRAWN BY:	DATE	**CAD Support Associates, Inc.**
		DRAWING TITLE: BUSHING MOUNT
		SIZE **B** · DRAWING NO. DRAWING 14-1 · REV.
		SCALE: · DATE: · SHEET · OF

LINK MOUNT
Drawing 14-2

Ø1.000
4 HOLES

R1.50
4 PL

5.000 TYP

2.500 TYP

4.00

0.50

8.00 SQ

0.50

1.00

Ø1.500

R1.50

3.88

Ø5.00

0.50

0.38

Ø2.375

.12

Ø4.75

3.00 (REF)

1.88

.12

Ø.375

1.25

.12

Ø.500 FLANGED HOLE

Ø1.500 CENTER HOLE

Ø3.5000 B.C.

HEX .56 ACROSS FLATS (BOLT & NUT)

Reference 14-3

CAD Support Associates

3D ASSEMBLY

Drawing 14-3

Drawing 14-4
Tapered Bushing

Drawing 14-5
Pivot Mount

0.250

6.000

3.000

R1.000

2.000

4.000

ø1.500 THRU
C'BORE ø2.500 × .125 DEEP

3.500

1.500

ø4.000

4.000

1.000

0.250

6.500

1.75

1.25

9.250

5.051

ø1.984

14.15   Drawings 14-6: A, B, C, and D

The drawings that follow, shown six to a page and labeled 14-6 A, B, C, and D, are 3D solid models derived from drawings done earlier in the book. You can start from scratch or begin with the 2D drawing and use some of the geometry as a guide to your 3D model. Either way, the dimensions for these drawings are those shown in preceding chapters.

Drawing 2-2

Drawing 3-4

Drawing 3-2

Drawing 3-6

Drawing 3-3

Drawing 4-4

DRAWING 14-6A

3D SOLIDS DRAWING

Drawing 5-1

Drawing 5-6

Drawing 5-2

Drawing 6-4

Drawing 5-4

Drawing 6-5

DRAWING 14-6B

3D SOLID DRAWINGS

Drawing 6-7

Drawing 8-3

Drawing 8-1

Drawing 8-4

Drawing 8-2

Drawing 8-7

DRAWING 14-6C

3D SOLID DRAWINGS

Drawing 9—6

Drawing 11—1

Drawing 10—2

Drawing 11—2

Drawing 10—3

Drawing 11—3

DRAWING 14—6D

3D SOLID DRAWINGS

Appendix A

Drawing Projects

The drawings on the following pages are offered as additional challenges and are presented without suggestions. They may be drawn in two or three dimensions and may be presented as multiple view drawings, hidden line drawings, or rendered drawings. In short, you are on your own to explore and master everything you have learned in this book.

ITEM NO.	DESCRIPTION	PART NO.	QTY.
20	FLAT HD SCREW #8-32 UNC X .25 LG	D400 F7	1
19	PAN HD SCREW 5/16-18 UNC X .18 LG	D400 F6	1
18	THREADED STUD 1/4-24 UNF X 1.25 LG	D400 F5	1
17	BINDER HD SCREW #10-24 UNC X 3.75 LG	D400 F4	1
16	BINDER HD SCREW #10-24 UNC X 1.62 LG	D400 F3	1
15	TRUSS HD SCREW 1/4-20 UNC X .88 LG	D400 F2	1
14	PAN HD SCREW #10-24 UNC X .38 LG	D400 F1	2
13	PIN .12 DIA (CUT LENGTH TO SUIT)	D400 C2	3
12	ANGLE ADJUSTOR	D400I	1
11	PIVOT	D400 H	1
10	THUMB KNOB	D400 G	1
9	BLADE	D400 E	1
8	CAP IRON	D400 D	1
7	WEDGE SPRING	D400 C1	1
6	WEDGE LEVER	D400 C	1
5	WEDGE IRON	D400 B	1
4	GRIP	D400 A	1
3	KNOB	D400F	1
2	MOUNTING PLATE	D400 K	1
1	BASE	D400 L	1

CAD Support Associates
P.O. Box 317, Needham, MA 02192
(617) 455-8670

JACK PLANE

DRAWN P. RILEY	DATE 5-22-87
CHECKED	
APPROVED	

SIZE C | DRAWING NO. D400 | REV. A
SCALE: 1/1 | SHEET 1 OF 1

NOTE: This Drawing of the Jack Plane Assembly was Drawn by Paul Riley and is used by AutoDESK for AutoCAD Release 13 Update training.

ITEM (7)
WEDGE SPRING
D400C1
MAT'L: .03 SPRING STEEL

ITEM (5)
WEDGE IRON
D400C
MAT'L: STEEL

ITEM (3)
KNOB
D400F
MAT'L: WOOD

ITEM (4)
GRIP
D400A
MAT'L: WOOD

ITEM (1)
BASE
D400L
MAT'L: C.I.

DETAILS-JACK PLANE
CSA5B

.56 R
4 PLACES

.62

.25

.06 .25 .157 DIA

.50 .25

.44 R
2 PLACES .56 .18 R

.88R

ITEM ⑥

WEDGE LEVER

D400C

MAT'L: STEEL

.38 DIA

3.12

.32

.06

.10 DIA

.19 R

0.13 .06

ITEM ⑫ 2.59 R

ANGLE ADJUSTOR

D400I

MAT'L: STEEL

ITEM ⑪

PIVOT

D400H

MAT'L: STEEL

.68 38 R

25

25
2 PL

1.00

.12 DIA

.44

.12

18

.25 DIA .56 R
2 PL

.88 45°

5.00

5/16-18 UNC

2.75

2.00

.75 1.25

.18

1.75

.50 .50

1.00

.38

.38 R
2 PL .75 1.00

.06

.54 ITEM ⑧

.58 D400D

CAP IRON
ITEM ⑧
MAT'L: STEEL CAP IRON

MAT'L: STEEL

DETAILS-JACK PLANE
CSA5C

ITEM ②
MOUNTING PLATE
D400K

MAT'L: STEEL

SECTION A-A

AUXILLARY VIEW

1/4-24 UNF X .25 DP

1/4-24 UNF
X .25 DEEP

1/4-20 UNC THRU

ITEM ⑨
BLADE
D400E

MAT'L: STEEL

DETAILS—JACK PLANE
CSA5D

ITEM (14)
D400F1
#10-24 UNC X .38 LG
PAN HD SCREW

ITEM (19)
D400F6
5/6-18 UNC X .18 LG
PAN HD SCREW

ITEM (15)
D400F2
#1/4-20 UNC X .88 LG
TRUSS HD SCREW

CUT TO FIT

.128 DIA

ITEM (13)
D400C2
PIN
MAT'L: STEEL

ITEM (16)
D400F3
#10-24 UNC X 1.62 LG
BINDER HD SCREW

ITEM (17)
D400F4
#10-24 UNC X 3.75 LG
BINDER HD SCREW

ITEM (18)
D400F3
#1/4-24 UNF X 1.25 LG
STUD

ITEM (20)
D400F7
#8-32 UNC X .25 LG
FLAT HD SCREW

.03 X 45° CHAMFER

.19
.38
.12

Ø.62

Ø.38
.32
1.00

MEDIUM KNURL

Ø1.00

ITEM (10)
THUMB KNOB
D400G
MAT'L: BRASS

Ø.88
X .12 DEEP C'BORE

#1/4-24 UNF THRU

DETAILS—JACK PLANE
CSA5E

PULLEY

CAD Support Associates
P.O. Box 317, Needham, MA 02192
(617) 455-8570

DRAWING NO. CSA6

REV. A

SHEET 1 OF 1

SIZE C

SCALE: 1/1

DRAWN

CHECKED

APPROVED

DATE

Ø4.25
0.25
0.13
2.13
1.75
0.50
0.75
0.75
R.25 TYP
2.50
R .12 TYP
6.50
2.38
1.50
Ø2.75
Ø3.38
Ø5.00
Ø1.50

FIRST FLOOR PLAN

SECOND FLOOR PLAN

HPA
DESIGN
Building Designers
1408 Providence Highway
Norwood, MA 02062
(617) 769-8001
(508) 520-3256
FAX (617) 769-7881

CSAB

SHEET NO. A-2

A SECOND FLOOR PLAN
1/4" = 1'

MASTER
BEDROOM

MASTER
BATH

WALK IN
CLOSET

BATH

HALLWAY

BEDROOM #2

BEDROOM #3

OPEN TO
BELOW

UNFINSHED

RIGHT SIDE ELEVATION

HPA
DESIGN

Building Designers
1408 Providence Highway
Norwood, MA 02062
(617) 769-8001
(508) 520-3256
FAX (617) 769-7881

CSA10

JOB NO. 95248
DATE: DECEMBER 13, 1995
DRAWN BY: ATK
CHECKED BY: HPA
REVISION DATE
PATH: MCHON\H4

SCALE: 1/4" = 1'-0"

SHEET NO. A-5

COR-A-VENT
RIDGE VENT

FIBERGLASS ROOF SHINGLES

COR-A-VENT
RIDGE VENT

LINE OF BITUTHENE
@ EAVE (TYPICAL)

ALUMINUM
FLASHING

ATTIC LEVEL
ALUM GUTTER
ALUM DOWNSPOUT

1x6 CORNER BOARD

SECOND FLOOR

WINDOW HEIGHT
@ FIRST FLOOR

FIRST FLOOR

BASEMENT SLAB

28X20
28X28
28X24

28X28

2836

2820

11-24x20

1/2"x6" CEDAR CLAPBOARDS
4" TO THE WEATHER

9070
OVERHEAD DOOR

9070
OVERHEAD DOOR

16X28

1x10 BAND BOARD
W/ 1x2 TRIM (TYP.)

FIRST FLOOR

SECOND FLOOR

1x6
CORNER BOARDS

ALUMINUM
DOWNSPOUT

ALUMINUM
GUTTER

ATTIC LEVEL

ⒷRIGHT SIDE ELEVATION
1/4" = 1'

PASSANGER
LOCOMOTIVE

PASSENGER LOCOMOTIVE

Scale

0   1   2   3   4   5

DRAWN	DATE	CAD Support Associates
P.RILEY		P.O. Box 317, Needham, MA 02192
CHECKED		(617) 456-9670
APPROVED		

SIZE | DRAWING NO. | REV
A | | A

SCALE: NONE | SHEET ___ OF ___

Menus and Macros

When you begin to look below the surface of AutoCAD as it is configured straight out of the box, you will find a whole world of customization possibilities. This "open architecture," which allows you to create your own menus, commands, toolbars, menus, and automated routines, is one of the reasons for AutoCAD's success. It is characteristic of all AutoCAD releases and has made room for a vast network of third-party developers to create custom software products tailoring AutoCAD to the particular needs of various industries.

Over time, the options for customizing AutoCAD have grown and become more powerful. Many of the basics of menu structure, however, have not changed. The intention of this discussion is not to make you an AutoCAD developer, but to give you a taste of what is going on in the menu system. After reading this, you should have a sense of what an AutoCAD menu is and how it works. You should also understand that menu development is a complex subject. Before you attempt any menu development of your own, you should study the *AutoCAD Customization Guide*.

True to form, AutoCAD provides several different ways to accomplish most customization tasks. A customized command sequence, for example, may result from a simple keyboard macro, an AutoLISP routine, a line of DIESEL string expression language, or a C language program connected to AutoCAD through ADS (AutoCAD Development System). We will confine our discussion to the organization of a menu file and the language of macros. These are easy to learn and require little programming background. AutoLISP, DIESEL, and C, on the other hand, are topics requiring a good deal of explanation and a knowledge of programming.

What Is an AutoCAD Menu?

Most likely, every time you have begun a drawing in AutoCAD you have used either the AutoCAD standard menu or some other menu that is available on your system. This menu is what makes it possible for you to select commands off of a menu, tablet, or toolbar. Without a menu you are limited to typing commands.

579

Menu files have a standard format that AutoCAD can read, and standard extensions so that AutoCAD can recognize them. In Release 14, menu file extensions include .mnc, .mnl, .mnr, .mns, and .mnu files. For example, the AutoCAD standard menu is contained in a file called ACAD.mnc. This file is loaded when you begin a new drawing from scratch or use any template drawing that was created using ACAD.mnc. The .mnc file is an executable file compiled in machine language. But there is also an ASCII version of ACAD.mnc called ACAD.mnu. ACAD.mnc was created by compiling ACAD.mnu into machine code. The importance of ACAD.mnu is that you can look at it with a word processor and revise it if you wish. The .mnu files can be created in any word processing program or text editor and are easy to read and understand once you know the syntax.

As you know, you also make frequent changes in menu items directly in the drawing editor (hiding, showing, or moving toolbars, for example). These changes are retained in a new ASCII file with the same name as the .mnc and .mnu files, but with an .mns extension. Once an .mns file is created, it is continually updated and used in lieu of the .mnc file. To return to the original menu configuration, you must use the MENU command to compile a new .mnc from the original .mnu file.

There are also two files that are loaded along with the .mnc file. The .mnl file contains AutoLISP expressions that are referred to in the menu. The .mnr file contains bitmap images that are used in the menu.

Once you know the language, you can create your own menu by modifying the ACAD files and giving the modified files a new name. You would make the changes to ACAD.mnu in any word processor or text editor with an ASCII format and give it a new name with a .mnu extension. Then when you wanted to load it into a drawing you would follow this procedure:

1. At the "Command:" prompt, type "menu".
2. Type your menu's name with no extension.
3. Wait.

AutoCAD will create the new .mnc, .mnl, .mnr, and .mns files and load them.

What Does a Menu Look Like?

If you go into whatever word processor or text editor you have available on your system and load the file ACAD.mnu (it usually will be located in a directory called \Prog\Acad\Support), you will see the first page of the menu. Menu files are quite large, and you will see only a small portion on your screen. The complete menu will be well over 100 pages long. A good way to learn about menus is to print out a few pages and study them, using the list of characters in Table A.1 and the *AutoCAD Customization Guide*. Comparing menu lines with menu items in the drawing editor is also an essential exercise, as we will demonstrate in the next section.

How Is a Menu Organized?

Menus consist of sections for button menus, pull-down menus, toolbars, tablets, the screen menu, and image tile menus. Each section type uses slightly different syntax, but there are certain generalizations that can be made. Take a look at this sec-

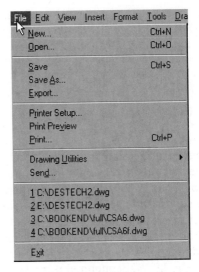

Figure B-1

tion from the Release 14 ACAD.mnu. It creates the File pull-down menu, shown in Figure B-1:

```
***POP1
**FILE
ID_MnFile     [&File]
ID_New        [&New...\tCtrl+N]^C^C_new
ID_Open       [&Open...\tCtrl+O]^C^C_open
      [-]
ID_Save       [&Save\tCtrl+S]^C^C_qsave
ID_Saveas     [Save &As...]^C^C_saveas
ID_Export     [&Export...]^C^C_export
      [-]
ID_Config     [P&rinter Setup...]^C^C_config
ID_Preview    [Print Pre&view]^C^C_preview
ID_Print      [&Print...\tCtrl+P]^C^C_plot
      [-]
ID_MnDrawing [->Drawing &Utilities]
ID_Audit        [&Audit]^C^C_audit
ID_Recover      [&Recover...]^C^C_recover
      [-]
ID_MnPurge      [->&Purge]
ID_PurgeAll       [&All]^C^C_purge _a
      [-]
ID_PurgeLay       [&Layers]^C^C_purge _la
ID_PurgeLin       [Li&netypes]^C^C_purge _lt
ID_PurgeTxt       [&Text Styles]^C^C_purge _st
ID_PurgeDim       [&Dimension Styles]^C^C_purge _d
ID_PurgeMln       [&Multiline Styles]^C^C_purge _m
ID_PurgeBlk       [&Blocks]^C^C_purge _b
```

```
ID_PurgeShp        [<-<-&Shapes]^C^C_purge _sh
ID_SendMail    [Sen&d...]
        [-]
ID_MRU         [Drawing Histo&ry]
        [-]
ID_Quit        [E&xit]^C^C_quit
```

Using this as an example, we can make the following points about menu organization, and pull-down menus in particular:

1. Menus are organized into lines. Each line is associated with a single item on a screen menu, an item on a pull-down menu, a tool on a toolbar, or a box on a tablet menu. There are also single lines for helpstrings, cursor buttons, image tile menus, and user-defined accelerator key sequences.

2. The only lines that are not associated with specific menu items and functions are those added for organizational purposes. These include lines with asterisks, called section headers, and lines with double slashes (//), which are comment lines. In the POP1 menu section, for example, "***POP1" is a section header.
   - Three-star headers like this one identify major sections, including the button functions, the pull-down menus, the screen menu, toolbars, image tile menus, and the four tablet areas. The pull-down menus are identified as POP1–POP16. The standard menu only uses POP1–POP7. POP0 is the object snap cursor menu.
   - Two-star headers identify individual toolbars and submenus of the screen menu.

3. In Windows, menu items have name tags. All of the ID_ labels in this example are name tags. These name tags can be referenced elsewhere in the menu. One common use of the name tag is to call out "Helpstrings", the short phrases on the status line that describe what a particular menu selection will do. These phrases are defined in the ***HELPSTRING section of the menu.

4. For pull-down menu sections, the words written in brackets, such as [&File], control the labels that actually appear in the drawing editor.
   - The "&" character is placed before a letter that can be used as a keyboard alternative to selecting the item with the pointing device.
   - "\t" is the tab character. Observe, for example, the space between "New" and "Ctrl+N" in the figure in relation to the third line of the POP1 menu section.

5. The action taken by selecting the menu item is controlled by the macro that comes after the brackets. In the fourth line of this section, "^C^C_new" is the macro. This macro is discussed in the following section.

6. The [-] lines create the line dividers in the pull-down menu.

7. The lines between ID_MnDrawing and ID_PurgeShp are the Drawing Utilities submenu. The line that calls the submenu is indicated by the characters "->"; in this case, "[->Drawing &Utilities]". The last line of the submenu is indicated by "<-<-"; in this case, "[<-<-&Shapes]".

What Is A MACRO?

The ability to define macros is available in many software packages. Macros have the function of storing lengthy and frequently used sequences of keystrokes in a shorthand form. Much of AutoCAD's menu system depends on macros. To understand and create simple macros in this system, there are a few items of syntax that you need to know. In the preceding example, "^C^C_new" is the macro in the fourth line. Look at the line again:

ID_New [&New...\tCtrl+N]^C^C_new

ID_New [&New...\tCtrl+N]: These are the item name tag and the label that appears on the menu, as discussed previously.

^C^C: This appears frequently in all menus. The "^" character is read by AutoCAD as the equivalent of the CTRL key on your keyboard. So what you see here is the menu equivalent of typing CTRL-C (Cancel) twice. CTRL-C works just like the Esc key to cancel commands. This ensures that any command in process is canceled before another one is entered. Often two cancels are required to bring you all the way out of one command before you enter another.

_new: This is the NEW command. Commands on the menu are typed exactly as they would be on the keyboard except that the _ is added as a flag identifying this as the English-language command. This allows foreign-language versions of AutoCAD to use menus developed in English.

Taken as a whole, then, this line does four things. First, it identifies the item and associates it with other related items. Second, it writes the label on the pull-down menu, identifying Ctrl+N as a keystroke alternative to making the menu selection. Third, it cancels any command in progress. Fourth, it initiates the New command.

With this basic understanding, you should be able to make use of the list of macro characters included at the end of this appendix.

What Other Languages Can Be Used in Menu Development?

AutoCAD Release 14 allows you to create customized routines in other languages in addition to the macro language presented here. AutoLISP is a programming language based on LISP. LISP is a "list processing" language. You will see AutoLISP statements in ACAD.mnu enclosed in parentheses.

DIESEL (Direct Interpretatively Evaluated String Expression Language) is a language that evaluates strings and returns string results. DIESEL borrows many of its terms from AutoLISP, and DIESEL expressions are also enclosed in parentheses. DIESEL expressions, however, are always proceeded by $. DIESEL is useful for such simple procedures as toggling the values of AutoCAD variables and writing helpstrings to the status line. AutoLISP can also be used in conjunction with DCL (Dialog Control Language) to create customized dialog boxes.

C or C++ language programs can be written and linked to AutoCAD through ARX, the AutoCAD Runtime Extension. ARX programs are read by the AutoLISP interpreter and then passed to AutoCAD as if they were AutoLISP. C is a high-level programming language. It has more power and is also significantly faster than AutoLISP. Programs written in C and run through ARX will run faster than AutoLISP programs.

In addition to these three languages, AutoCAD also includes a language for interface with database programs such as PARADOX or dBASE IV. This is called the AutoCAD SQL Extension (ASE). (SQL stands for Structured Query Language.)

How Is a Tablet Configured to Match a Menu?

AutoCAD reads the tablet sections of a menu file in a particular way that must correspond to the configuration of the physical tablet overlay that is attached to the digitizer. In ACAD.mnu there are four tablet sections, each corresponding to an area on the tablet overlay. Each line of the menu file corresponds to a box on the overlay, and boxes are read from left to right, top to bottom, area by area. This means that there must be a way to tell AutoCAD how many rows and columns are contained in each tablet area. This is done using the TABLET command and the following procedure (the tablet overlay must be securely in place on your digitizer before you begin):

1. Type "Tablet".
2. Type "cfg" (configure).
3. Enter the number of tablet areas on your overlay.
4. Type "y" to indicate that you want to realign the tablet menu areas.
5. In response to AutoCAD's prompts, point to the upper left, lower right, and lower left corners of each tablet menu area. Be sure that you do this in the same order as the tablets are named in the .mnu file.
6. After the outline of each area is specified, also specify the number of columns and rows in that area.

For additional information on tablets, see the *AutoCAD Customization Guide*.
The following table lists some macro characters you will find in any AutoCAD menu, along with their functions.

Most Common AutoCAD Macro Characters
(in order of appearance in Release 14 ACAD.mnu)

//	Identifies a comment line for documentation. Items on these lines will not be interpreted or executed.
***	Major section header.
;	Same as pressing enter while typing.
$	Begins any screen or pull-down menu call, or a Diesel expression.
$pn=*	Pulls down the menu called for pull down area n.
^	CTRL
^C	CTRL-C
^C^C	Double cancel: cancels any command, ensures a return to the "Command:" prompt before a new command is issued.
***POPn	Section header, where n is a number between 1 and 16, identifying one of the 16 possible pull-down menu areas. POP0 refers to the cursor menu.
[ ]	Brackets enclose text to be written directly to the screen or pull-down menu area. Eight characters are printed on the screen menu. The size of menu items on the pull-down menu varies.
[–]	Writes a blank line on a pull-down menu.
_	English-language flag.
'	Transparent command modifier.
->	Indicates the first item in a cascading menu.
<-	Indicates the last item in a cascading menu.

^P	Toggles menu echo off and on so that macro characters do not appear on the command line as they are being entered via the menu.
( )	Parentheses enclose AutoLISP and DIESEL expressions.
$S=	Calls a menu. If there is no menu name following the equal sign, the previous menu is called.
$M=	Introduces a DIESEL expression.
\	Pause for user input. Allows for keyboard entry, point selection, and object selection. Terminated by press of Enter or pickbutton.
~	Begins a pull-down menu label that is "grayed out." May be used to indicate a function not presently in use.
*^C^C	This set of characters will cause the menu item to repeat.
space	A single blank space in the middle of a line is treated as a press of the enter key.
$i=name	Calls an icon menu.
$i=*	Displays an icon menu.
+	Used at the end of a line to indicate that the menu item continues on the next line.

AutoCAD on the Internet and Other Data Exchange Formats

Release 14 is the first AutoCAD release to have direct links to the Internet. A new drawing format, the Drawing Web Format, or DWF file, allows you to publish designs on the Web. If you have Microsoft Network or Netscape, you can access the Internet from within AutoCAD. From there you can view files that have been posted by other designers at other sites, and you can post drawings of your own that you wish to make available. You can get a detailed discussion of AutoCAD Internet features and issues through the Autodesk home page, as discussed at the end of this appendix.

The DWF format is one of several drawing exchange formats that allow you to translate AutoCAD drawings for use with other software and to bring drawings from other programs into AutoCAD. This appendix will introduce you to importing and exporting data in different formats and will show you how to access the Internet from within AutoCAD. Following is a list of available drawing file types, listed by extenson, with descriptions of each and commands used to import and export them.

FILE EXTENSION	PURPOSE
3DS	3d Studio. 3DS files are used by Autodesk's 3D Studio software. 3D Studio is an Autodesk rendering program with advanced lighting and material capabilities. 3DSOUT, 3DSIN
BMP	Bitmap. Bitmap files use a pixel by pixel digital representation of screen images. BMPOUT, PASTECLIP
DWF	Drawing Web Format. For publishing drawings on the World Wide Web. DWF files can be viewed on the Internet by others who have a Web browser and the AutoCAD plug-in *WHIP!* DWF files are created for viewing and publishing; they are not

	read by AutoCAD for editing and information exchange, as regular DWG files would be. DWFOUT
DXB	Drawing Exchange Binary. A binary-coded format used by AutoSHADE. DXBIN
DXF	Data Exchange Format. A text file format for exchanging drawings between different CAD programs. AutoCAD reads and writes DXF files for exchange with other systems. DXFOUT, DXFIN
EPS	Encapsulated Postscript. For printing and plotting on machines with postscript capability. PSOUT, PSIN
SAT	ACIS (*.sat extension) files capture regions, solids, and NURB (NonUniform Rational B-spline) surfaces in an ASCII format for exchange with other modeling software. ACISOUT, ACISIN
STL	Stereolithograph Apparatus. For translating solid object data into a format compatible with a Stereolithograph machine. Stereolithography is a technology that creates actual physical models from CAD solid model data. STLOUT
WMF	Windows Metafile. For saving objects in a raster or vector image format for use with other Windows programs. WMFOUT, WMFIN

In addition to these file types, also remember that images can be transferred among Windows applications using the clipboard (Chapter 10). These exchanges are made using CUTCLIP, COPYCLIP, and COPYLINK commands for exporting and PASTECLIP, PASTELINK, and PASTESPEC for importing. When importing through the clipboard, AutoCAD automatically recognizes and uses the most efficient format among its options of DWG, WMP, and BMP files.

Creating Export Files

Although the file formats that AutoCAD can export to vary widely and are used for quite different purposes, the procedure for creating them is identical. As long as you know what type of file you want to create, all you need to do is open the Export Data dialog box from the File menu (Figure C-1), give the export file a

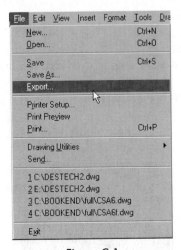

Figure C-1

name, and select the type of file you want to save it as. To create a DWF (Drawing Web File) for example, follow this procedure:

1. Open the File menu and select Export.
2. In the Export Data dialog box, type a name for the file.
3. Open the Save As Type list and select Drawing Web Format (*.dwf).
4. Click on Save.

For other drawing exchange formats, follow the same procedure, selecting the file type you want from the Save As Type file list.

Importing Files in other Formats

Many of the drawing file types listed previously can be imported into AutoCAD as well. Importing most drawing file types is handled through the Insert menu. In most cases you will select a file type, select a file, and open it. An example of an import procedure for a WMF follows:

1. Open the Insert menu and select Windows Metafile....
2. In the Import WMF file dialog box, select the name of a WMF file to insert.
3. Select Open.
4. Specify an insertion point and scale factors, just as you would when inserting a block with the INSERT command.

Different types of files require different insertion specifications, as shown in their respective Import dialog boxes. File types on the Insert menu are shown in Figure C-2. DXF files are opened using the OPEN command, selecting DXF from the Files of Type list.

Figure C-2

Accessing the Internet

Direct access to the Internet is available from within an AutoCAD Release 14 drawing session. This cabability makes it possible to publish designs on the Web, to access drawing files anywhere on the Web, to embed DWF files in Internet home pages, and to link individual objects within a drawing to remote URLs. With full use of these capacities, the Web becomes a vast network through which you can collaborate and exchange drawing data with other designers and engineers in distant sites.

To gain Internet access from within AutoCAD, you need to have either Microsoft Network or Netscape Navigator on your system and be connected to your server. To open and view AutoCAD drawings from other sites, you must also have the AutoCAD *WHIP!* program. *WHIP!* is not included in the standard Release 14 package but can be downloaded from Autodesk at http://www.autodesk.com/whip/.

Following is a procedure for going online from within AutoCAD:

1. Assuming you are already in AutoCAD but are not connected to the Web, minimize the AutoCAD window and then use whatever procedure your system requires to dial your server and get you online.
2. Maximize the AutoCAD Drawing window.
3. Type "Browser", or select Connect to Internet from the Help menu, or click the Browser icon on the Standard toolbar, as shown in Figure C-3.

Ordinarily your browser will take you directly to the Autodesk home page. The Autodesk home page is the default URL, so that is where you will go unless someone has changed the default in your system. The Autodesk home page is shown in Figure C-4. From here you can access many Autodesk options or use your browser to search out other sites. For more information on Release 14 Internet capabilities, try the following:

1. From the Autodesk home page, select Features & Benefits.
2. From the Features & Benefits page, select AutoCAD and the Web.

This will bring you to a 16-page document containing crucial information on AutoCAD Internet access and capabilities.

Figure C-3

Figure C-4

INDEX